Slumbering Beauty 2

story & art by YUMI UNITA

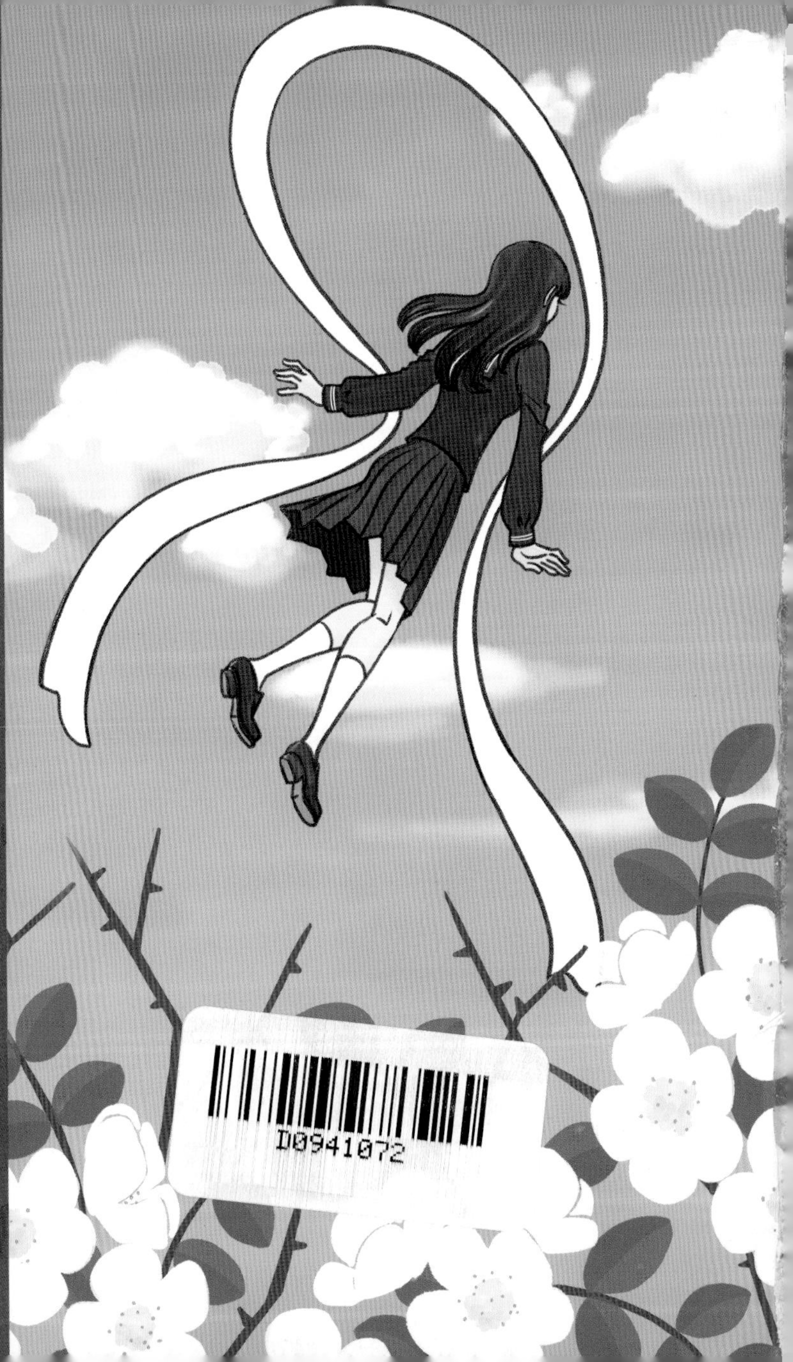

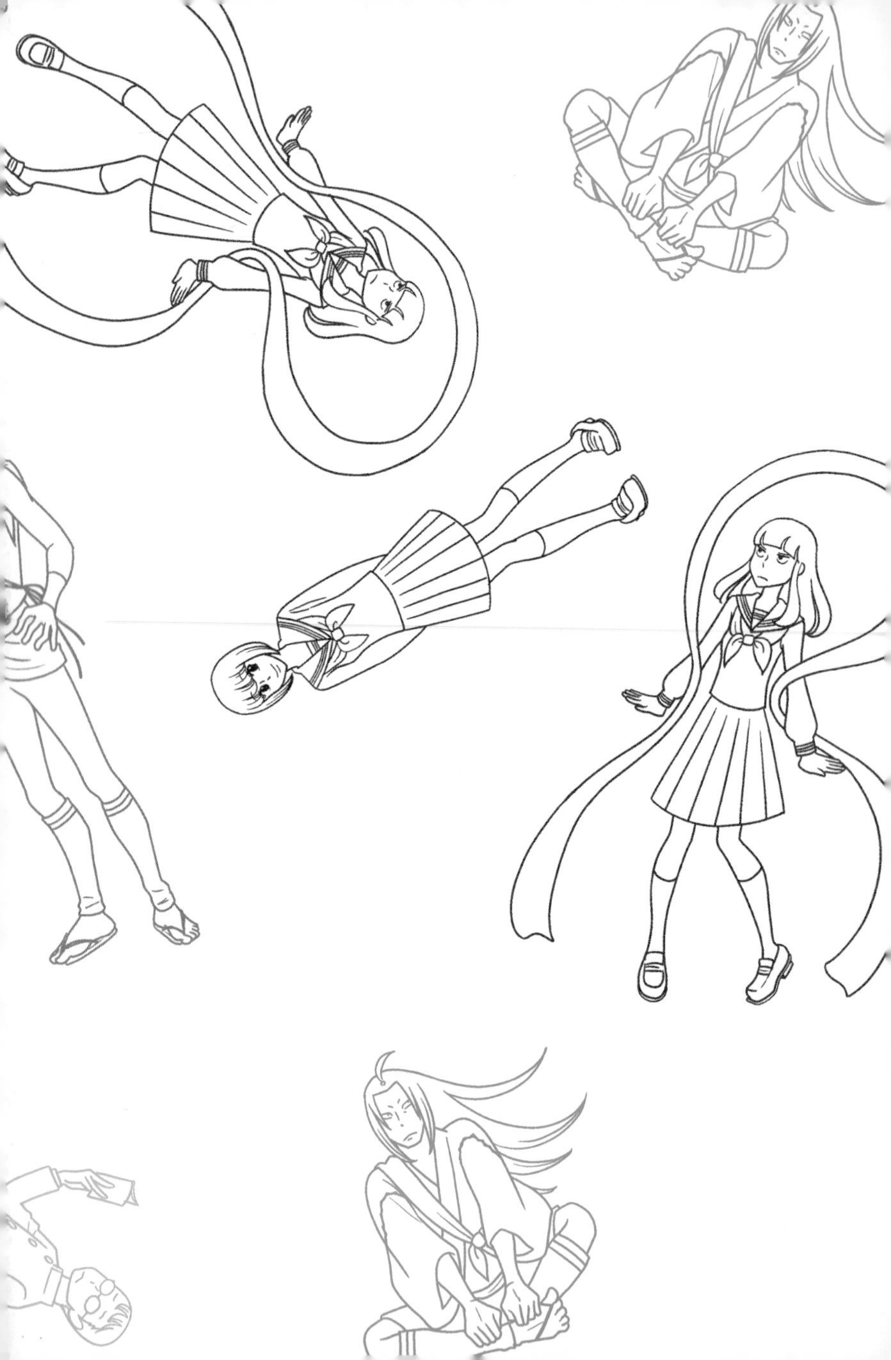

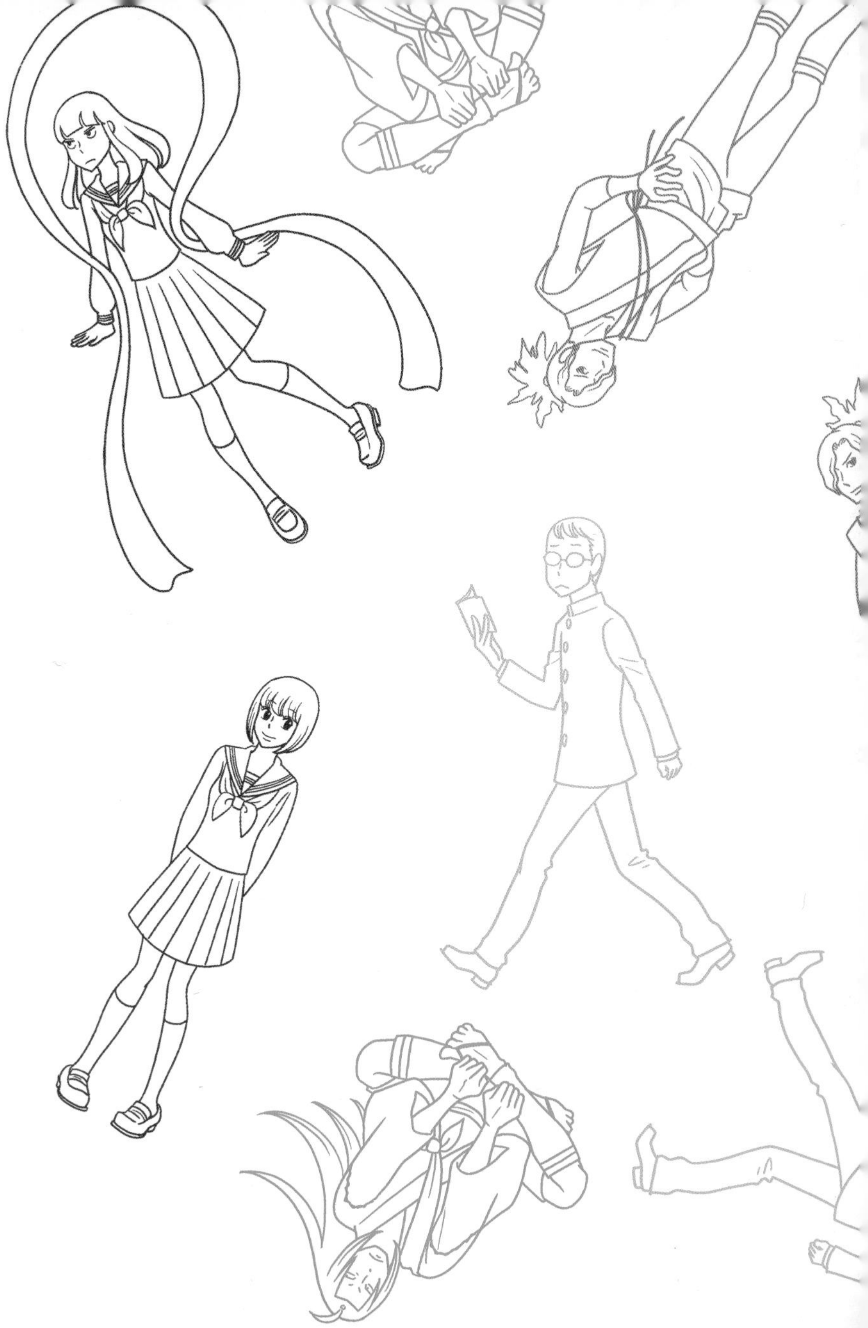

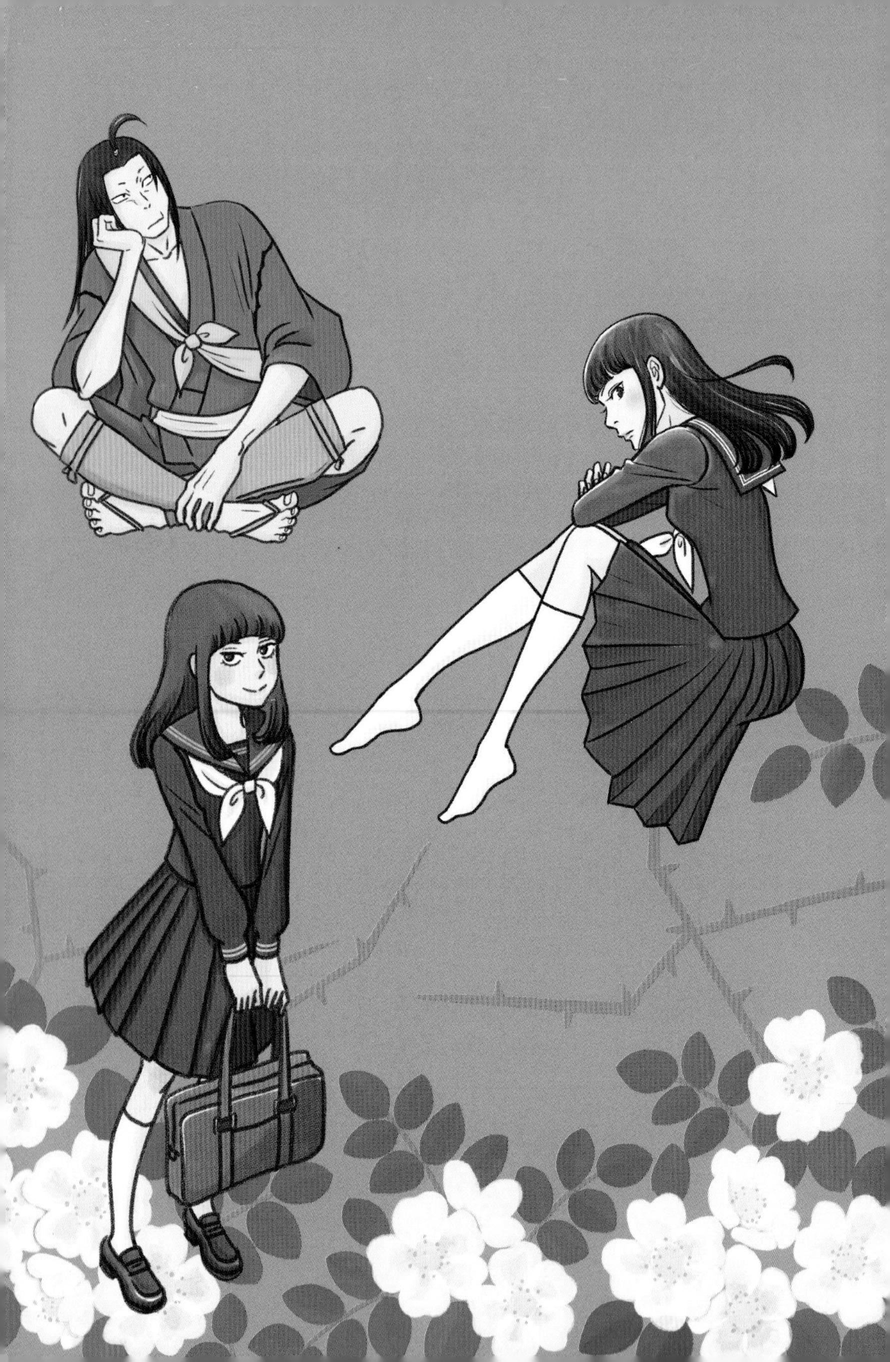

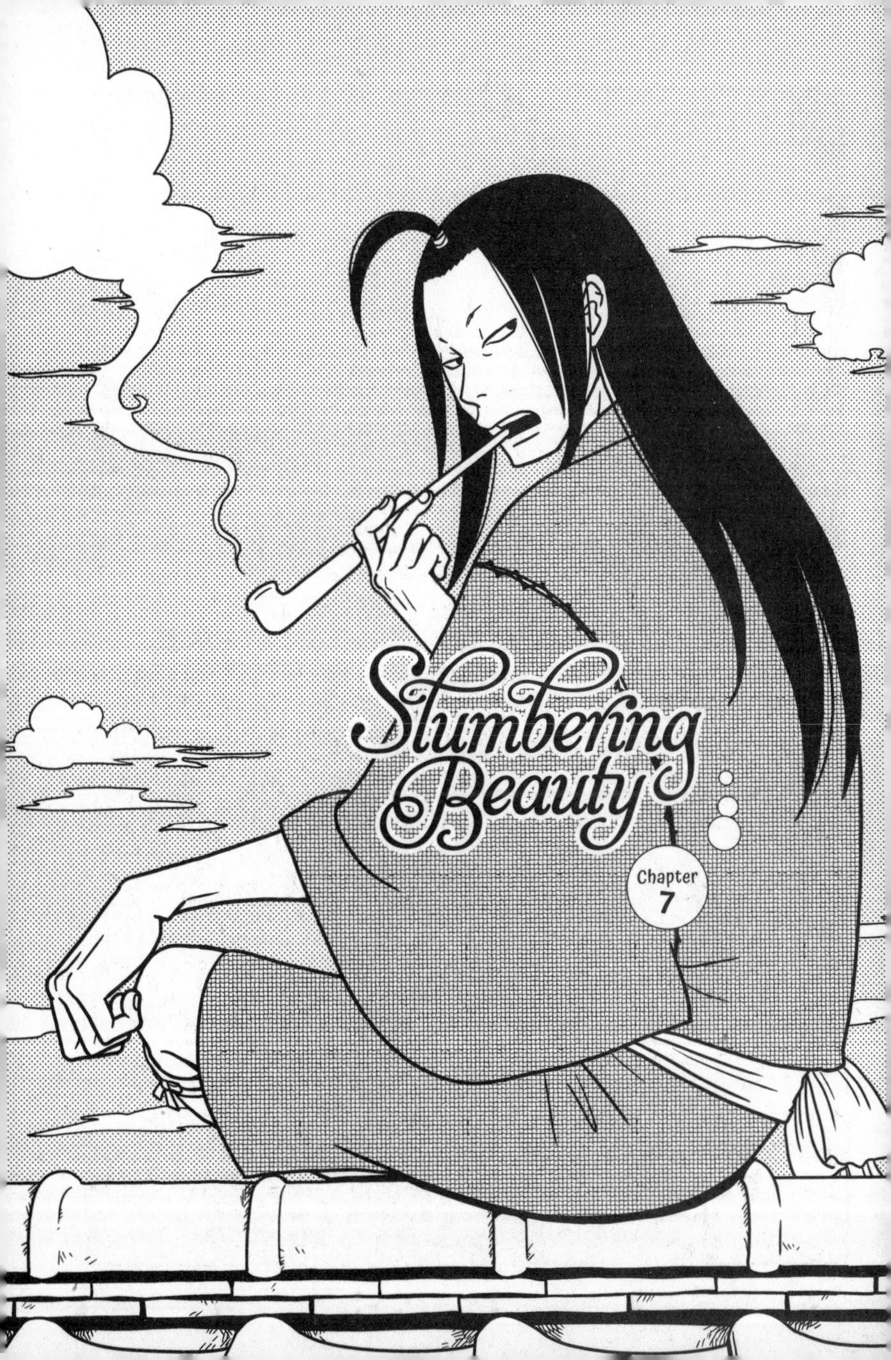
Slumbering Beauty
Chapter 7

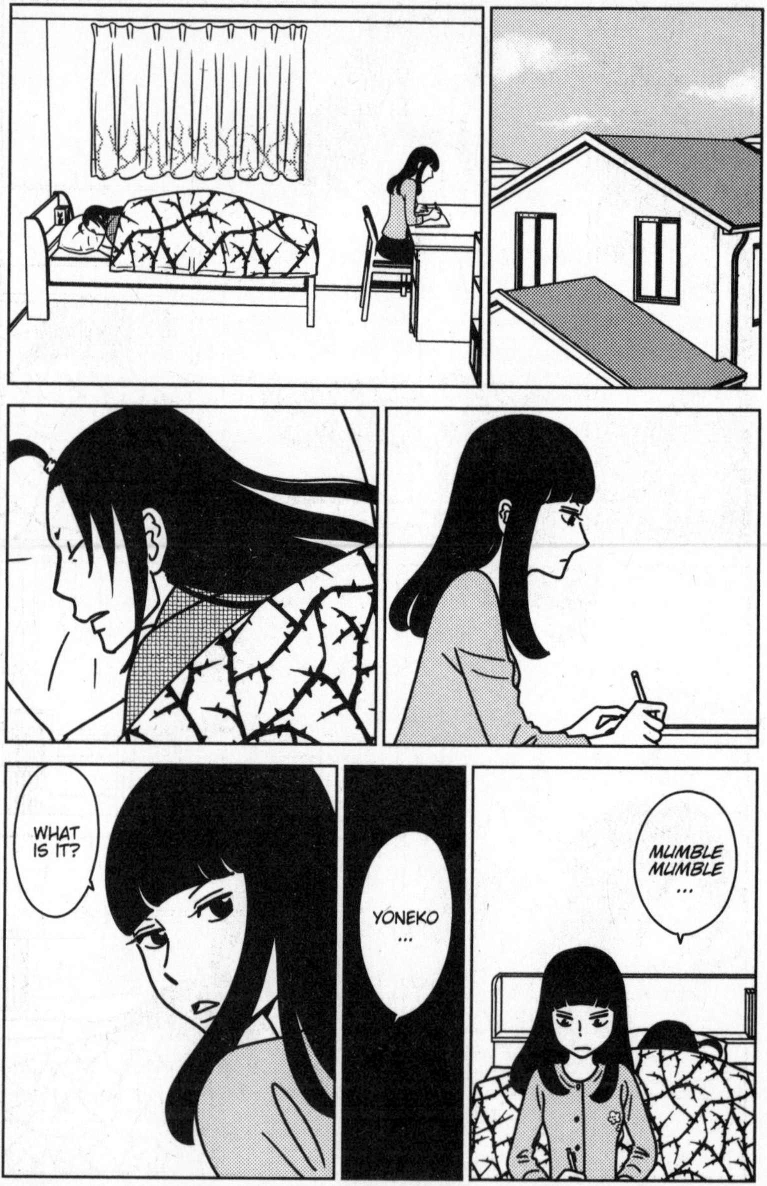
MUMBLE MUMBLE ...
YONEKO ...
WHAT IS IT?

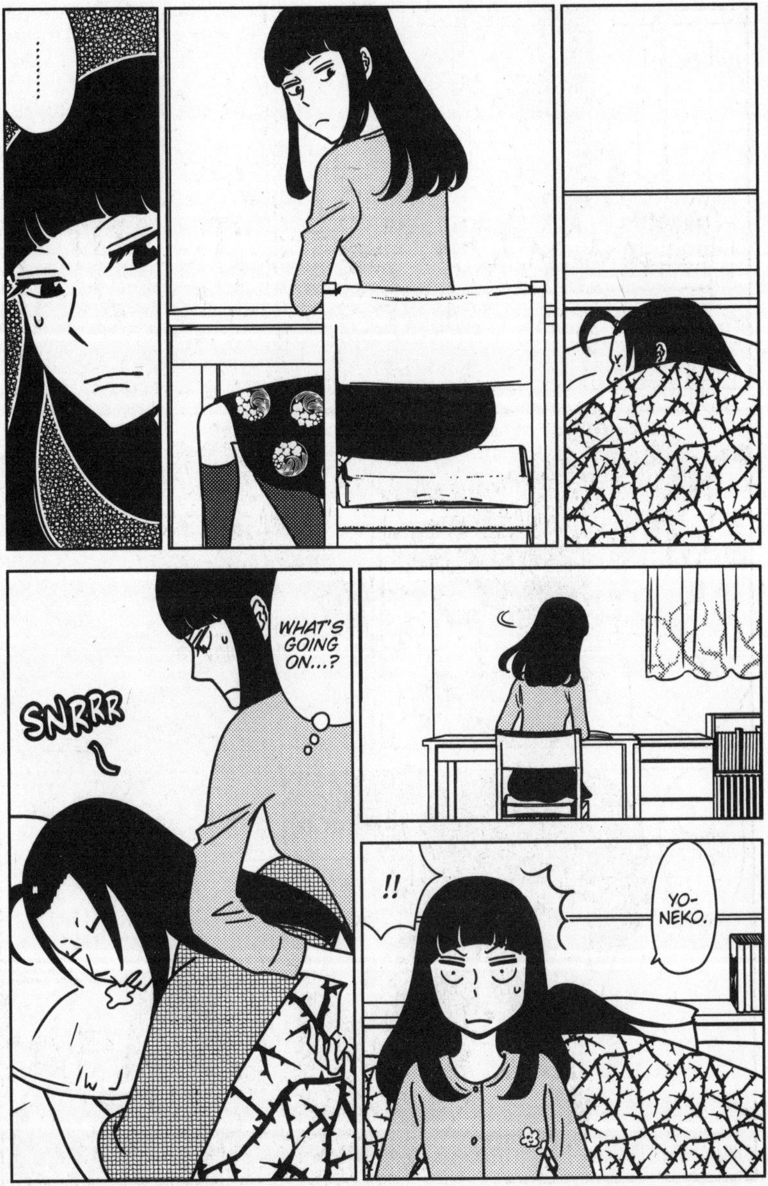
......
YO-NEKO.
!!
WHAT'S GOING ON...?
SNRRR

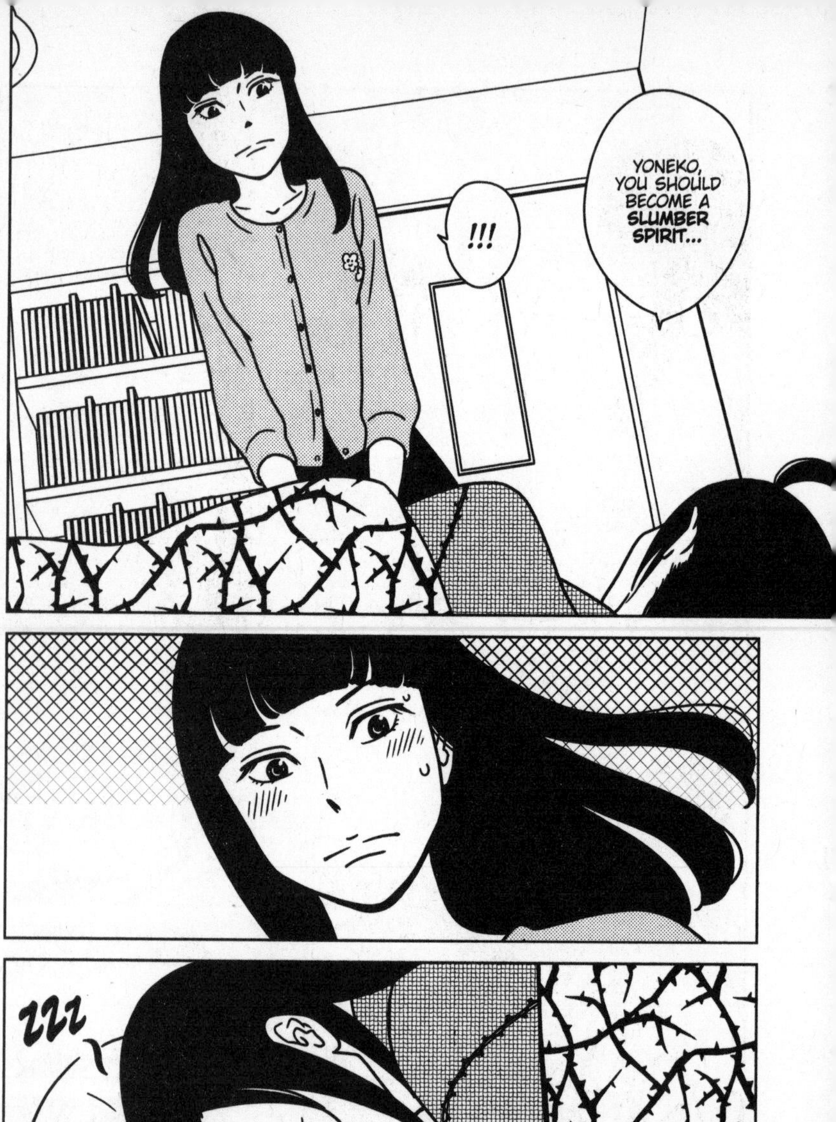
YONEKO, YOU SHOULD BECOME A SLUMBER SPIRIT...
!!!
ZZZ

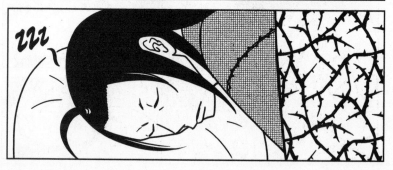

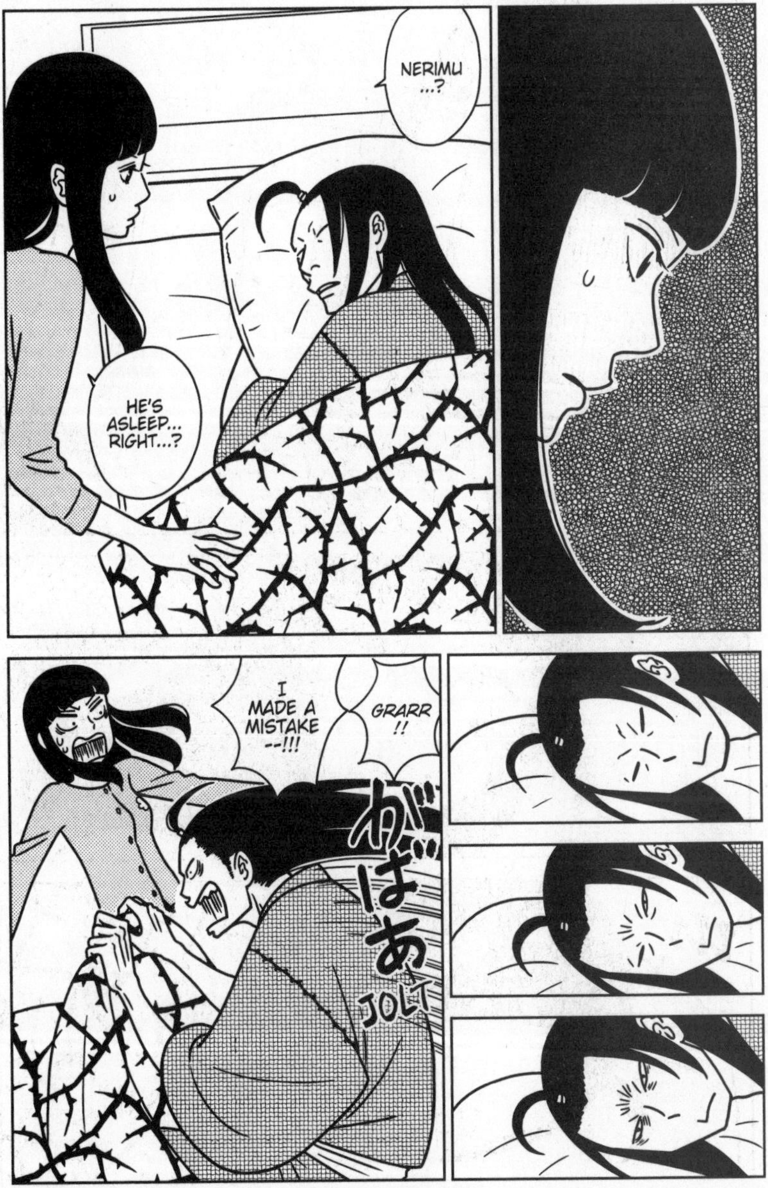
NERIMU ...?
HE'S ASLEEP... RIGHT...?
GRARR !!
I MADE A MISTAKE --!!!
がばあ
JOLT

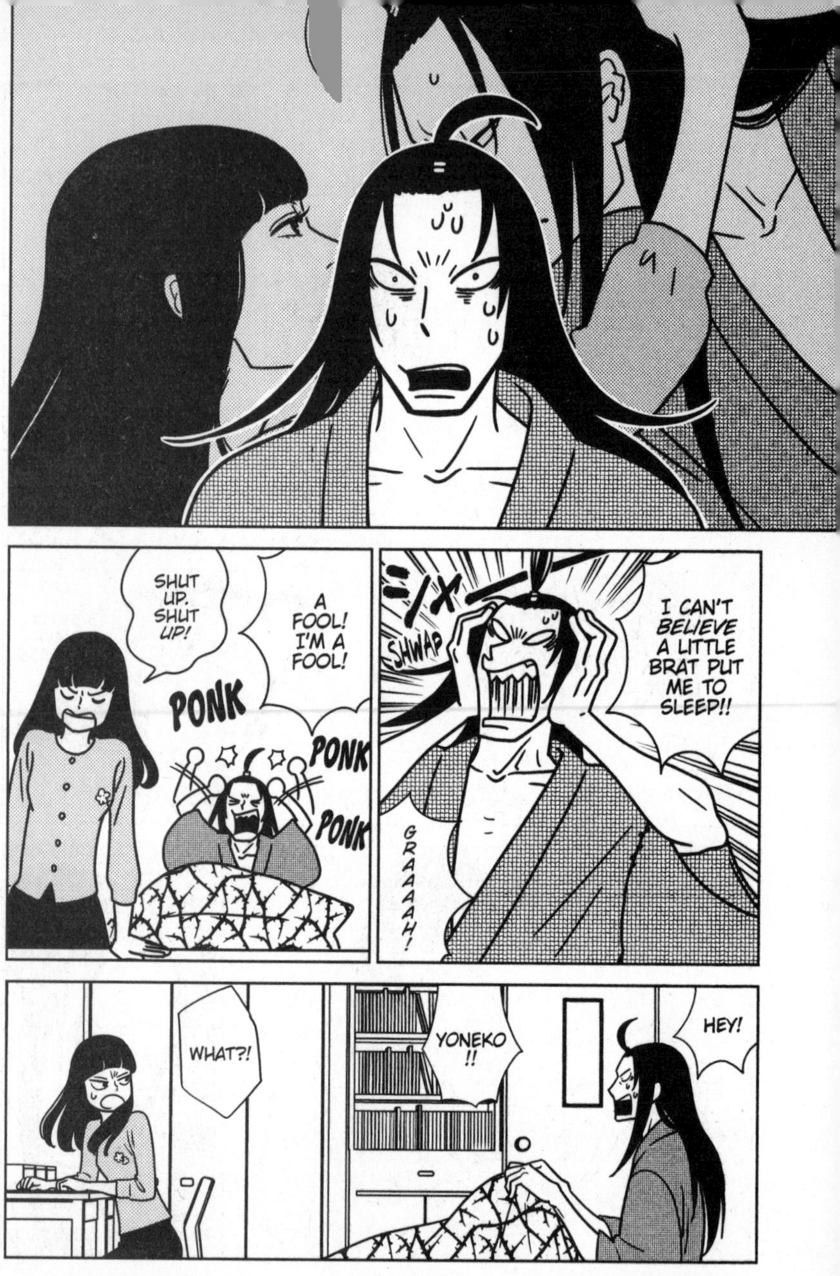
I CAN'T BELIEVE A LITTLE BRAT PUT ME TO SLEEP!!
SHWAP
GRAAAAAH!
A FOOL! I'M A FOOL!
SHUT UP. SHUT UP!
PONK
PONK
PONK
HEY!
YONEKO !!
WHAT?!

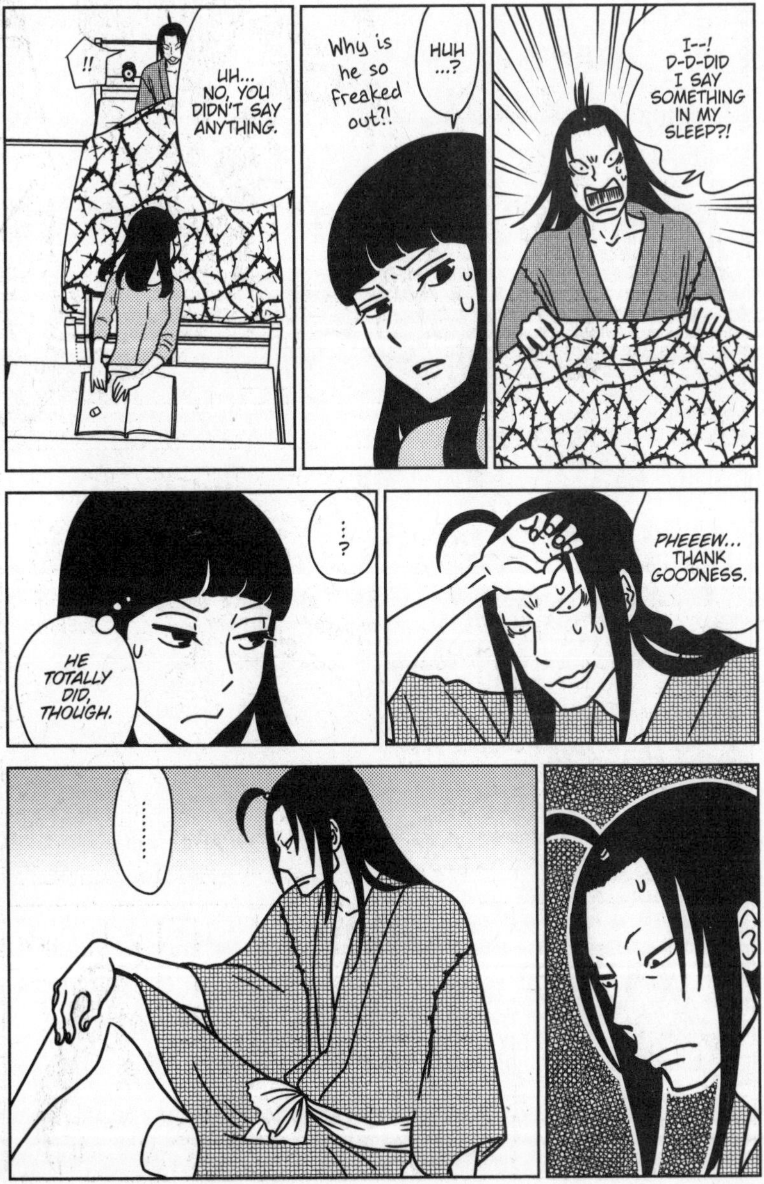
I--! D-D-DID I SAY SOMETHING IN MY SLEEP?!
HUH ...?
Why is he so freaked out?!
UH... NO, YOU DIDN'T SAY ANYTHING.
!!
PHEEEW... THANK GOODNESS.
...?
HE TOTALLY DID, THOUGH.
......

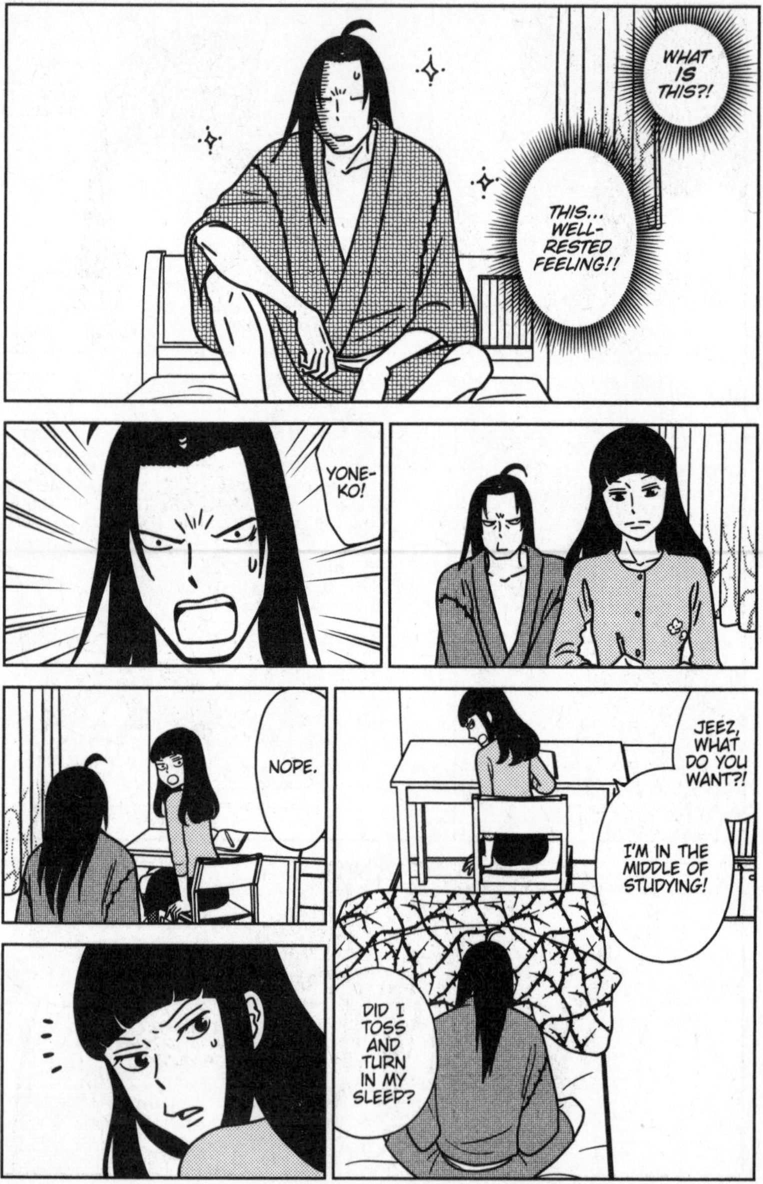
WHAT IS THIS?!
THIS... WELL-RESTED FEELING!!
YONE-KO!
JEEZ, WHAT DO YOU WANT?!
I'M IN THE MIDDLE OF STUDYING!
DID I TOSS AND TURN IN MY SLEEP?
NOPE.

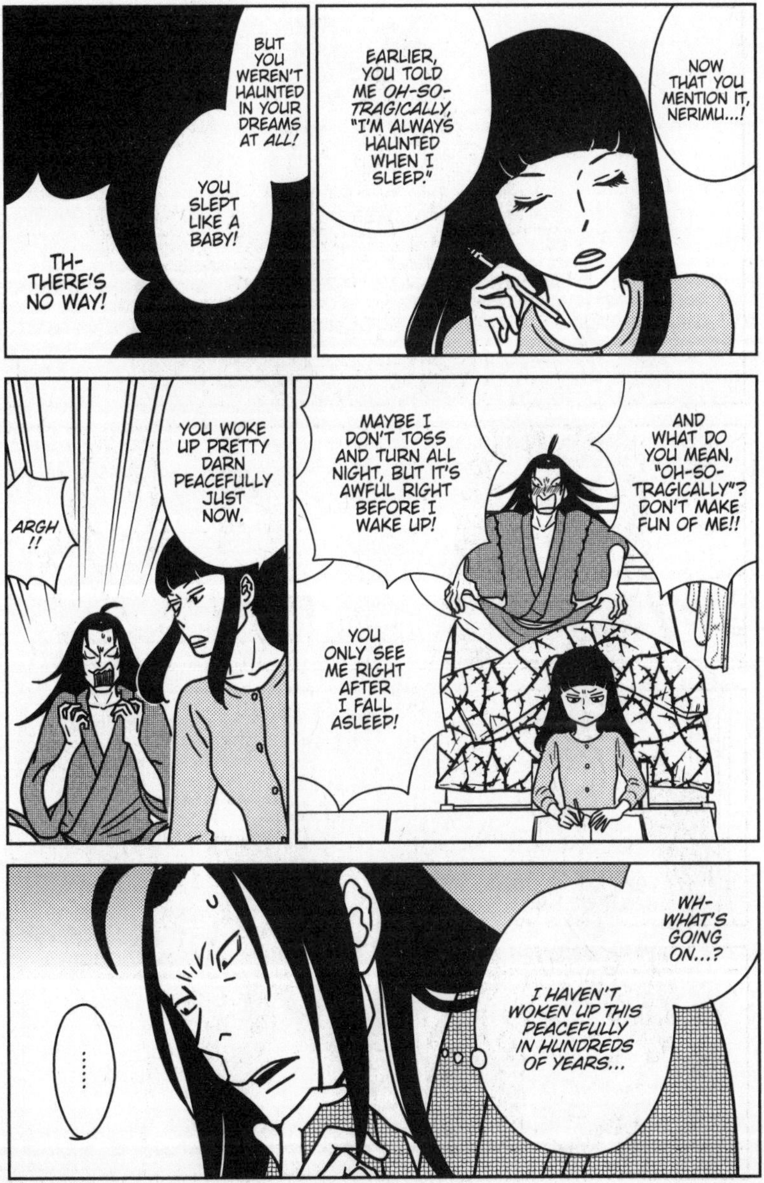
NOW THAT YOU MENTION IT, NERIMU...!
EARLIER, YOU TOLD ME *OH-SO-TRAGICALLY*, "I'M ALWAYS HAUNTED WHEN I SLEEP."
BUT YOU WEREN'T HAUNTED IN YOUR DREAMS AT *ALL*!
YOU SLEPT LIKE A BABY!
TH-THERE'S NO WAY!
AND WHAT DO YOU MEAN, "OH-SO-TRAGICALLY"? DON'T MAKE FUN OF ME!!
MAYBE I DON'T TOSS AND TURN ALL NIGHT, BUT IT'S AWFUL RIGHT BEFORE I WAKE UP!
YOU ONLY SEE ME RIGHT AFTER I FALL ASLEEP!
YOU WOKE UP PRETTY DARN PEACEFULLY JUST NOW.
ARGH!!
WH-WHAT'S GOING ON...?
I HAVEN'T WOKEN UP THIS PEACEFULLY IN HUNDREDS OF YEARS...
......

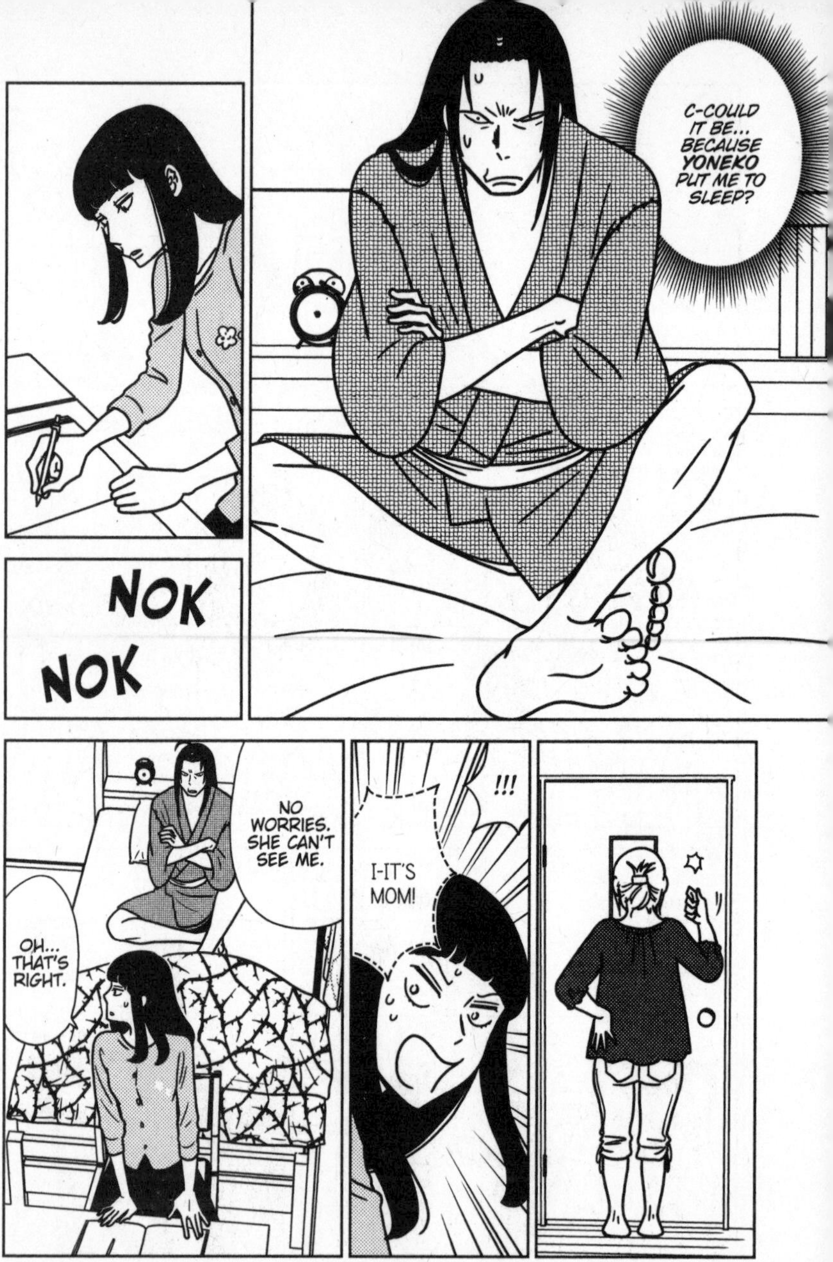
C-COULD IT BE... BECAUSE YONEKO PUT ME TO SLEEP?
NOK
NOK
!!!
I-IT'S MOM!
NO WORRIES. SHE CAN'T SEE ME.
OH... THAT'S RIGHT.

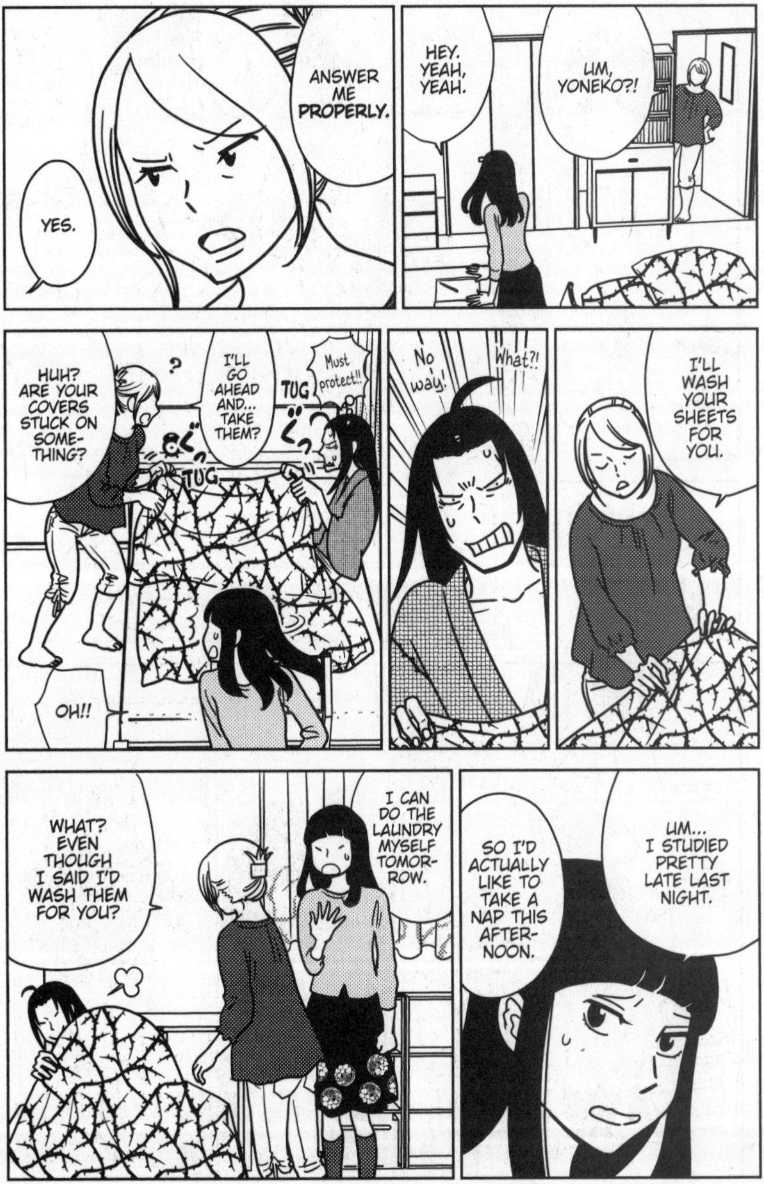
UM, YONEKO?!
HEY. YEAH, YEAH.
ANSWER ME PROPERLY.
YES.
I'LL WASH YOUR SHEETS FOR YOU.
What?!
No way!
Must protect!!
TUG
I'LL GO AHEAD AND... TAKE THEM?
?
HUH? ARE YOUR COVERS STUCK ON SOME-THING?
TUG
OH!!
UM... I STUDIED PRETTY LATE LAST NIGHT.
SO I'D ACTUALLY LIKE TO TAKE A NAP THIS AFTER-NOON.
I CAN DO THE LAUNDRY MYSELF TOMOR-ROW.
WHAT? EVEN THOUGH I SAID I'D WASH THEM FOR YOU?

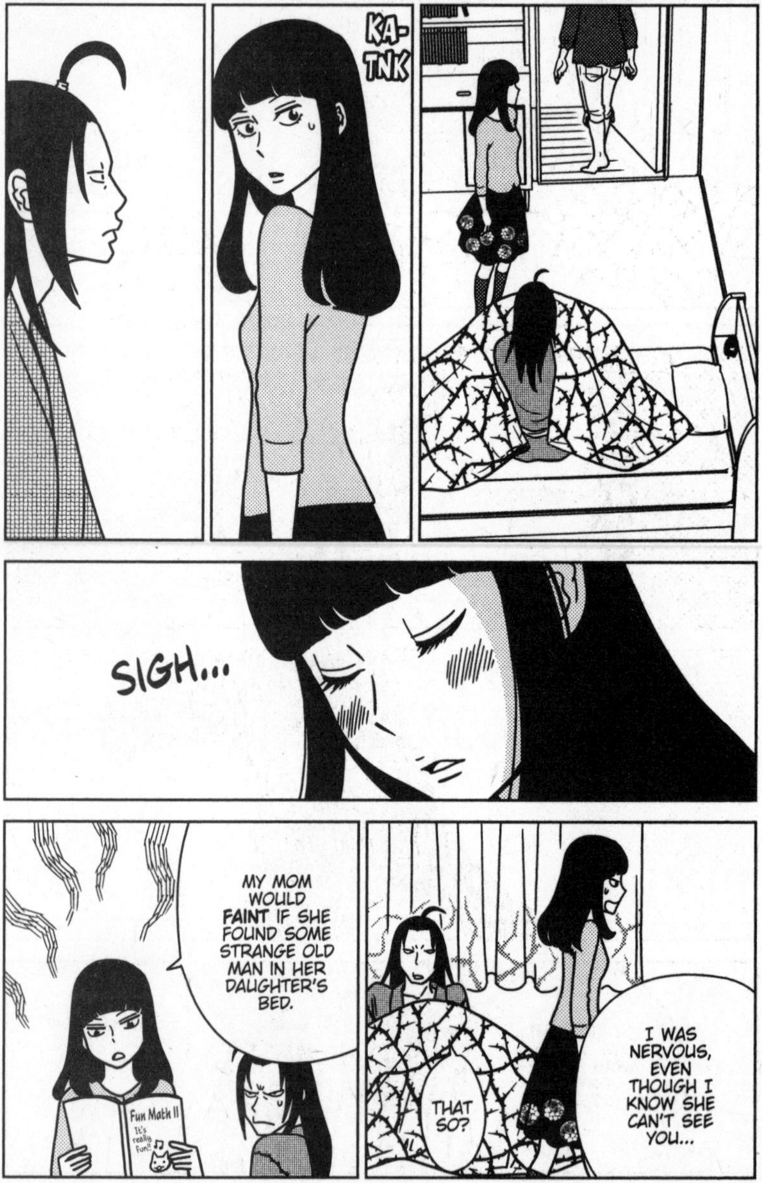
KA-TNK
SIGH...
I WAS NERVOUS, EVEN THOUGH I KNOW SHE CAN'T SEE YOU...
THAT SO?
MY MOM WOULD FAINT IF SHE FOUND SOME STRANGE OLD MAN IN HER DAUGHTER'S BED.
Fun Math II
It's really Fun!!

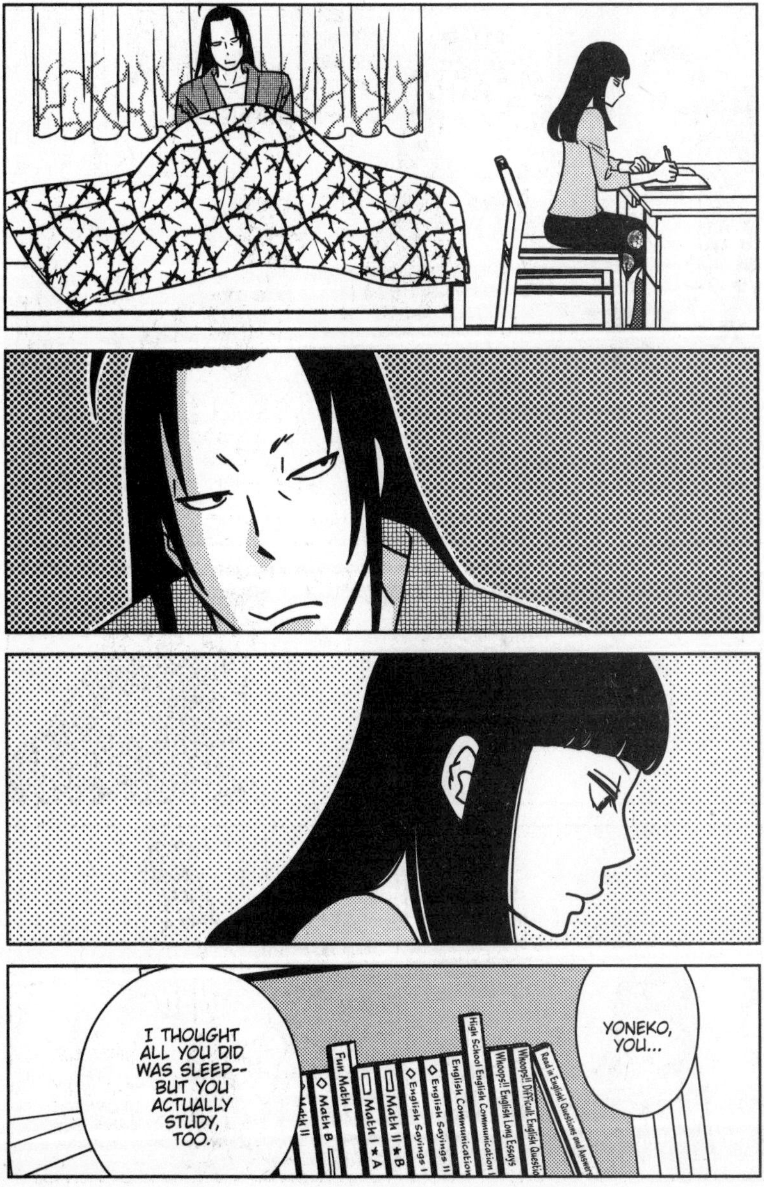
YONEKO, YOU...
I THOUGHT ALL YOU DID WAS SLEEP-- BUT YOU ACTUALLY STUDY, TOO.
Read in English: Questions and Answers
Whoops!! Difficult English Questio
Whoops!! English Long Essays
High School English Communication I
English Communication
English Sayings I
English Sayings II
Math II ★ B
Math I ★ A
Fun Math I
Math B

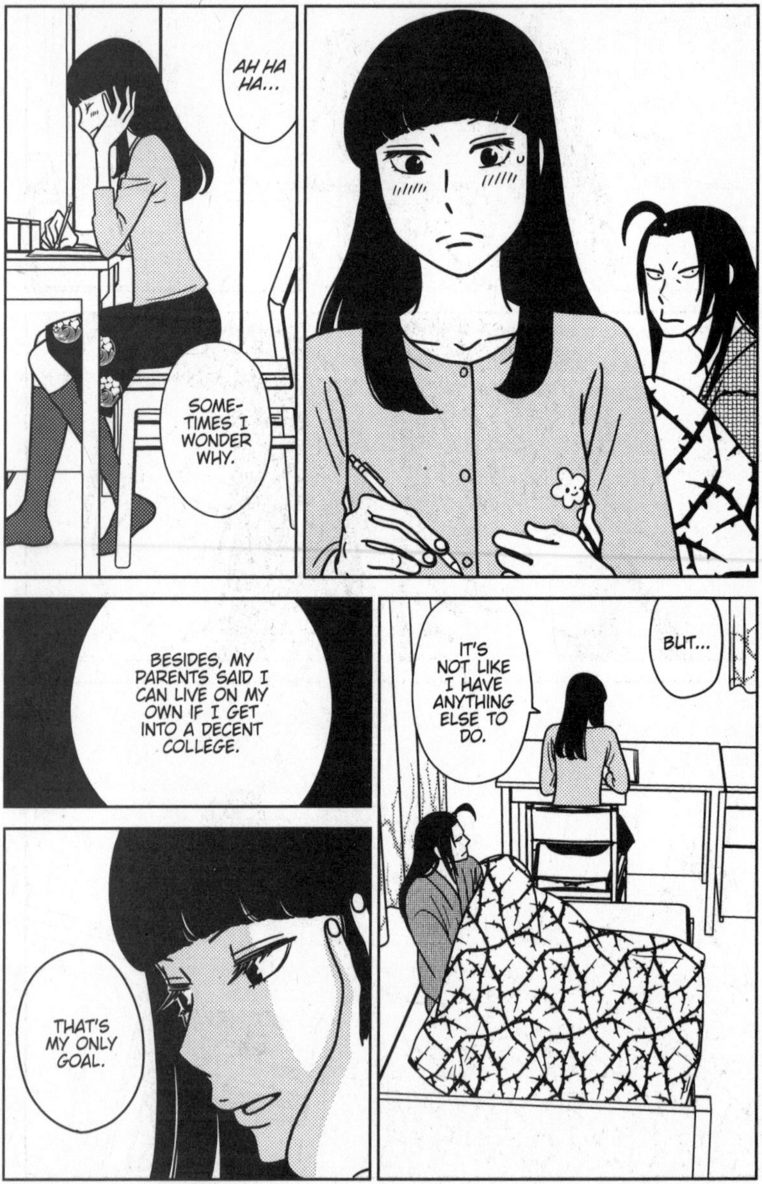
AH HA HA...
SOME-TIMES I WONDER WHY.
BUT...
IT'S NOT LIKE I HAVE ANYTHING ELSE TO DO.
BESIDES, MY PARENTS SAID I CAN LIVE ON MY OWN IF I GET INTO A DECENT COLLEGE.
THAT'S MY ONLY GOAL.

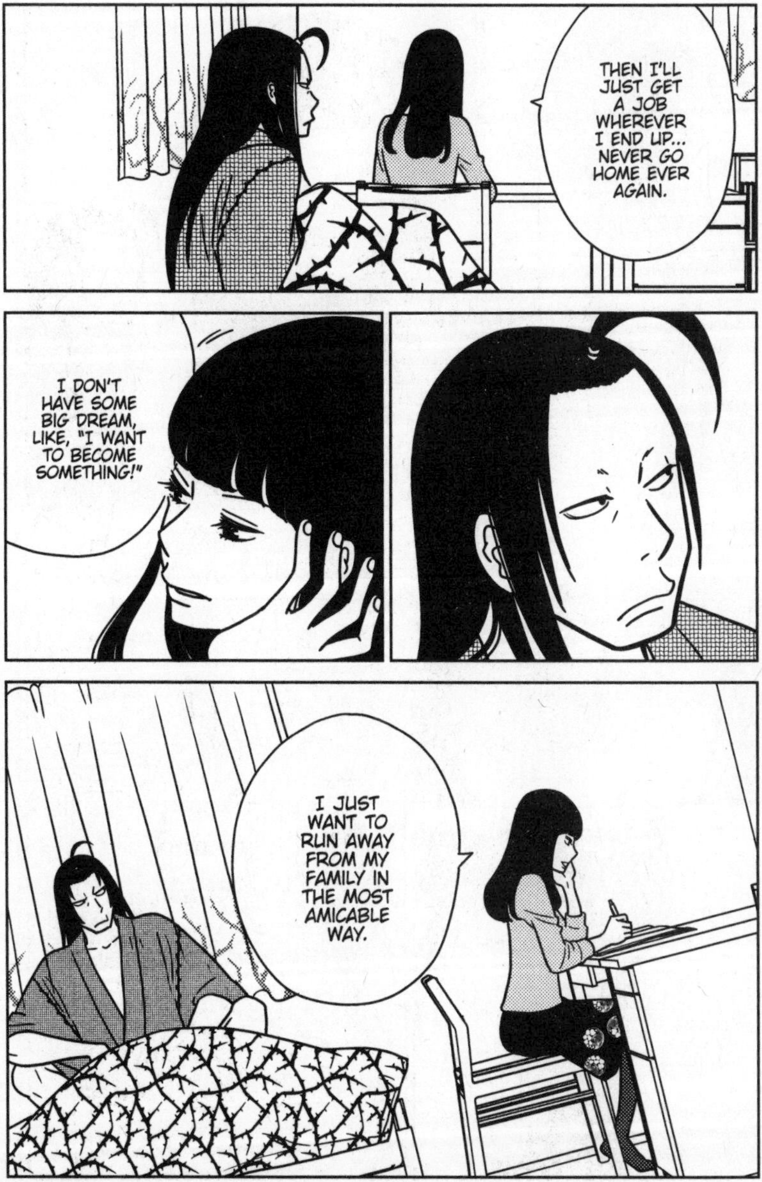
THEN I'LL JUST GET A JOB WHEREVER I END UP... NEVER GO HOME EVER AGAIN.
I DON'T HAVE SOME BIG DREAM, LIKE, "I WANT TO BECOME SOMETHING!"
I JUST WANT TO RUN AWAY FROM MY FAMILY IN THE MOST AMICABLE WAY.

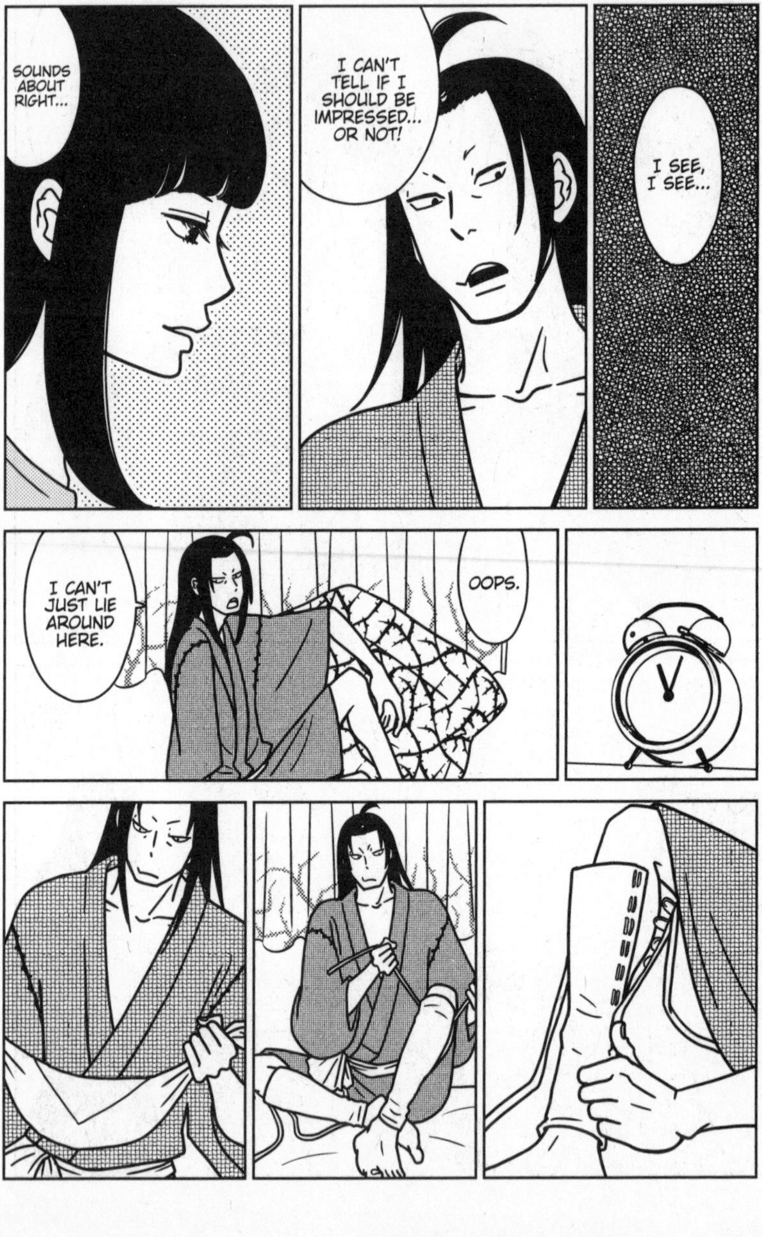
I SEE, I SEE...
I CAN'T TELL IF I SHOULD BE IMPRESSED... OR NOT!
SOUNDS ABOUT RIGHT...
OOPS.
I CAN'T JUST LIE AROUND HERE.

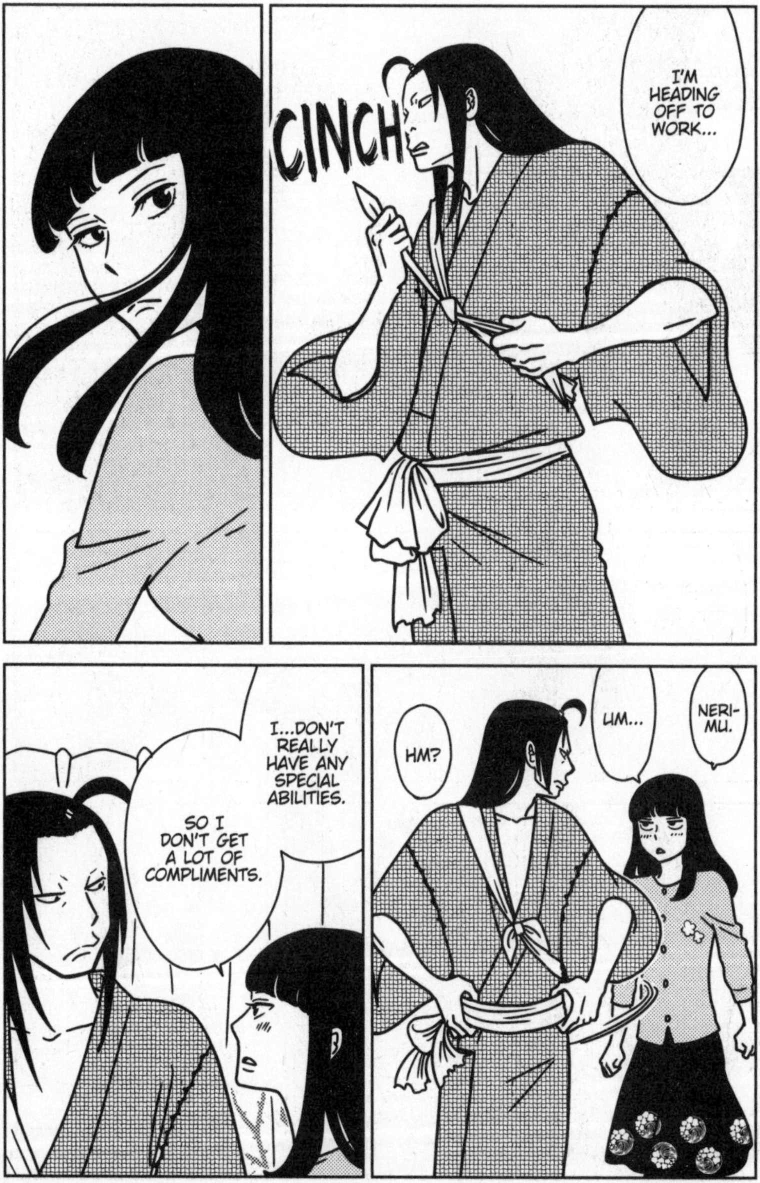
I'M HEADING OFF TO WORK...
CINCH
NERI-MU.
UM...
HM?
I...DON'T REALLY HAVE ANY SPECIAL ABILITIES.
SO I DON'T GET A LOT OF COMPLIMENTS.

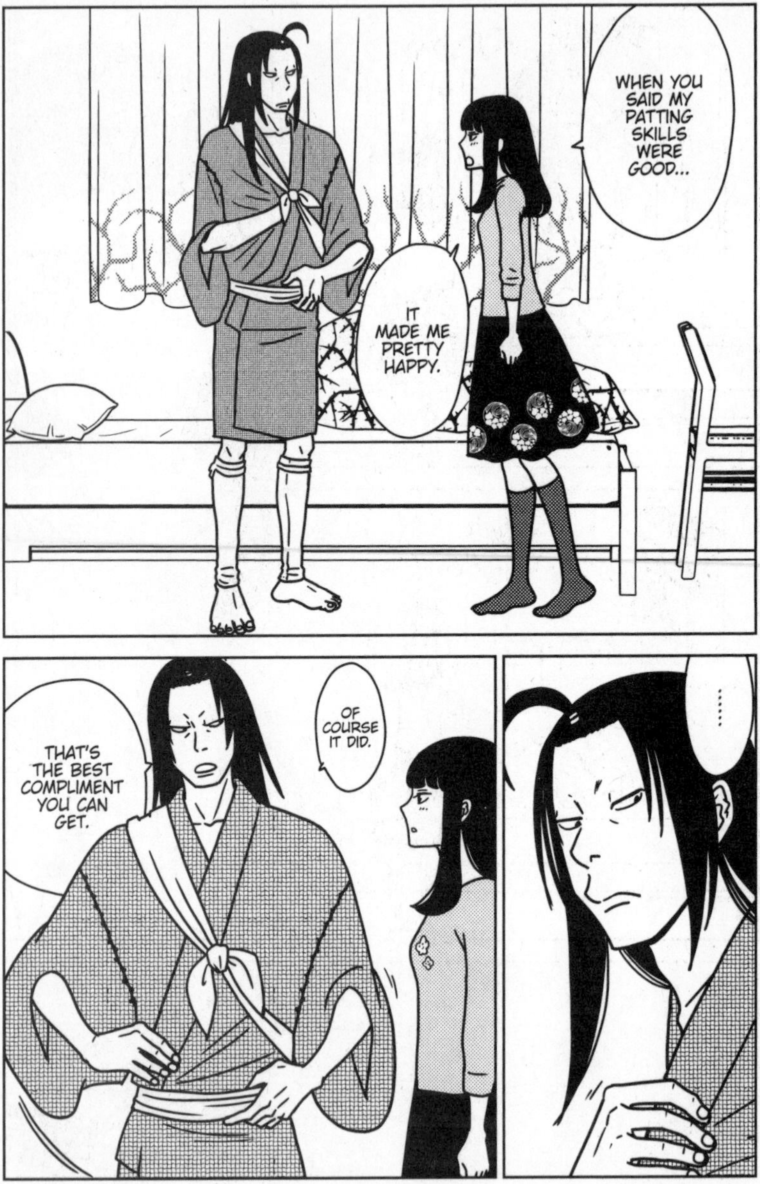
WHEN YOU SAID MY PATTING SKILLS WERE GOOD...
IT MADE ME PRETTY HAPPY.
......
OF COURSE IT DID.
THAT'S THE BEST COMPLIMENT YOU CAN GET.

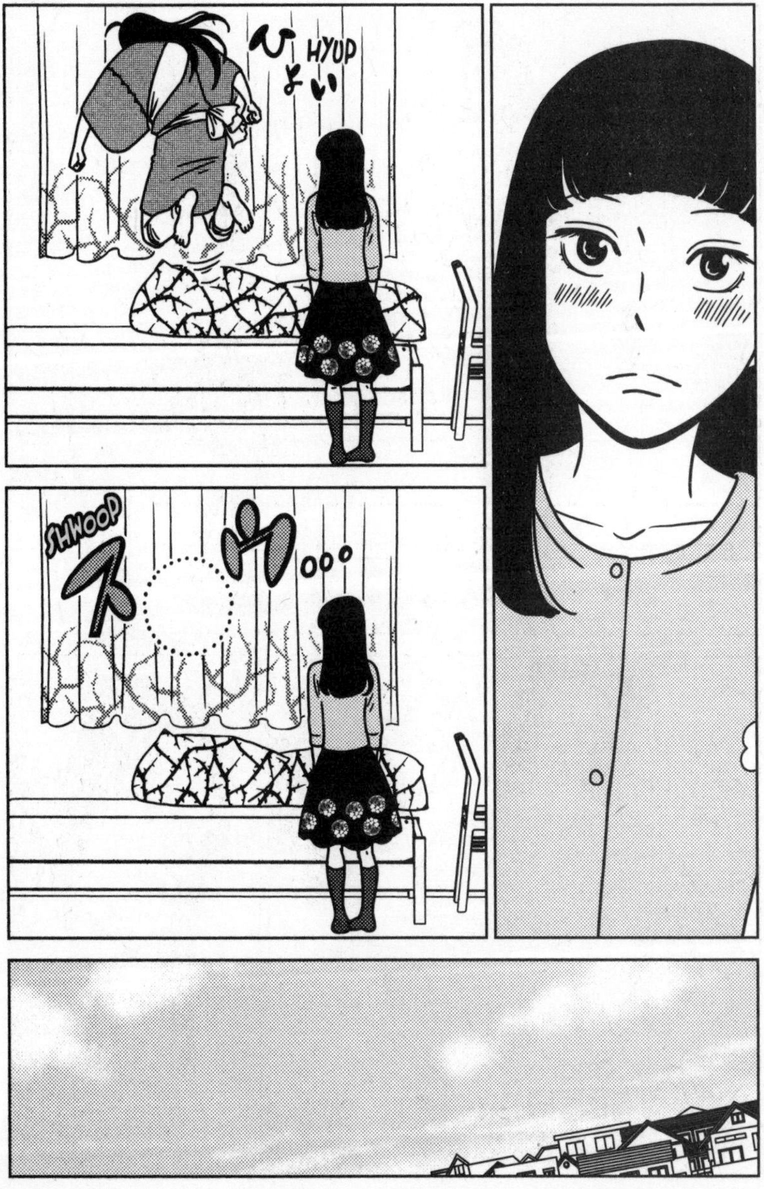
ひょい
HYUP
SHWOOP

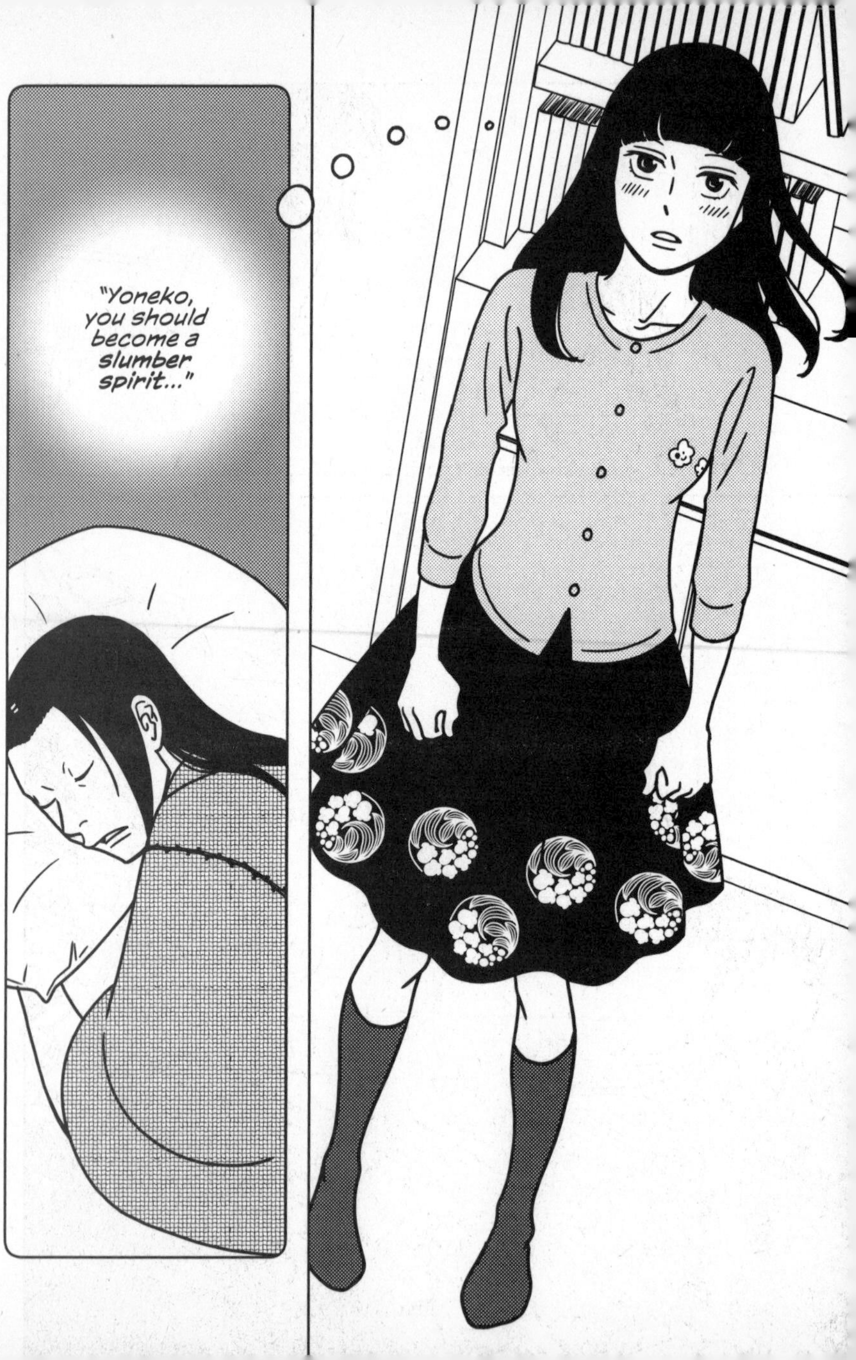
"Yoneko, you should become a slumber spirit..."

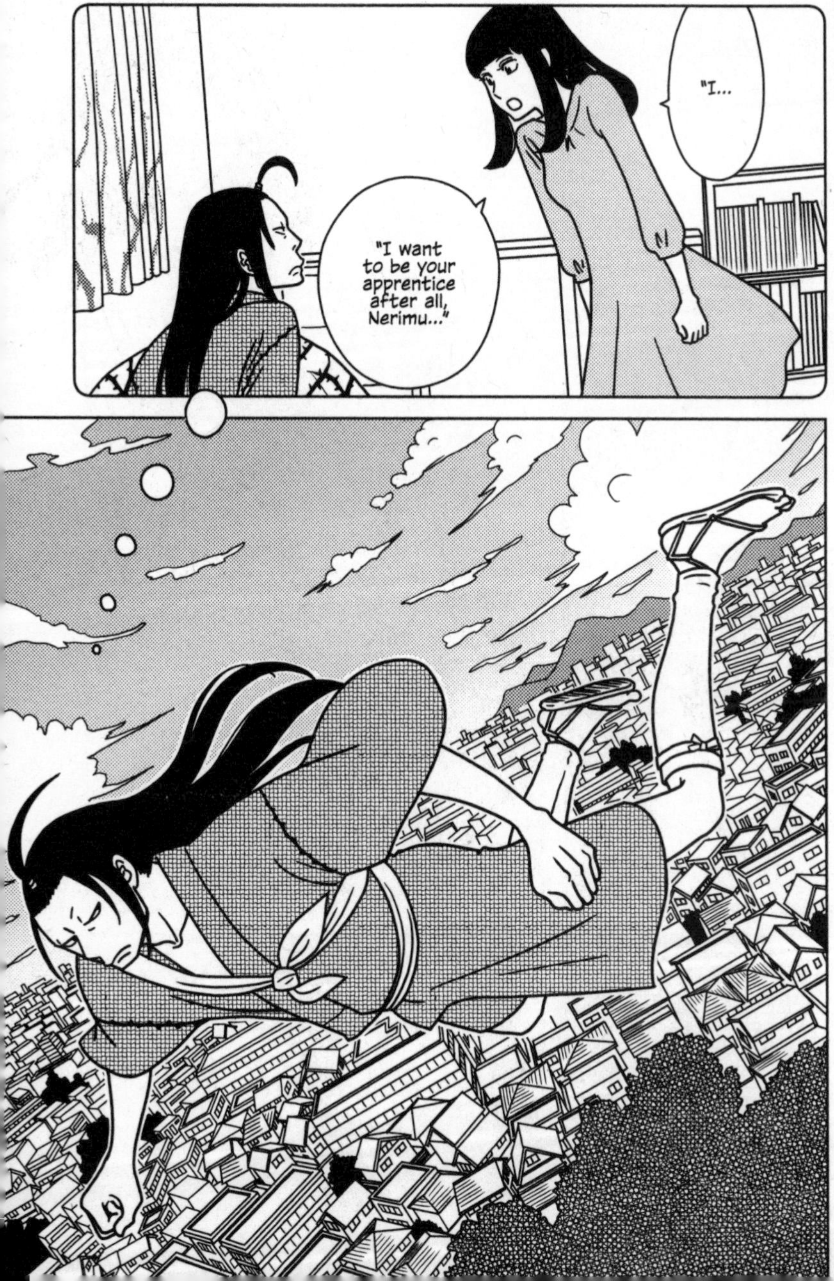
"I...
"I want to be your apprentice after all, Nerimu..."

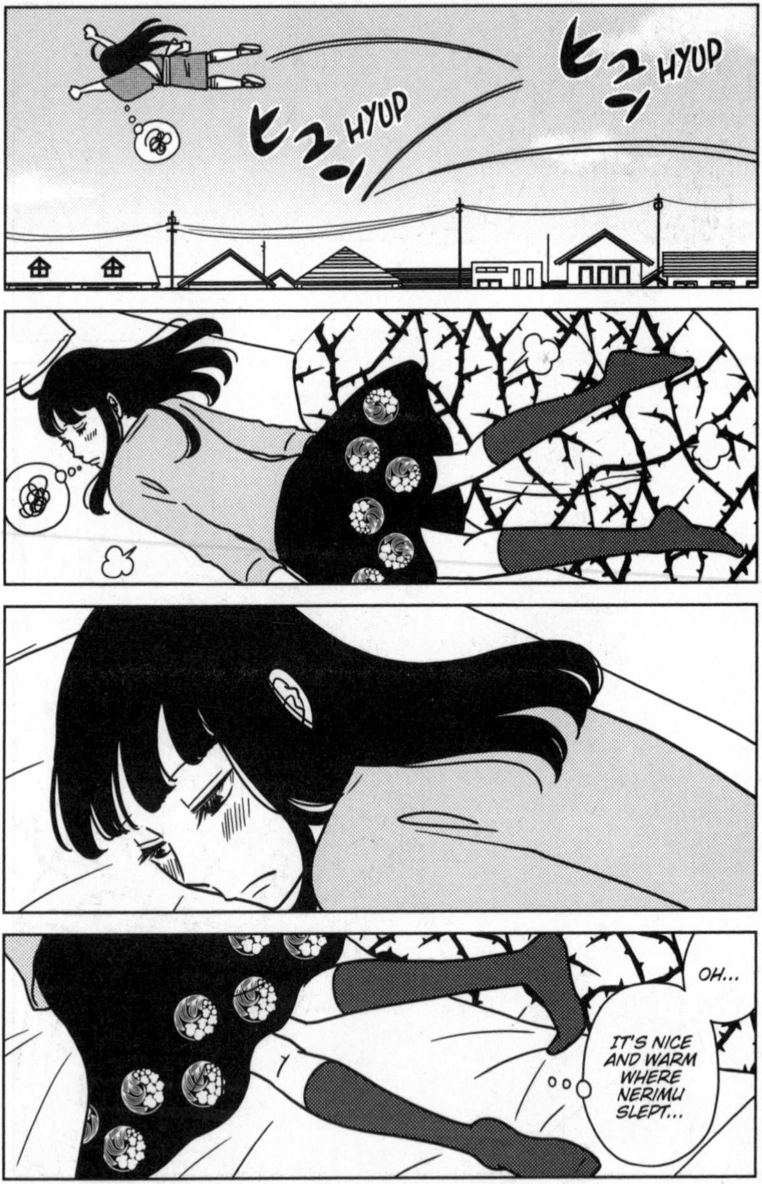
ヒュッ HYUP
ヒュッ HYUP
OH...
IT'S NICE AND WARM WHERE NERIMU SLEPT...

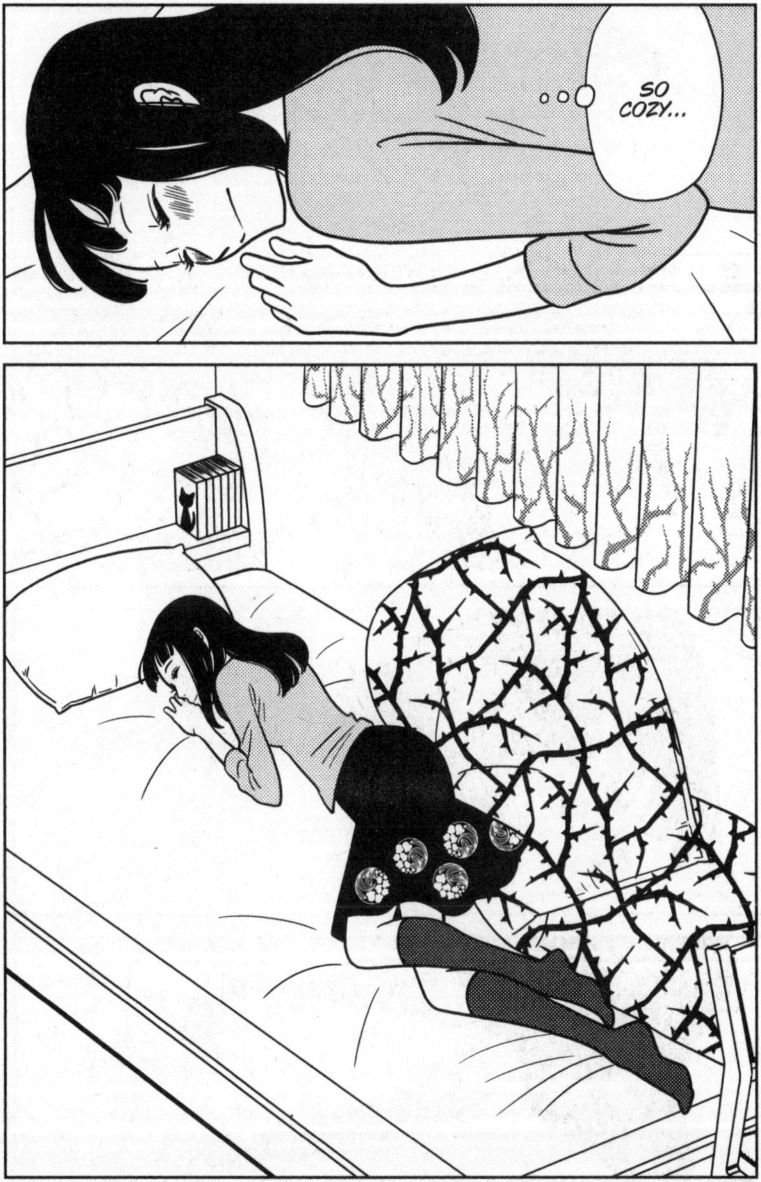
SO COZY...

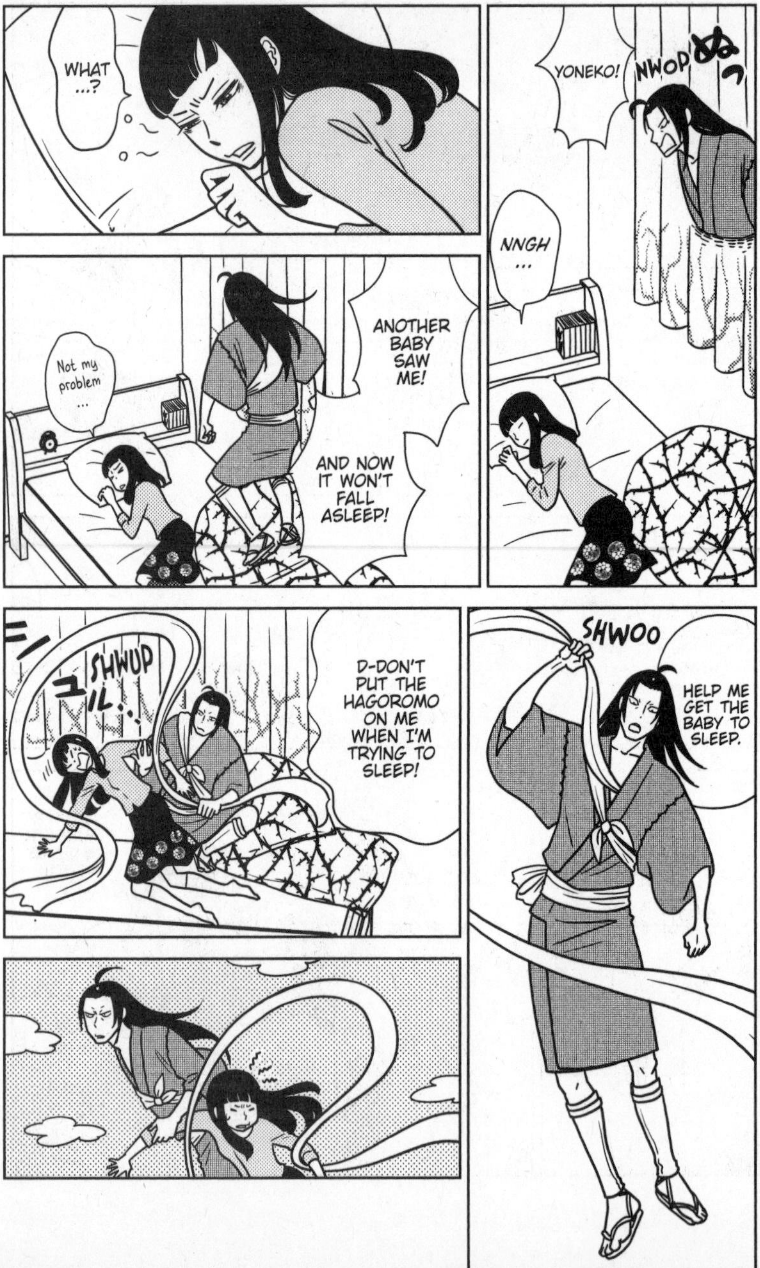
YONEKO!
NWOP ぬっ
NNGH ...
WHAT ...?
Not my problem ...
ANOTHER BABY SAW ME!
AND NOW IT WON'T FALL ASLEEP!
SHWOO
HELP ME GET THE BABY TO SLEEP.
D-DON'T PUT THE HAGOROMO ON ME WHEN I'M TRYING TO SLEEP!
SHWUP ユル...

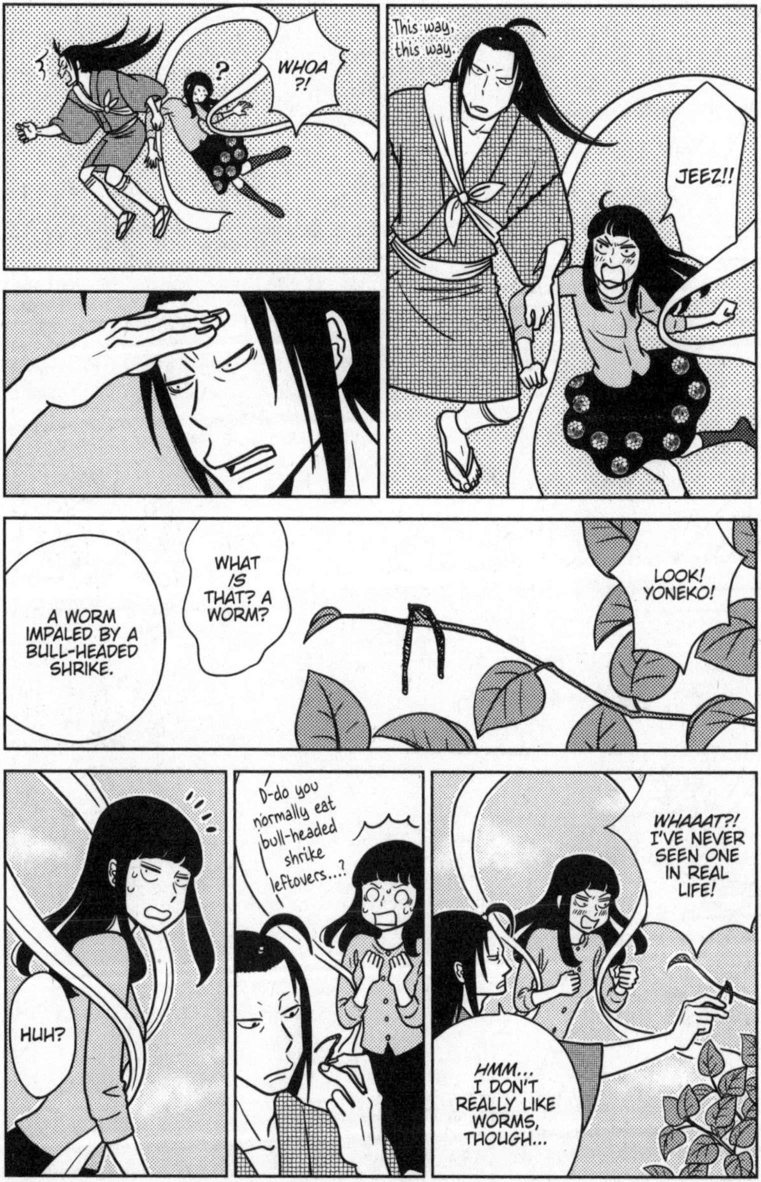
This way, this way.
JEEZ!!
WHOA ?!
LOOK! YONEKO!
WHAT IS THAT? A WORM?
A WORM IMPALED BY A BULL-HEADED SHRIKE.
WHAAAT?! I'VE NEVER SEEN ONE IN REAL LIFE!
HMM... I DON'T REALLY LIKE WORMS, THOUGH...
D-do you normally eat bull-headed shrike leftovers...?
HUH?

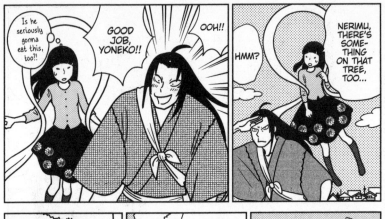

NERIMU, THERE'S SOME-THING ON THAT TREE, TOO...
HMM?
OOH!!
GOOD JOB, YONEKO!!
Is he seriously gonna eat this, too?!
?
DO THOSE PROPORTIONS LOOK A LITTLE...OFF TO YOU?
HUH...? IT LOOKS LIKE A PERSON...
IT'S UTSURA!!
THAT'S AWFUL!
C-COULD HE BE...?

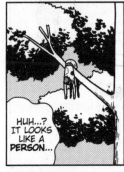

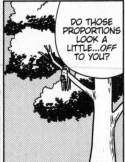

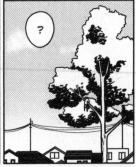

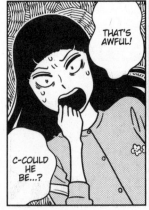

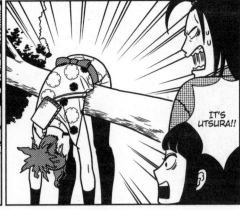

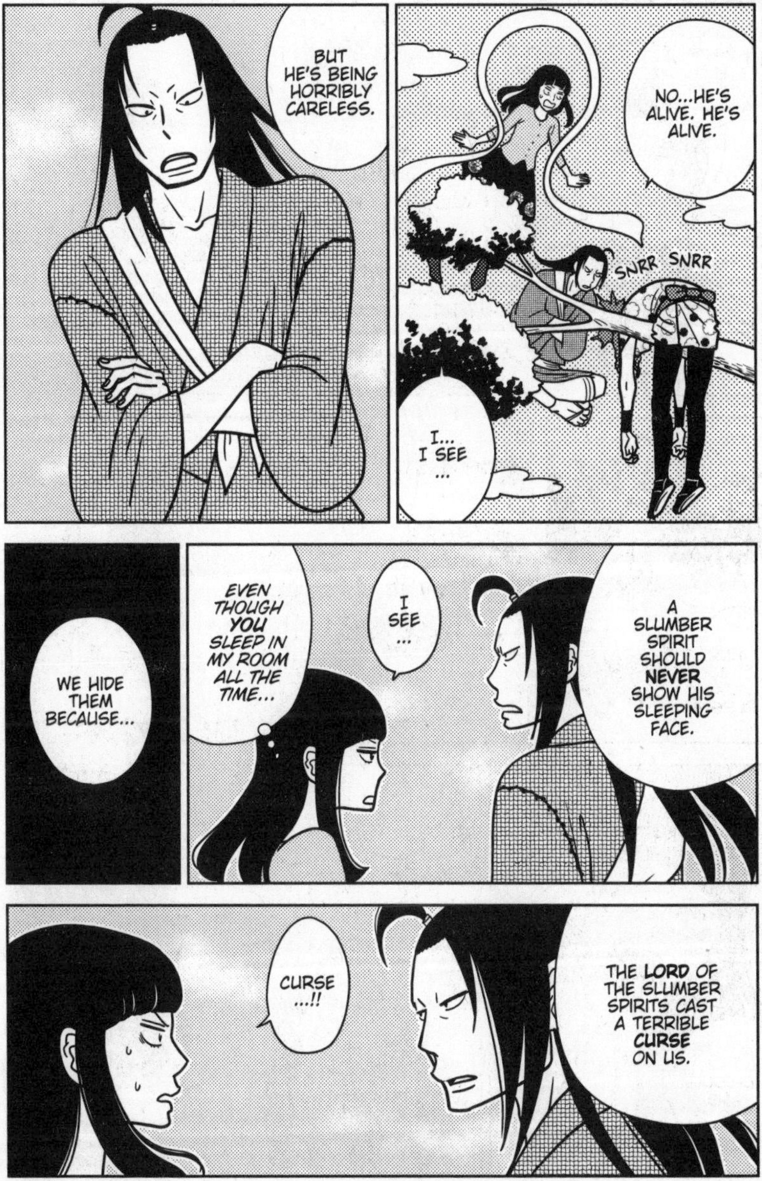
NO...HE'S ALIVE. HE'S ALIVE.
SNRR SNRR
I... I SEE ...
BUT HE'S BEING HORRIBLY CARELESS.
A SLUMBER SPIRIT SHOULD **NEVER** SHOW HIS SLEEPING FACE.
I SEE ...
EVEN THOUGH ***YOU*** *SLEEP IN MY ROOM ALL THE TIME...*
WE HIDE THEM BECAUSE...
THE **LORD** OF THE SLUMBER SPIRITS CAST A TERRIBLE **CURSE** ON US.
CURSE ...!!

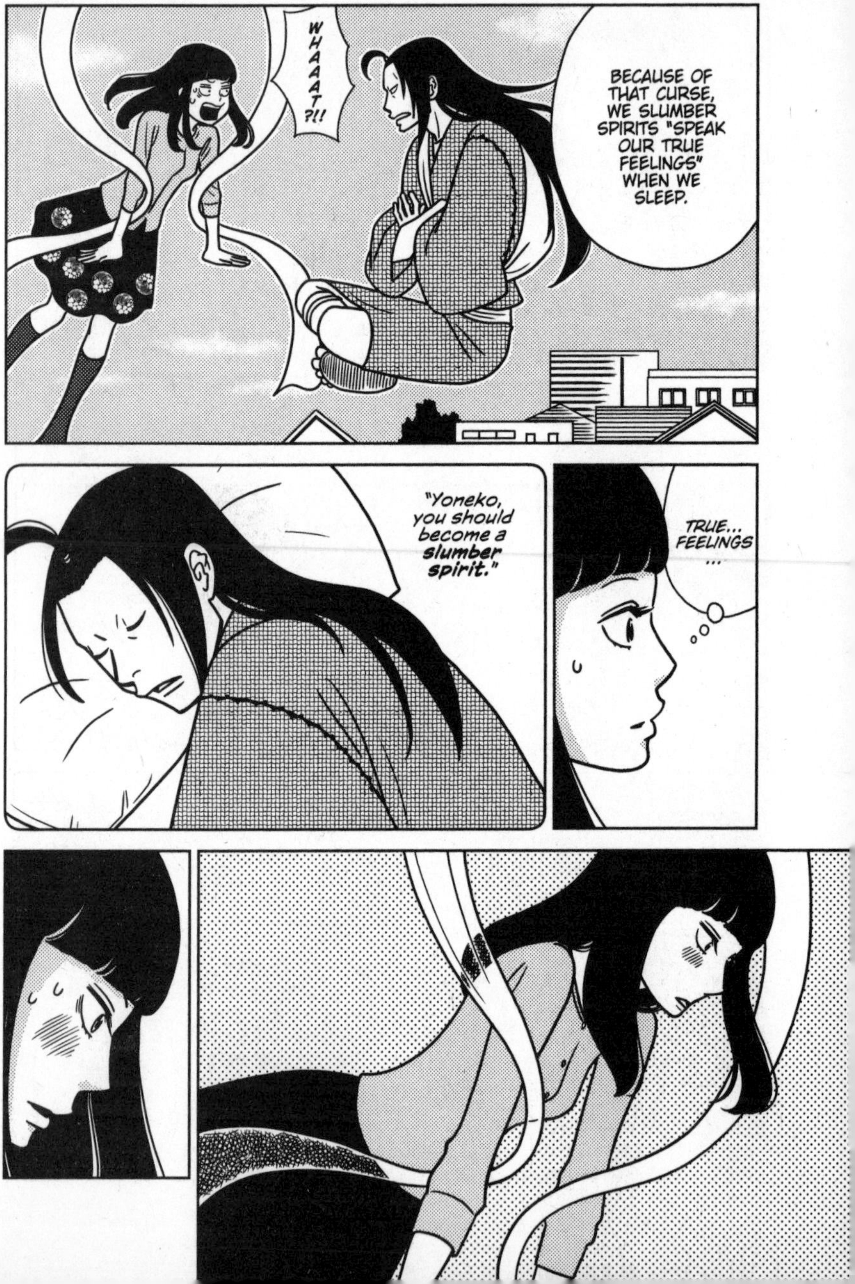
BECAUSE OF THAT CURSE, WE SLUMBER SPIRITS "SPEAK OUR TRUE FEELINGS" WHEN WE SLEEP.
WHAAAT?!!
TRUE... FEELINGS...
"Yoneko, you should become a **slumber spirit.**"

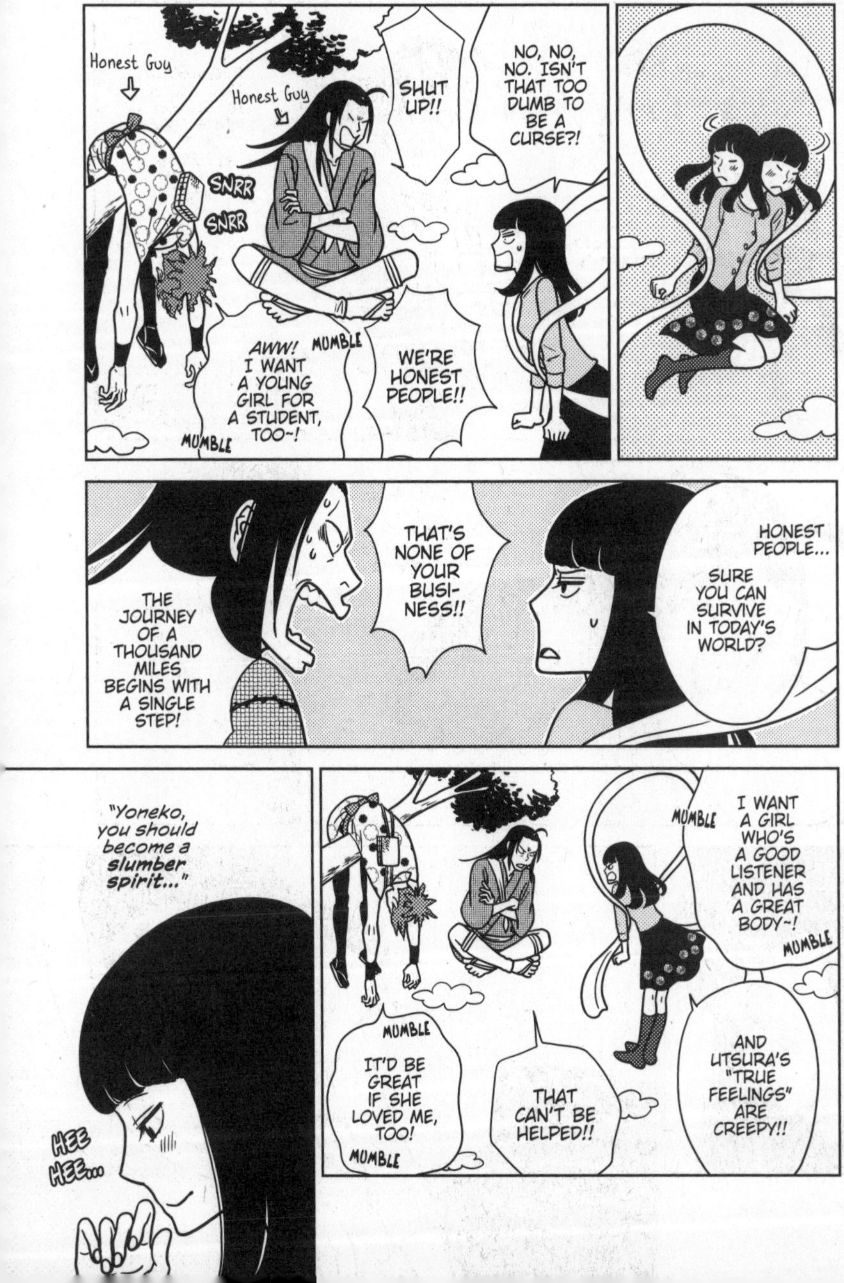
NO, NO, NO. ISN'T THAT TOO DUMB TO BE A CURSE?!
SHUT UP!!
Honest Guy
Honest Guy
SNRR
SNRR
WE'RE HONEST PEOPLE!!
MUMBLE
AWW! I WANT A YOUNG GIRL FOR A STUDENT, TOO~!
MUMBLE
HONEST PEOPLE...
SURE YOU CAN SURVIVE IN TODAY'S WORLD?
THAT'S NONE OF YOUR BUSI-NESS!!
THE JOURNEY OF A THOUSAND MILES BEGINS WITH A SINGLE STEP!
MUMBLE
I WANT A GIRL WHO'S A GOOD LISTENER AND HAS A GREAT BODY~!
MUMBLE
AND UTSURA'S "TRUE FEELINGS" ARE CREEPY!!
THAT CAN'T BE HELPED!!
MUMBLE
IT'D BE GREAT IF SHE LOVED ME, TOO!
MUMBLE
"Yoneko, you should become a slumber spirit..."
HEE HEE...

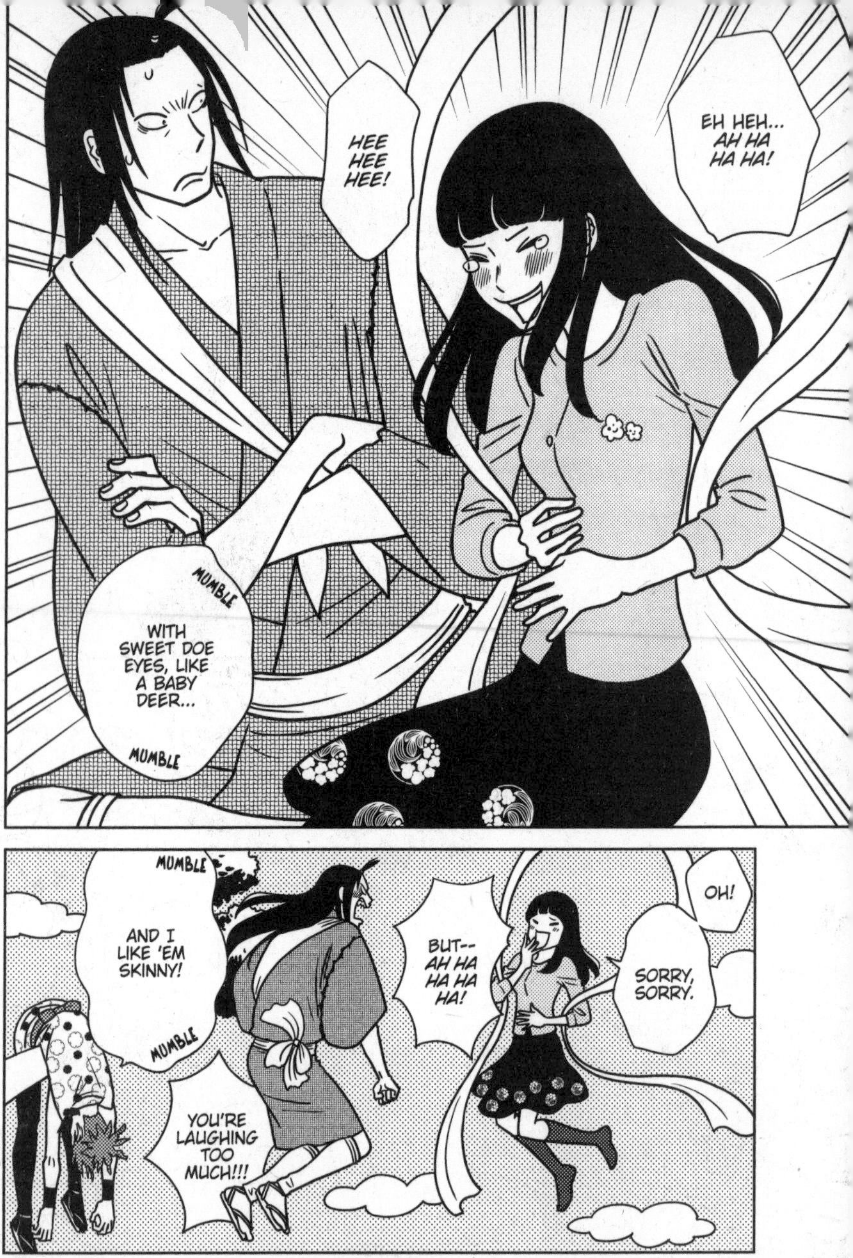
EH HEH... AH HA HA HA!
HEE HEE HEE!
MUMBLE
WITH SWEET DOE EYES, LIKE A BABY DEER...
MUMBLE
OH!
SORRY, SORRY.
BUT-- AH HA HA HA HA!
MUMBLE
AND I LIKE 'EM SKINNY!
MUMBLE
YOU'RE LAUGHING TOO MUCH!!!

Fin

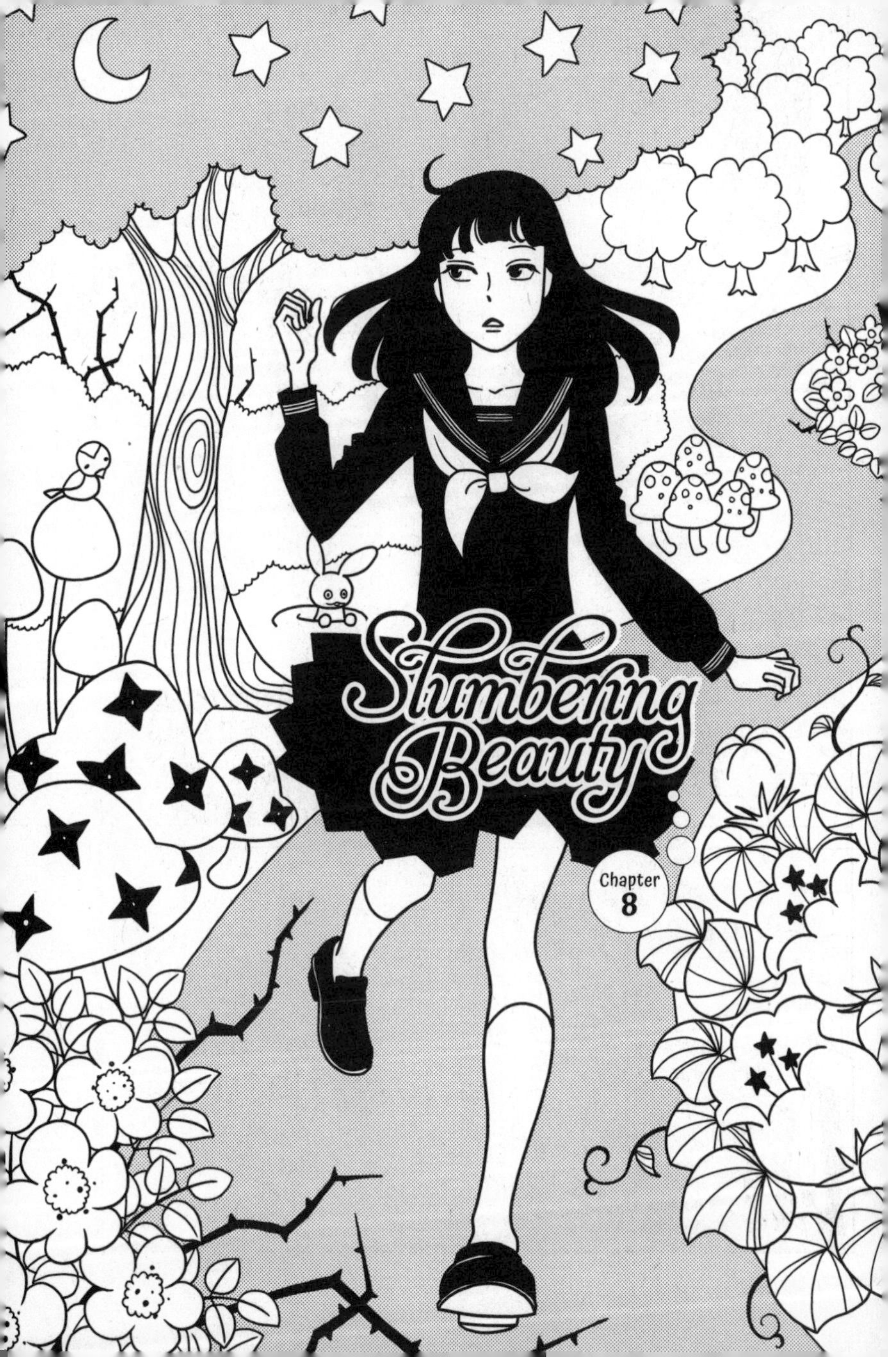

Slumbering Beauty
Chapter 8

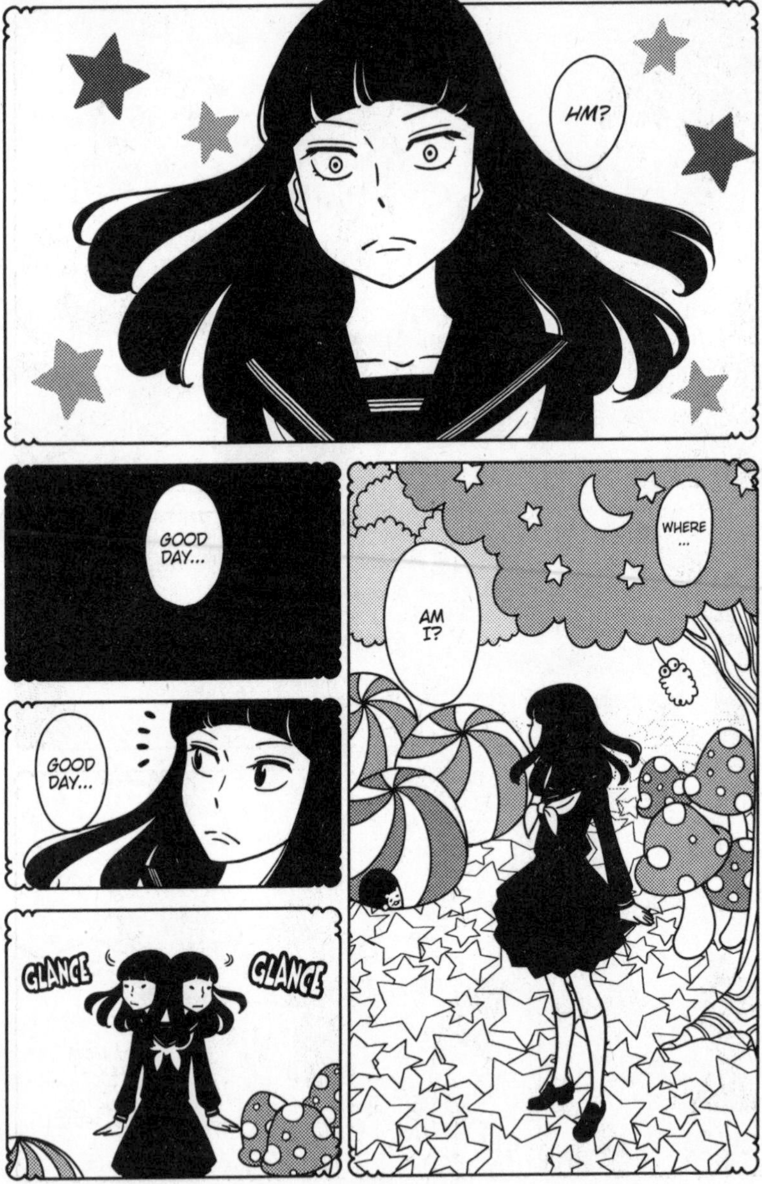
HM?
WHERE ...
AM I?
GOOD DAY...
GOOD DAY...
GLANCE
GLANCE

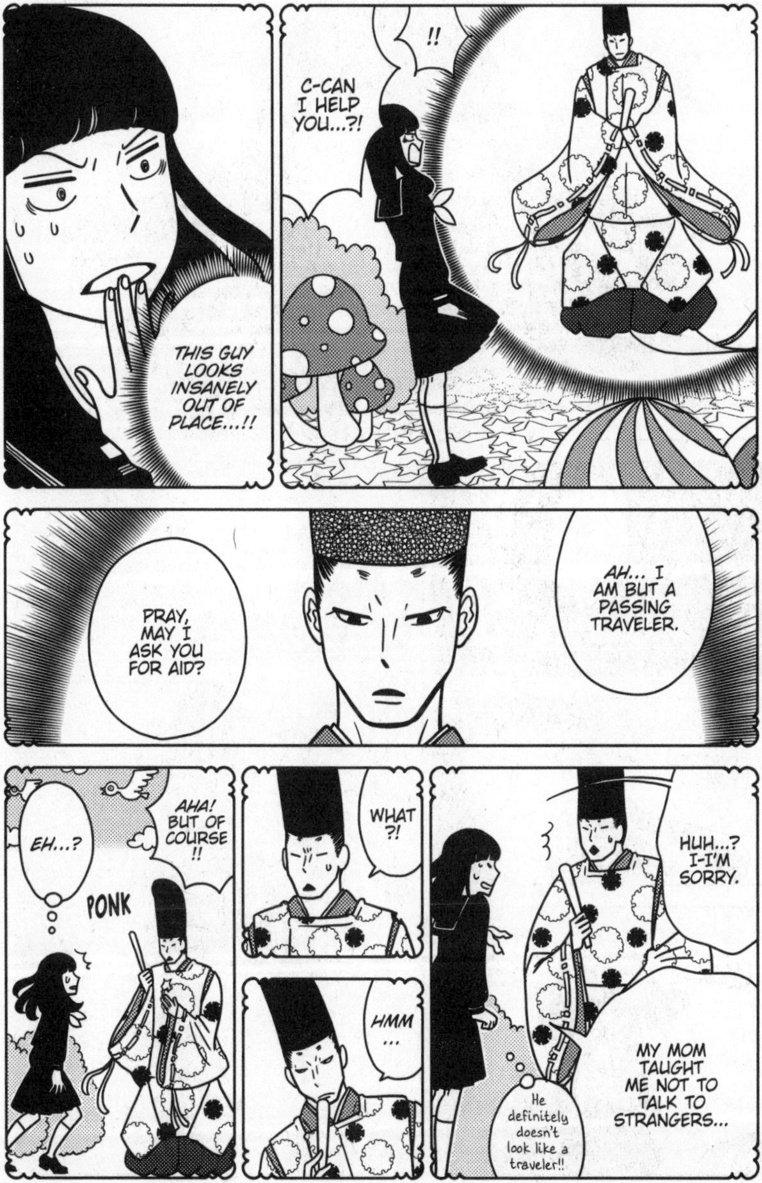
!!
C-CAN I HELP YOU...?!
THIS GUY LOOKS INSANELY OUT OF PLACE...!!
AH... I AM BUT A PASSING TRAVELER.
PRAY, MAY I ASK YOU FOR AID?
HUH...? I-I'M SORRY.
MY MOM TAUGHT ME NOT TO TALK TO STRANGERS...
He definitely doesn't look like a traveler!!
WHAT?!
HMM...
AHA! BUT OF COURSE!!
PONK
EH...?

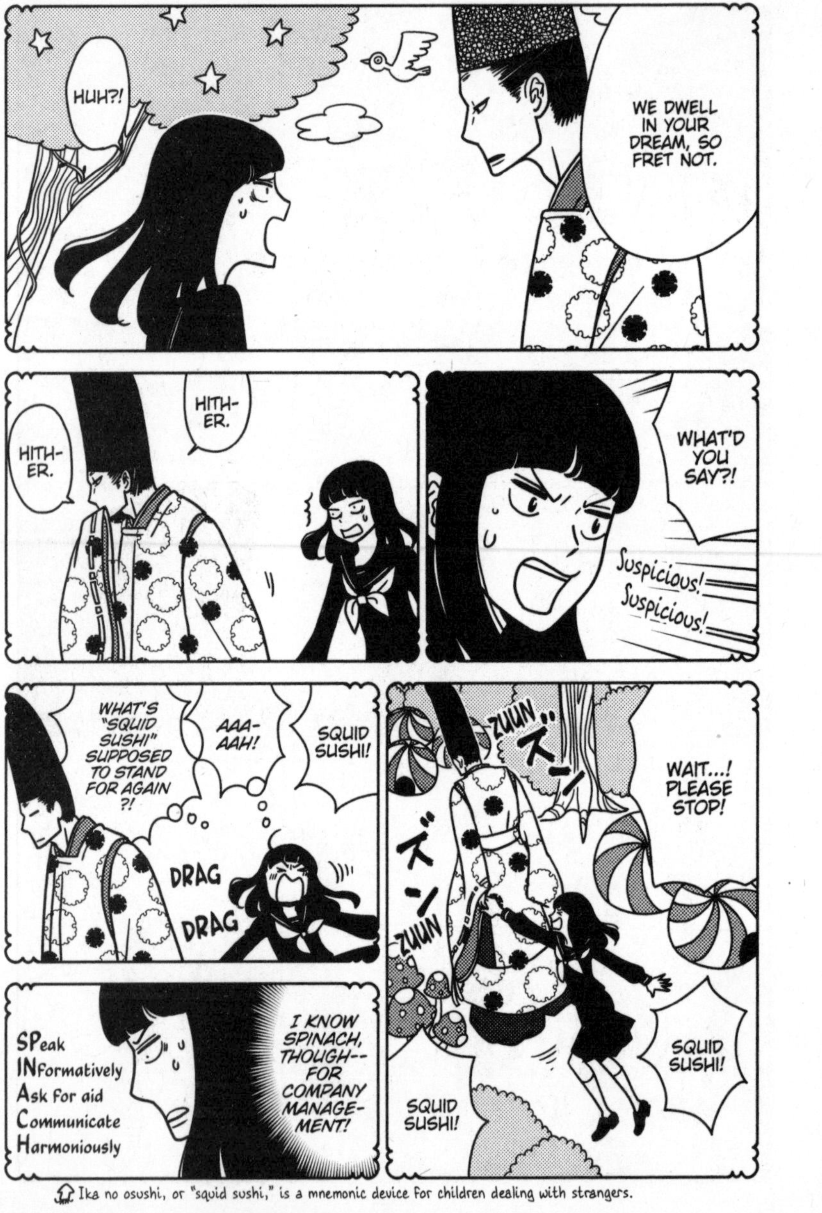
WE DWELL IN YOUR DREAM, SO FRET NOT.
HUH?!
WHAT'D YOU SAY?!
Suspicious! Suspicious!
HITH-ER.
HITH-ER.
WAIT...! PLEASE STOP!
ZUUN
ズーン
SQUID SUSHI!
ズーン
ZUUN
SQUID SUSHI!
SQUID SUSHI!
AAA-AAH!
WHAT'S "SQUID SUSHI" SUPPOSED TO STAND FOR AGAIN ?!
DRAG
DRAG
I KNOW SPINACH, THOUGH-- FOR COMPANY MANAGEMENT!
SPeak
INformatively
Ask for aid
Communicate
Harmoniously

Ika no osushi, or "squid sushi," is a mnemonic device for children dealing with strangers.

MEOW!
NOW! DRIVE THESE CATS TO THEIR REST.
MEOW!
MEOW!
MEOW!
MEOW!
MEOW!
HUH...?
MEOW!
WHY SHOULD I?
MEOW!
MEOW!
CATS CAN SLEEP WHENEVER THEY WANT TO!
WHY SHOULD I HELP SOMEONE I DON'T KNOW WITH A TASK THAT SOLVES NOTHING?!
......

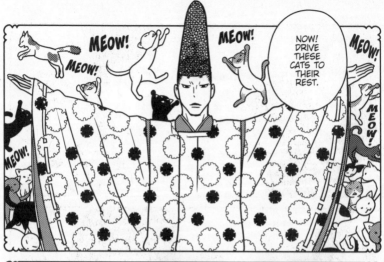

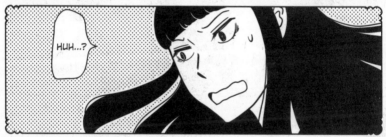

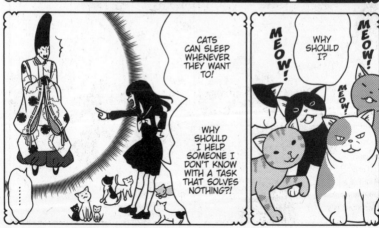

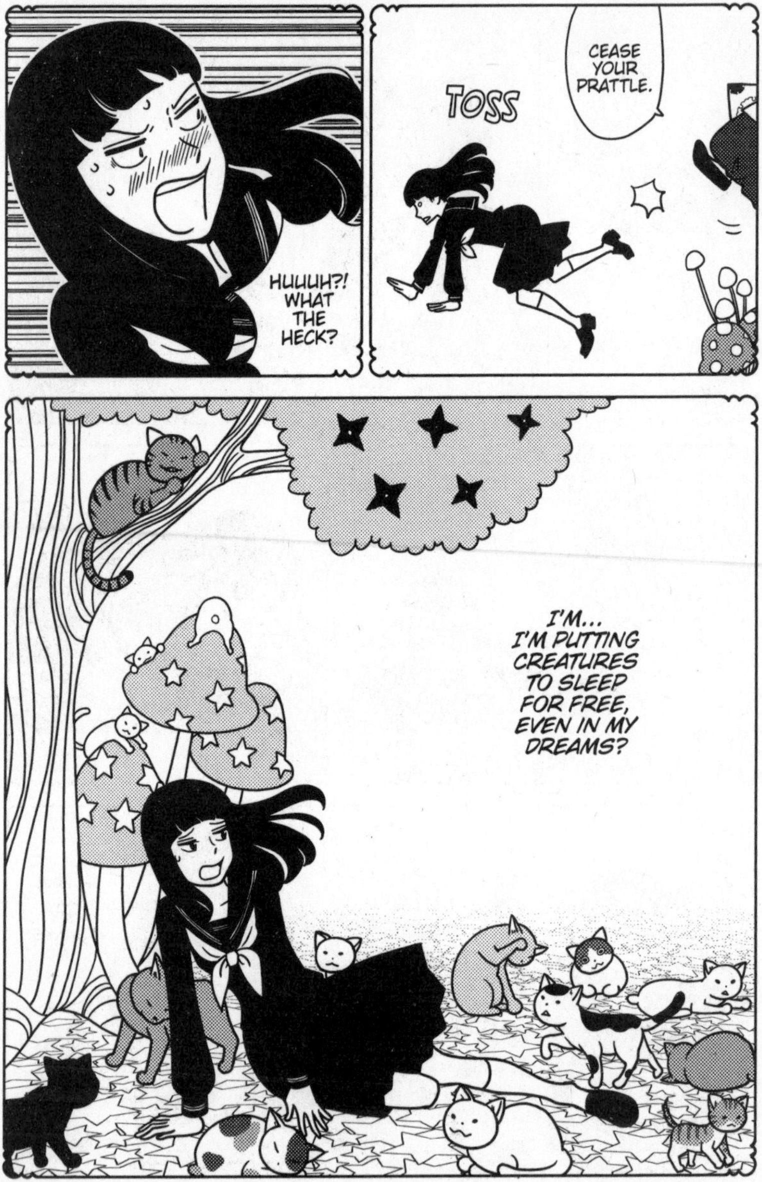
CEASE YOUR PRATTLE.
TOSS
HUUUH?! WHAT THE HECK?
I'M... I'M PUTTING CREATURES TO SLEEP FOR FREE, EVEN IN MY DREAMS?

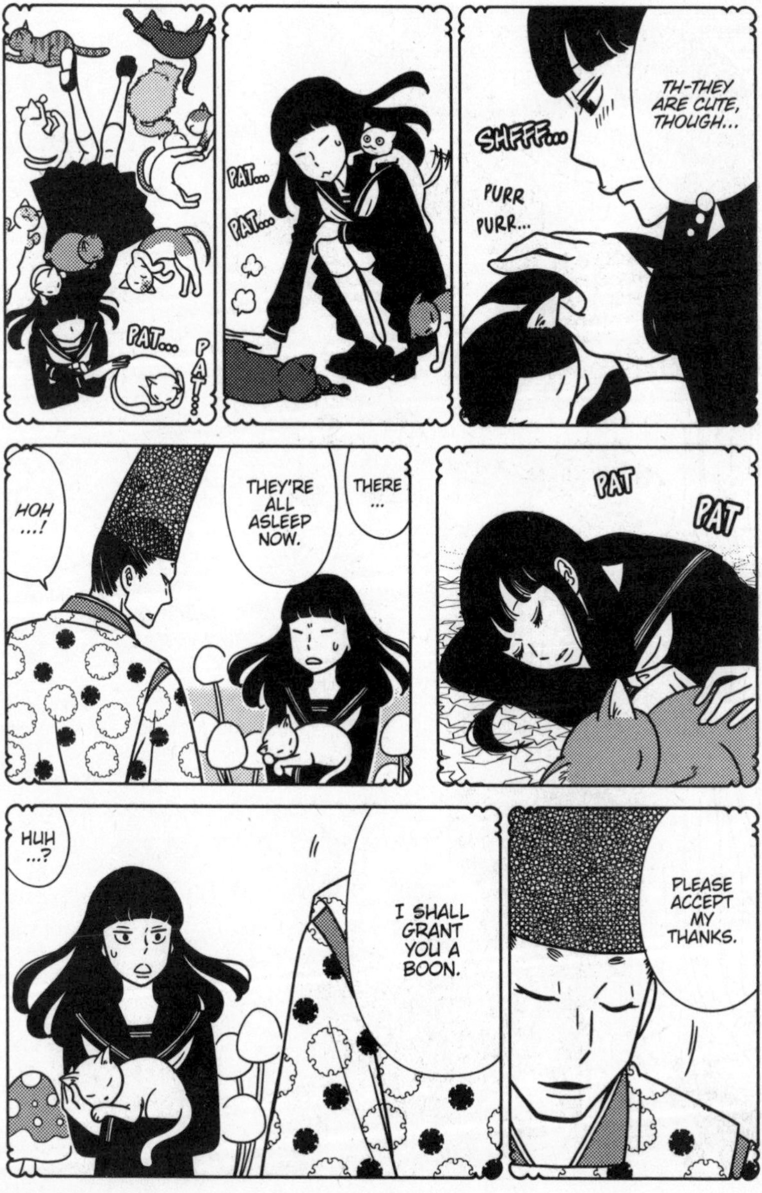
TH-THEY ARE CUTE, THOUGH...
SHFFF...
PURR PURR...
PAT...
PAT...
PAT...
PAT...
PAT
PAT
THERE ...
THEY'RE ALL ASLEEP NOW.
HOH ...!
PLEASE ACCEPT MY THANKS.
I SHALL GRANT YOU A BOON.
HUH ...?

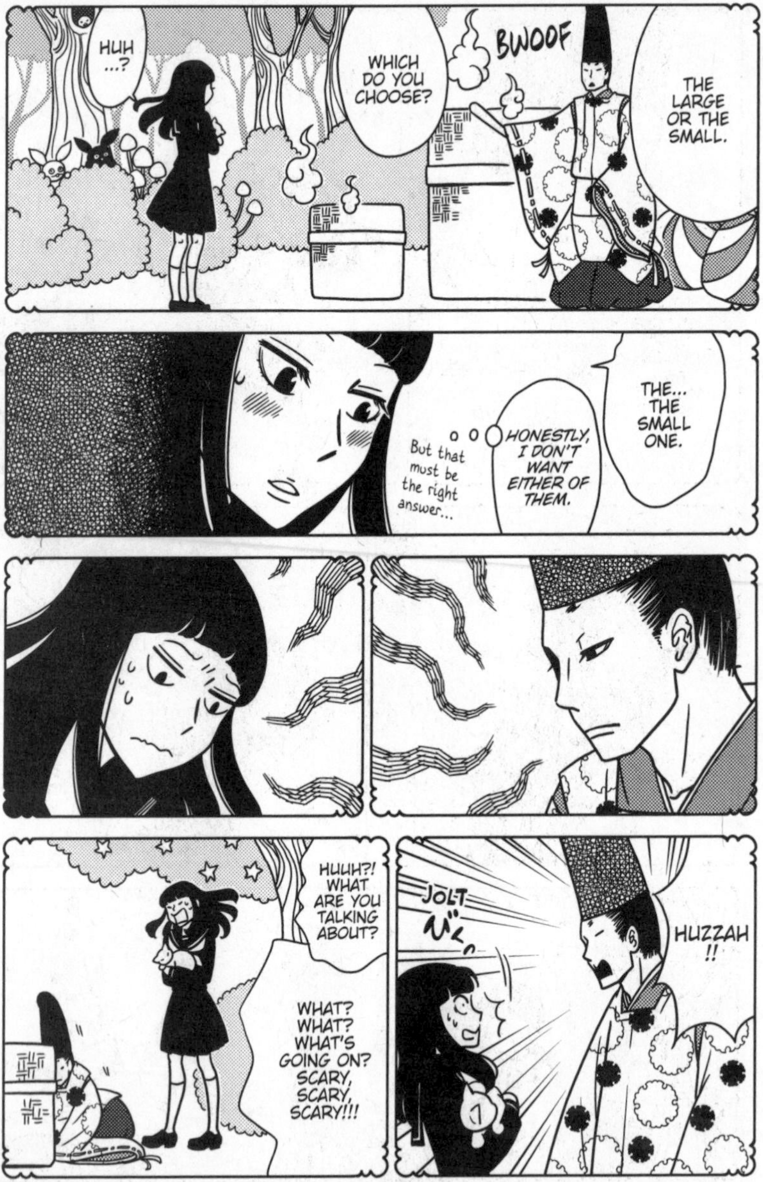
THE LARGE OR THE SMALL.
BWOOF
WHICH DO YOU CHOOSE?
HUH ...?
THE... THE SMALL ONE.
HONESTLY, I DON'T WANT EITHER OF THEM.
But that must be the right answer...
HUZZAH !!
JOLT
びく
HUUH?! WHAT ARE YOU TALKING ABOUT?
WHAT? WHAT? WHAT'S GOING ON? SCARY, SCARY, SCARY!!!

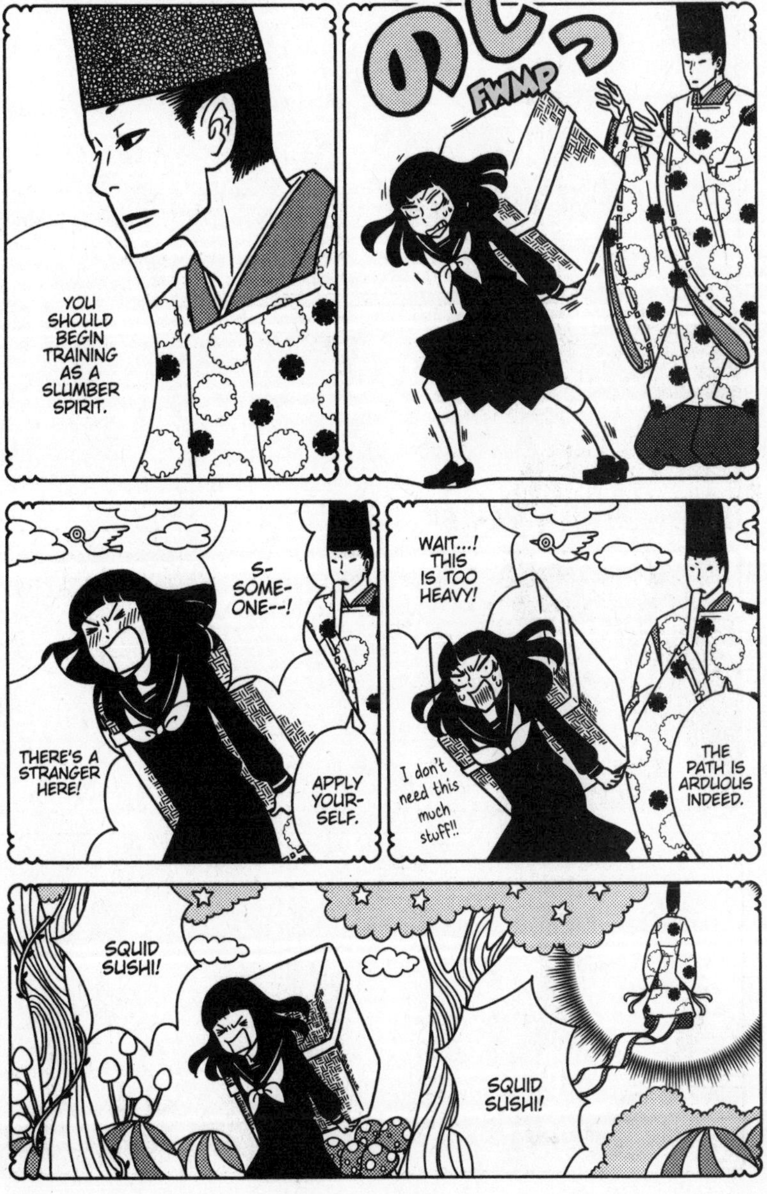
のしっ
FWMP
YOU SHOULD BEGIN TRAINING AS A SLUMBER SPIRIT.
WAIT...! THIS IS TOO HEAVY!
THE PATH IS ARDUOUS INDEED.
I don't need this much stuff!!
S-SOME-ONE--!
APPLY YOUR-SELF.
THERE'S A STRANGER HERE!
SQUID SUSHI!
SQUID SUSHI!

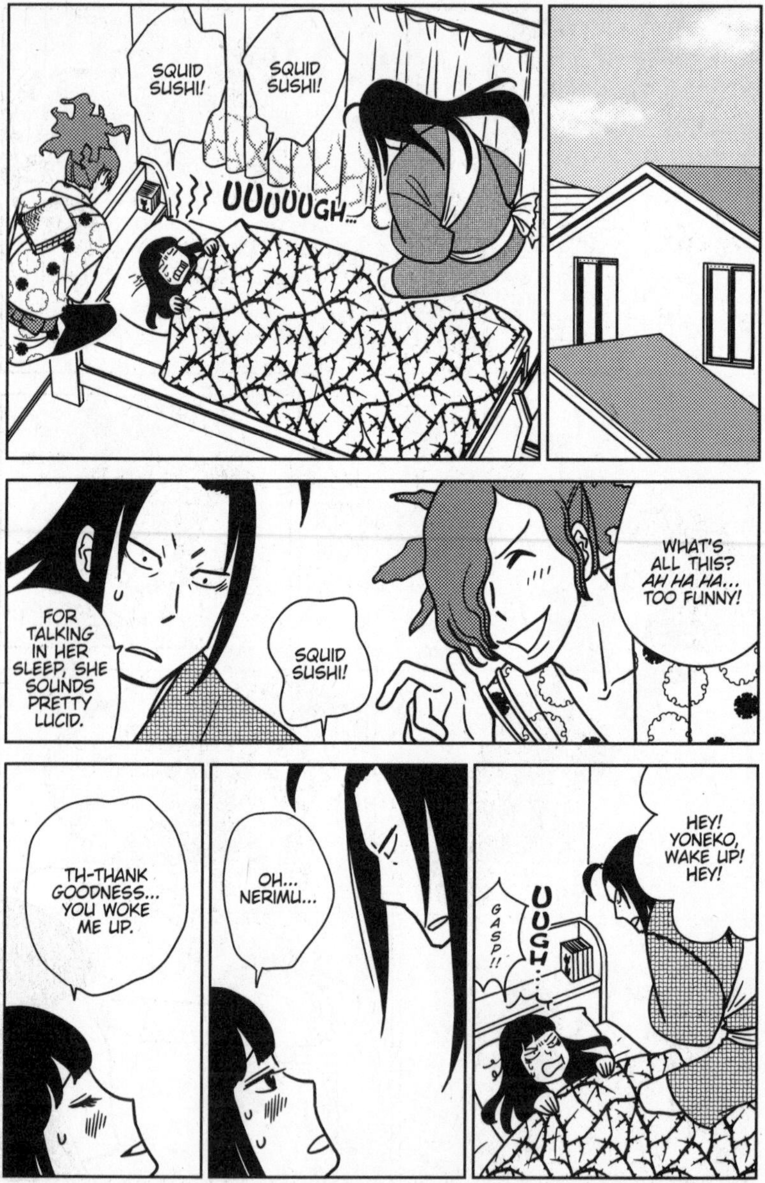
SQUID SUSHI!
SQUID SUSHI!
UUUUUGH...
WHAT'S ALL THIS? AH HA HA... TOO FUNNY!
SQUID SUSHI!
FOR TALKING IN HER SLEEP, SHE SOUNDS PRETTY LUCID.
HEY! YONEKO, WAKE UP! HEY!
UUGH...
GASP!!
OH... NERIMU...
TH-THANK GOODNESS... YOU WOKE ME UP.

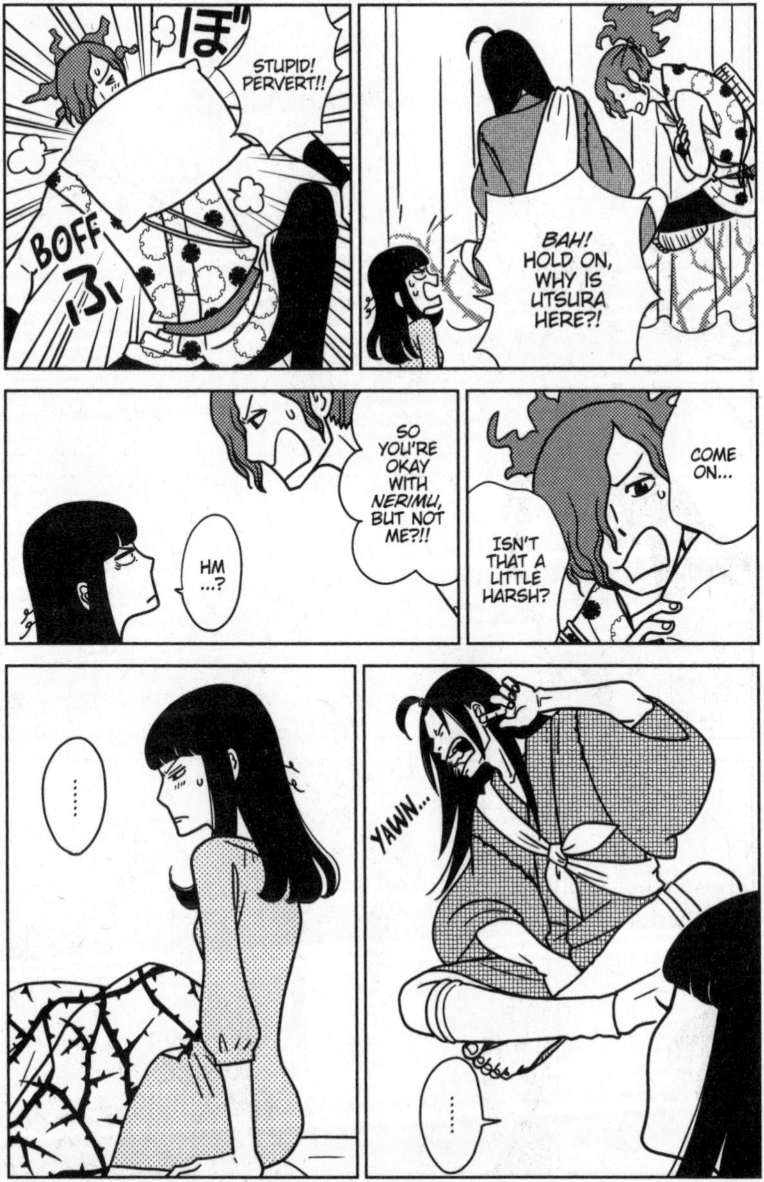
BAH! HOLD ON, WHY IS UTSURA HERE?!
STUPID! PERVERT!!
ぼ
BOFF
ふ
COME ON...
ISN'T THAT A LITTLE HARSH?
SO YOU'RE OKAY WITH NERIMU, BUT NOT ME?!!
HM ...?
YAWN...
......
......

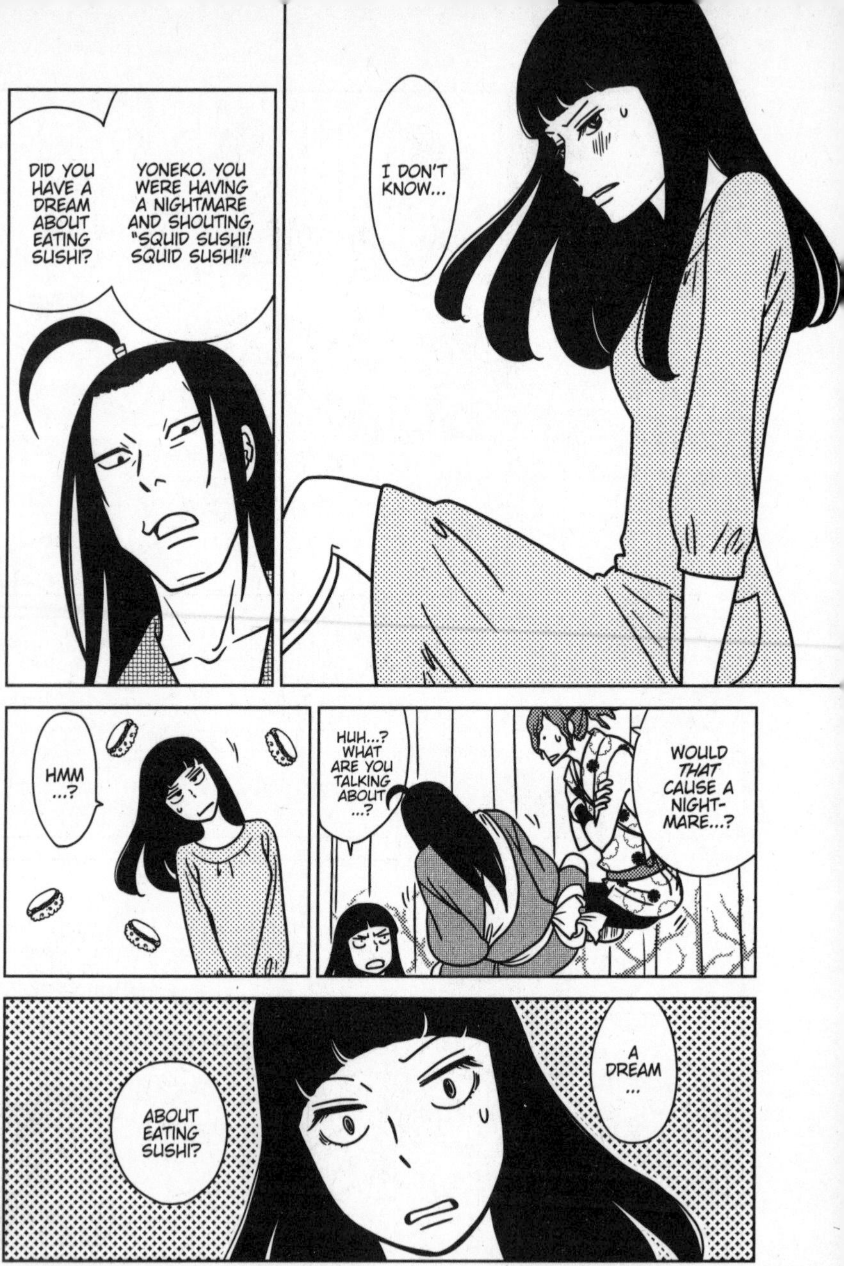
I DON'T KNOW...
YONEKO. YOU WERE HAVING A NIGHTMARE AND SHOUTING, "SQUID SUSHI! SQUID SUSHI!"
DID YOU HAVE A DREAM ABOUT EATING SUSHI?
WOULD *THAT* CAUSE A NIGHT-MARE...?
HUH...? WHAT ARE YOU TALKING ABOUT...?
HMM...?
A DREAM...
ABOUT EATING SUSHI?

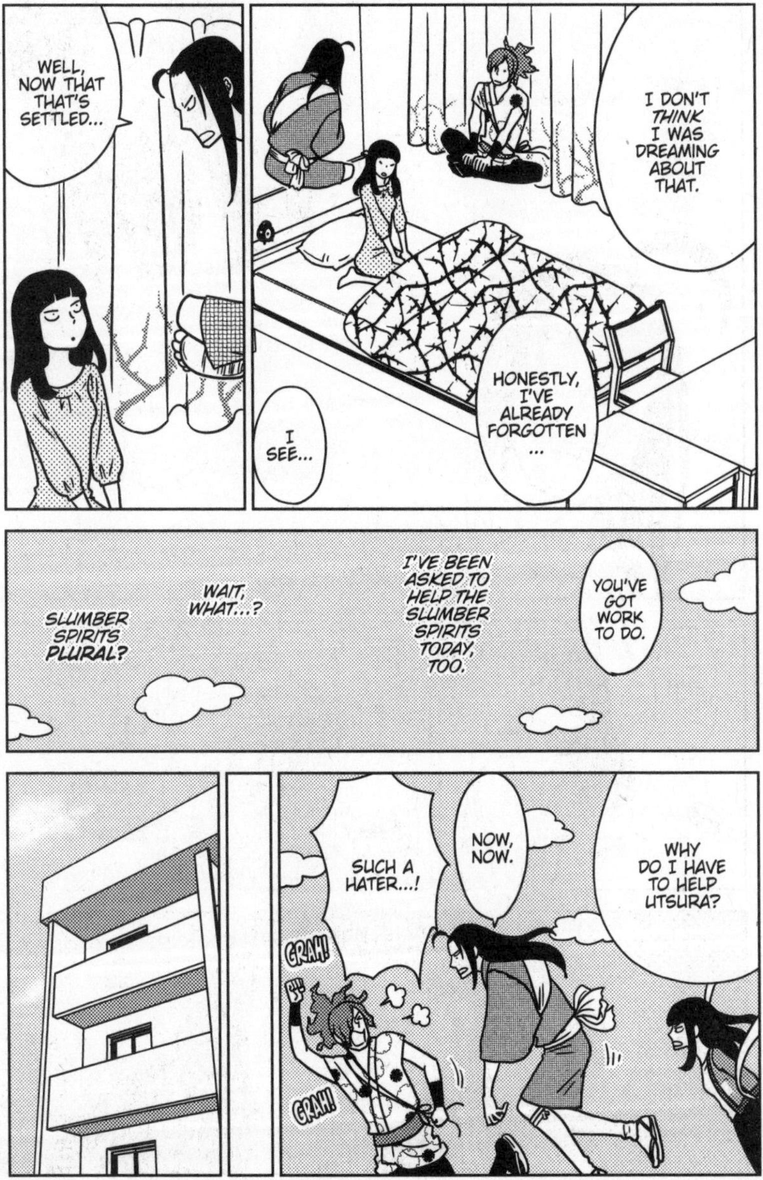
I DON'T *THINK* I WAS DREAMING ABOUT THAT.
HONESTLY, I'VE ALREADY FORGOTTEN ...
I SEE...
WELL, NOW THAT THAT'S SETTLED...
YOU'VE GOT WORK TO DO.
I'VE BEEN ASKED TO HELP THE SLUMBER SPIRITS TODAY, TOO.
WAIT, WHAT...?
SLUMBER SPIRITS **PLURAL?**
WHY DO I HAVE TO HELP UTSURA?
NOW, NOW.
SUCH A HATER...!
GRAH!
GRAH!

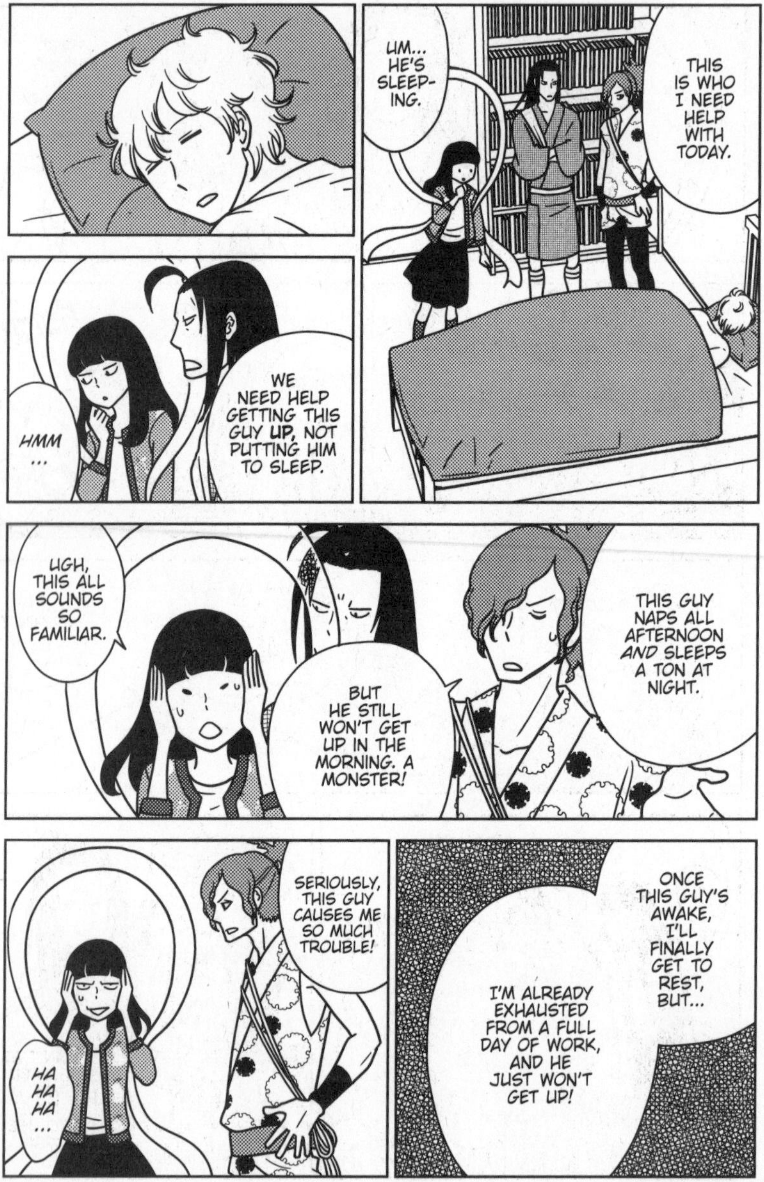
THIS IS WHO I NEED HELP WITH TODAY.
UM... HE'S SLEEP-ING.
WE NEED HELP GETTING THIS GUY **UP**, NOT PUTTING HIM TO SLEEP.
HMM...
THIS GUY NAPS ALL AFTERNOON *AND* SLEEPS A TON AT NIGHT.
BUT HE STILL WON'T GET UP IN THE MORNING. A MONSTER!
UGH, THIS ALL SOUNDS SO FAMILIAR.
ONCE THIS GUY'S AWAKE, I'LL FINALLY GET TO REST, BUT...
I'M ALREADY EXHAUSTED FROM A FULL DAY OF WORK, AND HE JUST WON'T GET UP!
SERIOUSLY, THIS GUY CAUSES ME SO MUCH TROUBLE!
HA HA HA...

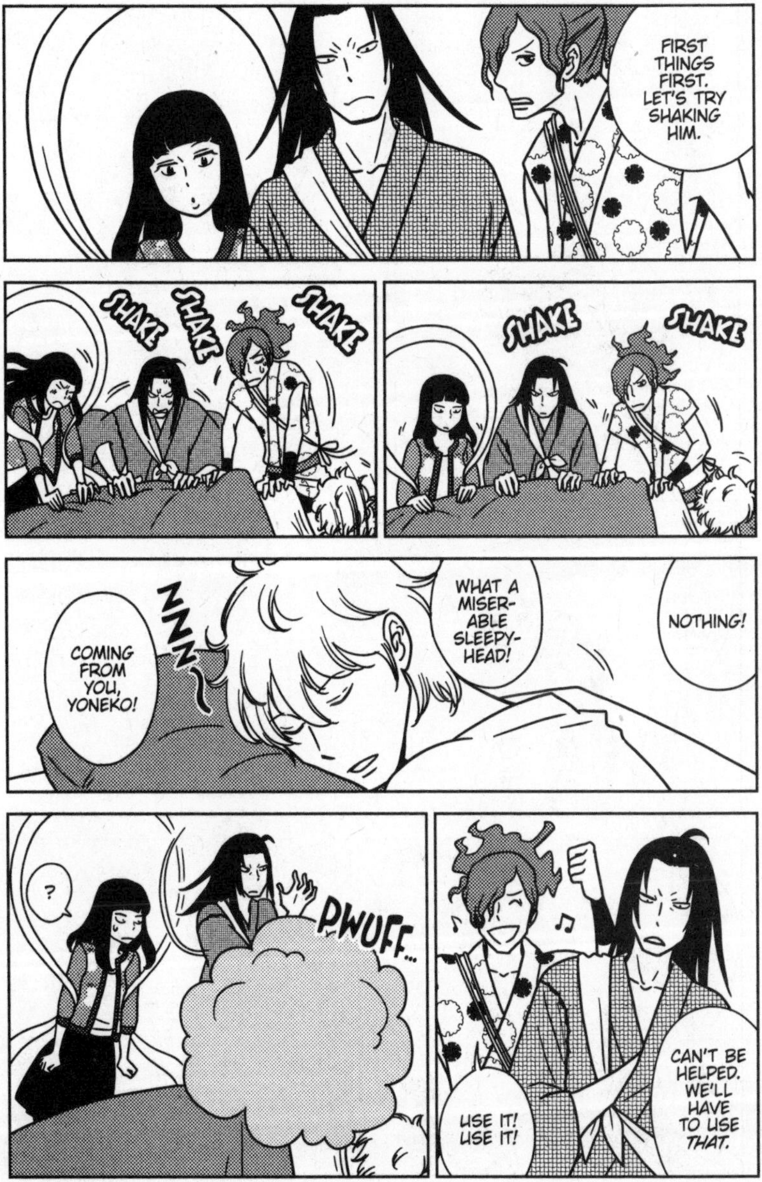
FIRST THINGS FIRST. LET'S TRY SHAKING HIM.
SHAKE
SHAKE
SHAKE
SHAKE
SHAKE
NOTHING!
WHAT A MISER-ABLE SLEEPY-HEAD!
NNN~
COMING FROM YOU, YONEKO!
CAN'T BE HELPED. WE'LL HAVE TO USE *THAT.*
USE IT! USE IT!
PWUFF...
?

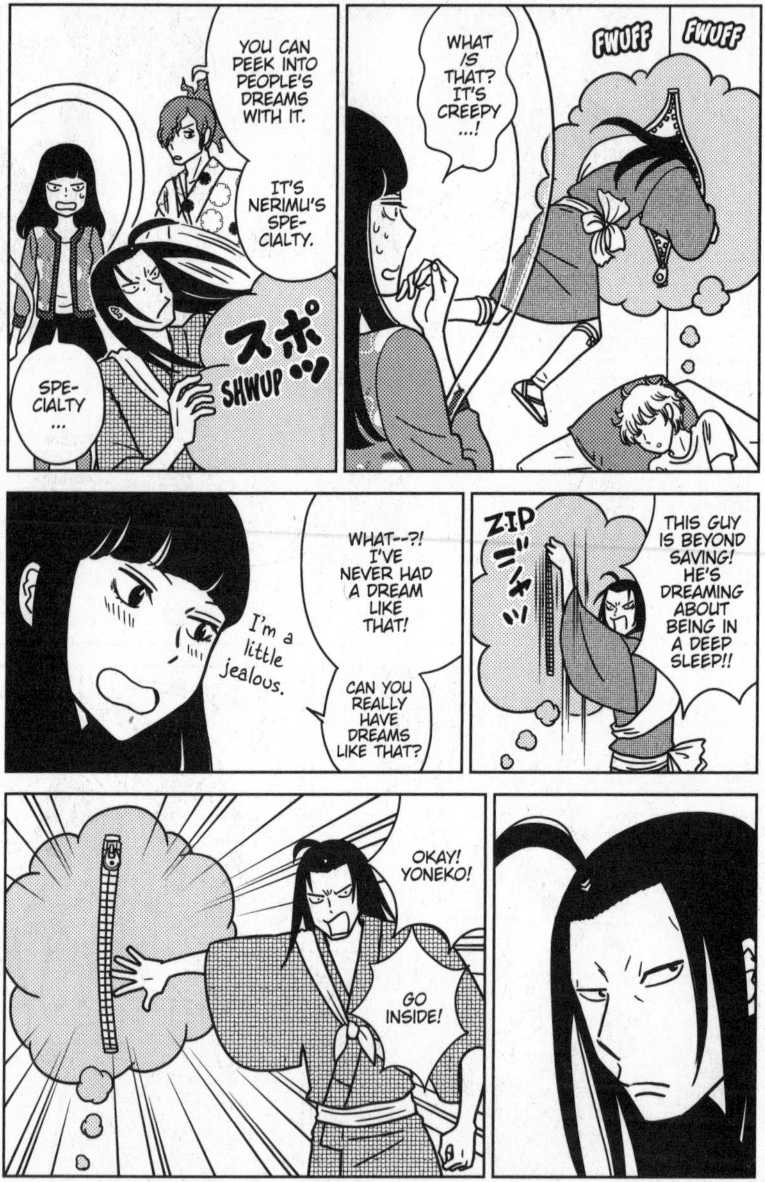
FWUFF
FWUFF
WHAT IS THAT? IT'S CREEPY ...!
YOU CAN PEEK INTO PEOPLE'S DREAMS WITH IT.
IT'S NERIMU'S SPE-CIALTY.
スポッ
SHWUP
SPE-CIALTY ...
THIS GUY IS BEYOND SAVING! HE'S DREAMING ABOUT BEING IN A DEEP SLEEP!!
ZIP
ジャッ
WHAT--?! I'VE NEVER HAD A DREAM LIKE THAT!
CAN YOU REALLY HAVE DREAMS LIKE THAT?
I'm a little jealous.
OKAY! YONEKO!
GO INSIDE!

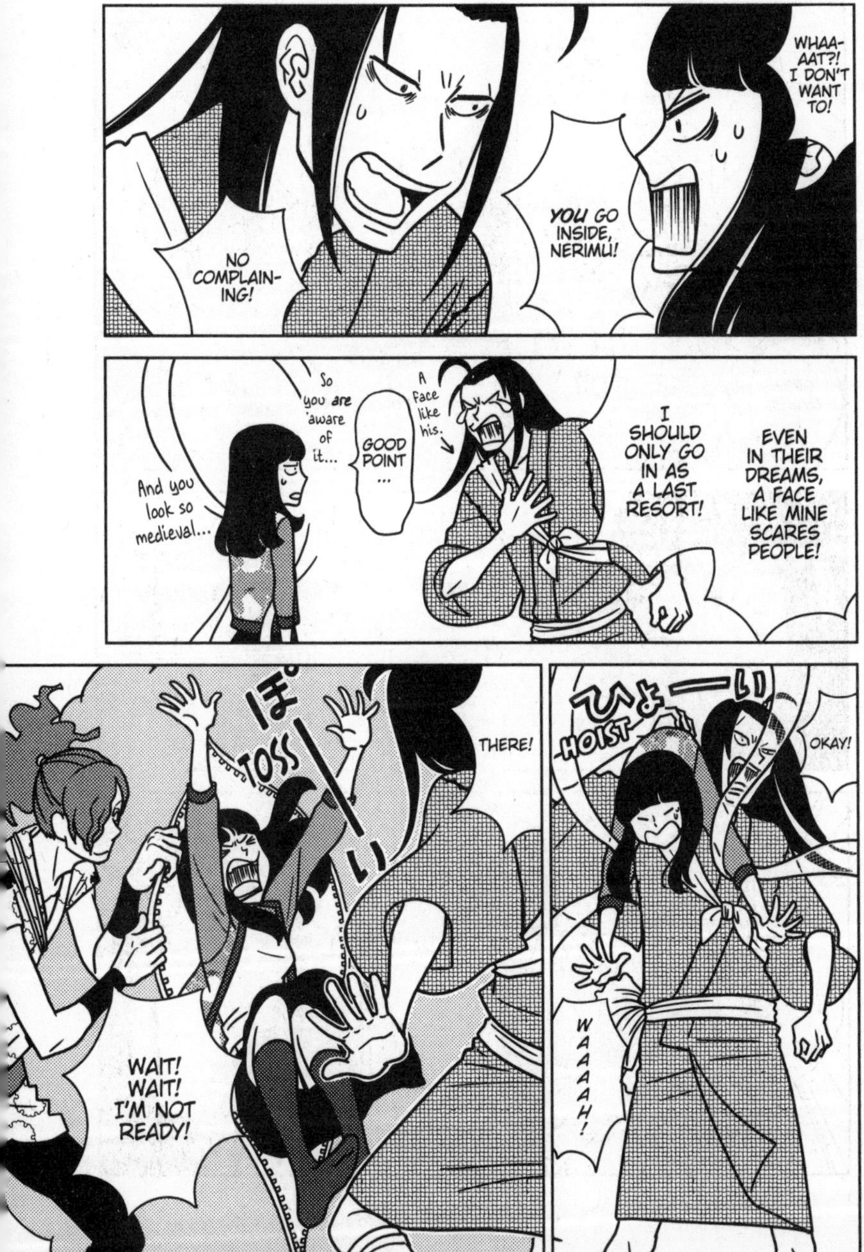

WHAA-AAT?! I DON'T WANT TO!
YOU GO INSIDE, NERIMU!
NO COMPLAIN-ING!
EVEN IN THEIR DREAMS, A FACE LIKE MINE SCARES PEOPLE!
I SHOULD ONLY GO IN AS A LAST RESORT!
A face like his.
GOOD POINT...
So you are aware of it...
And you look so medieval...
ひょーーい
HOIST
OKAY!
WAAAAAH!
THERE!
ぽーい
TOSS
WAIT! WAIT! I'M NOT READY!

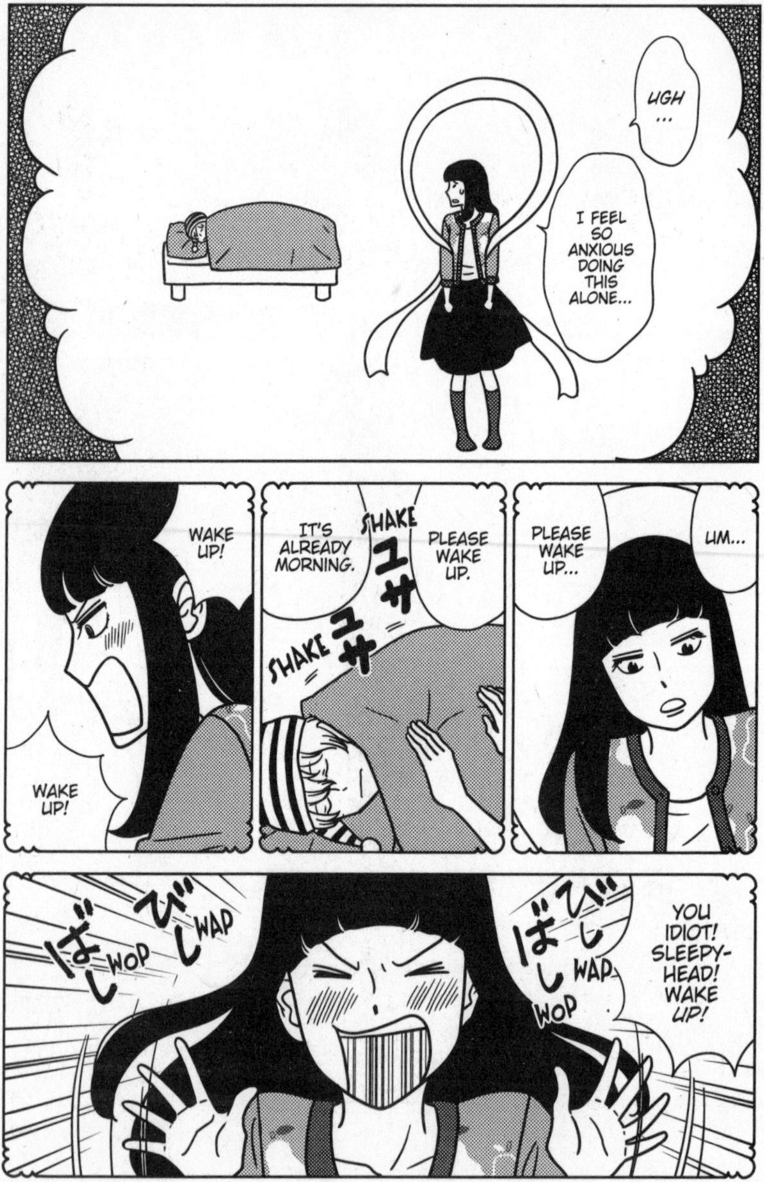
UGH ...
I FEEL SO ANXIOUS DOING THIS ALONE...
UM...
PLEASE WAKE UP...
PLEASE WAKE UP.
SHAKE ユサ
IT'S ALREADY MORNING.
SHAKE ユサ
WAKE UP!
WAKE UP!
YOU IDIOT! SLEEPY-HEAD! WAKE UP!
びし WAP
ばし WOP
びし WAP
ばし WOP

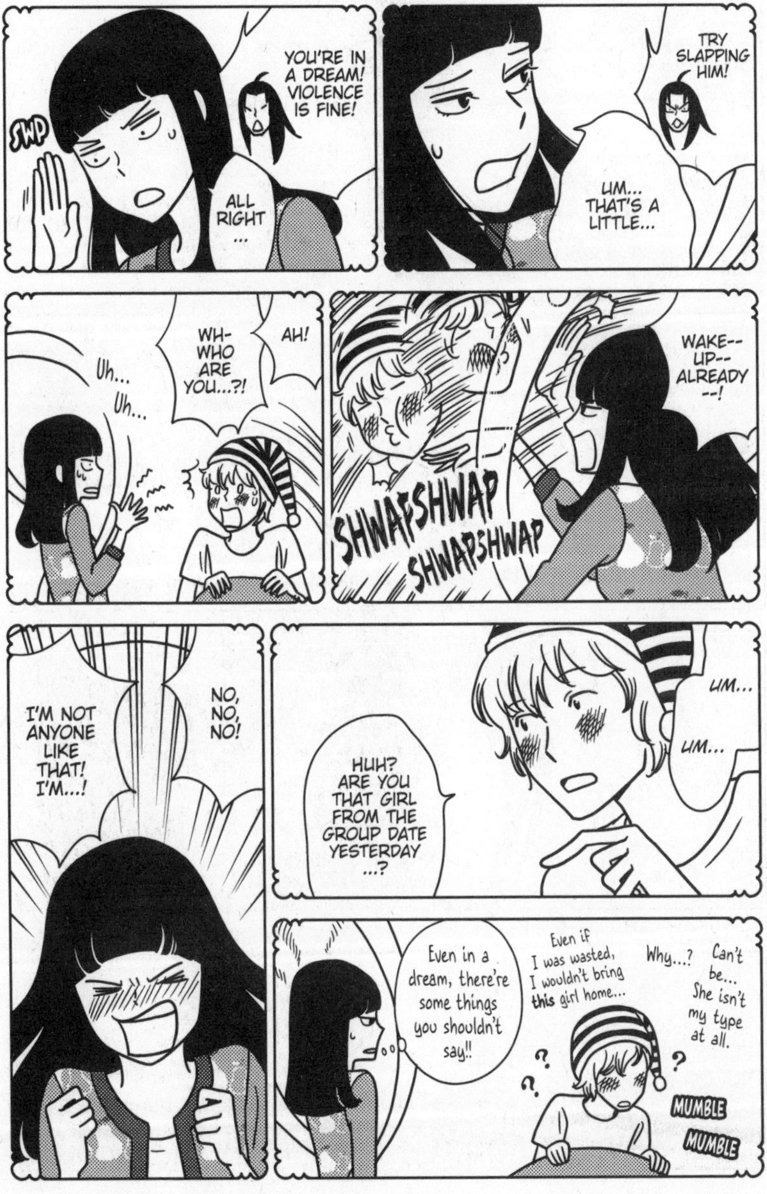
TRY SLAPPING HIM!
UM... THAT'S A LITTLE...
YOU'RE IN A DREAM! VIOLENCE IS FINE!
SWP
ALL RIGHT ...
WAKE-- UP-- ALREADY --!
SHWAPSHWAP
SHWAPSHWAP
AH!
WH- WHO ARE YOU...?!
Uh...
Uh...
UM...
UM...
HUH? ARE YOU THAT GIRL FROM THE GROUP DATE YESTERDAY ...?
Can't be... She isn't my type at all.
Why...?
Even if I was wasted, I wouldn't bring **this** girl home...
Even in a dream, there're some things you shouldn't say!!
MUMBLE
MUMBLE
NO, NO, NO!
I'M NOT ANYONE LIKE THAT! I'M...!

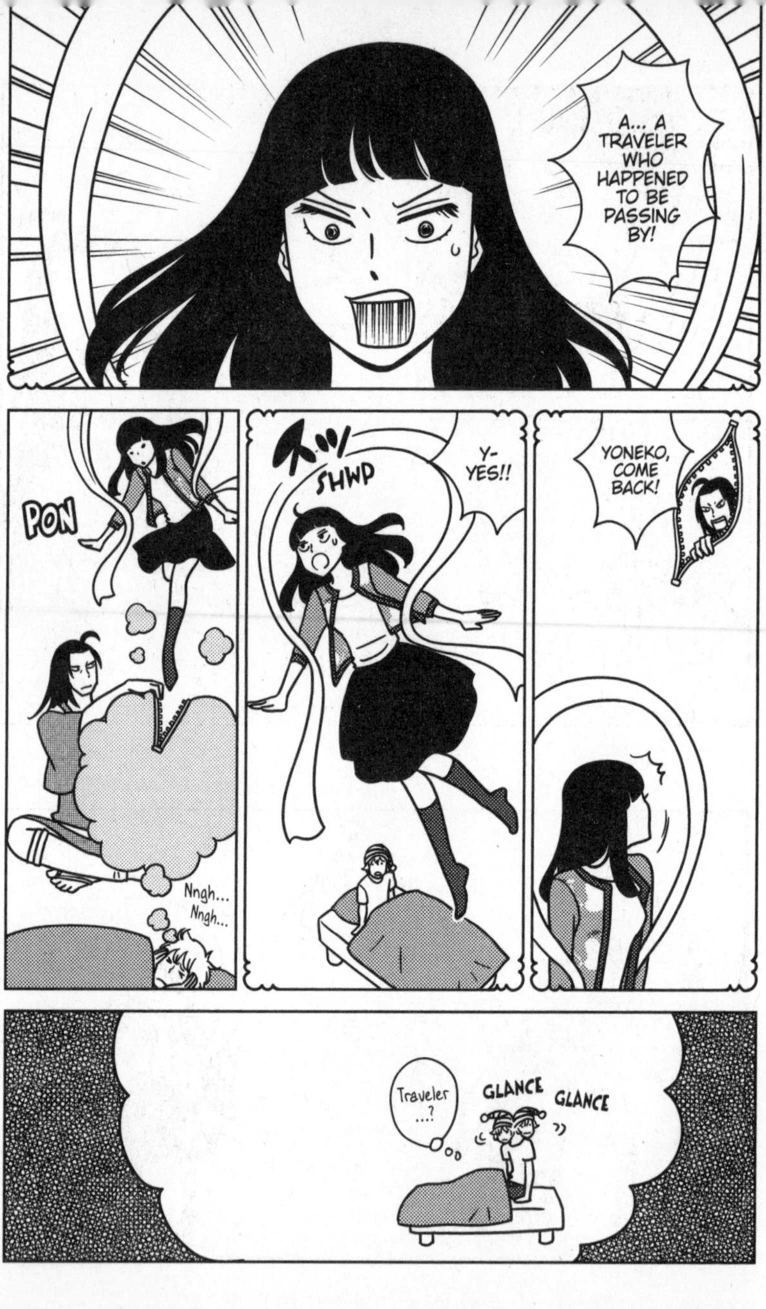
A... A TRAVELER WHO HAPPENED TO BE PASSING BY!
YONEKO, COME BACK!
SHWP
Y- YES!!
PON
Nngh... Nngh...
GLANCE
GLANCE
Traveler ...?

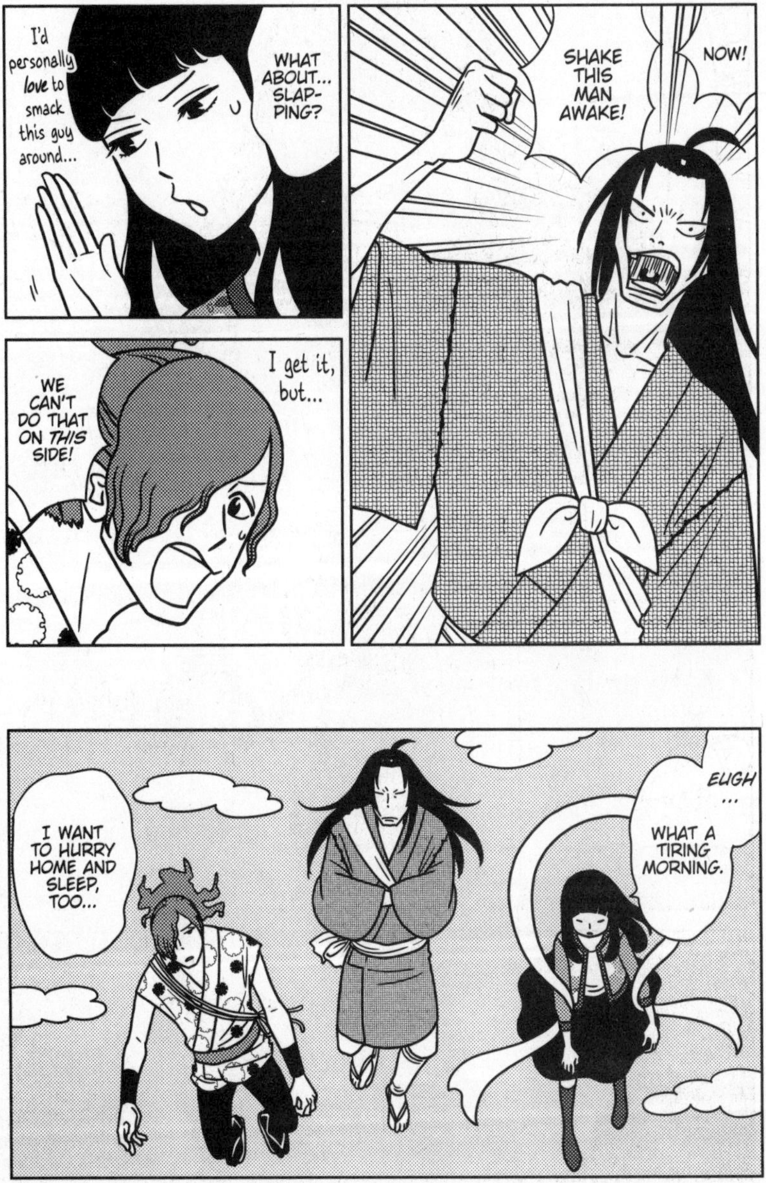
NOW!
SHAKE THIS MAN AWAKE!
WHAT ABOUT... SLAP-PING?
I'd personally *love* to smack this guy around...
I get it, but...
WE CAN'T DO THAT ON *THIS* SIDE!
EUGH ...
WHAT A TIRING MORNING.
I WANT TO HURRY HOME AND SLEEP, TOO...

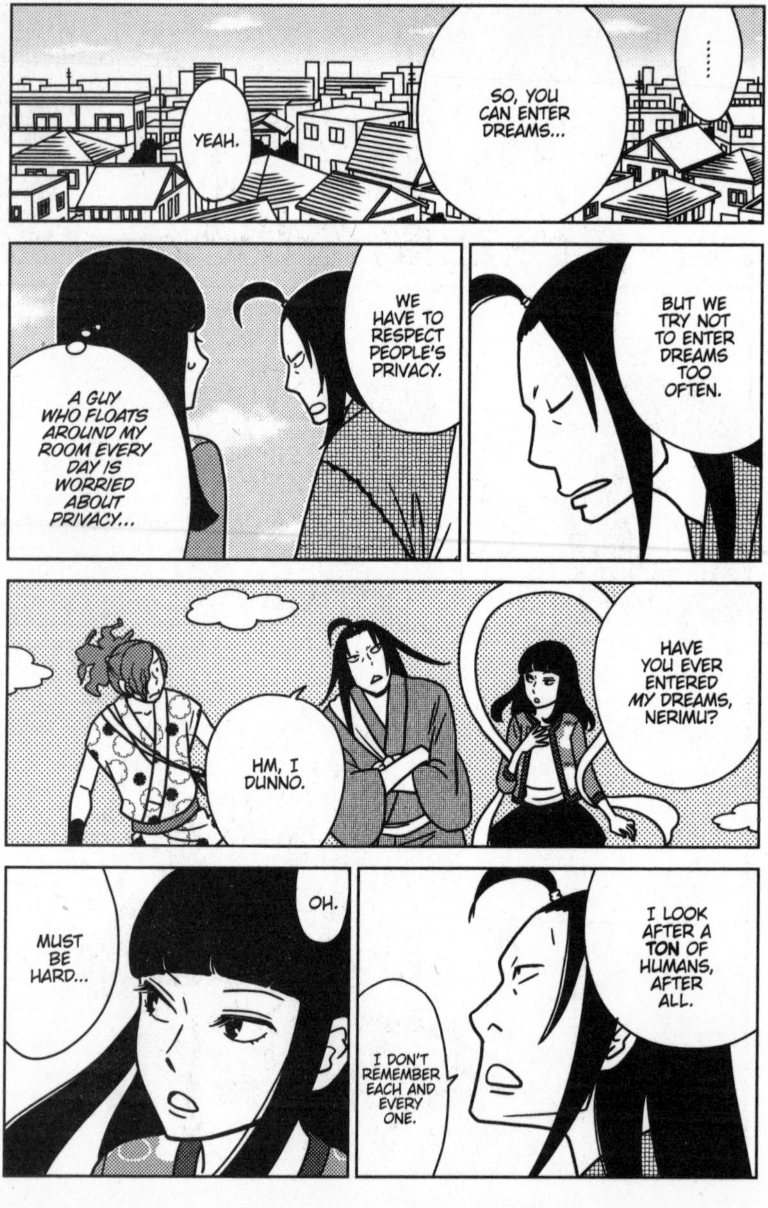
......
SO, YOU CAN ENTER DREAMS...
YEAH.
BUT WE TRY NOT TO ENTER DREAMS TOO OFTEN.
WE HAVE TO RESPECT PEOPLE'S PRIVACY.
A GUY WHO FLOATS AROUND MY ROOM EVERY DAY IS WORRIED ABOUT PRIVACY...
HAVE YOU EVER ENTERED MY DREAMS, NERIMU?
HM, I DUNNO.
I LOOK AFTER A **TON** OF HUMANS, AFTER ALL.
I DON'T REMEMBER EACH AND EVERY ONE.
OH.
MUST BE HARD...

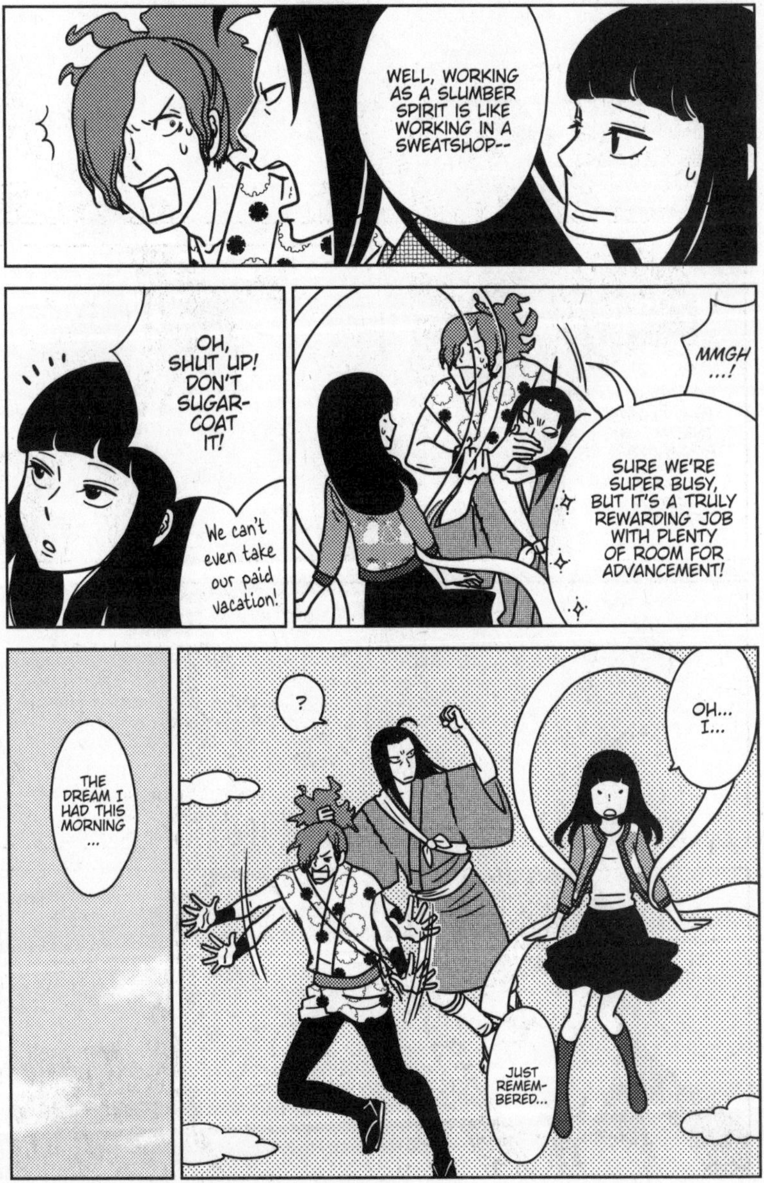
WELL, WORKING AS A SLUMBER SPIRIT IS LIKE WORKING IN A SWEATSHOP--
MMGH ...!
SURE WE'RE SUPER BUSY, BUT IT'S A TRULY REWARDING JOB WITH PLENTY OF ROOM FOR ADVANCEMENT!
OH, SHUT UP! DON'T SUGAR-COAT IT!
We can't even take our paid vacation!
OH... I...
?
JUST REMEM-BERED...
THE DREAM I HAD THIS MORNING ...

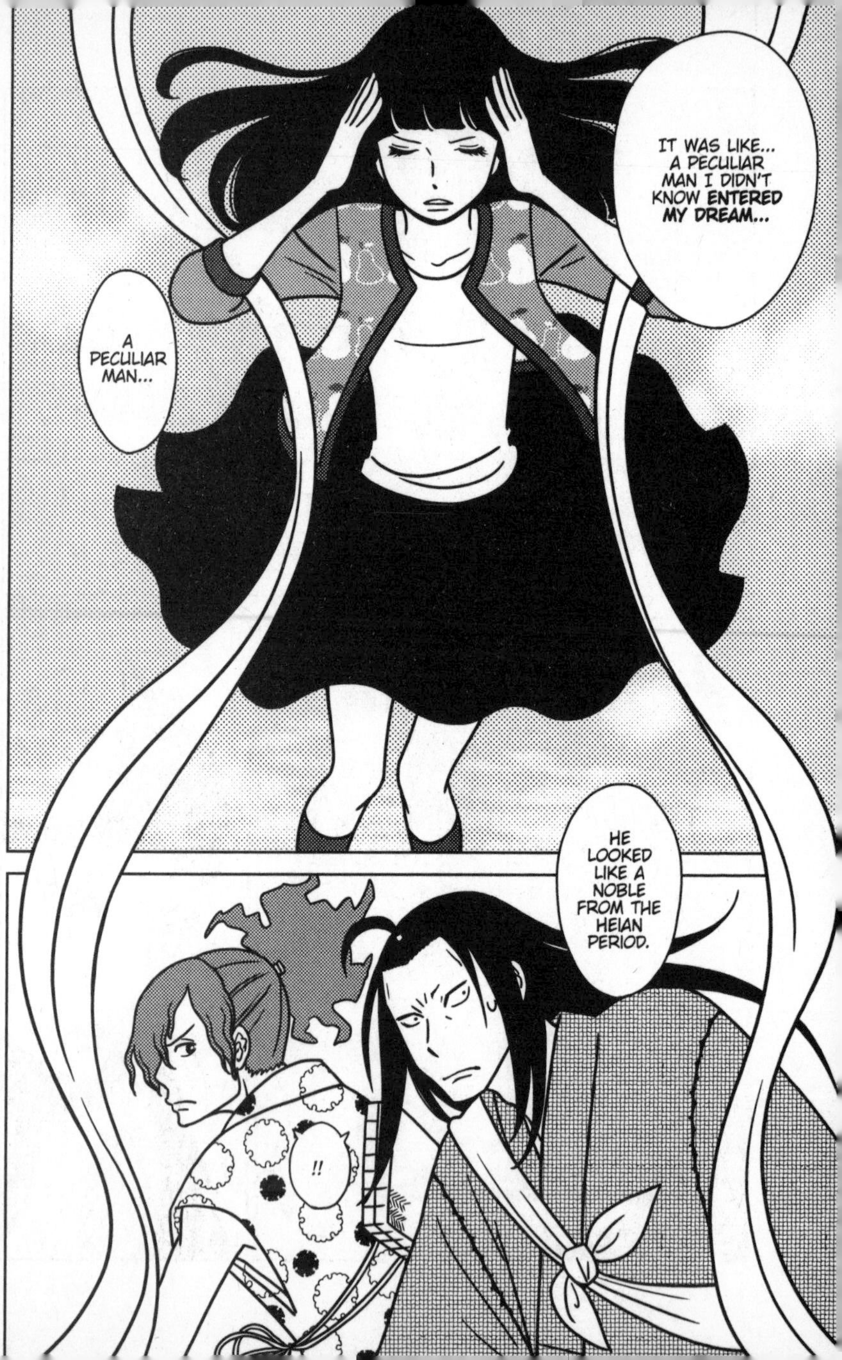
IT WAS LIKE... A PECULIAR MAN I DIDN'T KNOW ENTERED MY DREAM...
A PECULIAR MAN...
HE LOOKED LIKE A NOBLE FROM THE HEIAN PERIOD.
!!

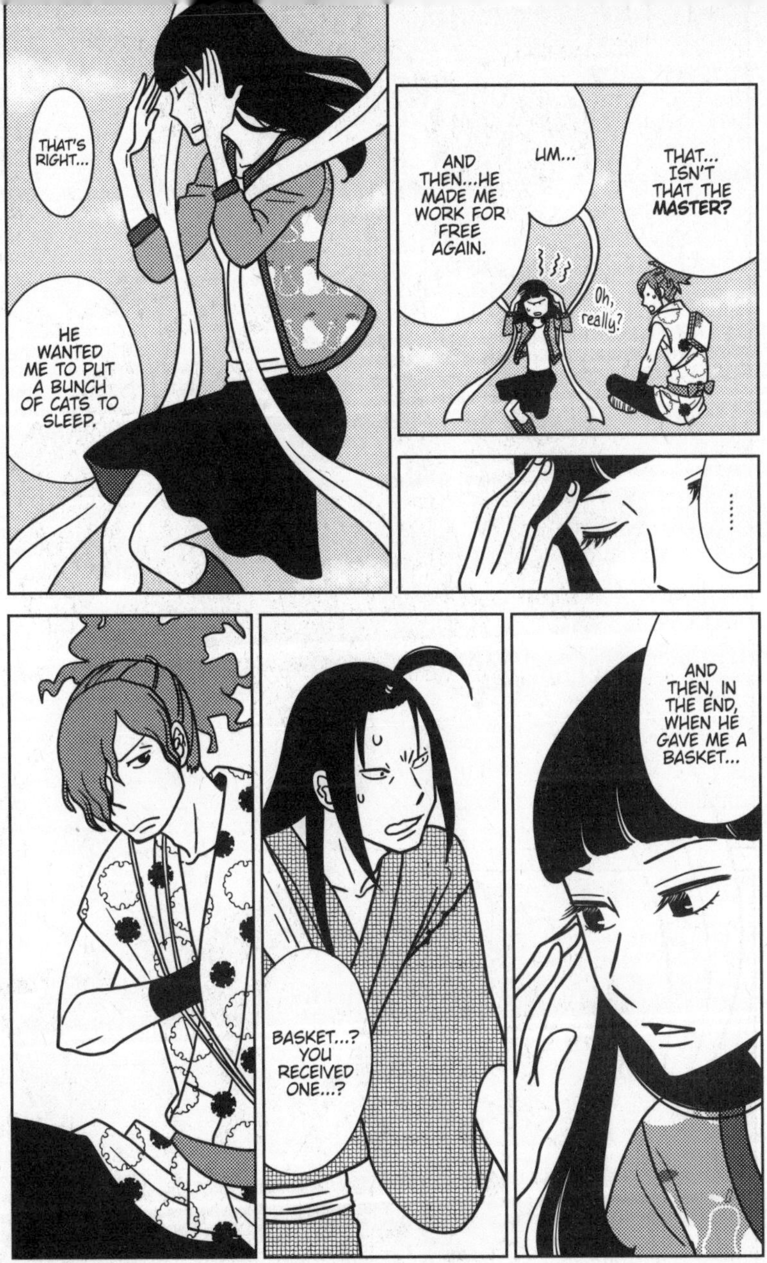
THAT... ISN'T THAT THE MASTER?
UM...
AND THEN...HE MADE ME WORK FOR FREE AGAIN.
Oh, really?
......
THAT'S RIGHT...
HE WANTED ME TO PUT A BUNCH OF CATS TO SLEEP.
AND THEN, IN THE END, WHEN HE GAVE ME A BASKET...
BASKET...? YOU RECEIVED ONE...?

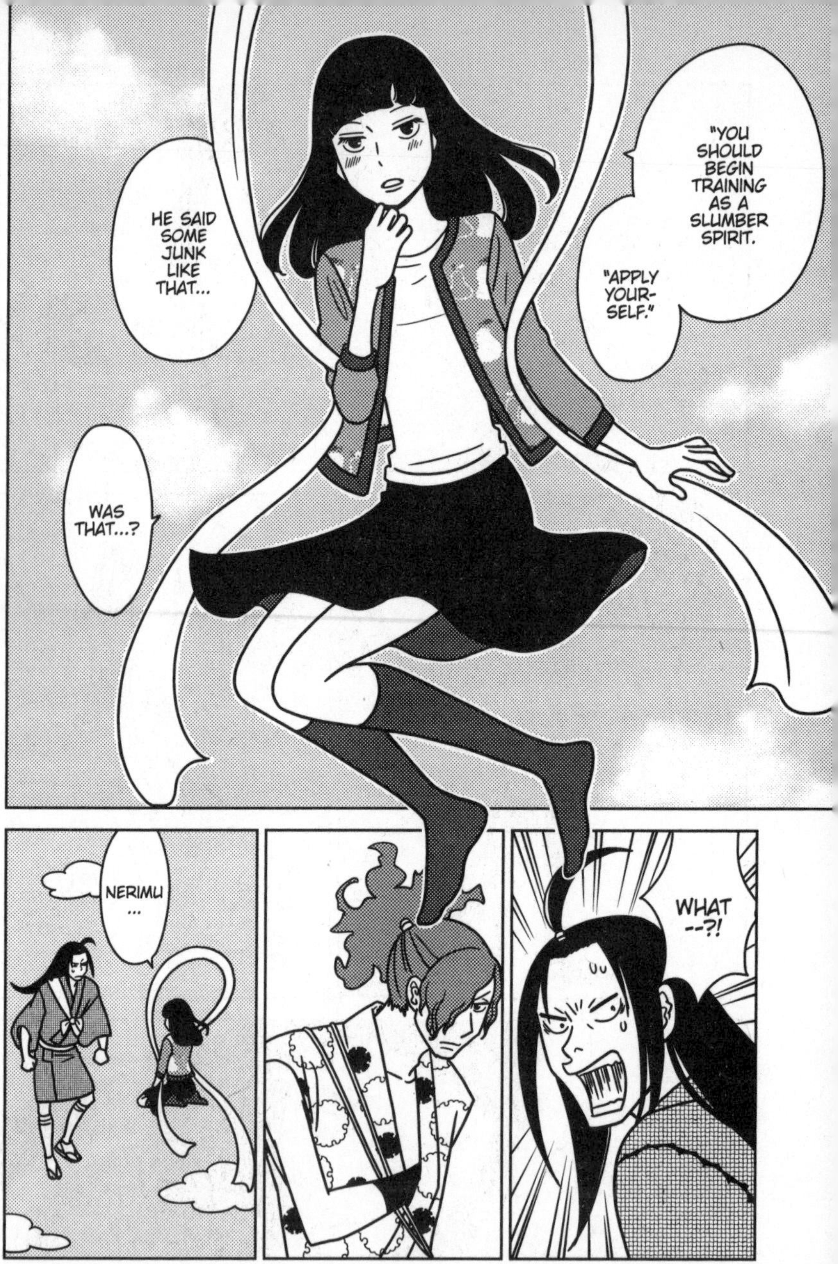
"YOU SHOULD BEGIN TRAINING AS A SLUMBER SPIRIT.
"APPLY YOUR-SELF."
HE SAID SOME JUNK LIKE THAT...
WAS THAT...?
WHAT--?!
NERIMU...

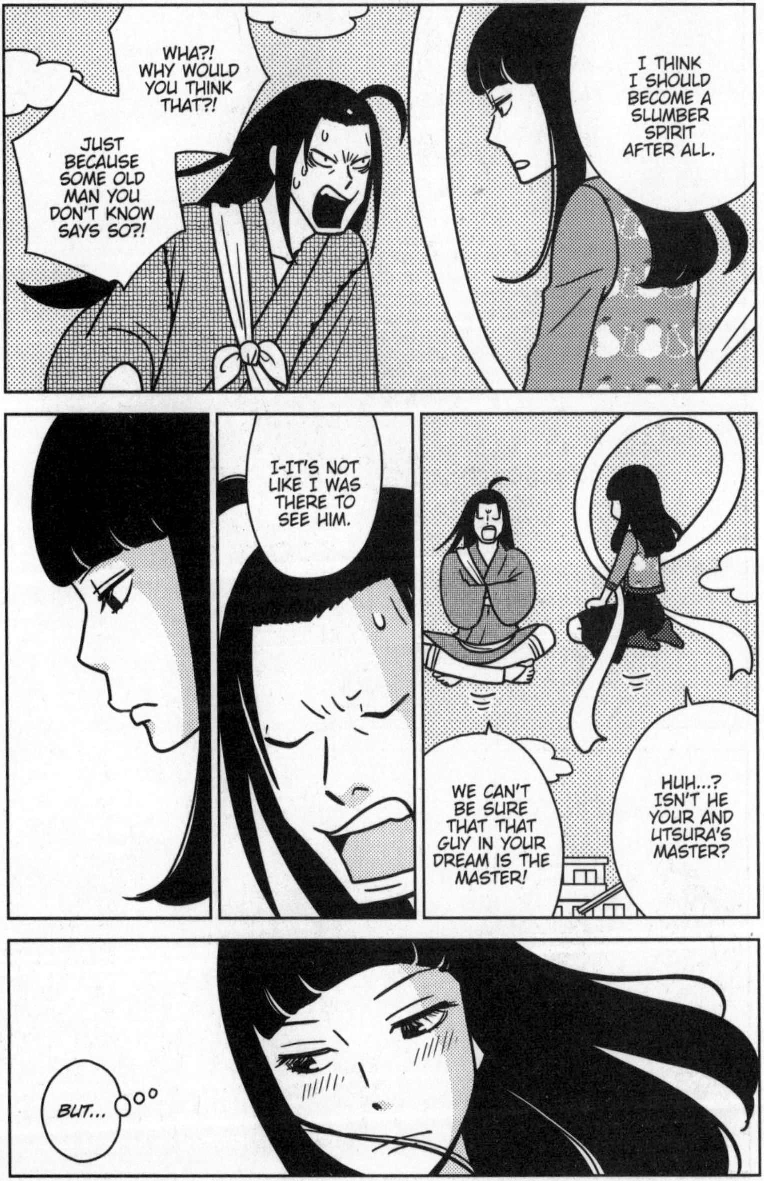
I THINK I SHOULD BECOME A SLUMBER SPIRIT AFTER ALL.
WHA?! WHY WOULD YOU THINK THAT?!
JUST BECAUSE SOME OLD MAN YOU DON'T KNOW SAYS SO?!
HUH...? ISN'T HE YOUR AND UTSURA'S MASTER?
WE CAN'T BE SURE THAT THAT GUY IN YOUR DREAM IS THE MASTER!
I-IT'S NOT LIKE I WAS THERE TO SEE HIM.
BUT...

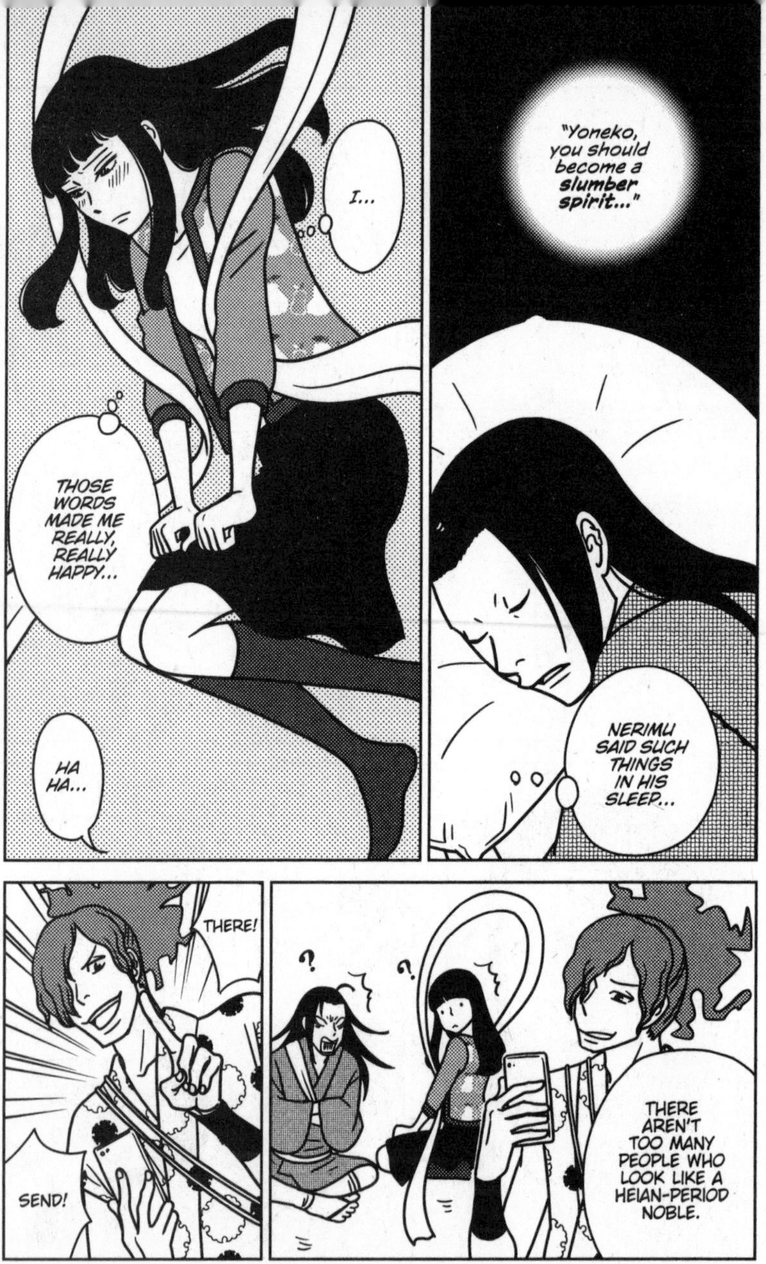
"Yoneko, you should become a slumber spirit..."
NERIMU SAID SUCH THINGS IN HIS SLEEP...
I...
THOSE WORDS MADE ME REALLY, REALLY HAPPY...
HA HA...
THERE AREN'T TOO MANY PEOPLE WHO LOOK LIKE A HEIAN-PERIOD NOBLE.
THERE!
SEND!

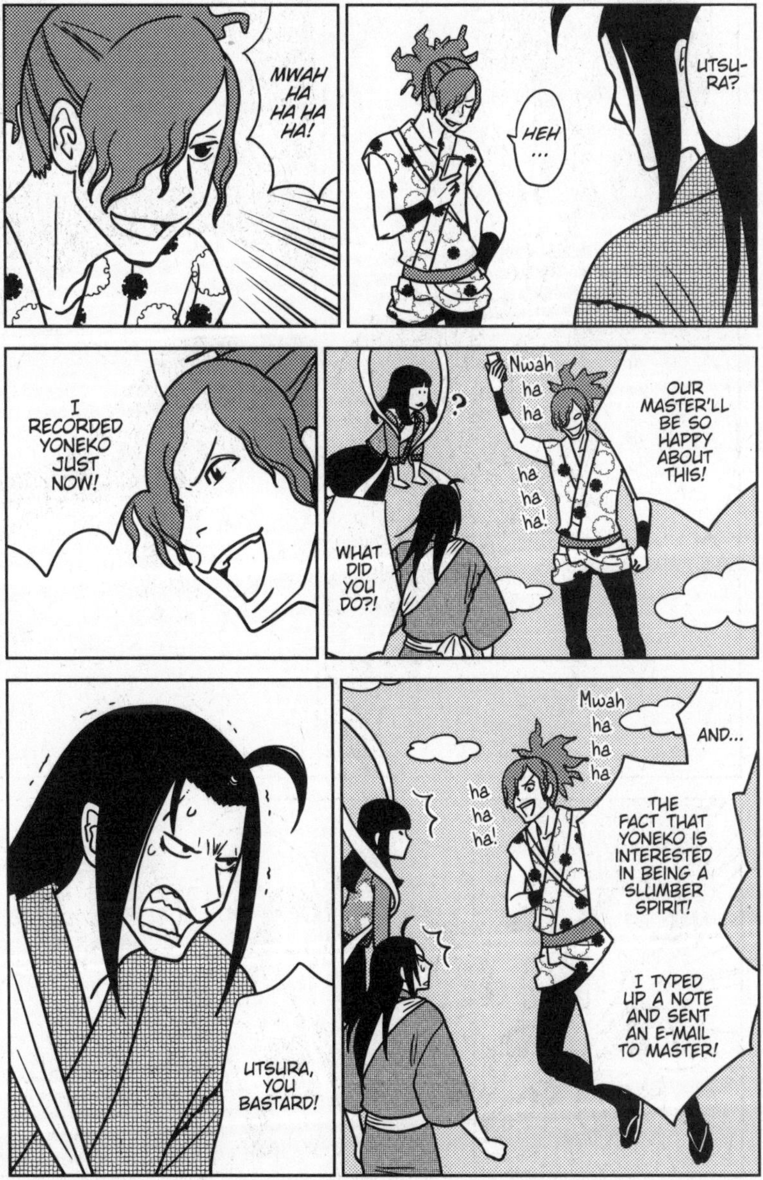
UTSURA?
HEH...
MWAH HA HA HA HA!
OUR MASTER'LL BE SO HAPPY ABOUT THIS!
Nwah ha ha
?
ha ha ha!
WHAT DID YOU DO?!
I RECORDED YONEKO JUST NOW!
AND...
Mwah ha ha ha
THE FACT THAT YONEKO IS INTERESTED IN BEING A SLUMBER SPIRIT!
ha ha ha!
I TYPED UP A NOTE AND SENT AN E-MAIL TO MASTER!
UTSURA, YOU BASTARD!

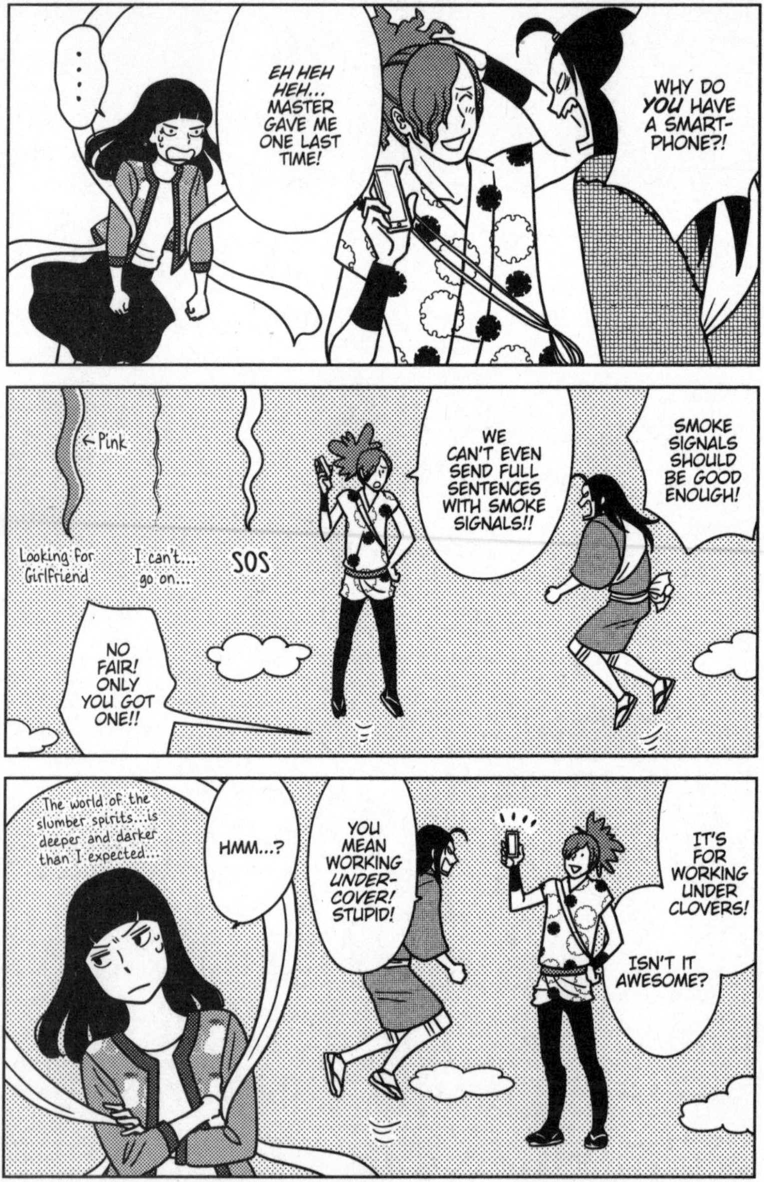
WHY DO YOU HAVE A SMARTPHONE?!
EH HEH HEH... MASTER GAVE ME ONE LAST TIME!
....
SMOKE SIGNALS SHOULD BE GOOD ENOUGH!
WE CAN'T EVEN SEND FULL SENTENCES WITH SMOKE SIGNALS!!
SOS
I can't... go on...
← Pink
Looking for Girlfriend
NO FAIR! ONLY YOU GOT ONE!!
IT'S FOR WORKING UNDER CLOVERS!
ISN'T IT AWESOME?
YOU MEAN WORKING UNDER-COVER! STUPID!
HMM...?
The world of the slumber spirits...is deeper and darker than I expected...

Fin

Slumbering Beauty

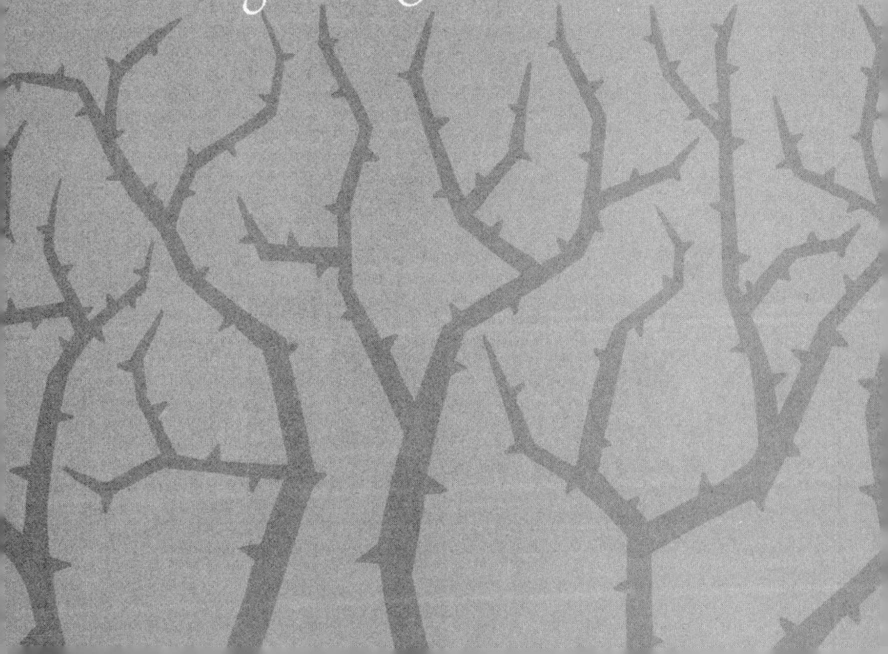

Nemurimehime by Yumi Unita

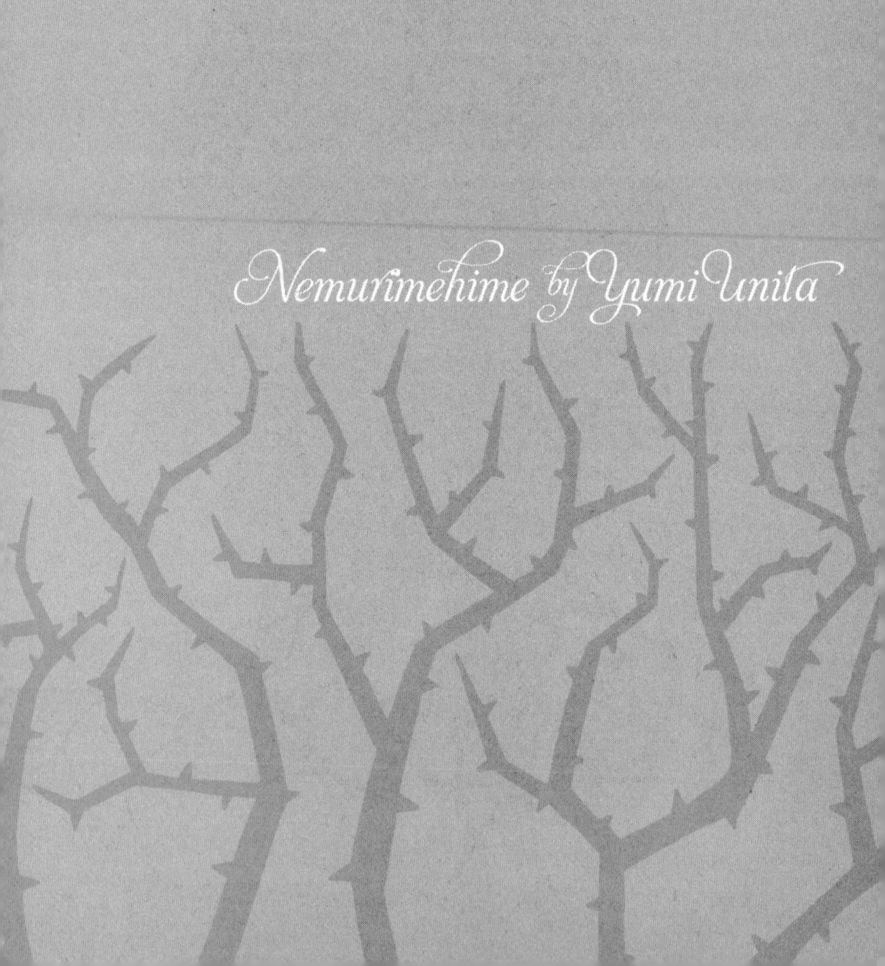

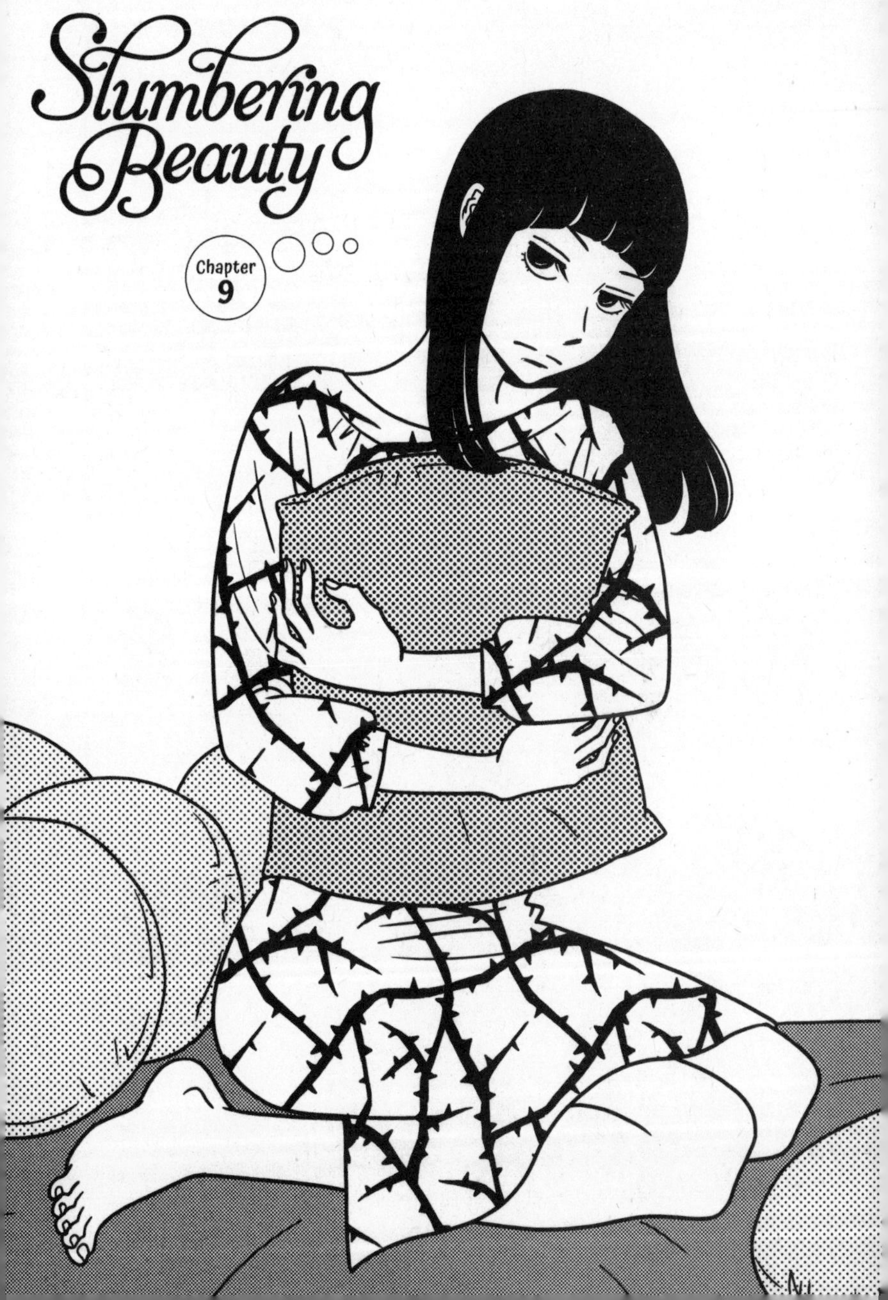
Slumbering Beauty
Chapter 9

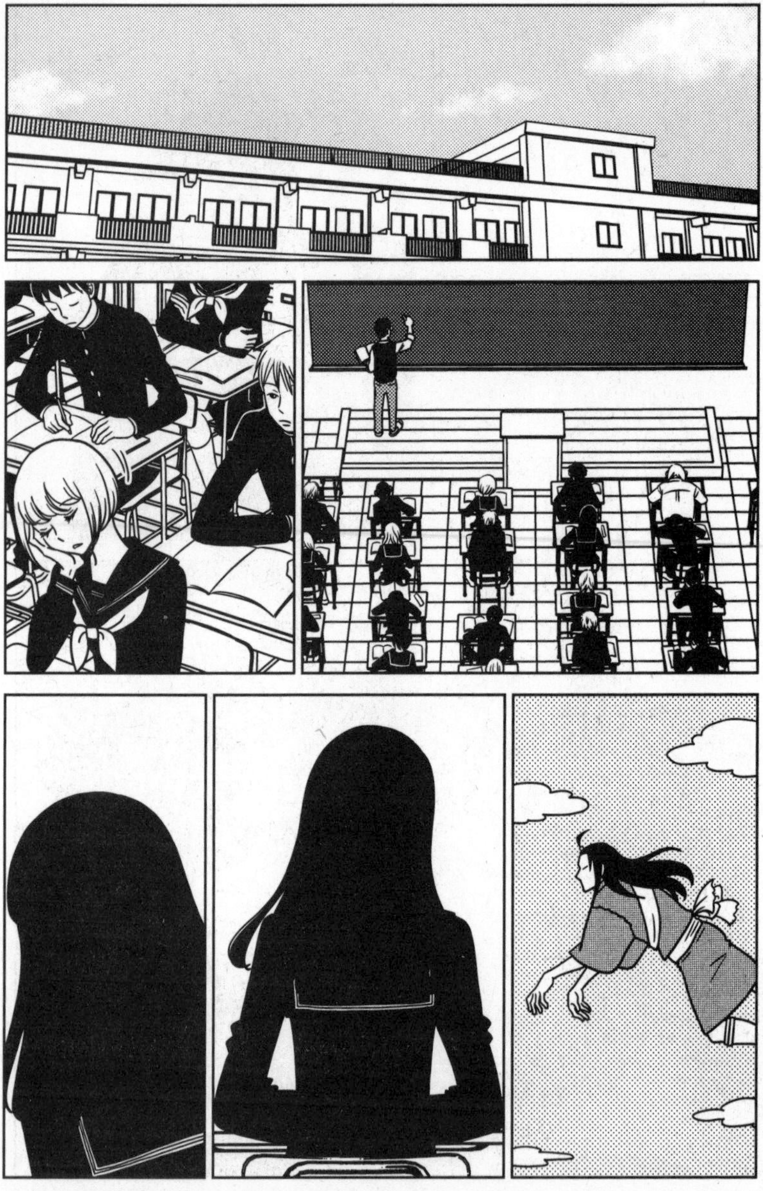

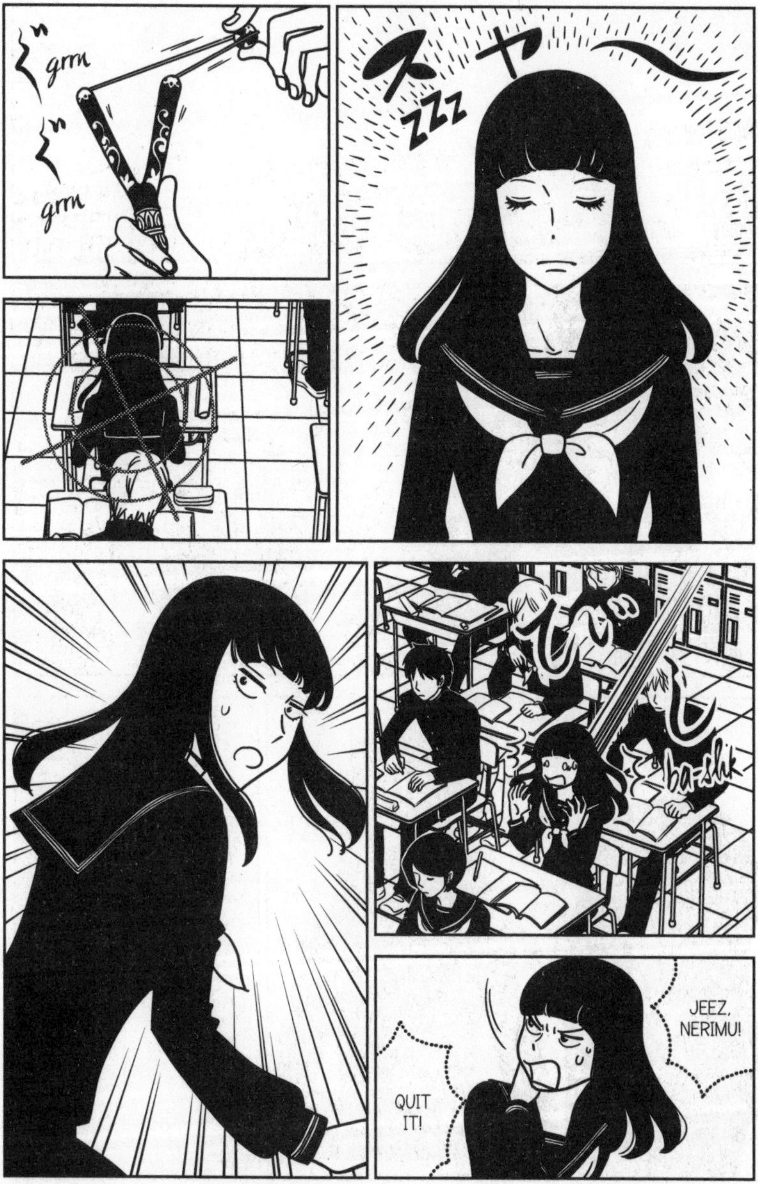
スヤ〜
zzz
grrn
grrn
ba-shik
JEEZ, NERIMU!
QUIT IT!

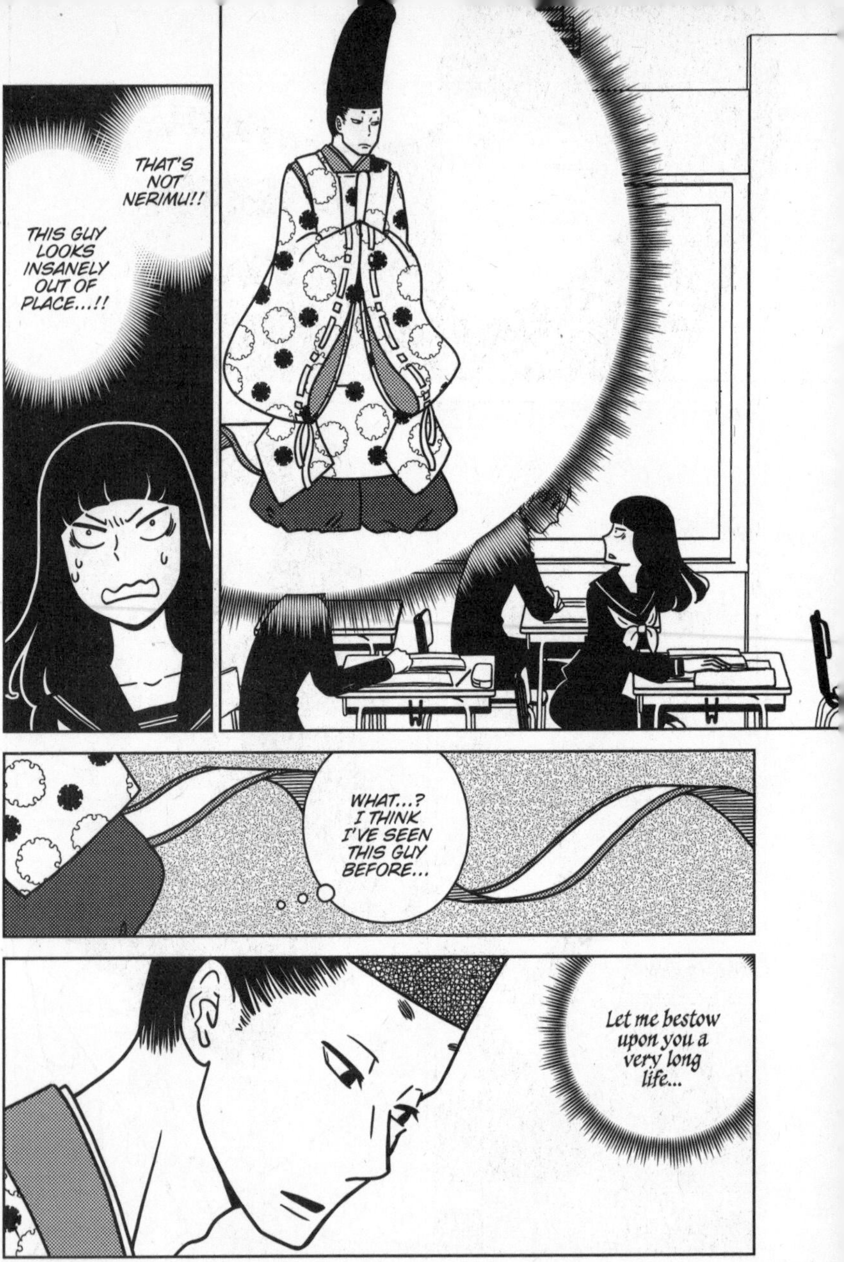
THAT'S NOT NERIMU!!
THIS GUY LOOKS INSANELY OUT OF PLACE...!!
WHAT...? I THINK I'VE SEEN THIS GUY BEFORE...
Let me bestow upon you a very long life...

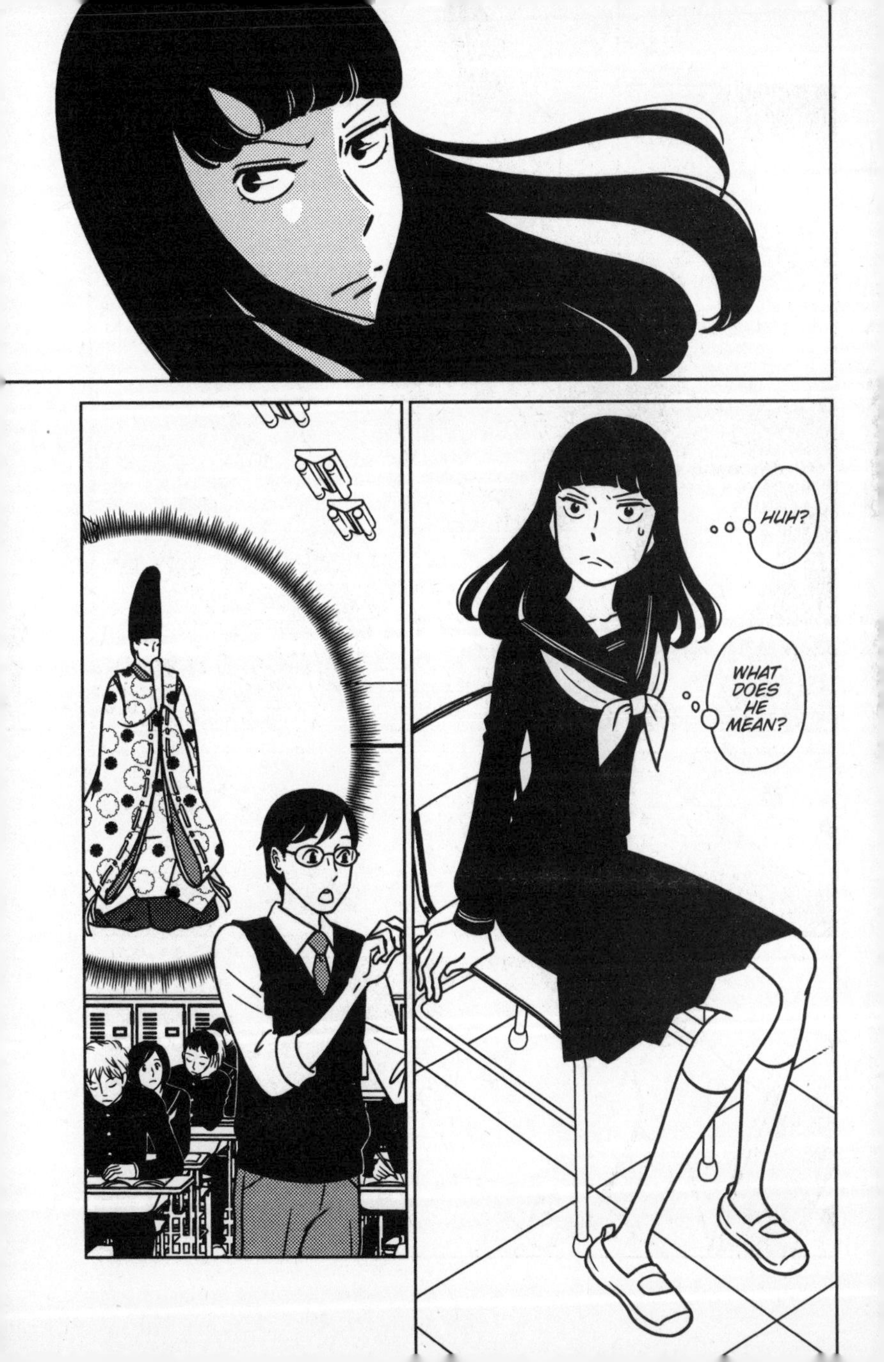
HUH?
WHAT DOES HE MEAN?

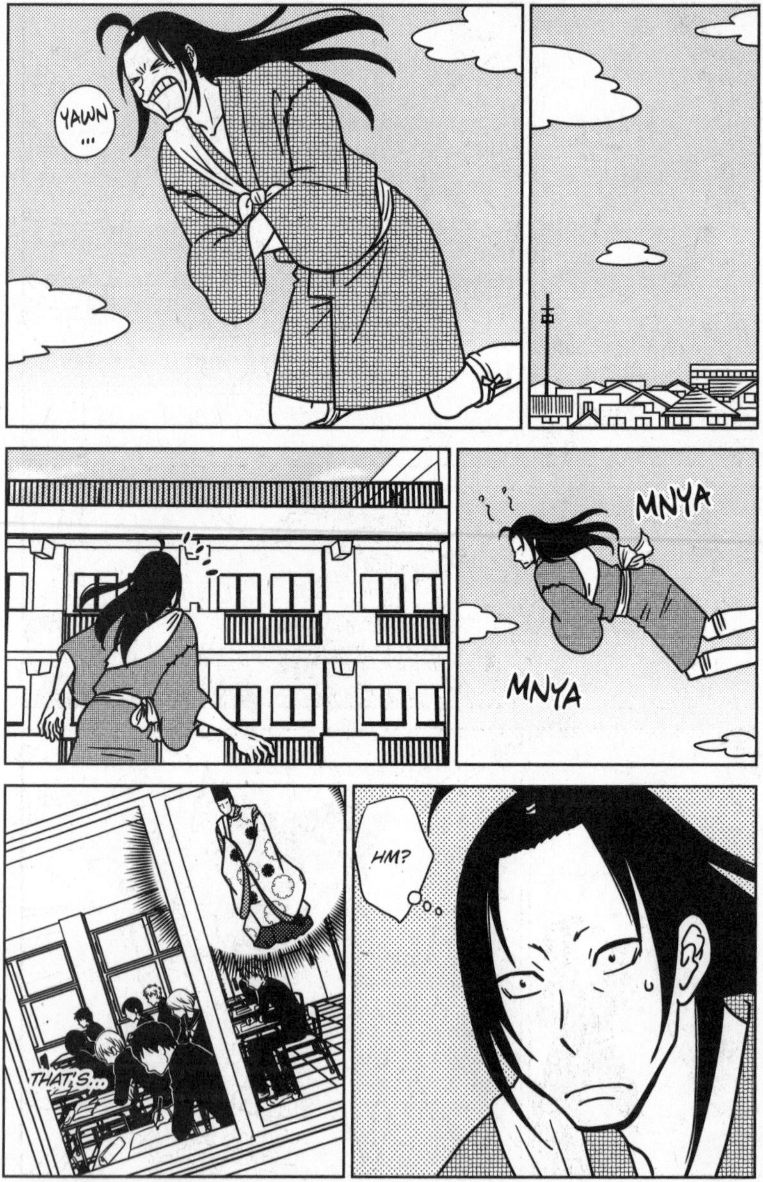
YAWN ...
MNYA
MNYA
HM?
THAT'S...

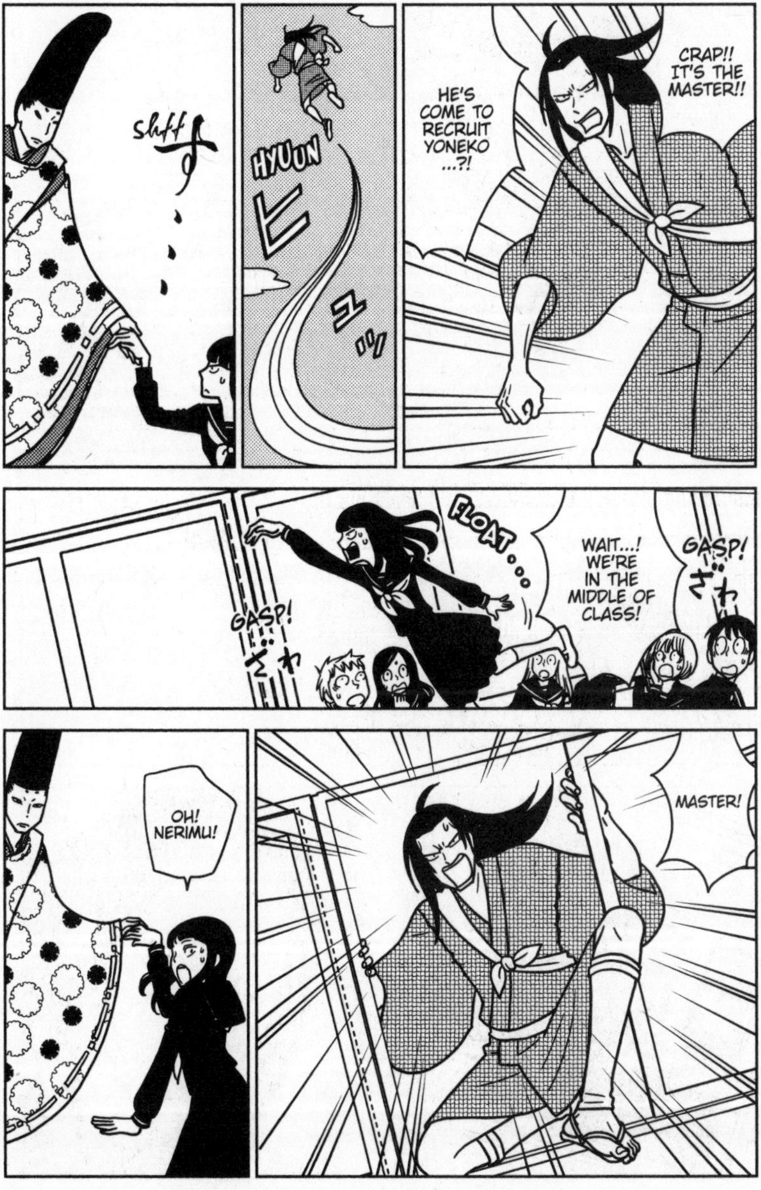
CRAP!! IT'S THE MASTER!!
HE'S COME TO RECRUIT YONEKO ...?!
HYUUN
ヒュッ
shff
す
GASP!
ざわ
WAIT...! WE'RE IN THE MIDDLE OF CLASS!
FLOAT...
GASP!
ざわ
MASTER!
OH! NERIMU!

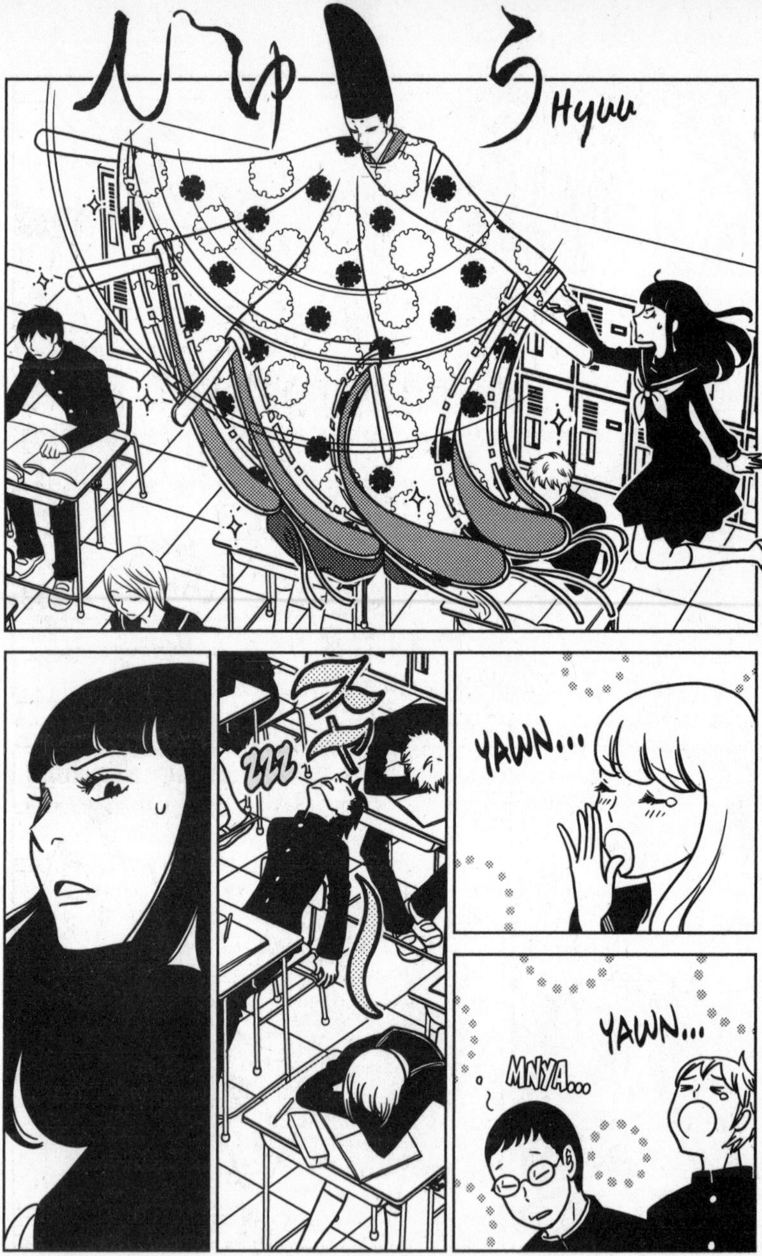

Hyuu
YAWN...
YAWN...
MNYA...
ZZZ

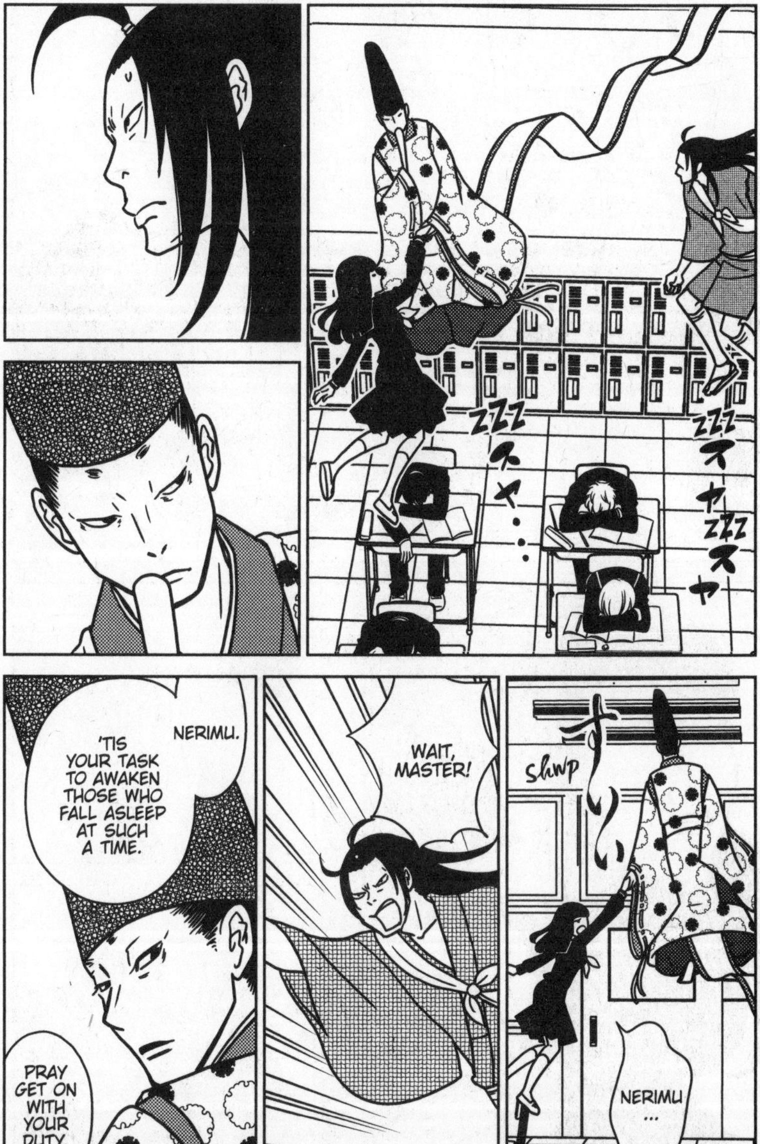
ZZZ
ZZZ
ZZZ
shwp
NERIMU ...
WAIT, MASTER!
NERIMU.
'TIS YOUR TASK TO AWAKEN THOSE WHO FALL ASLEEP AT SUCH A TIME.
PRAY GET ON WITH YOUR DUTY.

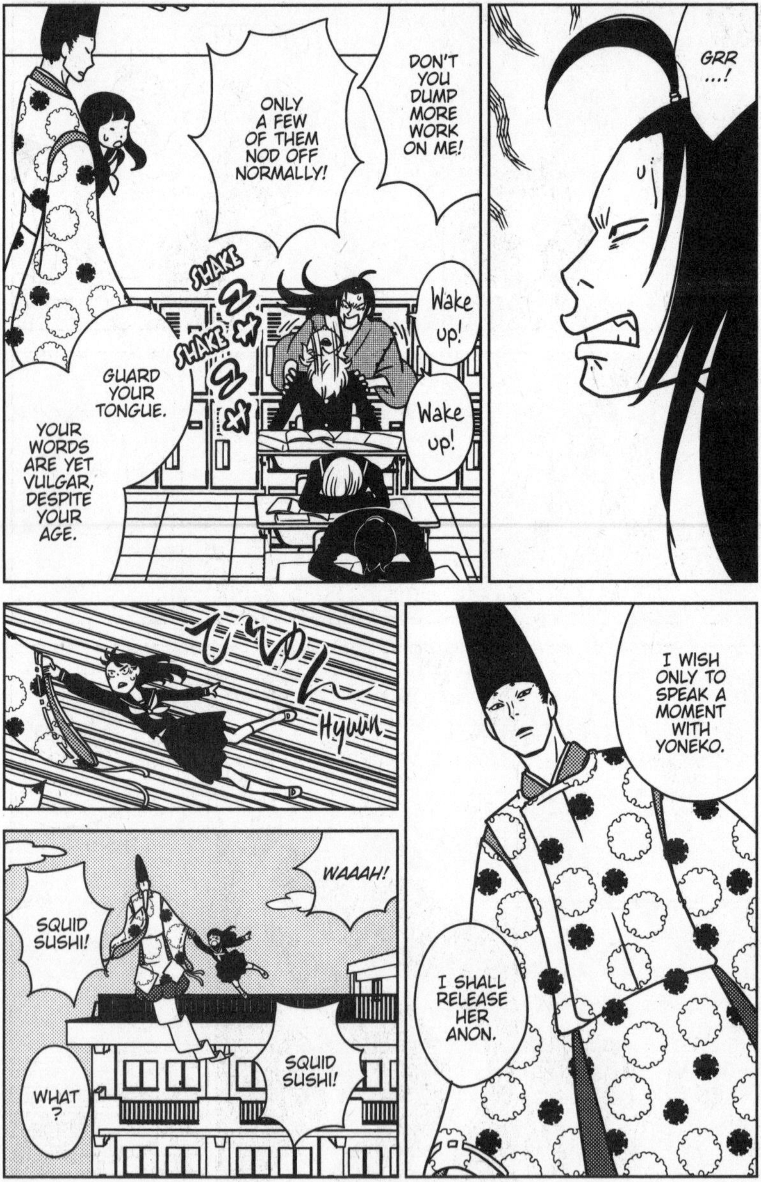
GRR ...!
DON'T YOU DUMP MORE WORK ON ME!
ONLY A FEW OF THEM NOD OFF NORMALLY!
Wake up!
Wake up!
SHAKE
SHAKE
GUARD YOUR TONGUE.
YOUR WORDS ARE YET VULGAR, DESPITE YOUR AGE.
I WISH ONLY TO SPEAK A MOMENT WITH YONEKO.
I SHALL RELEASE HER ANON.
Hyuun
WAAAH!
SQUID SUSHI!
SQUID SUSHI!
WHAT?

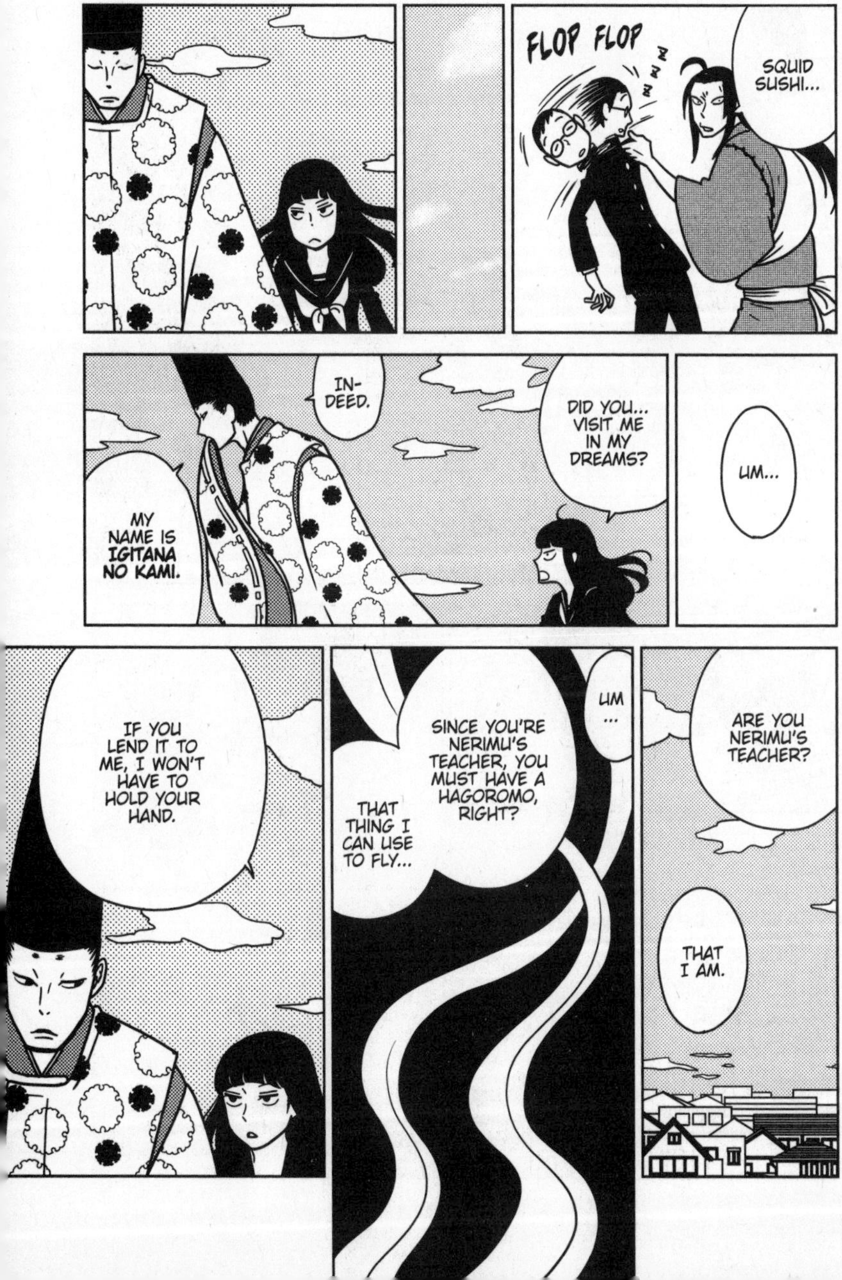
FLOP FLOP
ZZZ
SQUID SUSHI...
UM...
DID YOU... VISIT ME IN MY DREAMS?
IN-DEED.
MY NAME IS IGITANA NO KAMI.
ARE YOU NERIMU'S TEACHER?
THAT I AM.
UM ...
SINCE YOU'RE NERIMU'S TEACHER, YOU MUST HAVE A HAGOROMO, RIGHT?
THAT THING I CAN USE TO FLY...
IF YOU LEND IT TO ME, I WON'T HAVE TO HOLD YOUR HAND.

YOU ARE CLEVER INDEED.

SHOULD I HAND YOU SUCH A THING, YOU WOULD SURELY FLEE.

HE SAW THROUGH ME!

. . . . .

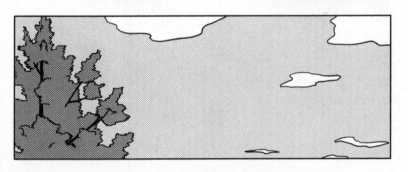

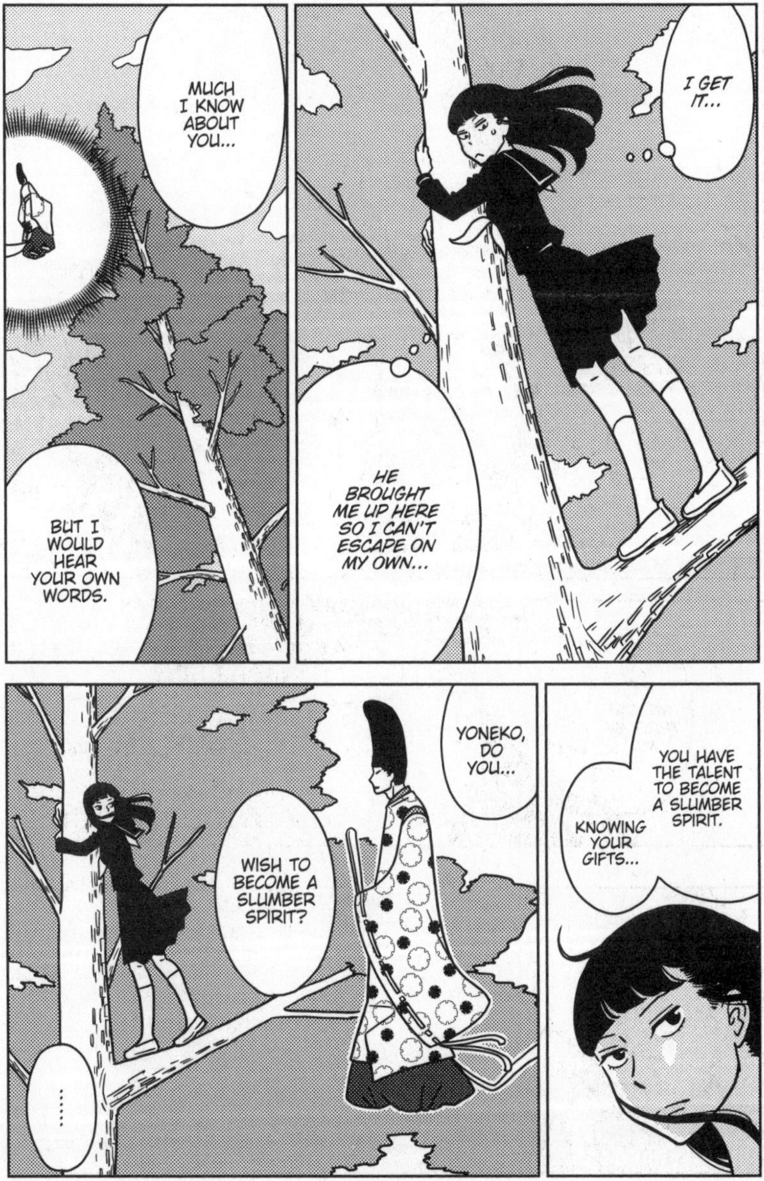
I GET IT...
HE BROUGHT ME UP HERE SO I CAN'T ESCAPE ON MY OWN...
MUCH I KNOW ABOUT YOU...
BUT I WOULD HEAR YOUR OWN WORDS.
YOU HAVE THE TALENT TO BECOME A SLUMBER SPIRIT.
KNOWING YOUR GIFTS...
YONEKO, DO YOU...
WISH TO BECOME A SLUMBER SPIRIT?
......

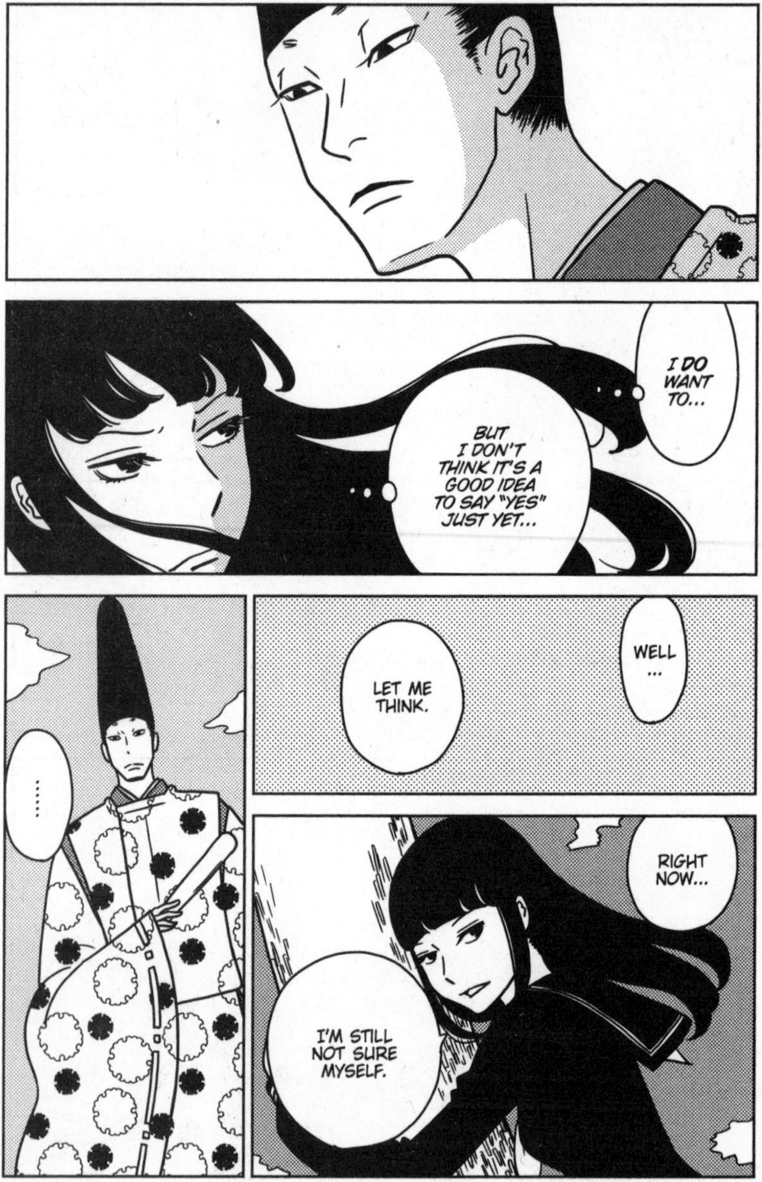
I DO WANT TO...
BUT I DON'T THINK IT'S A GOOD IDEA TO SAY "YES" JUST YET...
WELL ...
LET ME THINK.
RIGHT NOW...
I'M STILL NOT SURE MYSELF.
......

I SHOULD NE'ER BE SO UNCOUTH...
AS TO DEMAND IMMEDIATE RESPONSE.
FIVE DAYS.
I SHALL WAIT FIVE DAYS.
AHH.
PRAY ALLOW ME TO SAY...
SHOULD YOU BECOME A SLUMBER SPIRIT...
YOU WOULD ENJOY A VERY LONG LIFE.
I DO NOT BELIEVE 'TIS A MEAN DEAL.

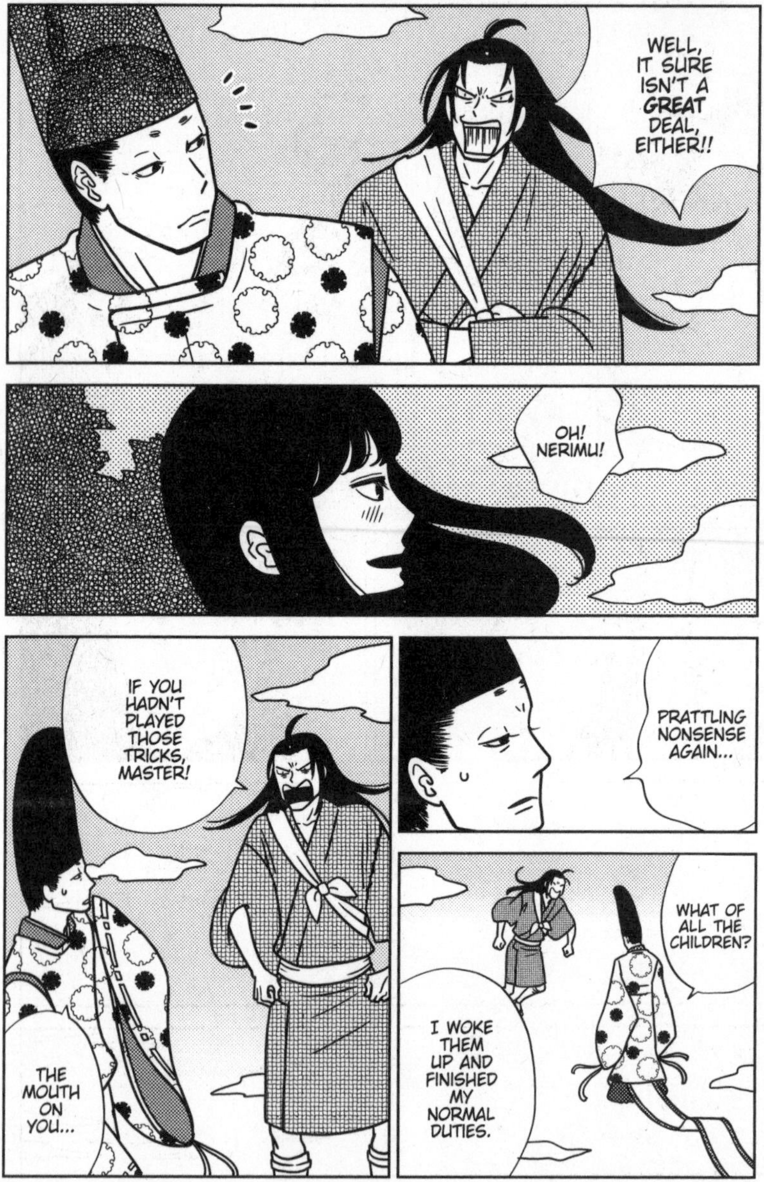
WELL, IT SURE ISN'T A GREAT DEAL, EITHER!!
OH! NERIMU!
PRATTLING NONSENSE AGAIN...
WHAT OF ALL THE CHILDREN?
I WOKE THEM UP AND FINISHED MY NORMAL DUTIES.
IF YOU HADN'T PLAYED THOSE TRICKS, MASTER!
THE MOUTH ON YOU...

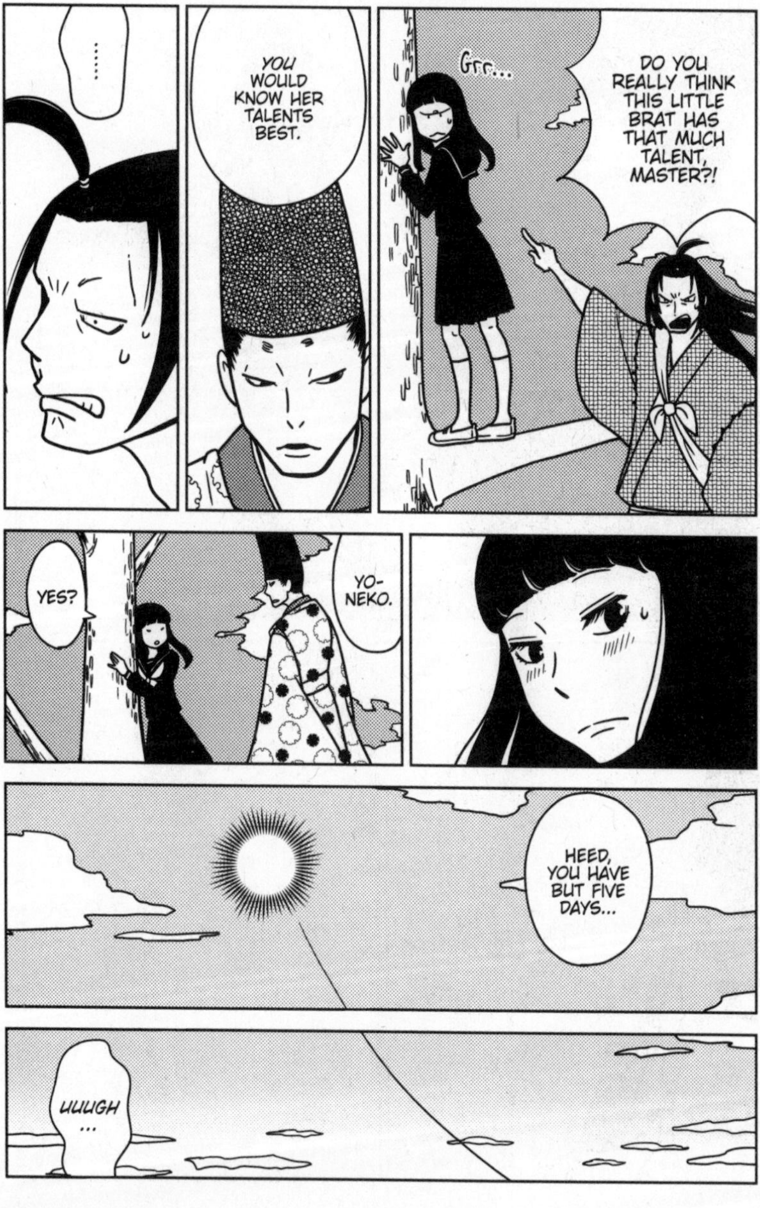
DO YOU REALLY THINK THIS LITTLE BRAT HAS THAT MUCH TALENT, MASTER?!
Grr...
YOU WOULD KNOW HER TALENTS BEST.
......
YO-NEKO.
YES?
HEED, YOU HAVE BUT FIVE DAYS...
UUUGH ...

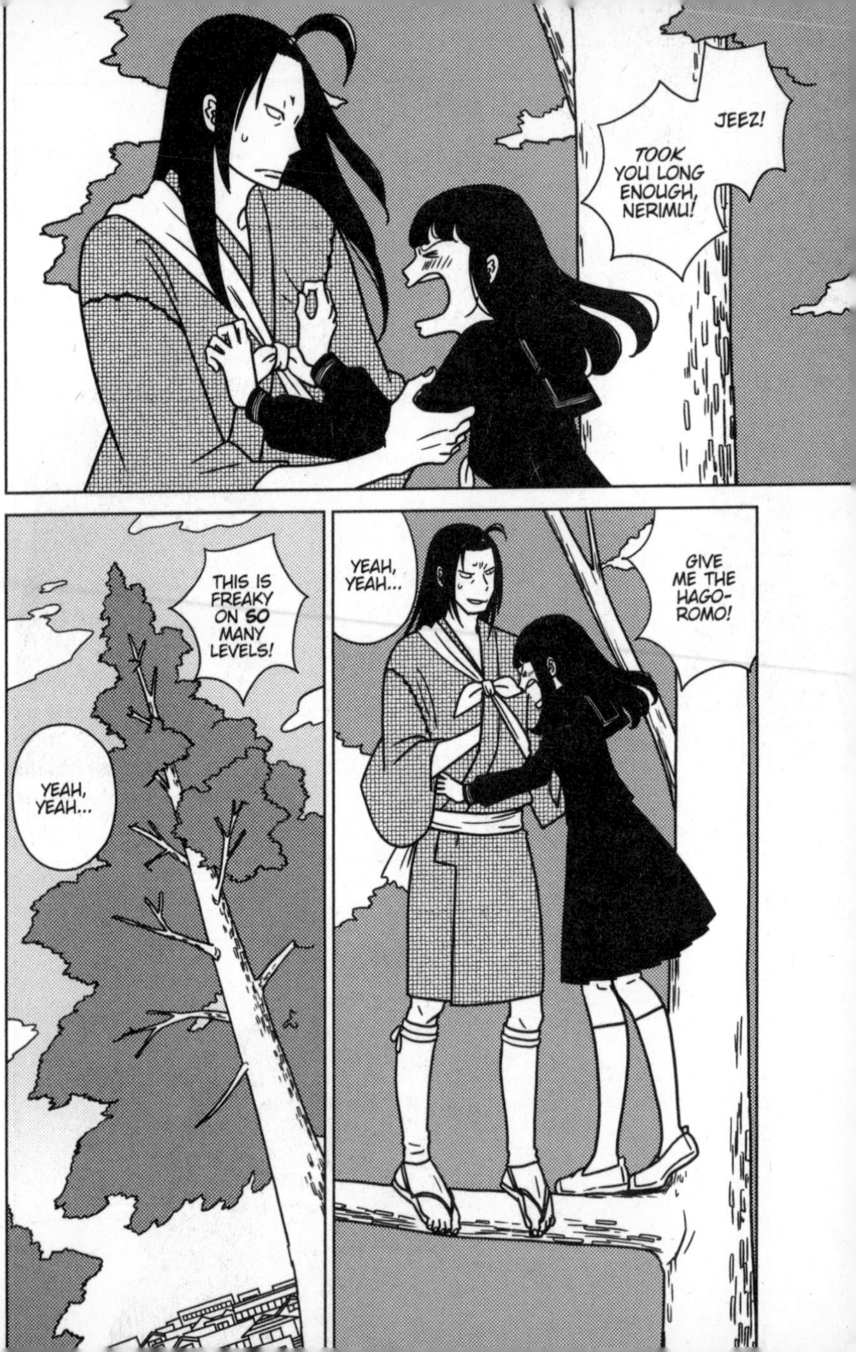
JEEZ!
TOOK YOU LONG ENOUGH, NERIMU!
GIVE ME THE HAGO-ROMO!
YEAH, YEAH...
THIS IS FREAKY ON SO MANY LEVELS!
YEAH, YEAH...

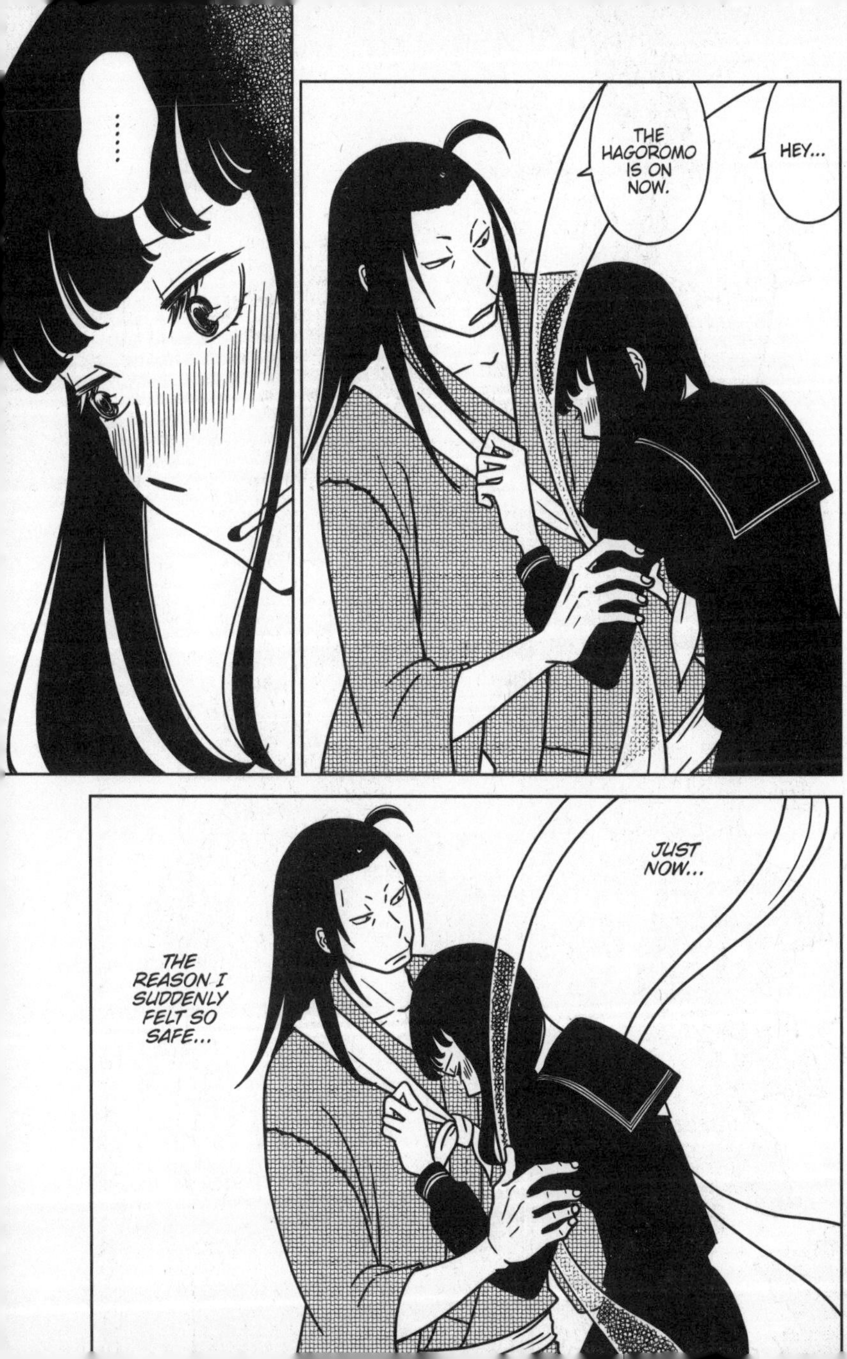
HEY...
THE HAGOROMO IS ON NOW.
......
JUST NOW...
THE REASON I SUDDENLY FELT SO SAFE...

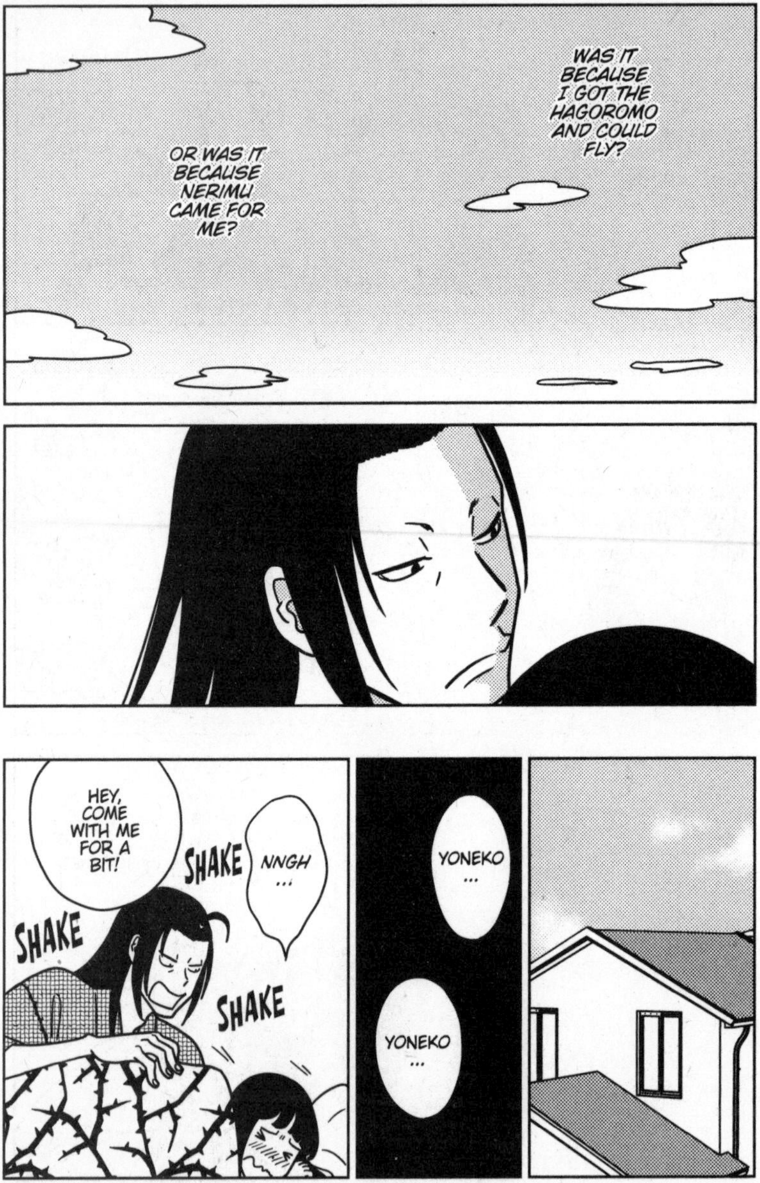
WAS IT BECAUSE I GOT THE HAGOROMO AND COULD FLY?
OR WAS IT BECAUSE NERIMU CAME FOR ME?
YONEKO ...
YONEKO ...
NNGH ...
HEY, COME WITH ME FOR A BIT!
SHAKE
SHAKE
SHAKE

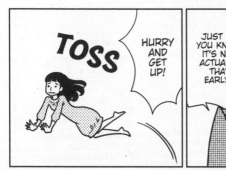

MMGH... WHAT DO YOU WANT THIS EARLY IN THE MORNING?
JUST SO YOU KNOW, IT'S NOT ACTUALLY THAT EARLY!!
HURRY AND GET UP!
TOSS
WAIT... HERE?
YOU WANT ME TO PAT YOU, NERIMU?
WELL, IT'S SOMETHING I WANTED TO TEST...
I SEE...
A...bird's nest? But isn't it too big?
HEY! HOW WILL I GET HOME?
OH... JUST USE THE HAGOROMO.
YOU CAN GIVE IT BACK TO ME LATER.
RUMMAGE
ごそごそ
RUMMAGE
OKAY...

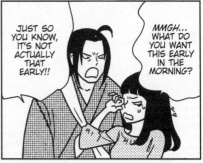

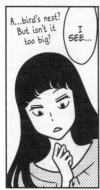

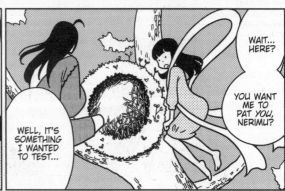

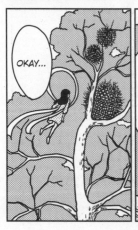

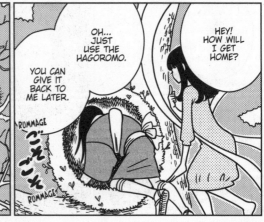

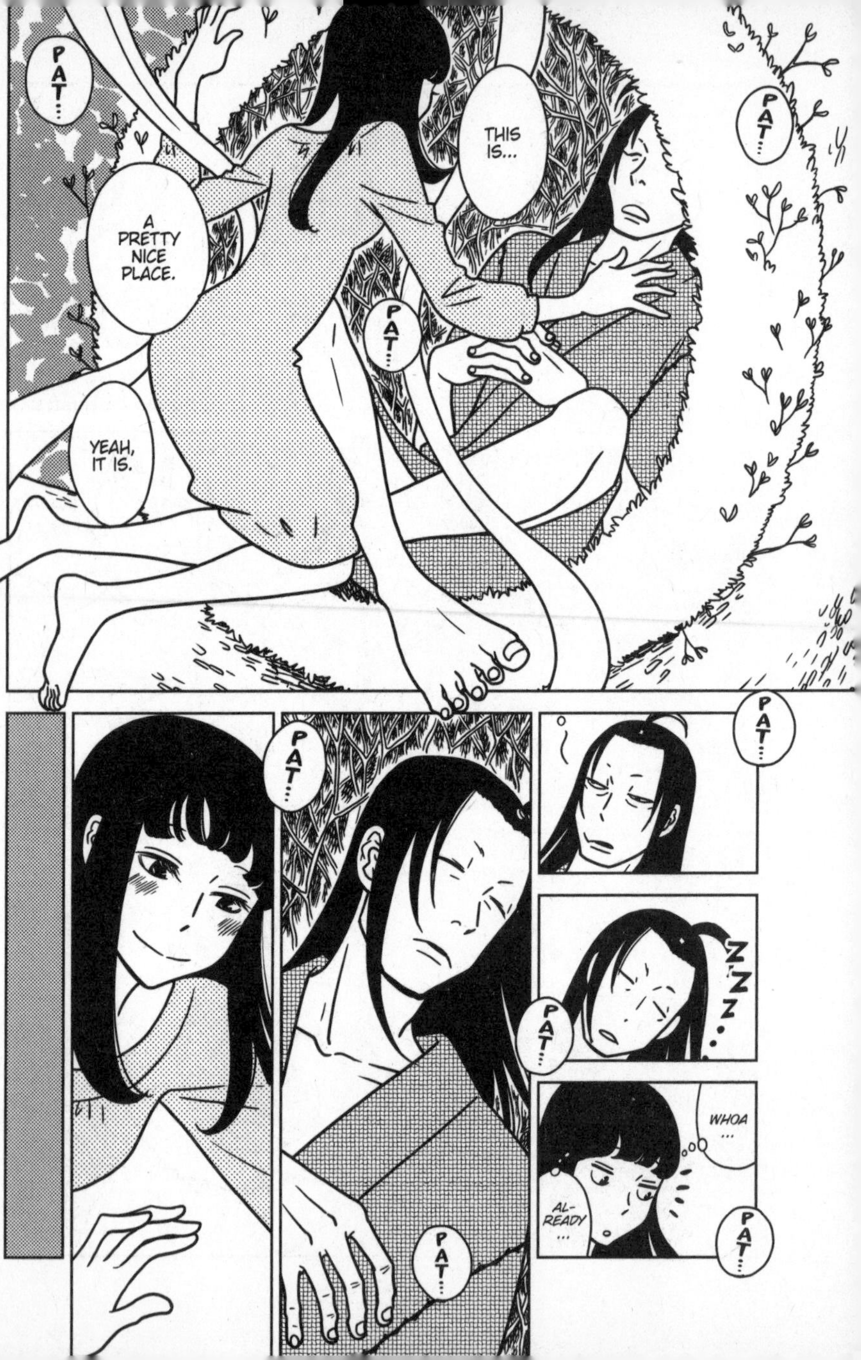

PAT...
THIS IS...
PAT...
A PRETTY NICE PLACE.
PAT...
YEAH, IT IS.
PAT...
ZZZ...
PAT...
WHOA...
ALREADY...
PAT...
PAT...
PAT...

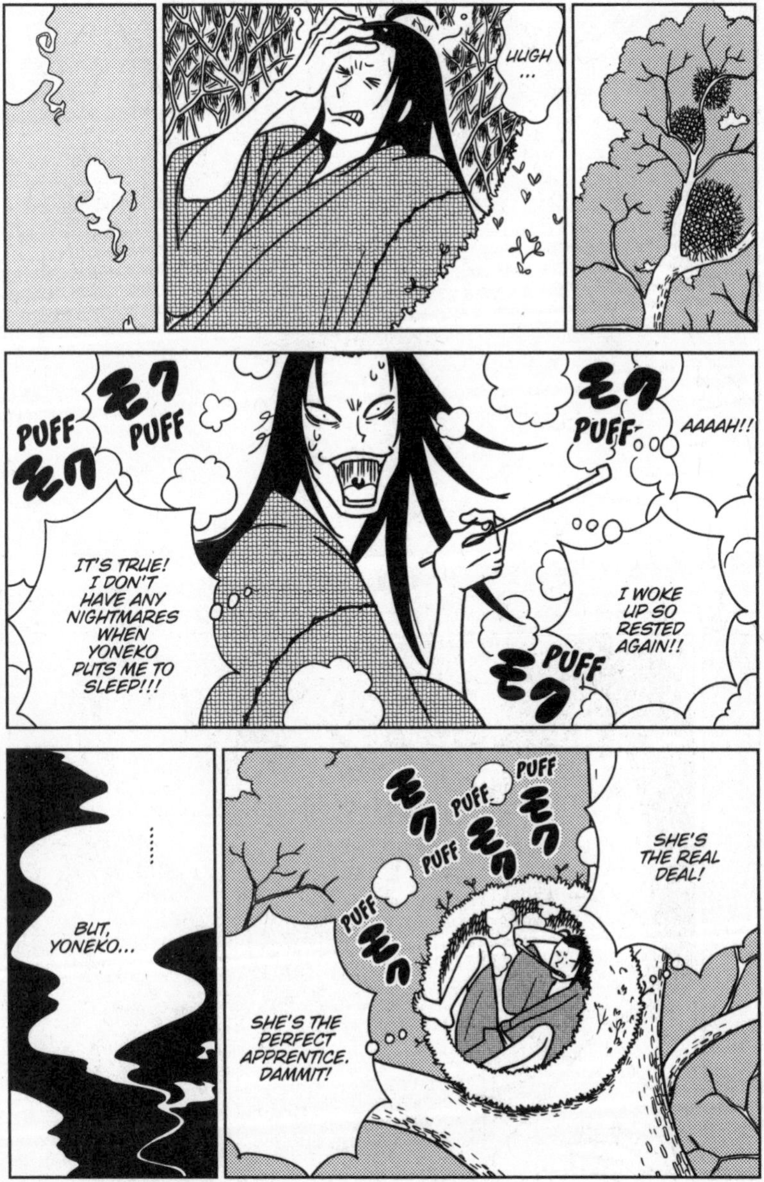
UUGH ...
モク PUFF
AAAAH!!
I WOKE UP SO RESTED AGAIN!!
PUFF モク
モク PUFF
PUFF モク
IT'S TRUE! I DON'T HAVE ANY NIGHTMARES WHEN YONEKO PUTS ME TO SLEEP!!!
PUFF モク
SHE'S THE REAL DEAL!
PUFF モク
PUFF モク
PUFF モク
SHE'S THE PERFECT APPRENTICE. DAMMIT!
......
BUT, YONEKO...

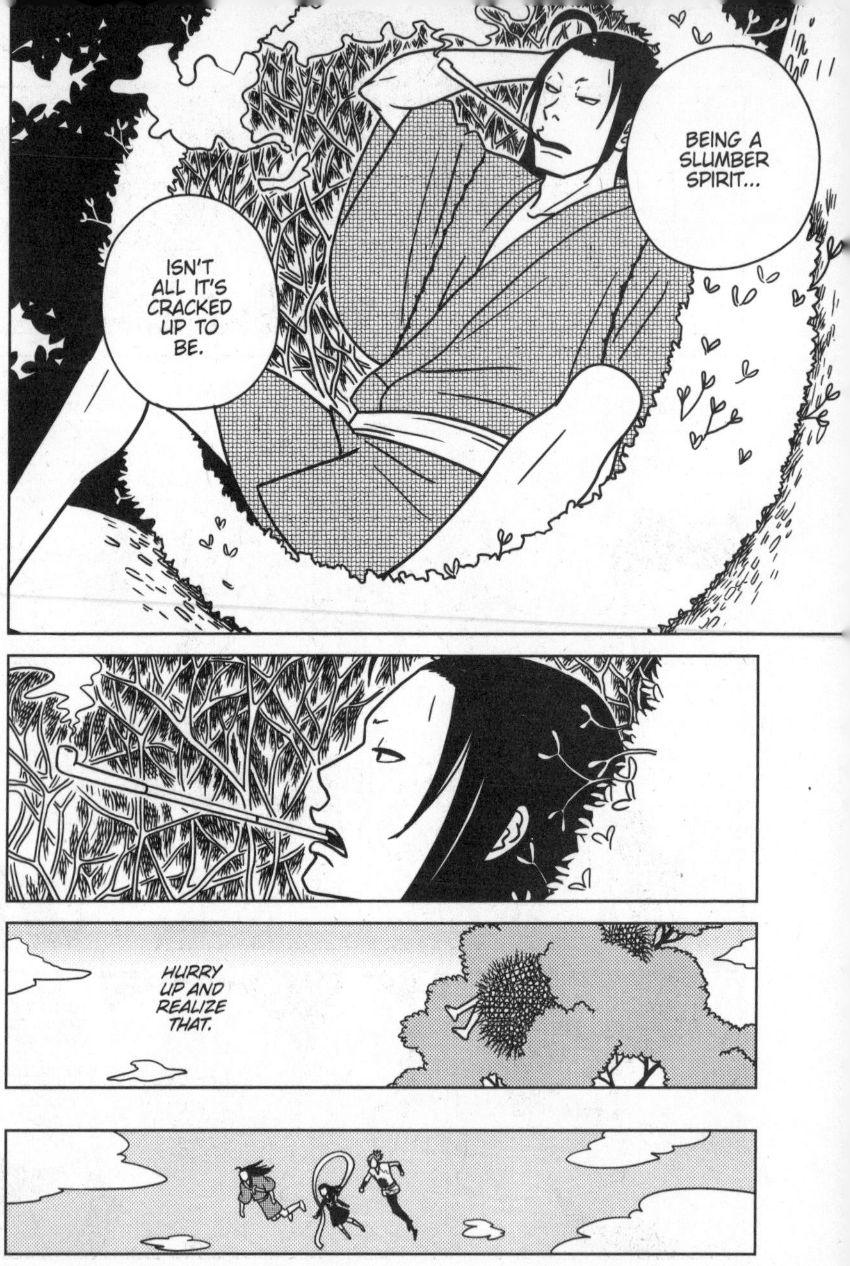
BEING A SLUMBER SPIRIT...
ISN'T ALL IT'S CRACKED UP TO BE.
HURRY UP AND REALIZE THAT.

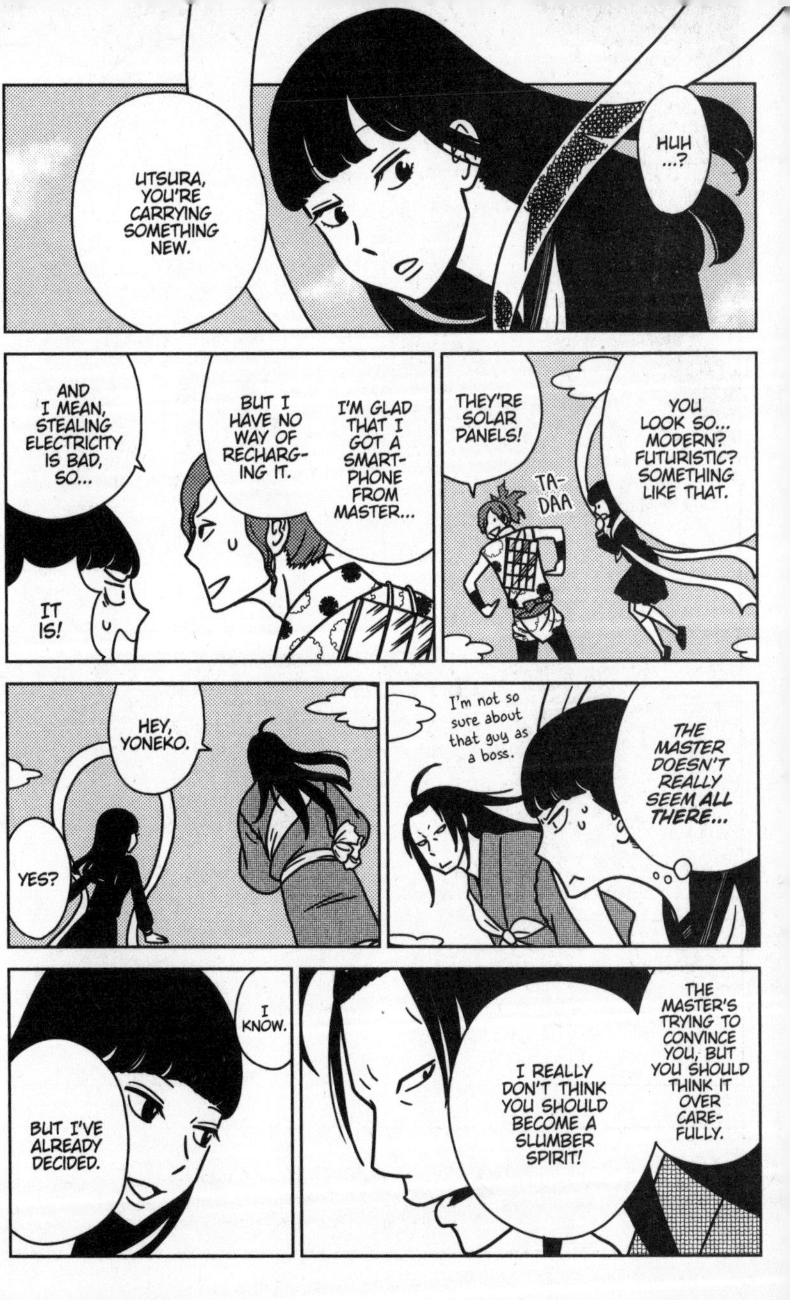
HUH ...?
UTSURA, YOU'RE CARRYING SOMETHING NEW.
YOU LOOK SO... MODERN? FUTURISTIC? SOMETHING LIKE THAT.
THEY'RE SOLAR PANELS!
TA-DAA
I'M GLAD THAT I GOT A SMARTPHONE FROM MASTER...
BUT I HAVE NO WAY OF RECHARGING IT.
AND I MEAN, STEALING ELECTRICITY IS BAD, SO...
IT IS!
THE MASTER DOESN'T REALLY SEEM ALL THERE...
I'm not so sure about that guy as a boss.
HEY, YONEKO.
YES?
THE MASTER'S TRYING TO CONVINCE YOU, BUT YOU SHOULD THINK IT OVER CAREFULLY.
I REALLY DON'T THINK YOU SHOULD BECOME A SLUMBER SPIRIT!
I KNOW.
BUT I'VE ALREADY DECIDED.

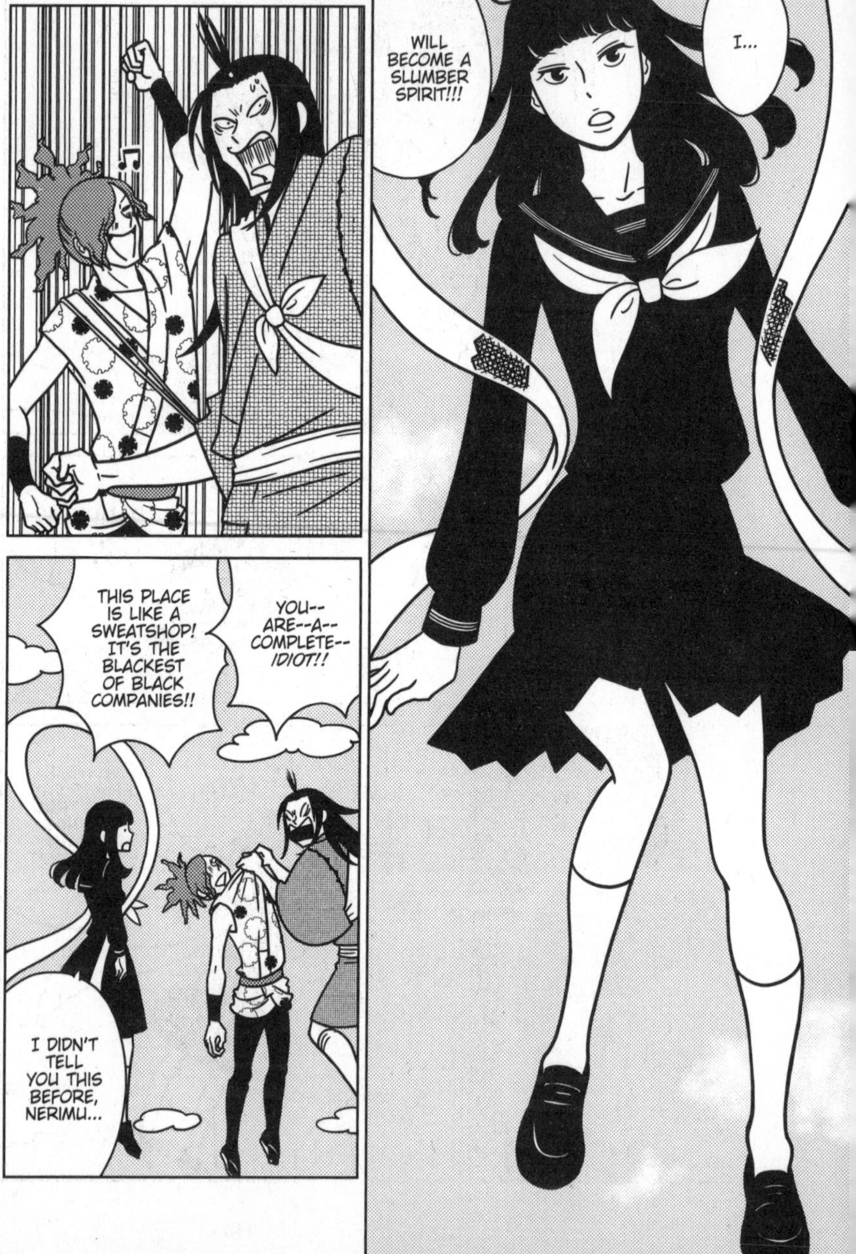
THIS PLACE IS LIKE A SWEATSHOP! IT'S THE BLACKEST OF BLACK COMPANIES!!
YOU--ARE--A--COMPLETE--IDIOT!!
I DIDN'T TELL YOU THIS BEFORE, NERIMU...
I...
WILL BECOME A SLUMBER SPIRIT!!!

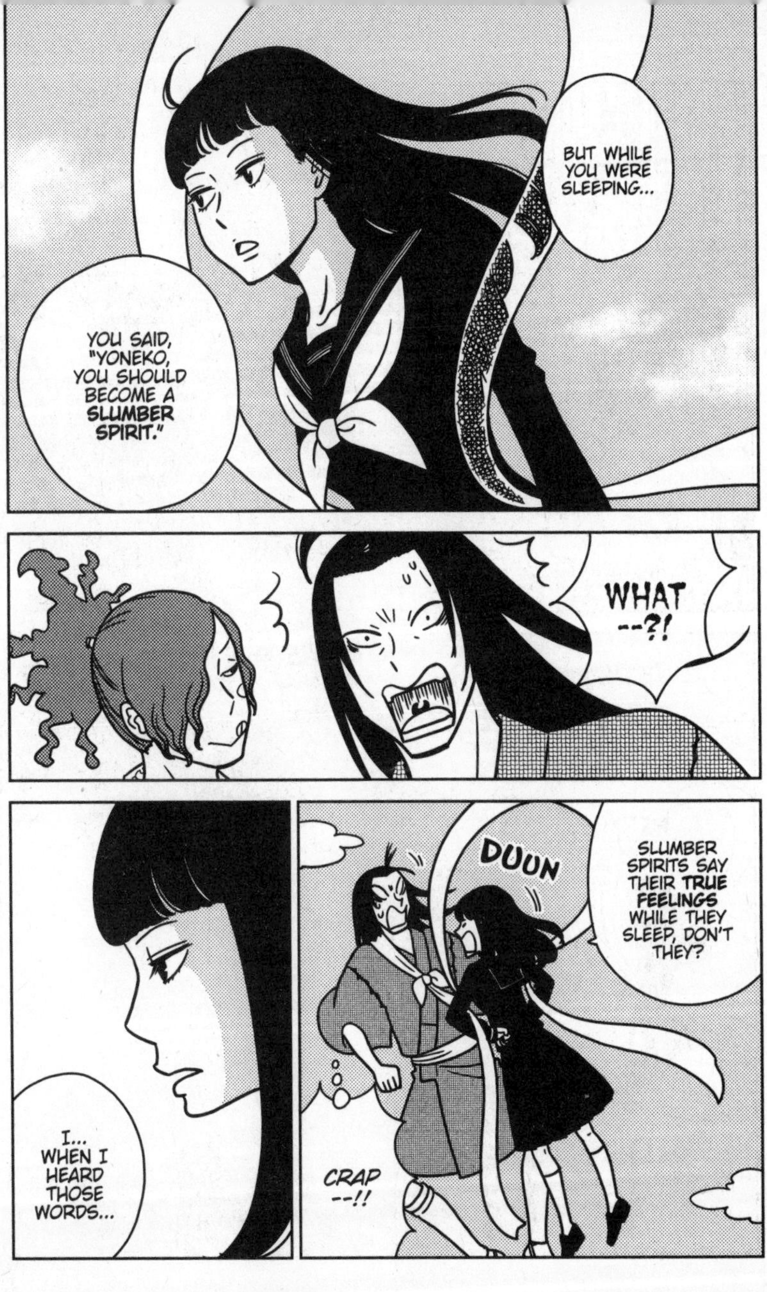
BUT WHILE YOU WERE SLEEPING...
YOU SAID, "YONEKO, YOU SHOULD BECOME A SLUMBER SPIRIT."
WHAT --?!
SLUMBER SPIRITS SAY THEIR TRUE FEELINGS WHILE THEY SLEEP, DON'T THEY?
DUUN
CRAP --!!
I... WHEN I HEARD THOSE WORDS...

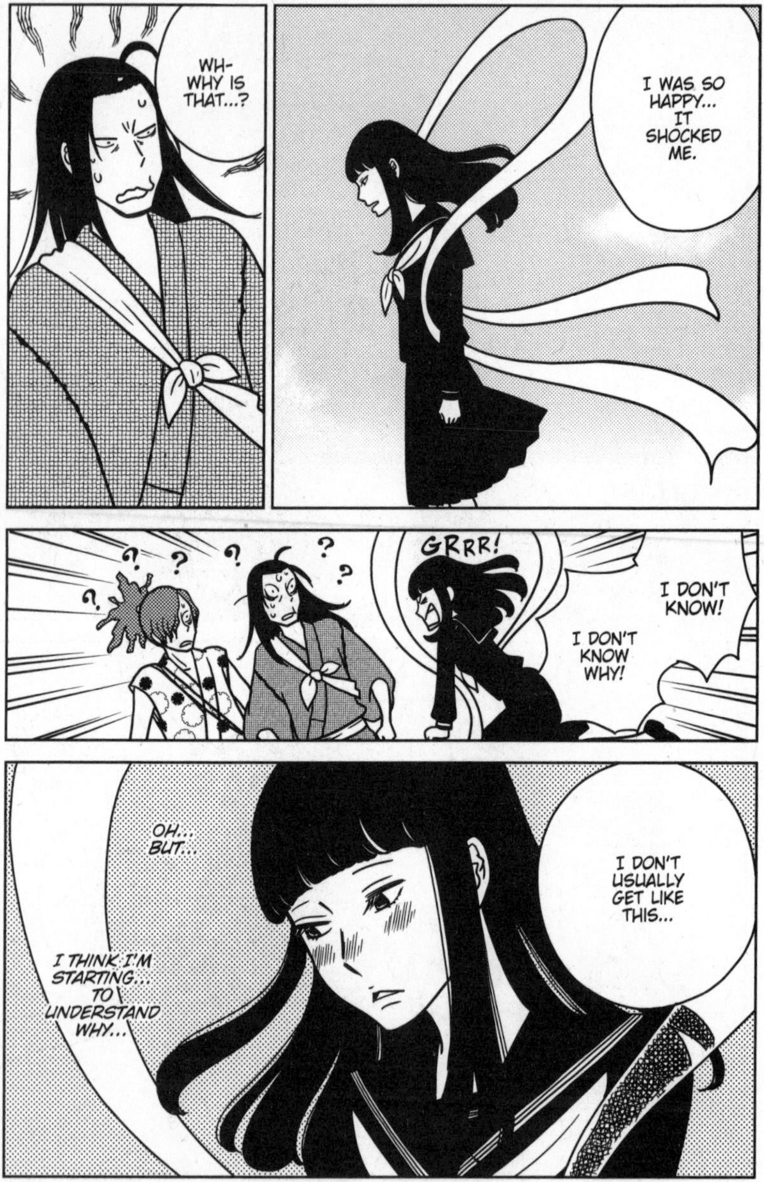
I WAS SO HAPPY... IT SHOCKED ME.
WH- WHY IS THAT...?
I DON'T KNOW!
I DON'T KNOW WHY!
GRRR!
I DON'T USUALLY GET LIKE THIS...
OH... BUT...
I THINK I'M STARTING... TO UNDERSTAND WHY...

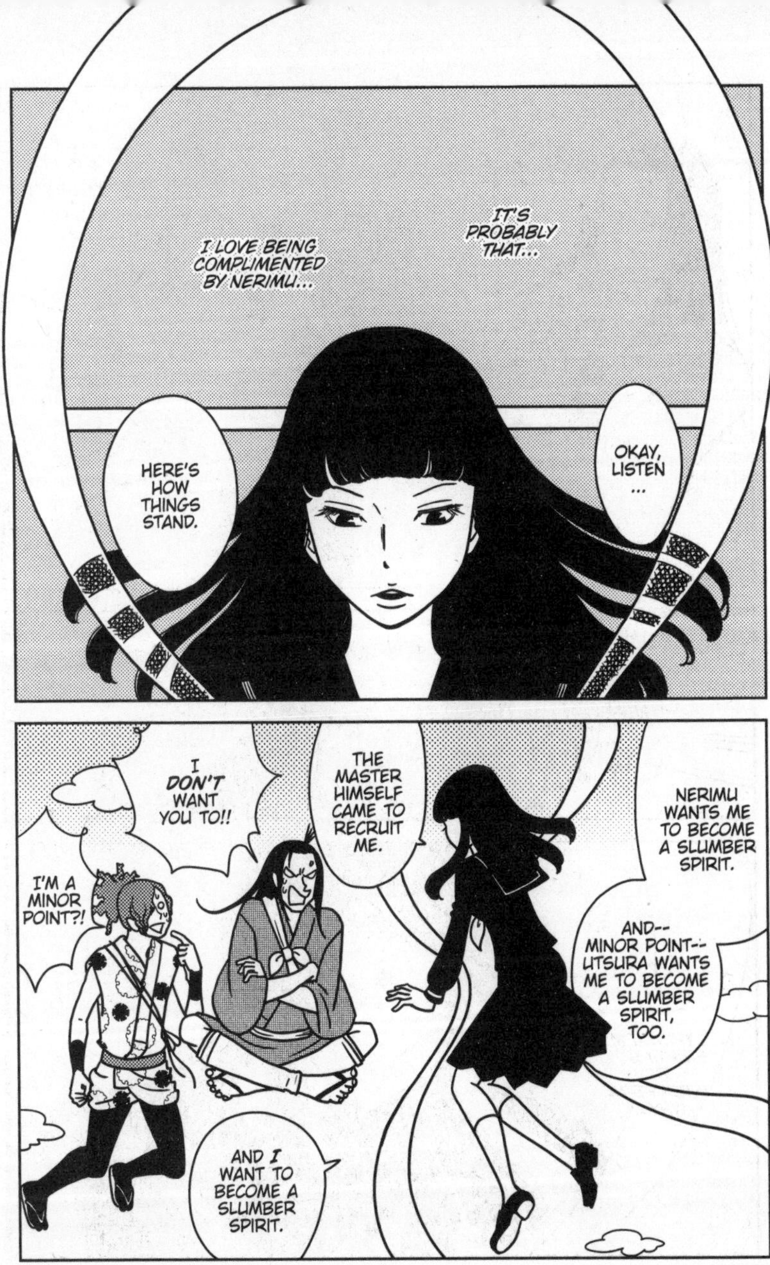
IT'S PROBABLY THAT...
I LOVE BEING COMPLIMENTED BY NERIMU...
OKAY, LISTEN...
HERE'S HOW THINGS STAND.
NERIMU WANTS ME TO BECOME A SLUMBER SPIRIT.
THE MASTER HIMSELF CAME TO RECRUIT ME.
I *DON'T* WANT YOU TO!!
AND--MINOR POINT--UTSURA WANTS ME TO BECOME A SLUMBER SPIRIT, TOO.
I'M A MINOR POINT?!
AND *I* WANT TO BECOME A SLUMBER SPIRIT.

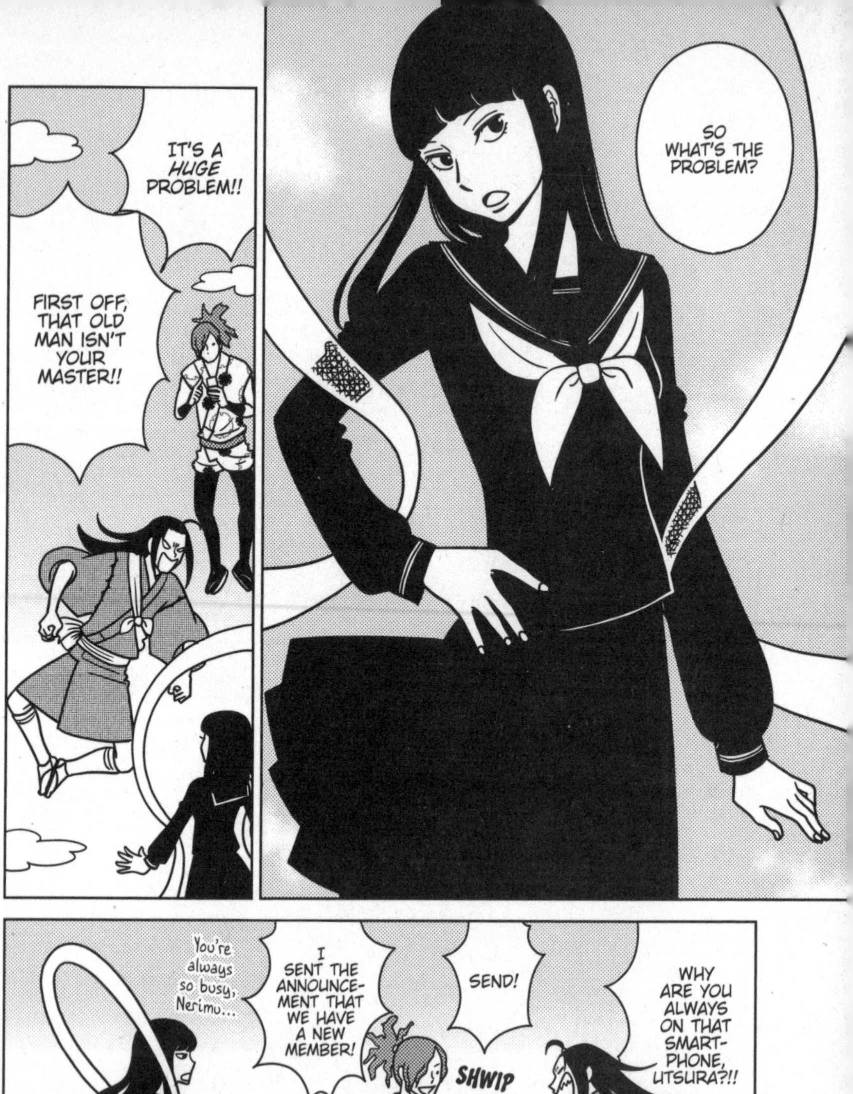
SO WHAT'S THE PROBLEM?
IT'S A *HUGE* PROBLEM!!
FIRST OFF, THAT OLD MAN ISN'T YOUR MASTER!!
WHY ARE YOU ALWAYS ON THAT SMART-PHONE, UTSURA?!!
SEND!
SHWIP
I SENT THE ANNOUNCE-MENT THAT WE HAVE A NEW MEMBER!
I properly reported you calling him an "old man," too!!
You're always so busy, Nerimu...

Fin

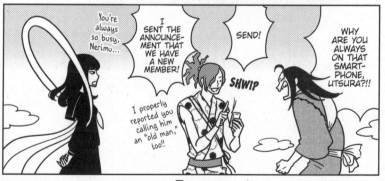

Slumbering Beauty

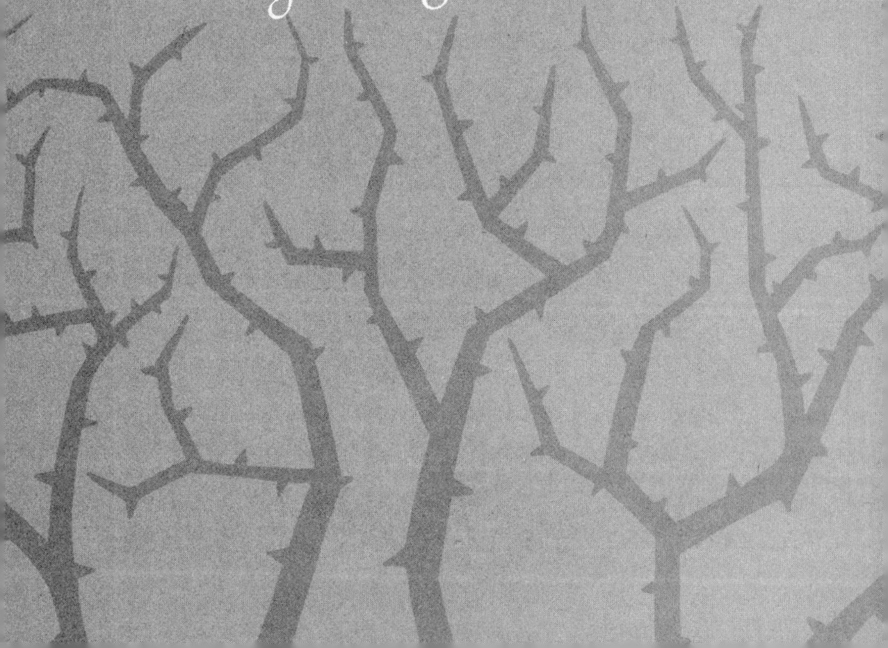

Nemurimehime by Yumi Unita

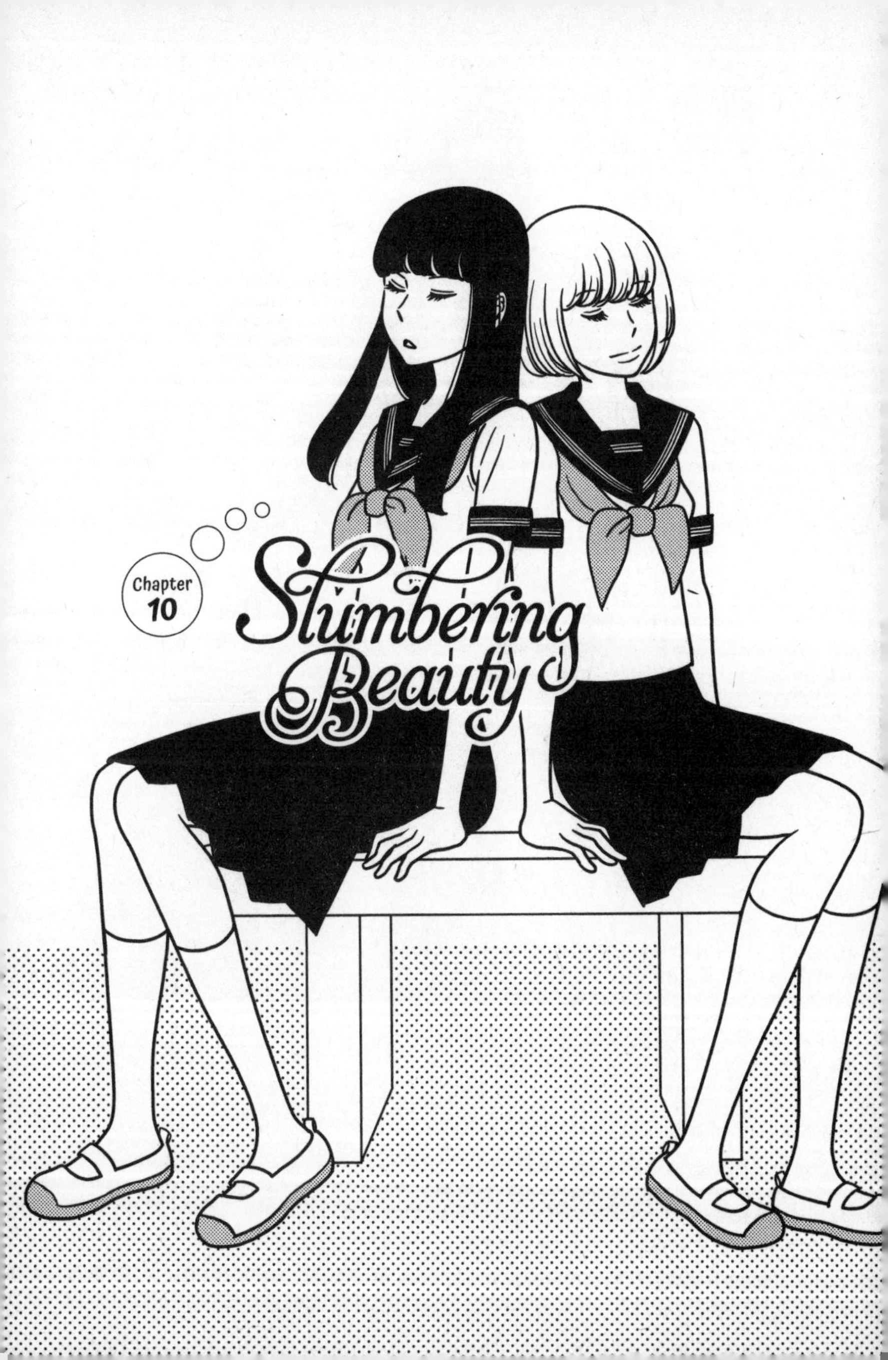
Chapter 10
Slumbering Beauty

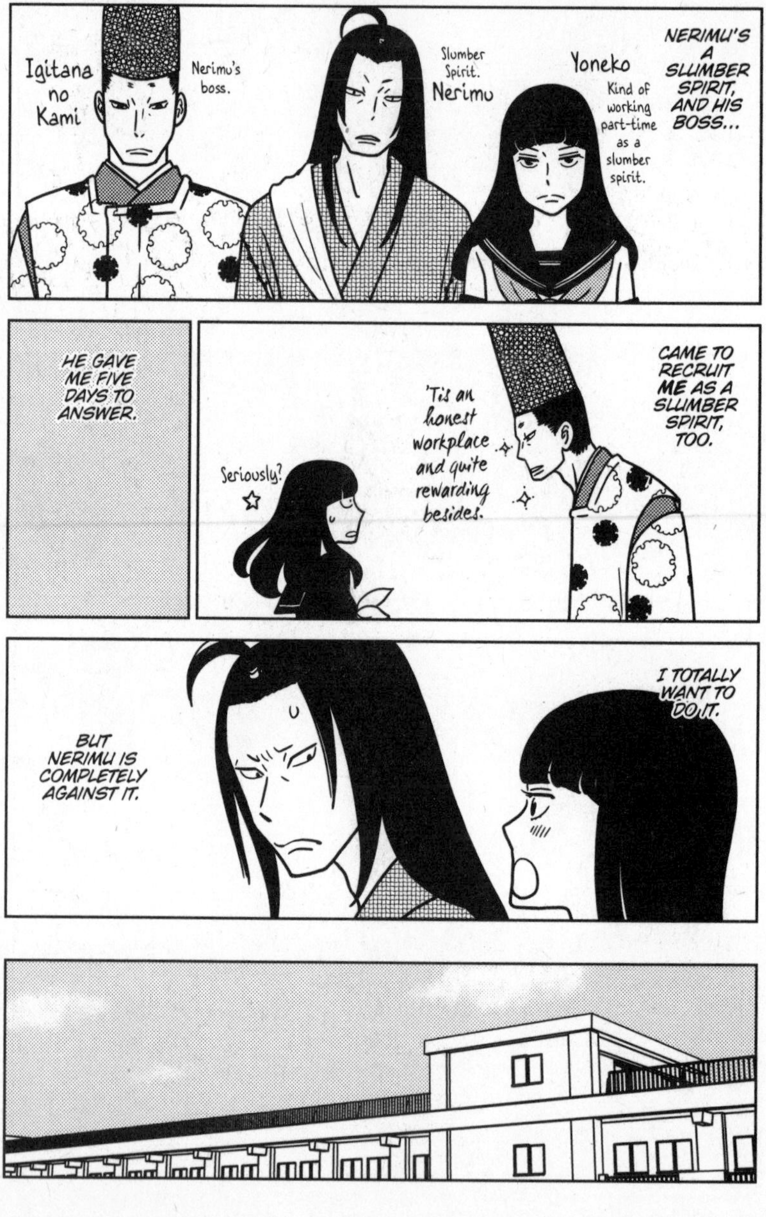
NERIMU'S A SLUMBER SPIRIT, AND HIS BOSS...
Yoneko
Kind of working part-time as a slumber spirit.
Slumber Spirit. Nerimu
Nerimu's boss.
Igitana no Kami
CAME TO RECRUIT ME AS A SLUMBER SPIRIT, TOO.
'Tis an honest workplace and quite rewarding besides.
Seriously?
HE GAVE ME FIVE DAYS TO ANSWER.
I TOTALLY WANT TO DO IT.
BUT NERIMU IS COMPLETELY AGAINST IT.

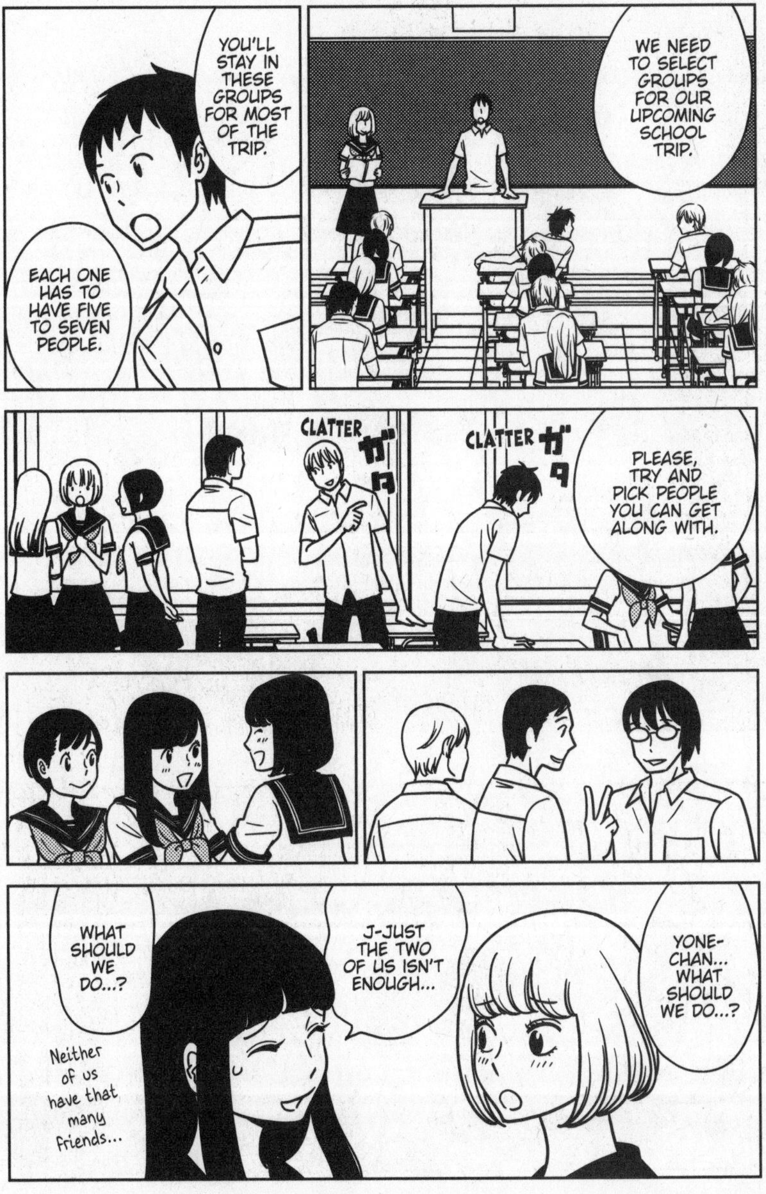
WE NEED TO SELECT GROUPS FOR OUR UPCOMING SCHOOL TRIP.
YOU'LL STAY IN THESE GROUPS FOR MOST OF THE TRIP.
EACH ONE HAS TO HAVE FIVE TO SEVEN PEOPLE.
PLEASE, TRY AND PICK PEOPLE YOU CAN GET ALONG WITH.
CLATTER ガタ
CLATTER ガタ
YONE-CHAN... WHAT SHOULD WE DO...?
J-JUST THE TWO OF US ISN'T ENOUGH...
WHAT SHOULD WE DO...?
Neither of us have that many friends...

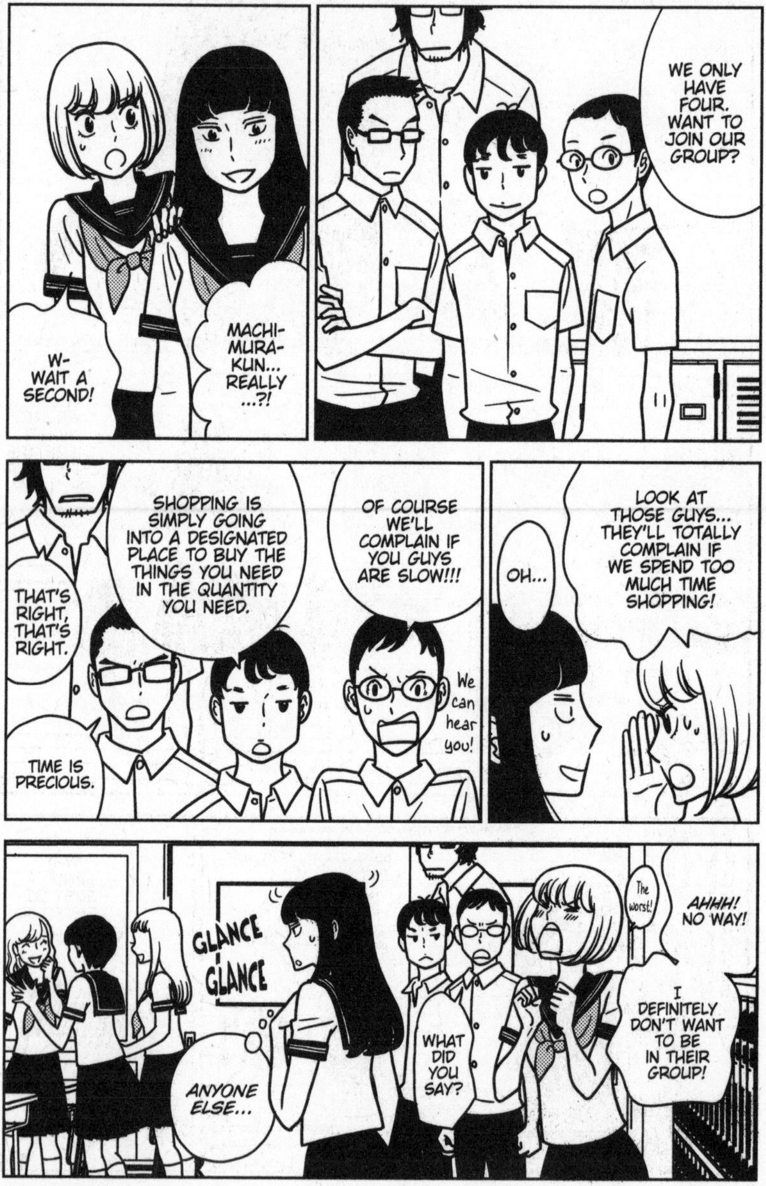
WE ONLY HAVE FOUR. WANT TO JOIN OUR GROUP?
MACHIMURA-KUN... REALLY ...?!
W-WAIT A SECOND!
LOOK AT THOSE GUYS... THEY'LL TOTALLY COMPLAIN IF WE SPEND TOO MUCH TIME SHOPPING!
OH...
OF COURSE WE'LL COMPLAIN IF YOU GUYS ARE SLOW!!!
We can hear you!
SHOPPING IS SIMPLY GOING INTO A DESIGNATED PLACE TO BUY THE THINGS YOU NEED IN THE QUANTITY YOU NEED.
THAT'S RIGHT, THAT'S RIGHT.
TIME IS PRECIOUS.
AHHH! NO WAY!
The worst!
I DEFINITELY DON'T WANT TO BE IN THEIR GROUP!
WHAT DID YOU SAY?
GLANCE GLANCE
ANYONE ELSE...

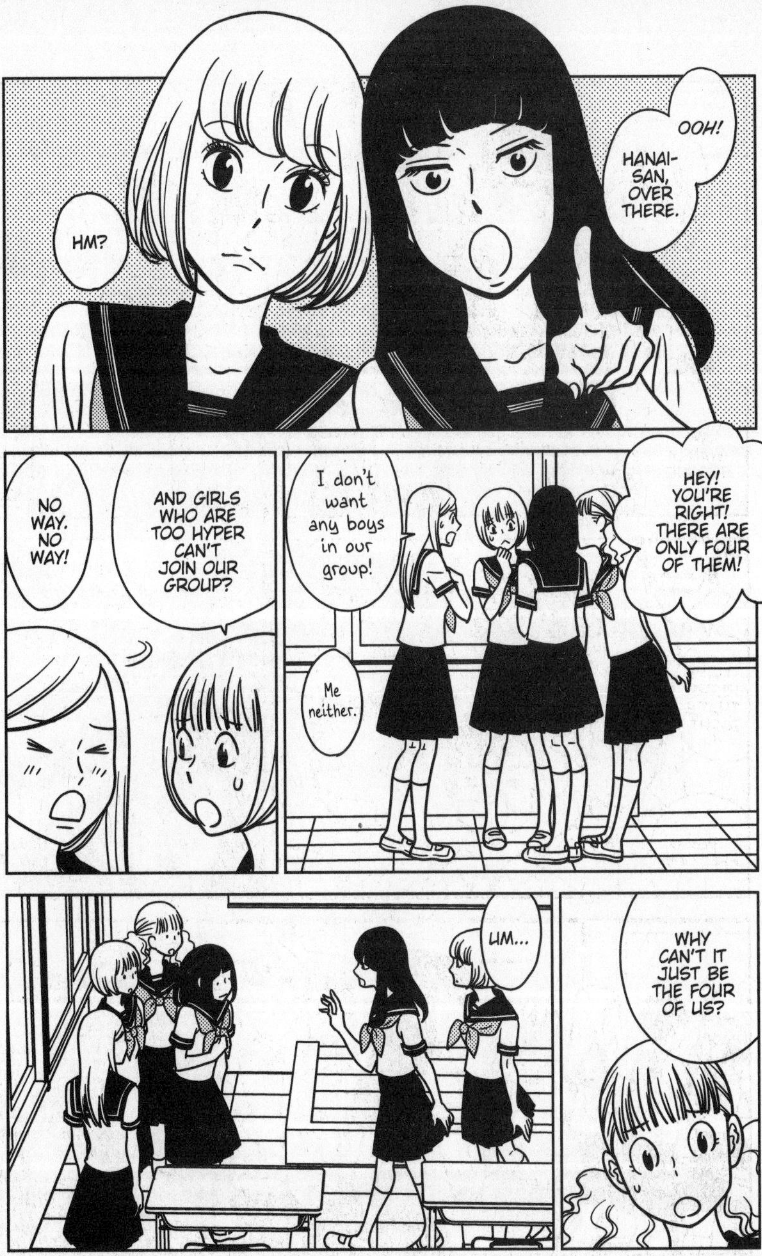
OOH!
HANAI-SAN, OVER THERE.
HM?
HEY! YOU'RE RIGHT! THERE ARE ONLY FOUR OF THEM!
I don't want any boys in our group!
Me neither.
AND GIRLS WHO ARE TOO HYPER CAN'T JOIN OUR GROUP?
NO WAY. NO WAY!
WHY CAN'T IT JUST BE THE FOUR OF US?
UM...

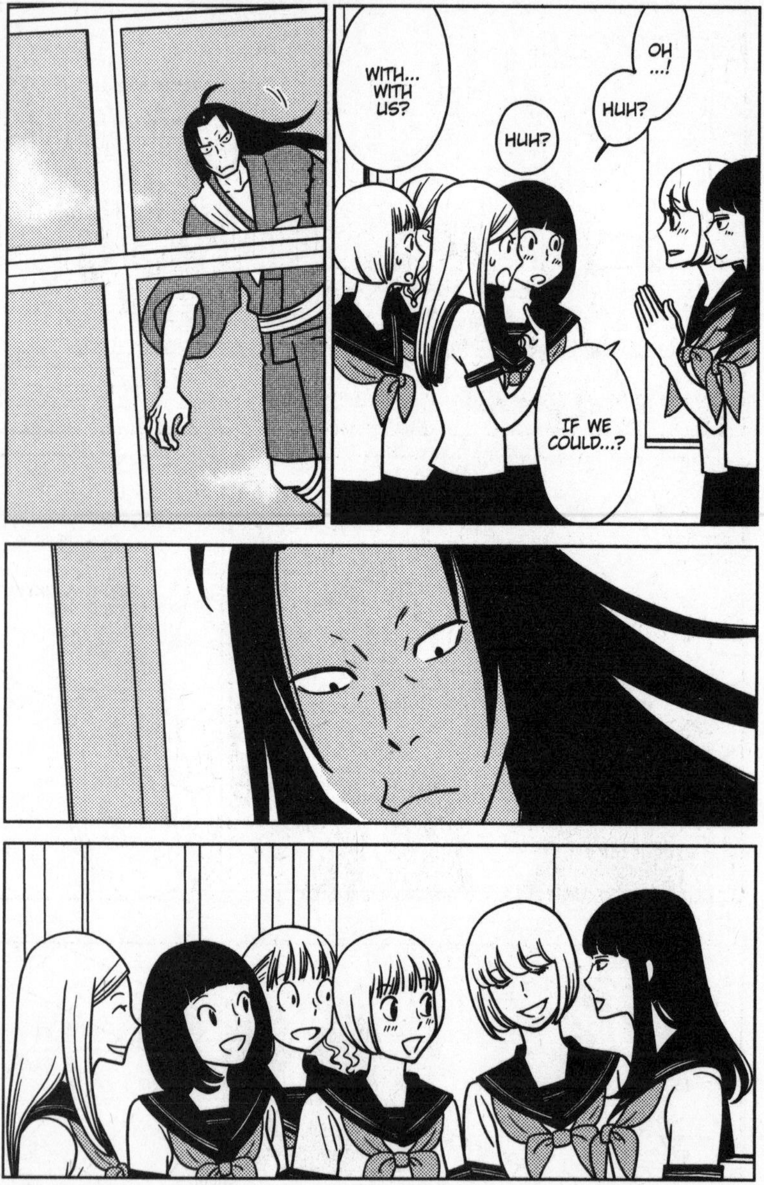
OH ...!
HUH?
HUH?
WITH... WITH US?
IF WE COULD...?

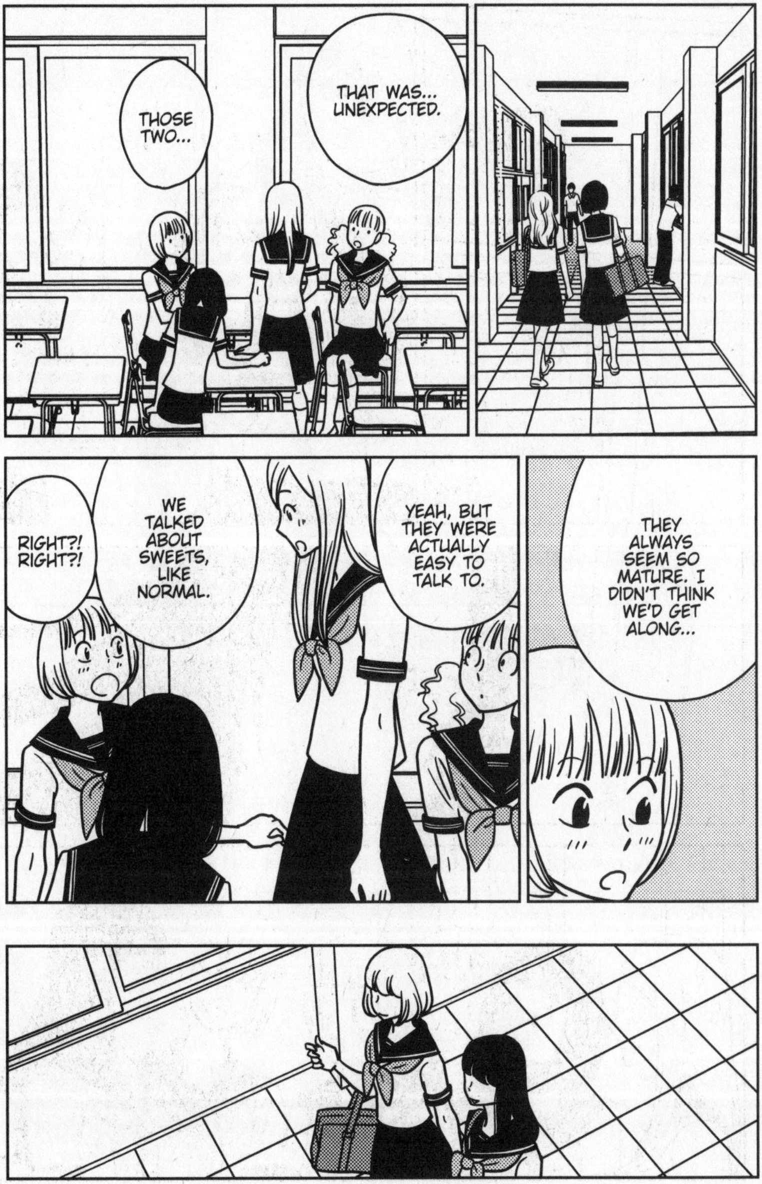
THAT WAS... UNEXPECTED.
THOSE TWO...
THEY ALWAYS SEEM SO MATURE. I DIDN'T THINK WE'D GET ALONG...
YEAH, BUT THEY WERE ACTUALLY EASY TO TALK TO.
WE TALKED ABOUT SWEETS, LIKE NORMAL.
RIGHT?! RIGHT?!

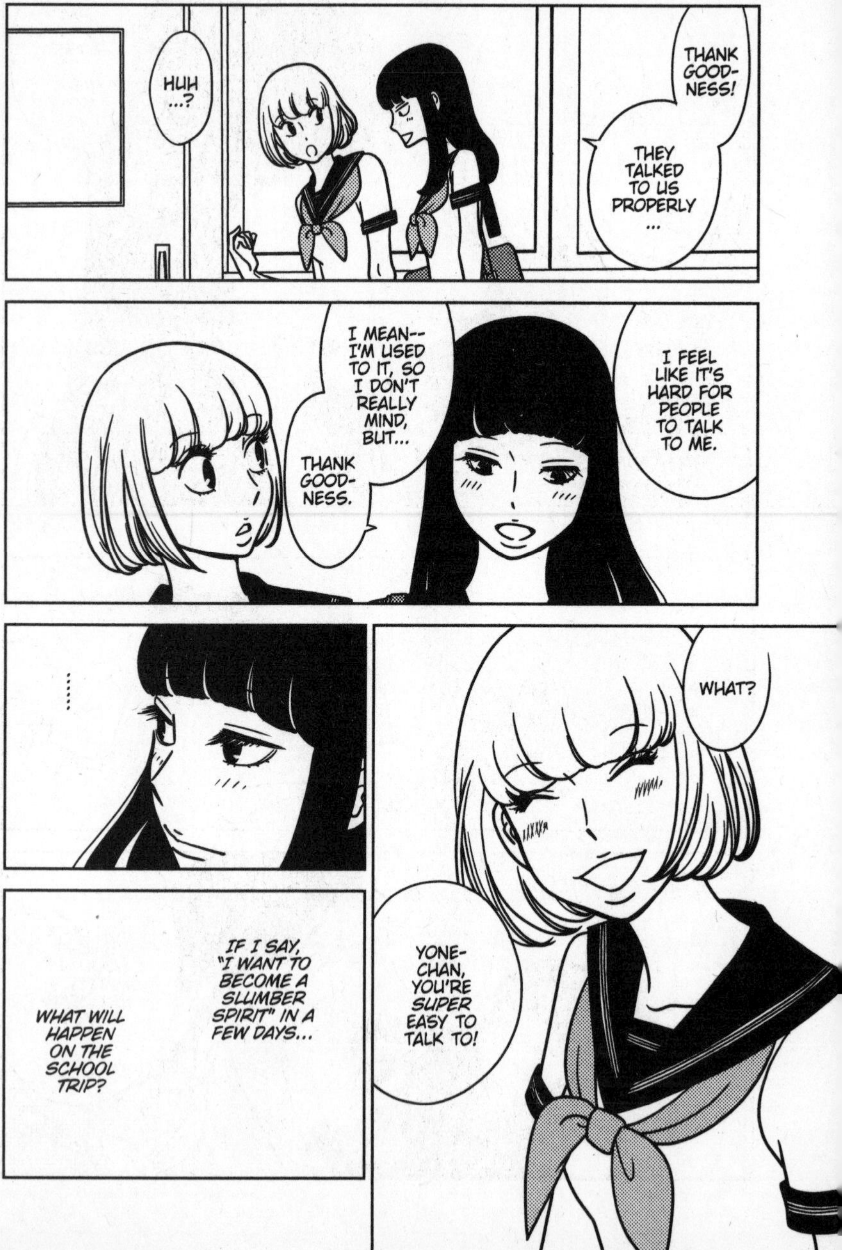
THANK GOODNESS!
THEY TALKED TO US PROPERLY...
HUH...?
I FEEL LIKE IT'S HARD FOR PEOPLE TO TALK TO ME.
I MEAN-- I'M USED TO IT, SO I DON'T REALLY MIND, BUT...
THANK GOODNESS.
WHAT?
YONE-CHAN, YOU'RE SUPER EASY TO TALK TO!
......
IF I SAY, "I WANT TO BECOME A SLUMBER SPIRIT" IN A FEW DAYS...
WHAT WILL HAPPEN ON THE SCHOOL TRIP?

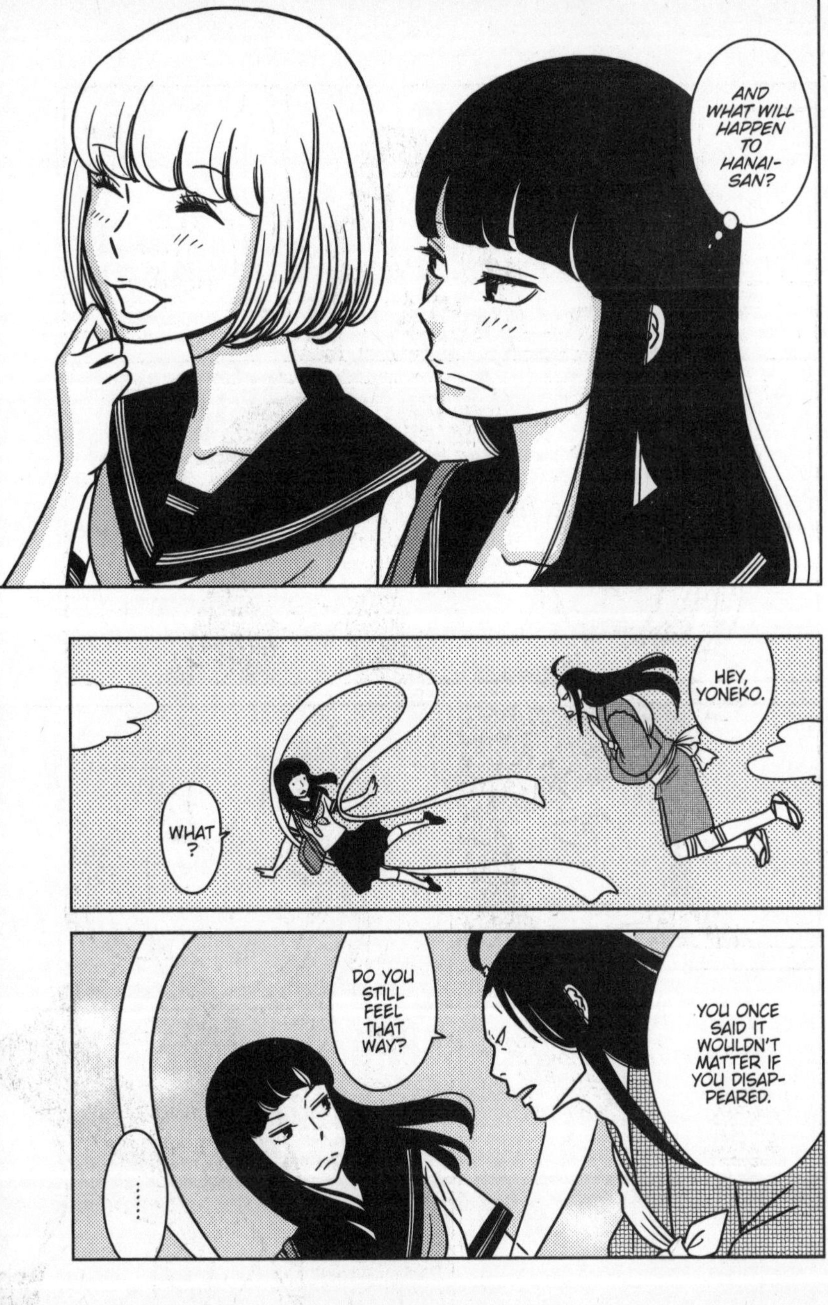
AND WHAT WILL HAPPEN TO HANAI-SAN?
HEY, YONEKO.
WHAT?
YOU ONCE SAID IT WOULDN'T MATTER IF YOU DISAP-PEARED.
DO YOU STILL FEEL THAT WAY?
......

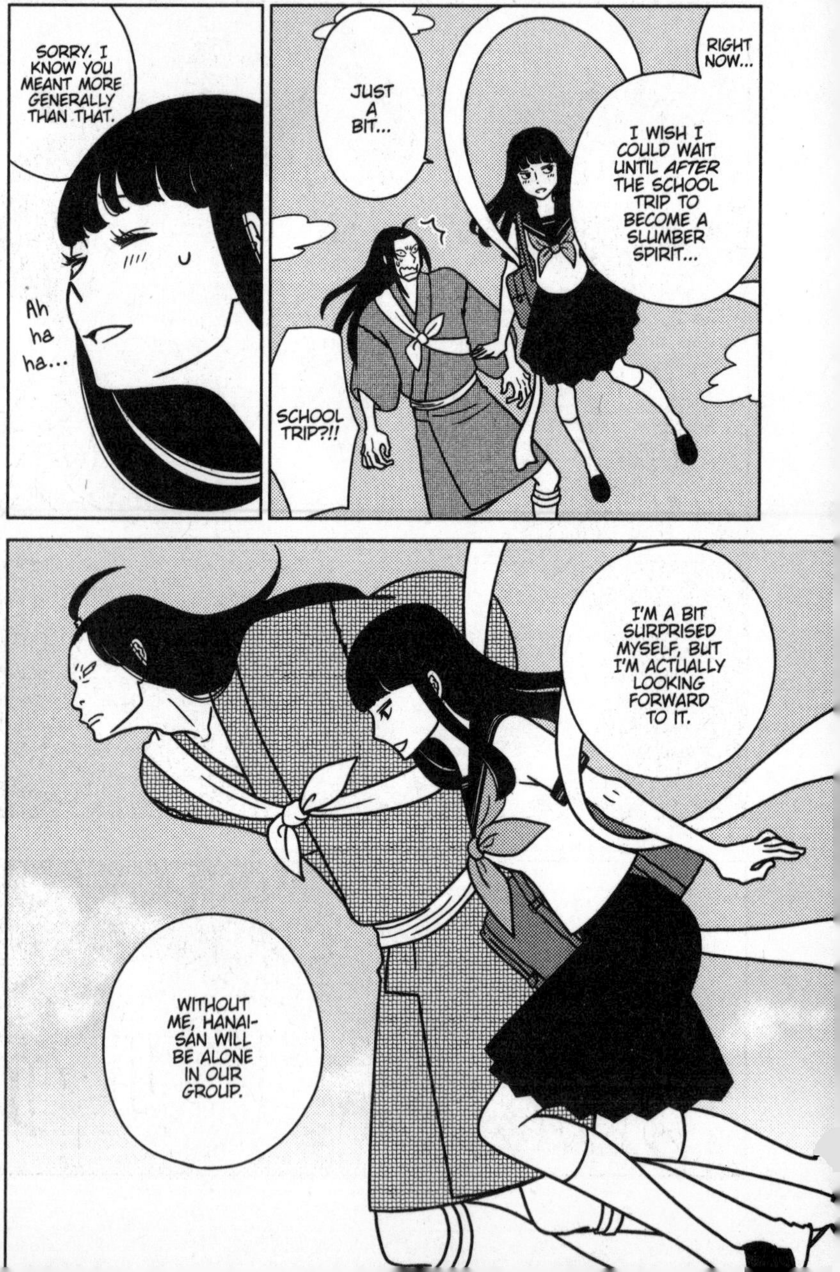
RIGHT NOW...
I WISH I COULD WAIT UNTIL *AFTER* THE SCHOOL TRIP TO BECOME A SLUMBER SPIRIT...
JUST A BIT...
SCHOOL TRIP?!!
SORRY. I KNOW YOU MEANT MORE GENERALLY THAN THAT.
Ah ha ha...
I'M A BIT SURPRISED MYSELF, BUT I'M ACTUALLY LOOKING FORWARD TO IT.
WITHOUT ME, HANAI-SAN WILL BE ALONE IN OUR GROUP.

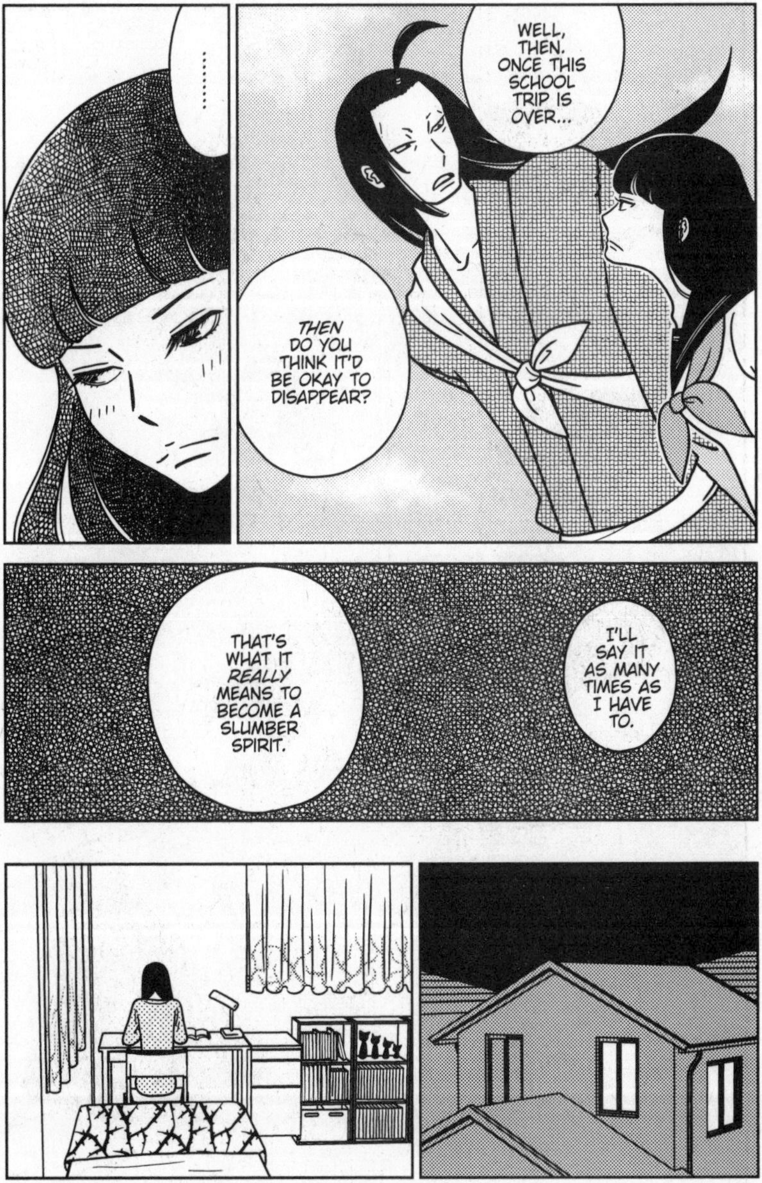
WELL, THEN. ONCE THIS SCHOOL TRIP IS OVER...
THEN DO YOU THINK IT'D BE OKAY TO DISAPPEAR?
......
I'LL SAY IT AS MANY TIMES AS I HAVE TO.
THAT'S WHAT IT *REALLY* MEANS TO BECOME A SLUMBER SPIRIT.

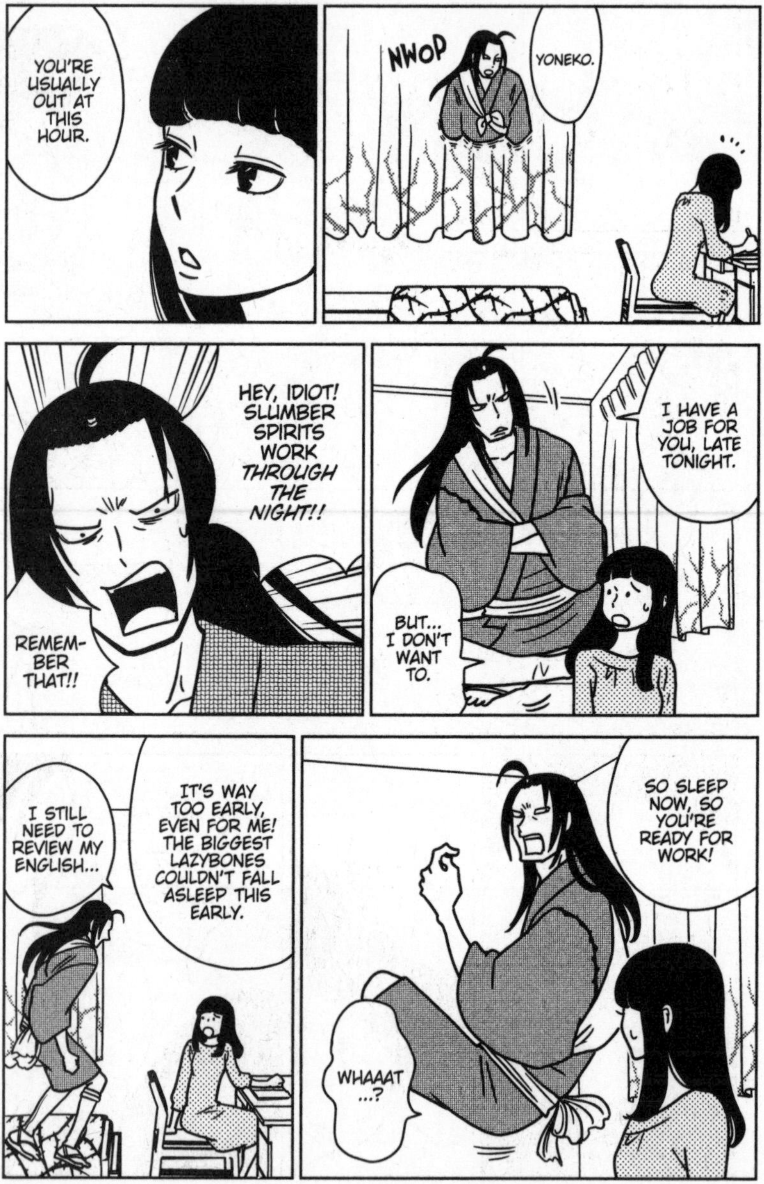
NWOP
YONEKO.
...
YOU'RE USUALLY OUT AT THIS HOUR.
I HAVE A JOB FOR YOU, LATE TONIGHT.
BUT... I DON'T WANT TO.
HEY, IDIOT! SLUMBER SPIRITS WORK *THROUGH THE NIGHT*!!
REMEM-BER THAT!!
SO SLEEP NOW, SO YOU'RE READY FOR WORK!
WHAAAT ...?
IT'S WAY TOO EARLY, EVEN FOR ME! THE BIGGEST LAZYBONES COULDN'T FALL ASLEEP THIS EARLY.
I STILL NEED TO REVIEW MY ENGLISH...

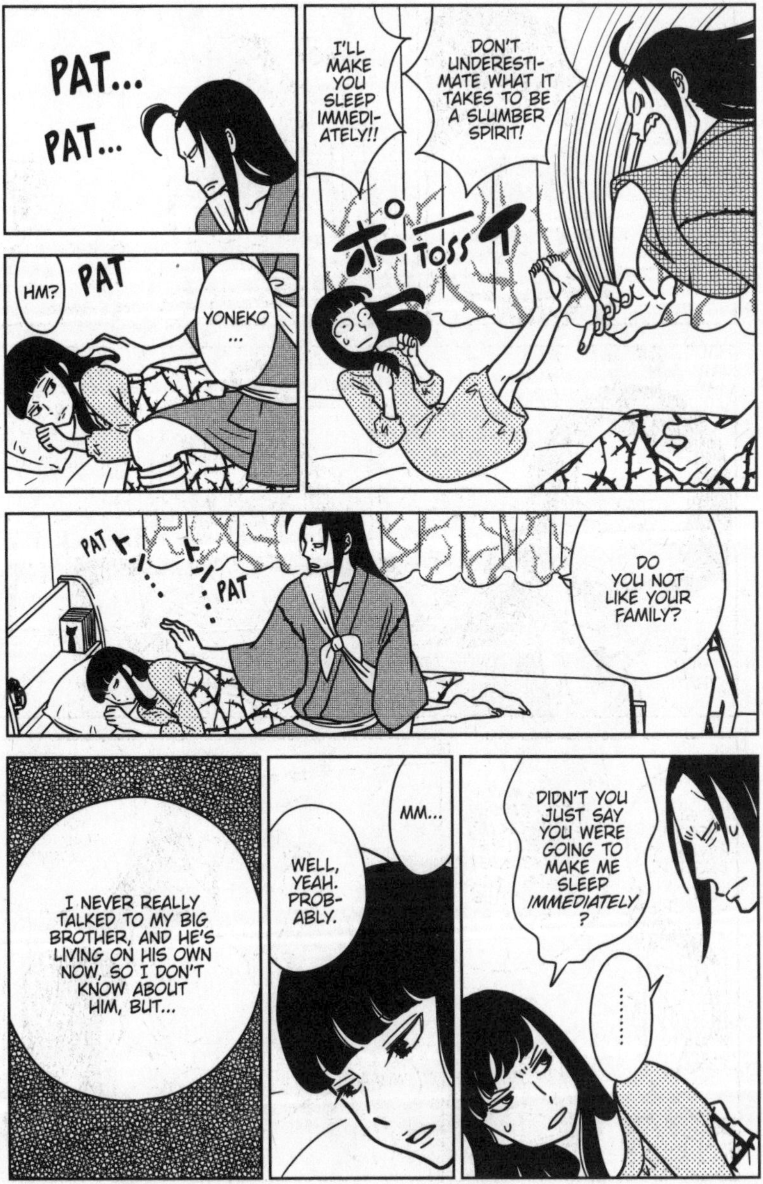
DON'T UNDERESTIMATE WHAT IT TAKES TO BE A SLUMBER SPIRIT!
I'LL MAKE YOU SLEEP IMMEDIATELY!!
ポーイ
TOSS
PAT...
PAT...
YONEKO ...
PAT
HM?
DO YOU NOT LIKE YOUR FAMILY?
PAT
トン
トン
PAT
DIDN'T YOU JUST SAY YOU WERE GOING TO MAKE ME SLEEP *IMMEDIATELY*?
......
MM...
WELL, YEAH. PROBABLY.
I NEVER REALLY TALKED TO MY BIG BROTHER, AND HE'S LIVING ON HIS OWN NOW, SO I DON'T KNOW ABOUT HIM, BUT...

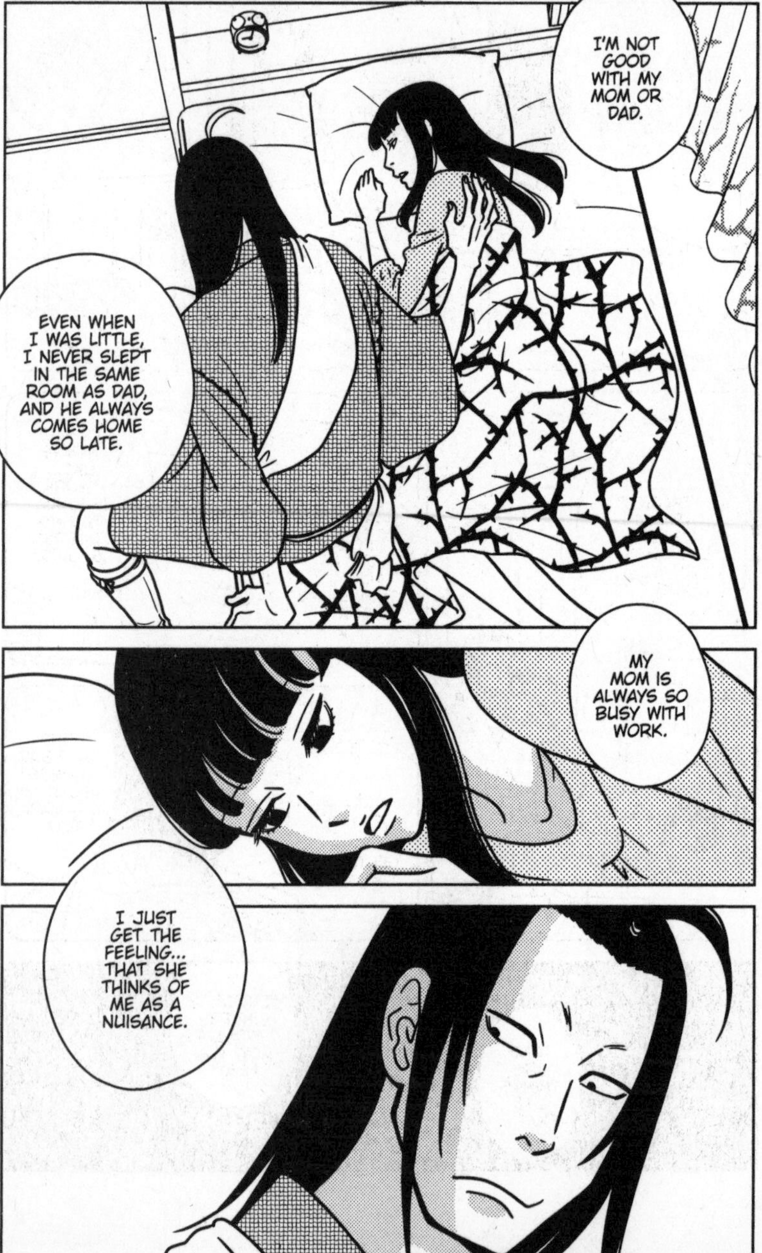
I'M NOT GOOD WITH MY MOM OR DAD.
EVEN WHEN I WAS LITTLE, I NEVER SLEPT IN THE SAME ROOM AS DAD, AND HE ALWAYS COMES HOME SO LATE.
MY MOM IS ALWAYS SO BUSY WITH WORK.
I JUST GET THE FEELING... THAT SHE THINKS OF ME AS A NUISANCE.

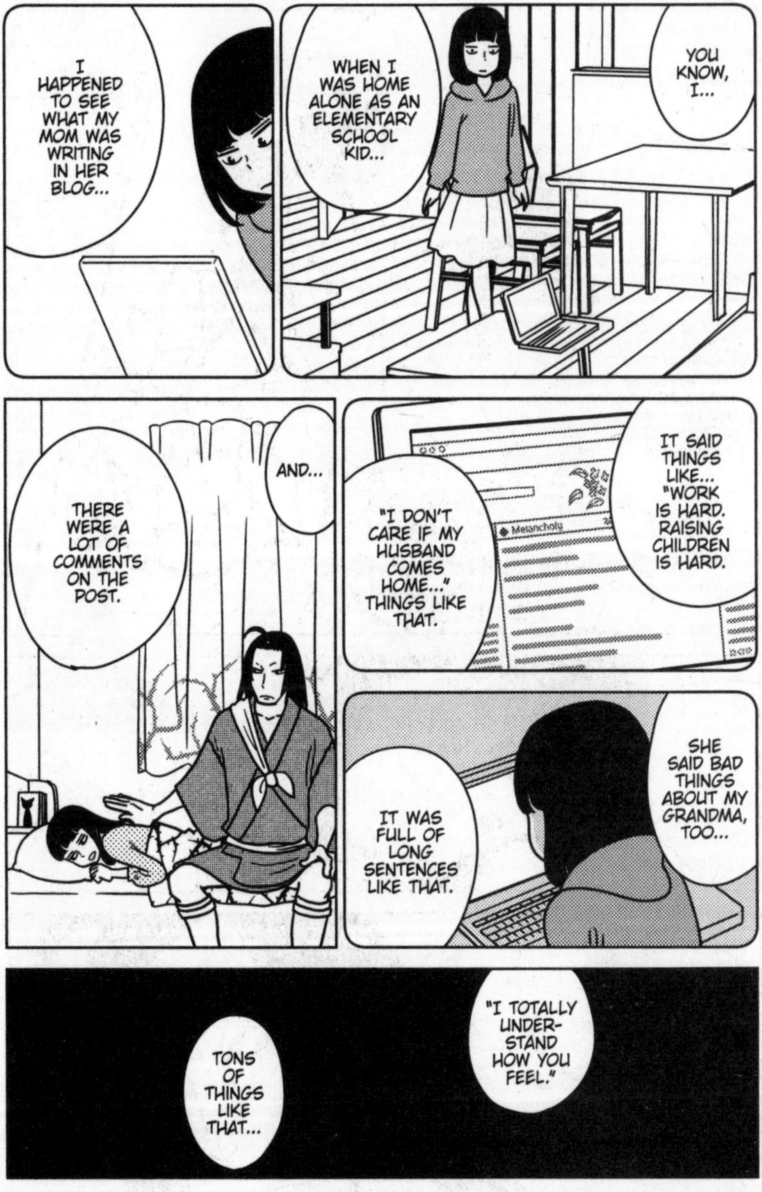
YOU KNOW, I...
WHEN I WAS HOME ALONE AS AN ELEMENTARY SCHOOL KID...
I HAPPENED TO SEE WHAT MY MOM WAS WRITING IN HER BLOG...
IT SAID THINGS LIKE... "WORK IS HARD. RAISING CHILDREN IS HARD.
Melancholy
"I DON'T CARE IF MY HUSBAND COMES HOME..." THINGS LIKE THAT.
SHE SAID BAD THINGS ABOUT MY GRANDMA, TOO...
IT WAS FULL OF LONG SENTENCES LIKE THAT.
AND...
THERE WERE A LOT OF COMMENTS ON THE POST.
"I TOTALLY UNDER-STAND HOW YOU FEEL."
TONS OF THINGS LIKE THAT...

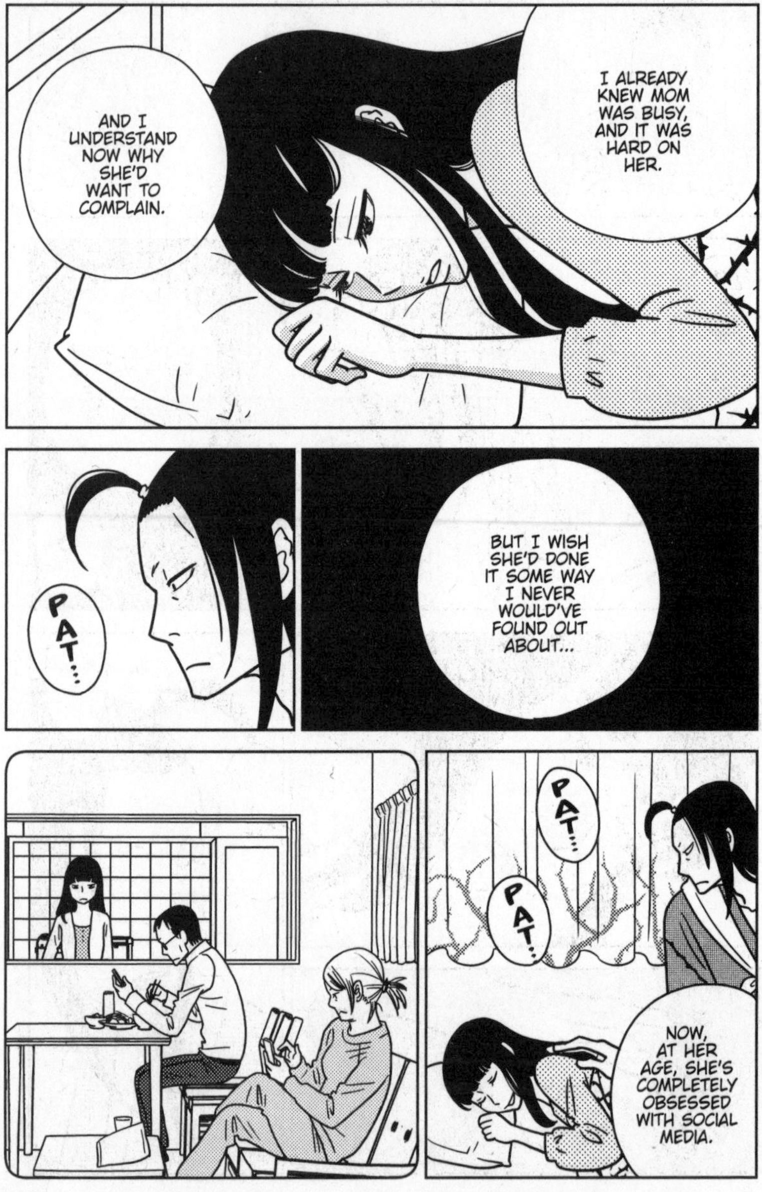
I ALREADY KNEW MOM WAS BUSY, AND IT WAS HARD ON HER.
AND I UNDERSTAND NOW WHY SHE'D WANT TO COMPLAIN.
BUT I WISH SHE'D DONE IT SOME WAY I NEVER WOULD'VE FOUND OUT ABOUT...
PAT...
PAT...
PAT...
NOW, AT HER AGE, SHE'S COMPLETELY OBSESSED WITH SOCIAL MEDIA.

My husband is silently eating the dinner I worked so hard to make, staring at his smartphone. \\(˘o˘)/

PAT...

PAT...

I'M SURE SHE'S WRITING BAD THINGS ABOUT DAD RIGHT NOW.

PAT...

PAT...

......

I SEE...

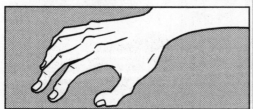

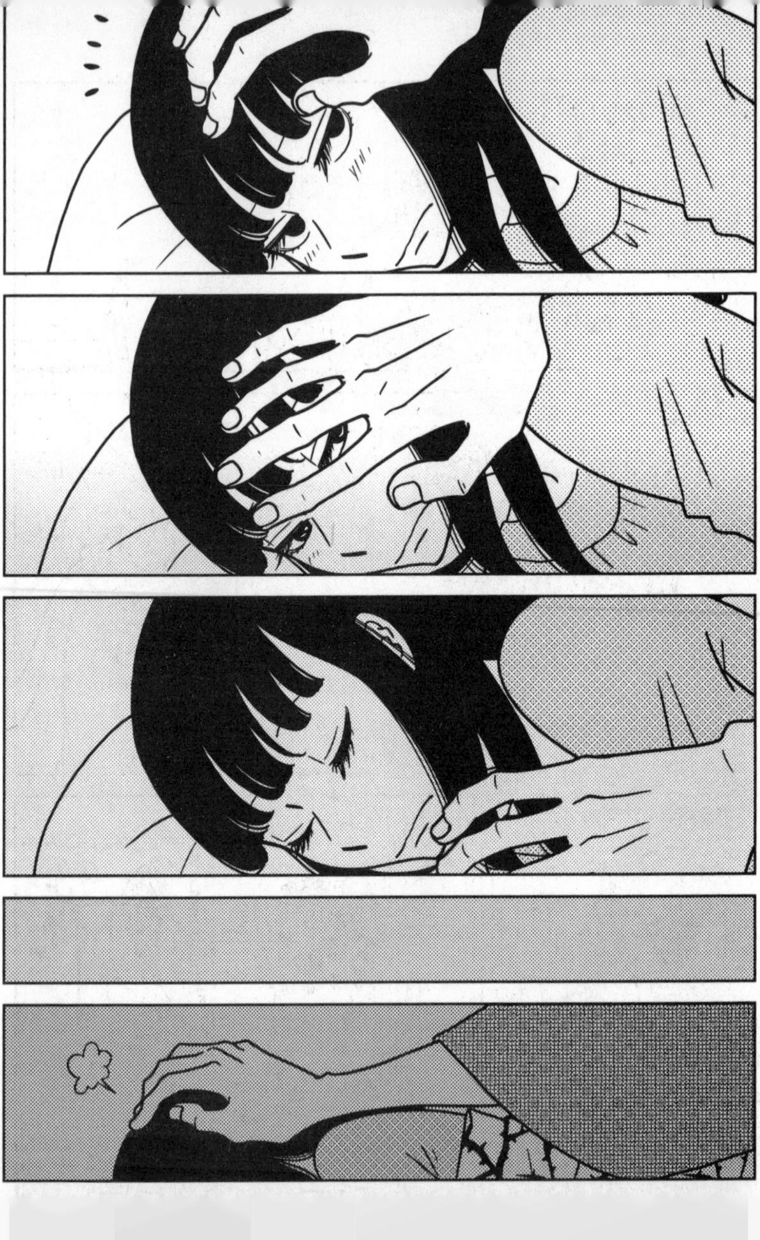

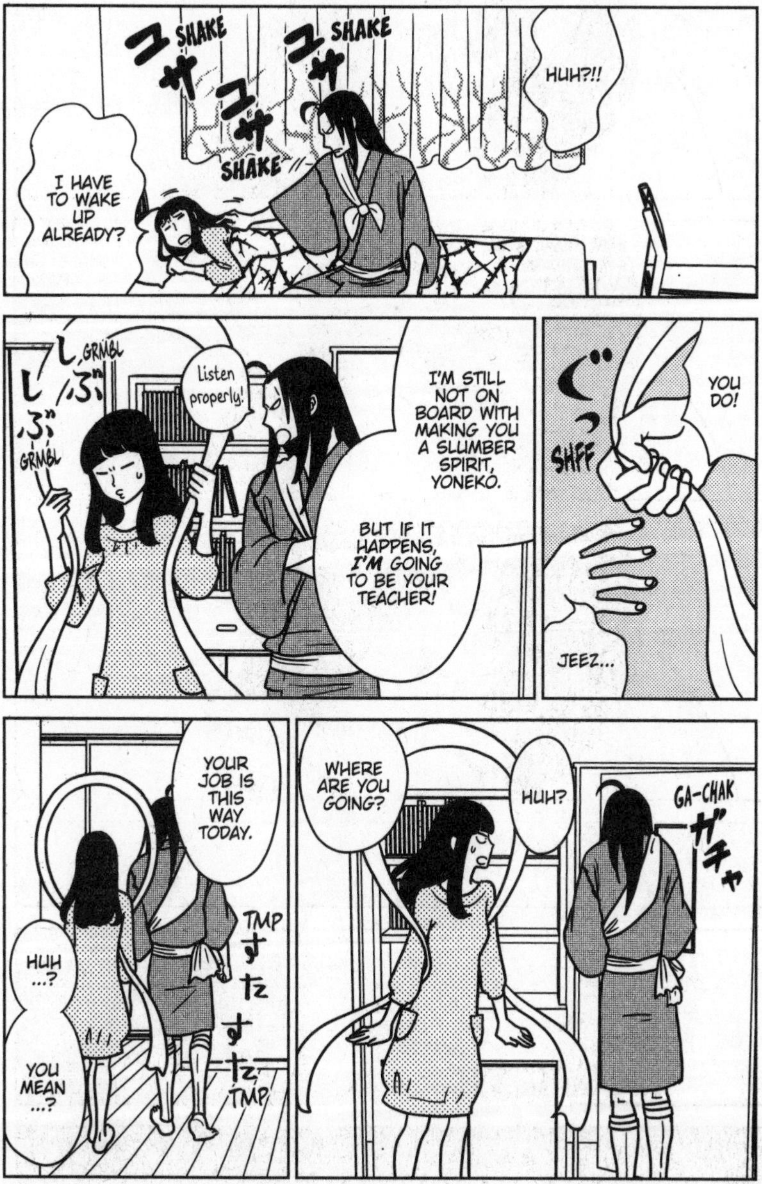
HUH?!!
ユサ SHAKE
ユサ SHAKE
ユサ SHAKE
I HAVE TO WAKE UP ALREADY?
YOU DO!
ぐっ SHFF
JEEZ...
I'M STILL NOT ON BOARD WITH MAKING YOU A SLUMBER SPIRIT, YONEKO.
BUT IF IT HAPPENS, *I'M* GOING TO BE YOUR TEACHER!
Listen properly!
しぶ GRMBL
しぶ GRMBL
GA-CHAK ガチャ
HUH?
WHERE ARE YOU GOING?
YOUR JOB IS THIS WAY TODAY.
TMP すた
すた TMP
HUH ...?
YOU MEAN ...?

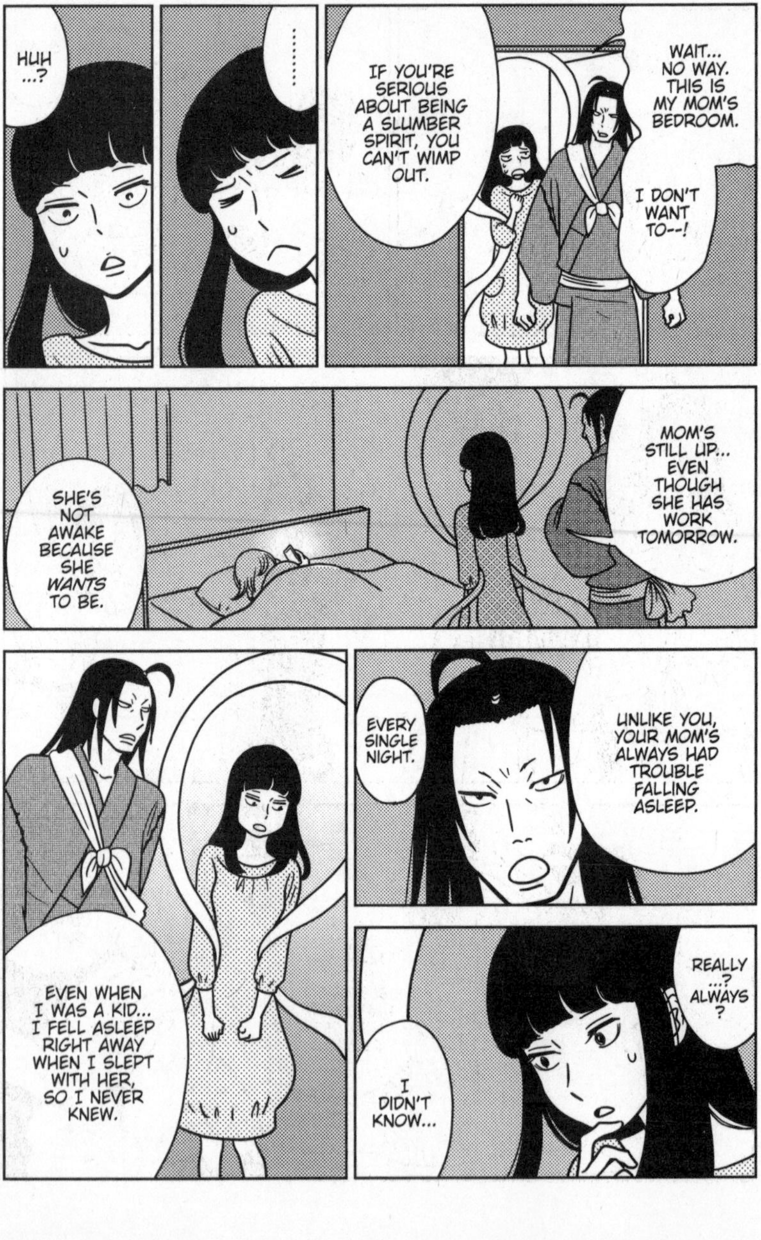
WAIT... NO WAY. THIS IS MY MOM'S BEDROOM.
I DON'T WANT TO--!
IF YOU'RE SERIOUS ABOUT BEING A SLUMBER SPIRIT, YOU CAN'T WIMP OUT.
......
HUH ...?
MOM'S STILL UP... EVEN THOUGH SHE HAS WORK TOMORROW.
SHE'S NOT AWAKE BECAUSE SHE *WANTS* TO BE.
UNLIKE YOU, YOUR MOM'S ALWAYS HAD TROUBLE FALLING ASLEEP.
EVERY SINGLE NIGHT.
REALLY ...? ALWAYS ?
I DIDN'T KNOW...
EVEN WHEN I WAS A KID... I FELL ASLEEP RIGHT AWAY WHEN I SLEPT WITH HER, SO I NEVER KNEW.

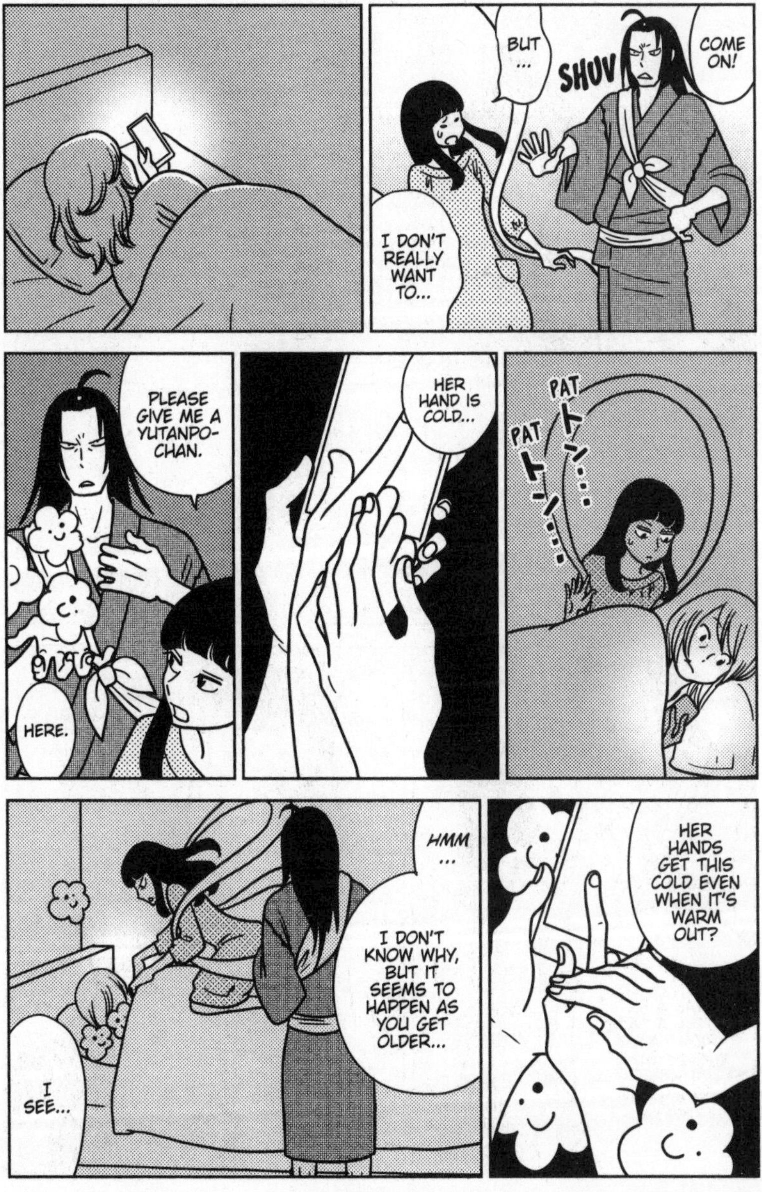
COME ON!
SHUV
BUT ...
I DON'T REALLY WANT TO...
PAT
トン…
PAT
トン…
HER HAND IS COLD...
PLEASE GIVE ME A YUTANPO-CHAN.
HERE.
HER HANDS GET THIS COLD EVEN WHEN IT'S WARM OUT?
HMM ...
I DON'T KNOW WHY, BUT IT SEEMS TO HAPPEN AS YOU GET OLDER...
I SEE...

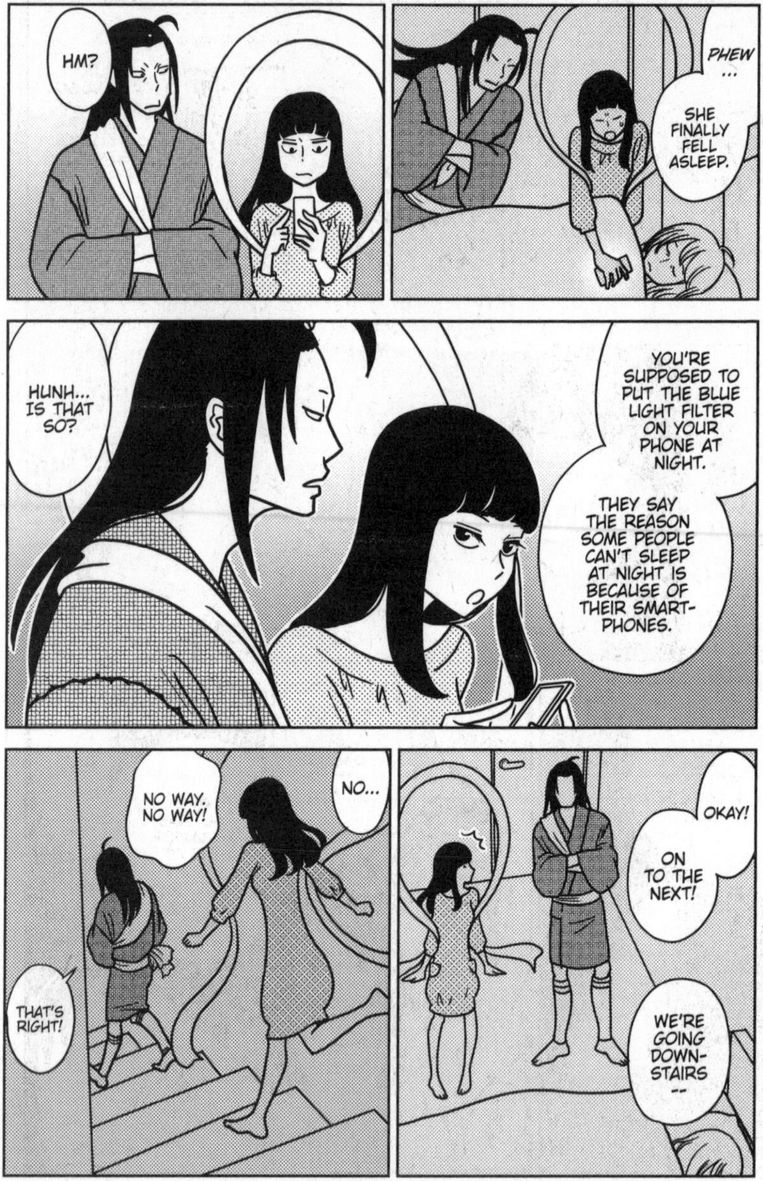
PHEW ...
SHE FINALLY FELL ASLEEP.
HM?
YOU'RE SUPPOSED TO PUT THE BLUE LIGHT FILTER ON YOUR PHONE AT NIGHT.
THEY SAY THE REASON SOME PEOPLE CAN'T SLEEP AT NIGHT IS BECAUSE OF THEIR SMART-PHONES.
HUNH... IS THAT SO?
OKAY!
ON TO THE NEXT!
WE'RE GOING DOWN-STAIRS --
NO...
NO WAY. NO WAY!
THAT'S RIGHT!

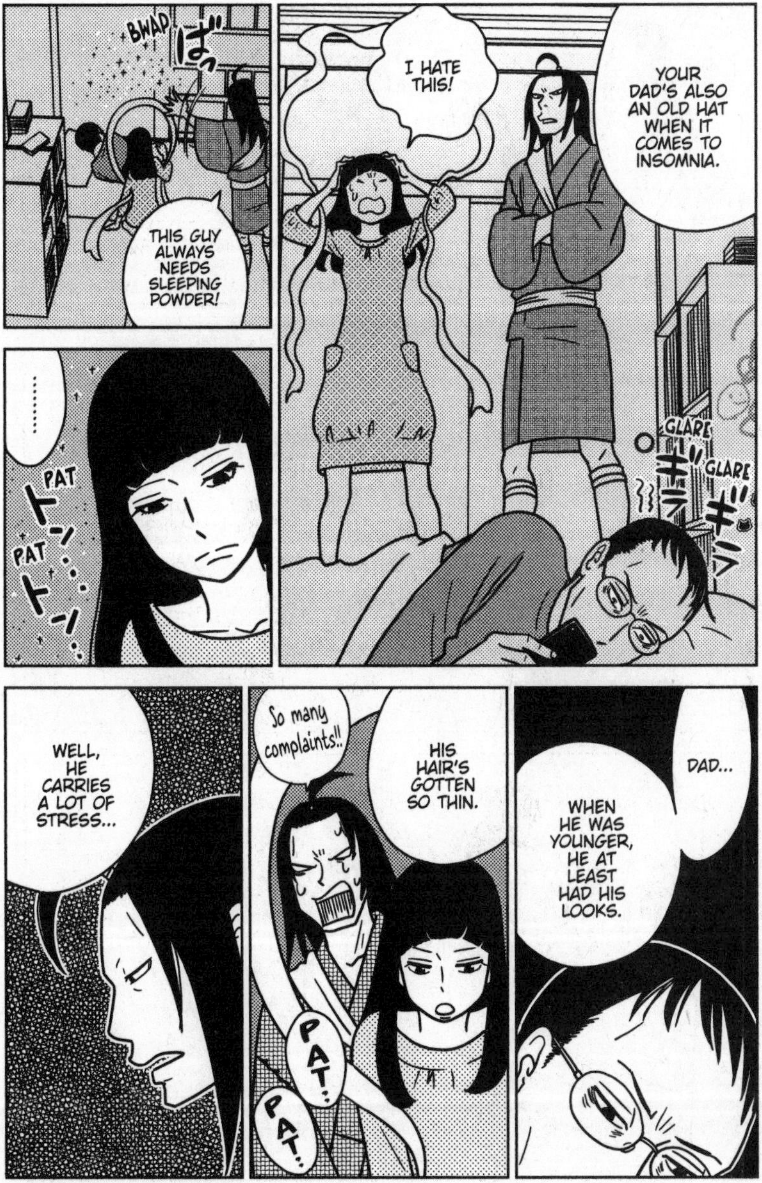
YOUR DAD'S ALSO AN OLD HAT WHEN IT COMES TO INSOMNIA.
I HATE THIS!
GLARE ギラ
GLARE ギラ
BWAP ばっ
THIS GUY ALWAYS NEEDS SLEEPING POWDER!
......
PAT トン
PAT トン
DAD...
WHEN HE WAS YOUNGER, HE AT LEAST HAD HIS LOOKS.
HIS HAIR'S GOTTEN SO THIN.
So many complaints!!
PAT..
PAT..
WELL, HE CARRIES A LOT OF STRESS...

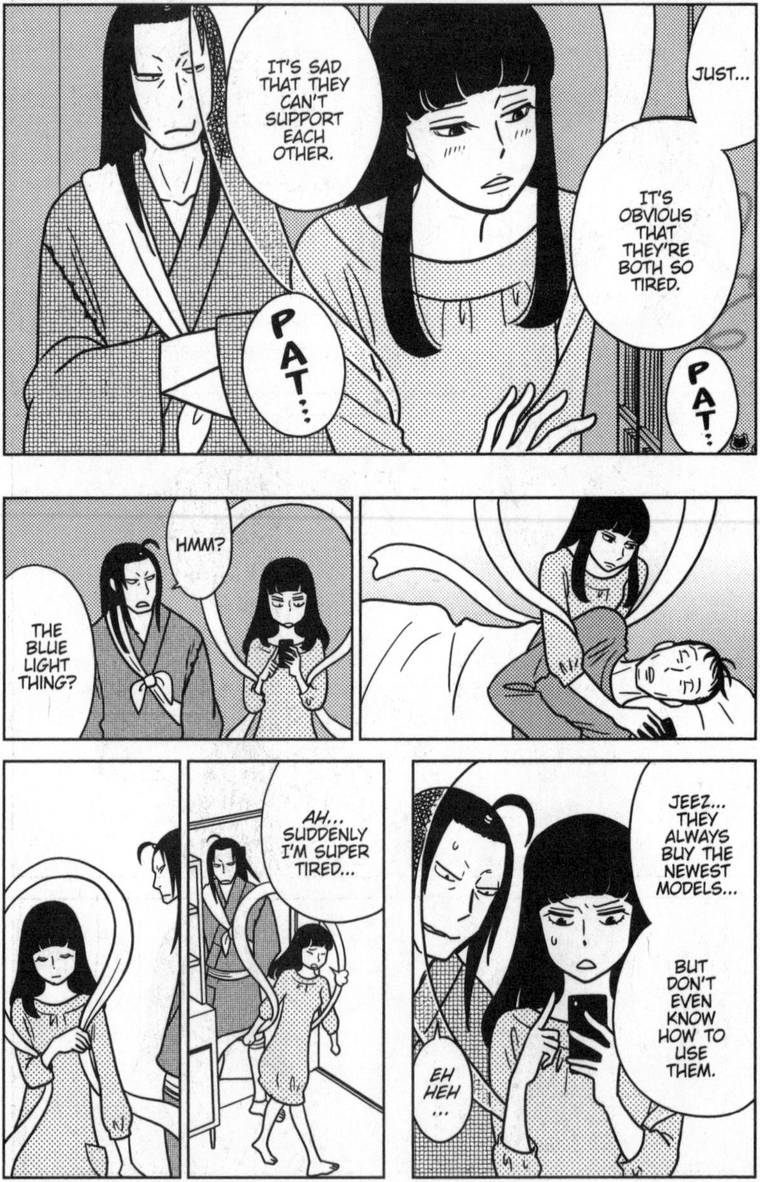
IT'S SAD THAT THEY CAN'T SUPPORT EACH OTHER.
JUST...
IT'S OBVIOUS THAT THEY'RE BOTH SO TIRED.
PAT...
PAT.
HMM?
THE BLUE LIGHT THING?
JEEZ... THEY ALWAYS BUY THE NEWEST MODELS...
BUT DON'T EVEN KNOW HOW TO USE THEM.
EH HEH ...
AH... SUDDENLY I'M SUPER TIRED...

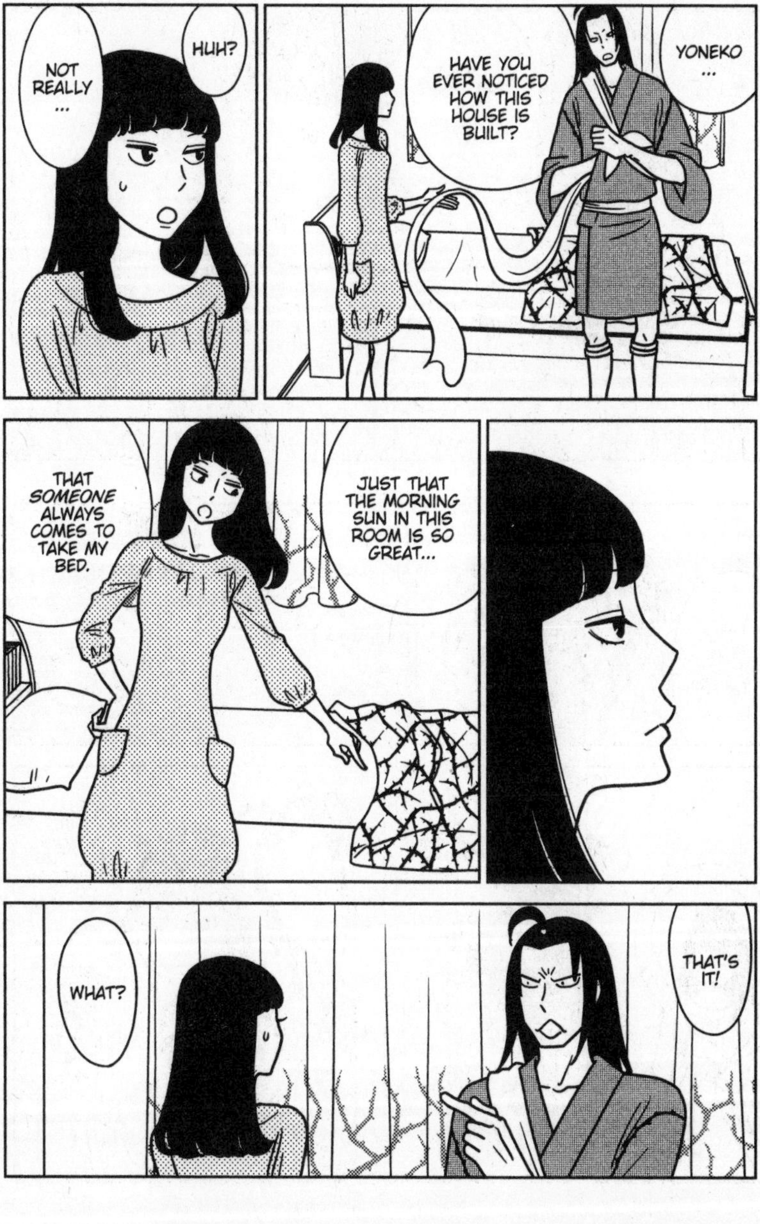
YONEKO ...
HAVE YOU EVER NOTICED HOW THIS HOUSE IS BUILT?
HUH?
NOT REALLY ...
JUST THAT THE MORNING SUN IN THIS ROOM IS SO GREAT...
THAT *SOMEONE* ALWAYS COMES TO TAKE MY BED.
THAT'S IT!
WHAT?

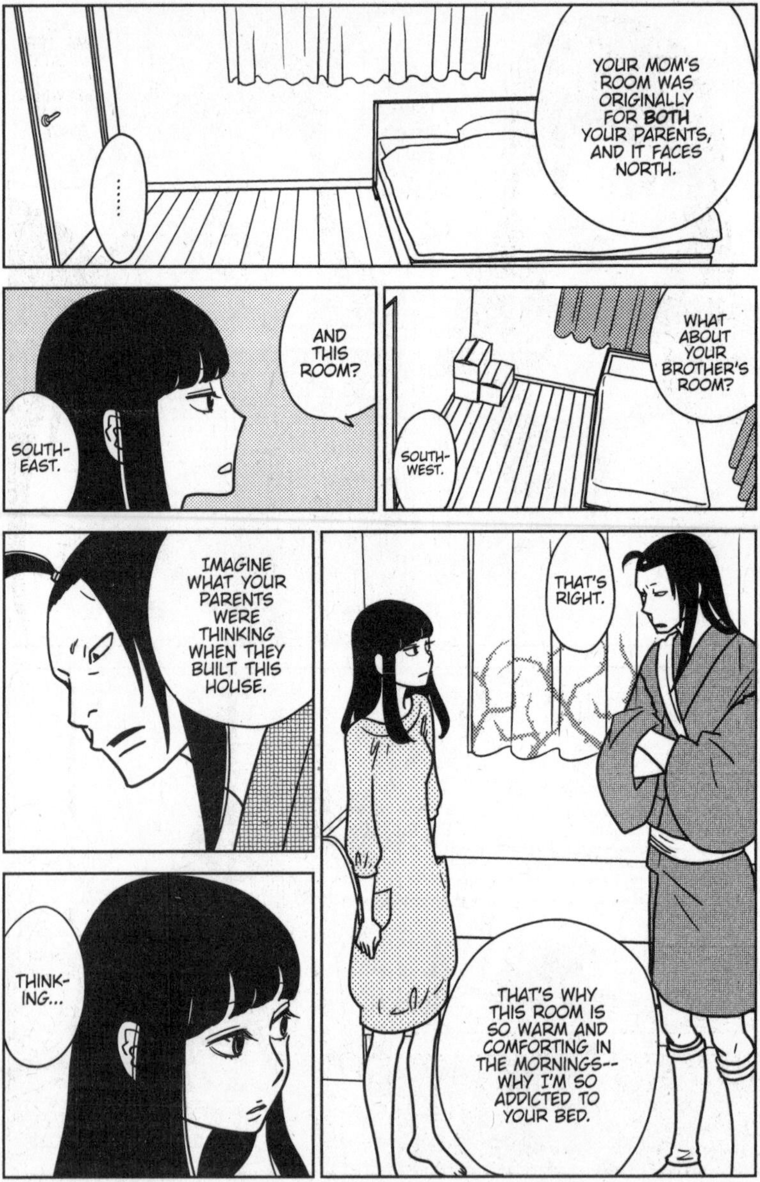
YOUR MOM'S ROOM WAS ORIGINALLY FOR **BOTH** YOUR PARENTS, AND IT FACES NORTH.
......
WHAT ABOUT YOUR BROTHER'S ROOM?
SOUTH-WEST.
AND THIS ROOM?
SOUTH-EAST.
THAT'S RIGHT.
THAT'S WHY THIS ROOM IS SO WARM AND COMFORTING IN THE MORNINGS-- WHY I'M SO ADDICTED TO YOUR BED.
IMAGINE WHAT YOUR PARENTS WERE THINKING WHEN THEY BUILT THIS HOUSE.
THINKING-ING...

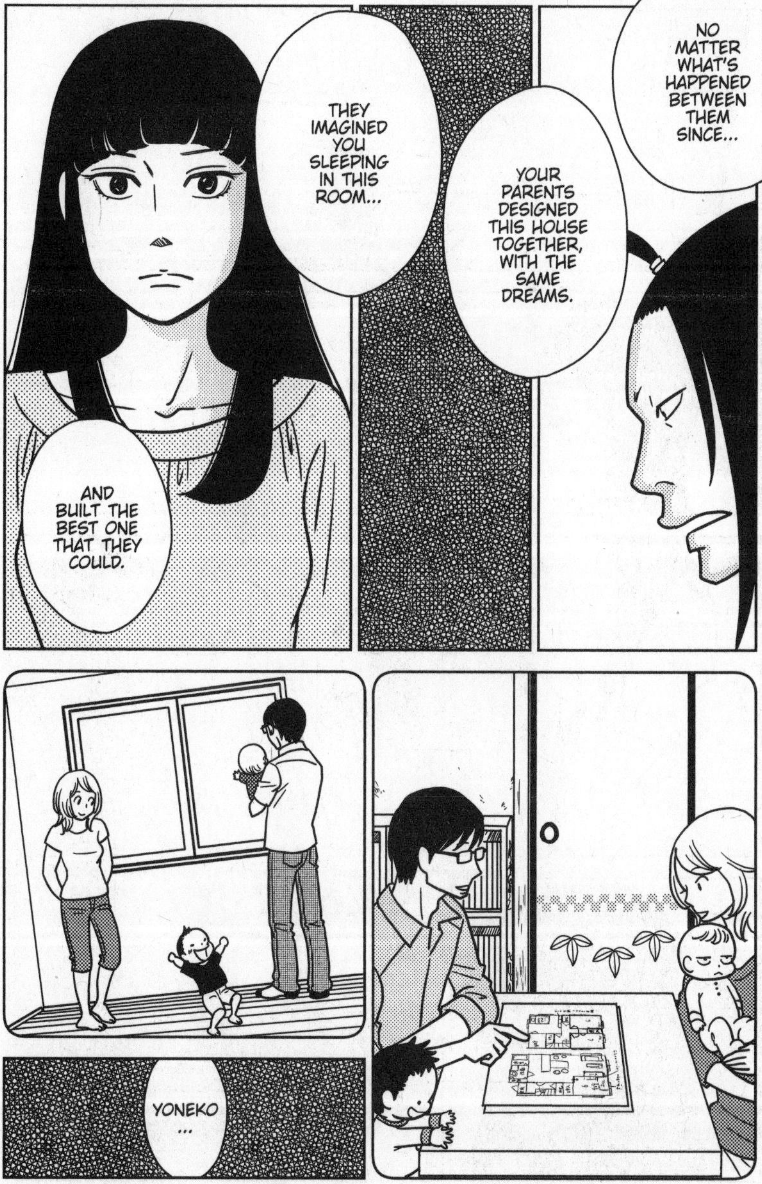
NO MATTER WHAT'S HAPPENED BETWEEN THEM SINCE...
YOUR PARENTS DESIGNED THIS HOUSE TOGETHER, WITH THE SAME DREAMS.
THEY IMAGINED YOU SLEEPING IN THIS ROOM...
AND BUILT THE BEST ONE THAT THEY COULD.
YONEKO ...

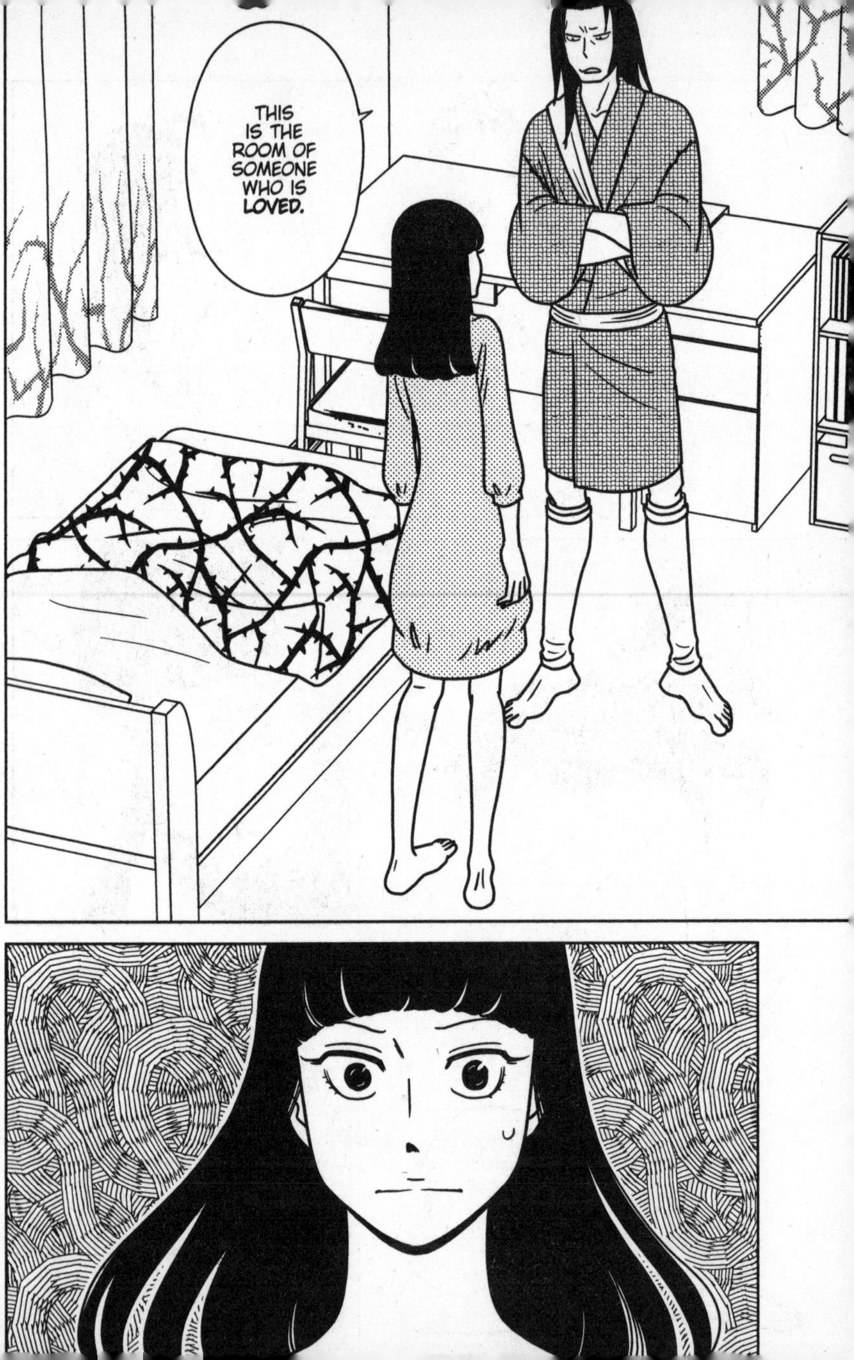
THIS IS THE ROOM OF SOMEONE WHO IS LOVED.

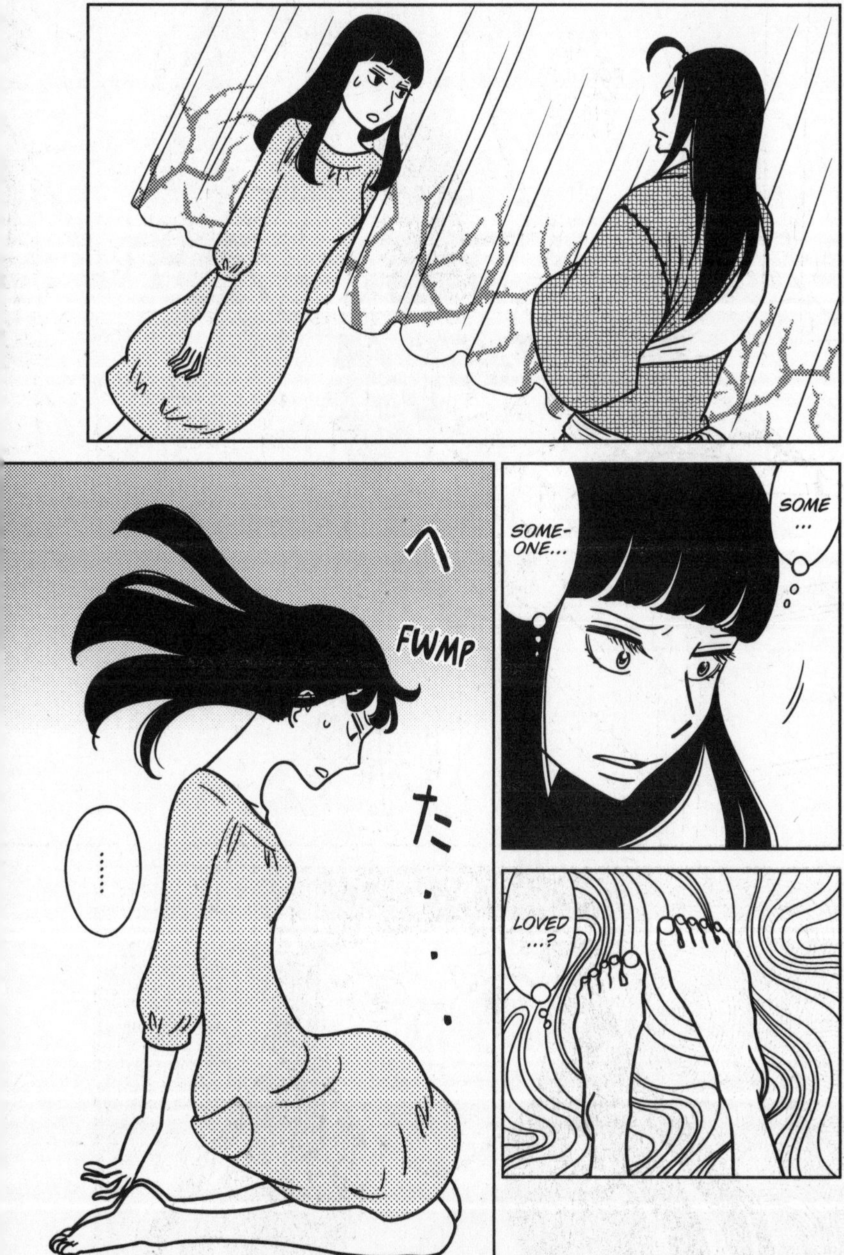
SOME ...
SOME-ONE...
LOVED ...?
へ
FWMP
た...
......

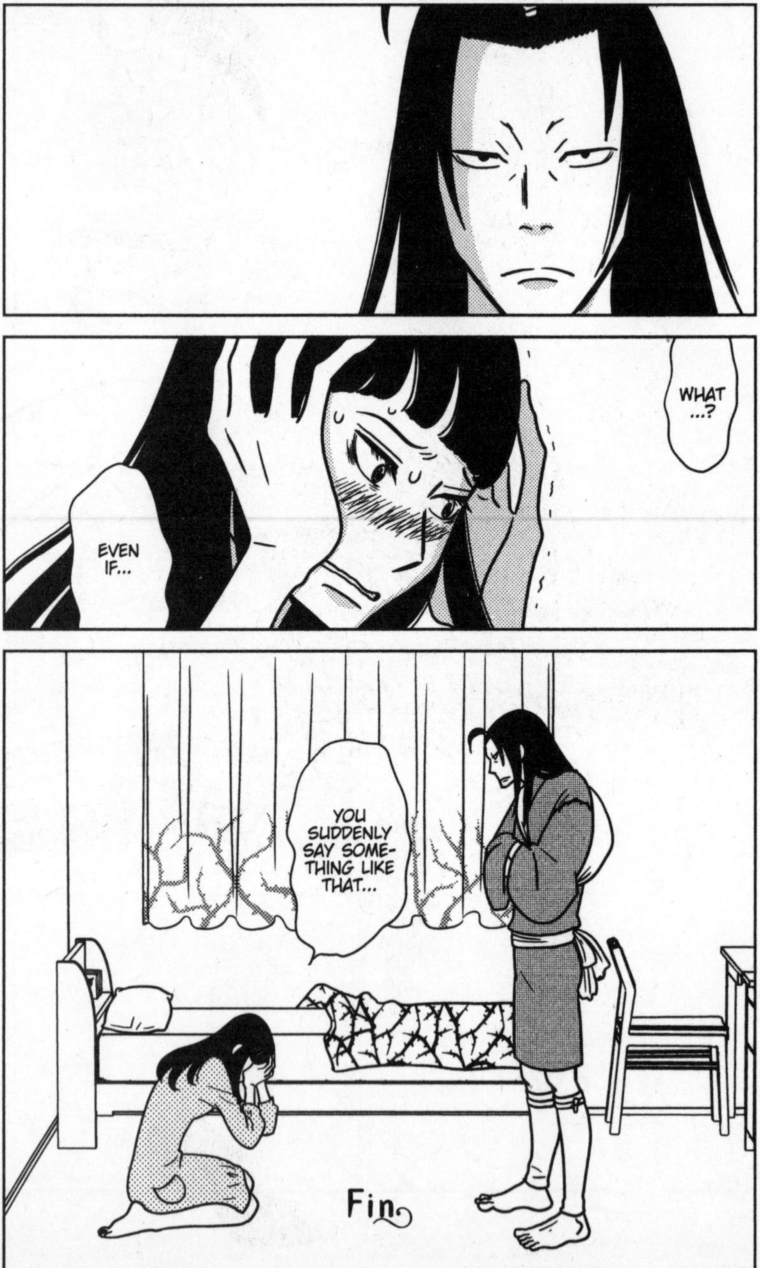
WHAT ...?
EVEN IF...
YOU SUDDENLY SAY SOME-THING LIKE THAT...
Fin

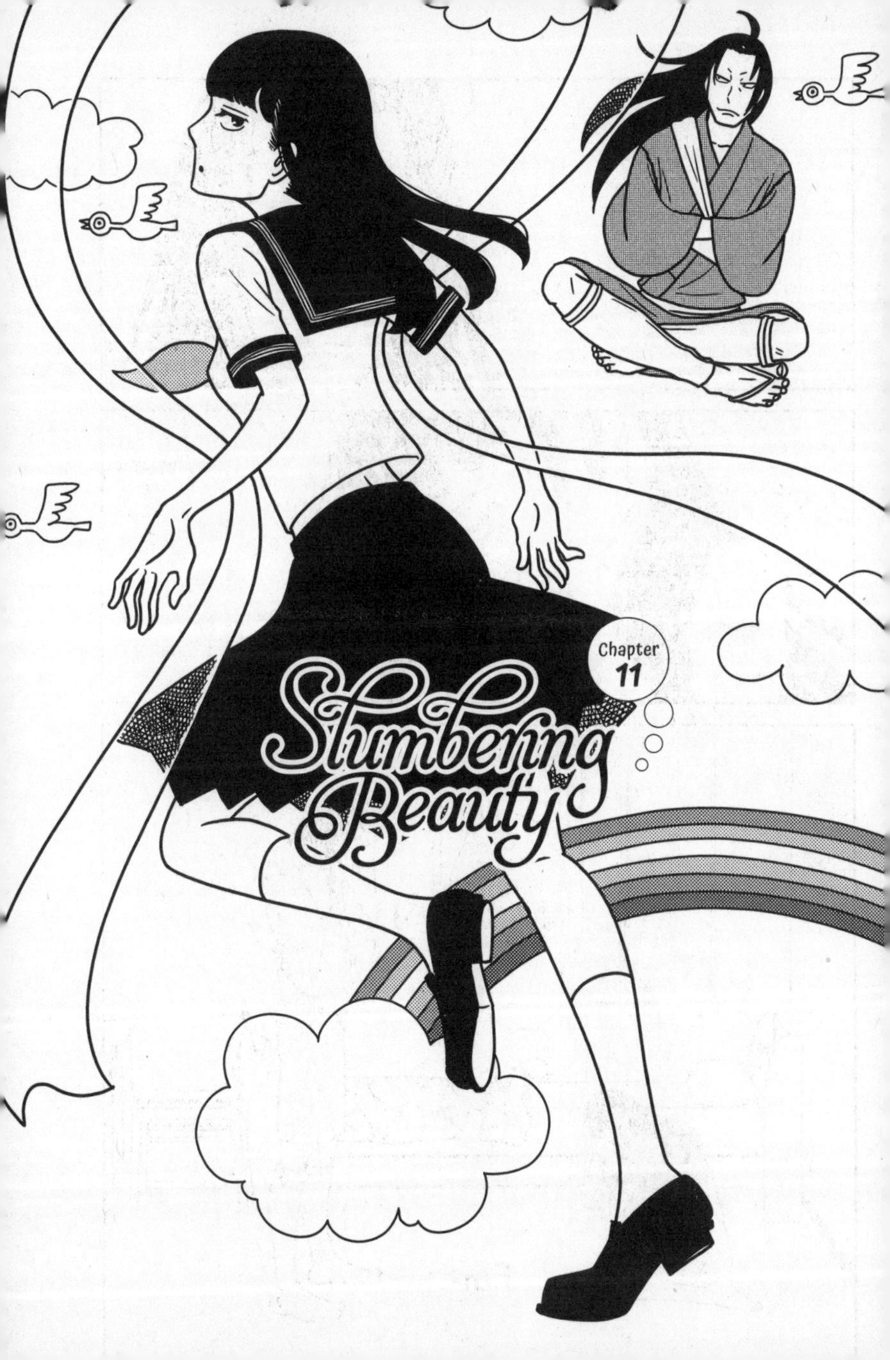
Chapter 11
Slumbering Beauty

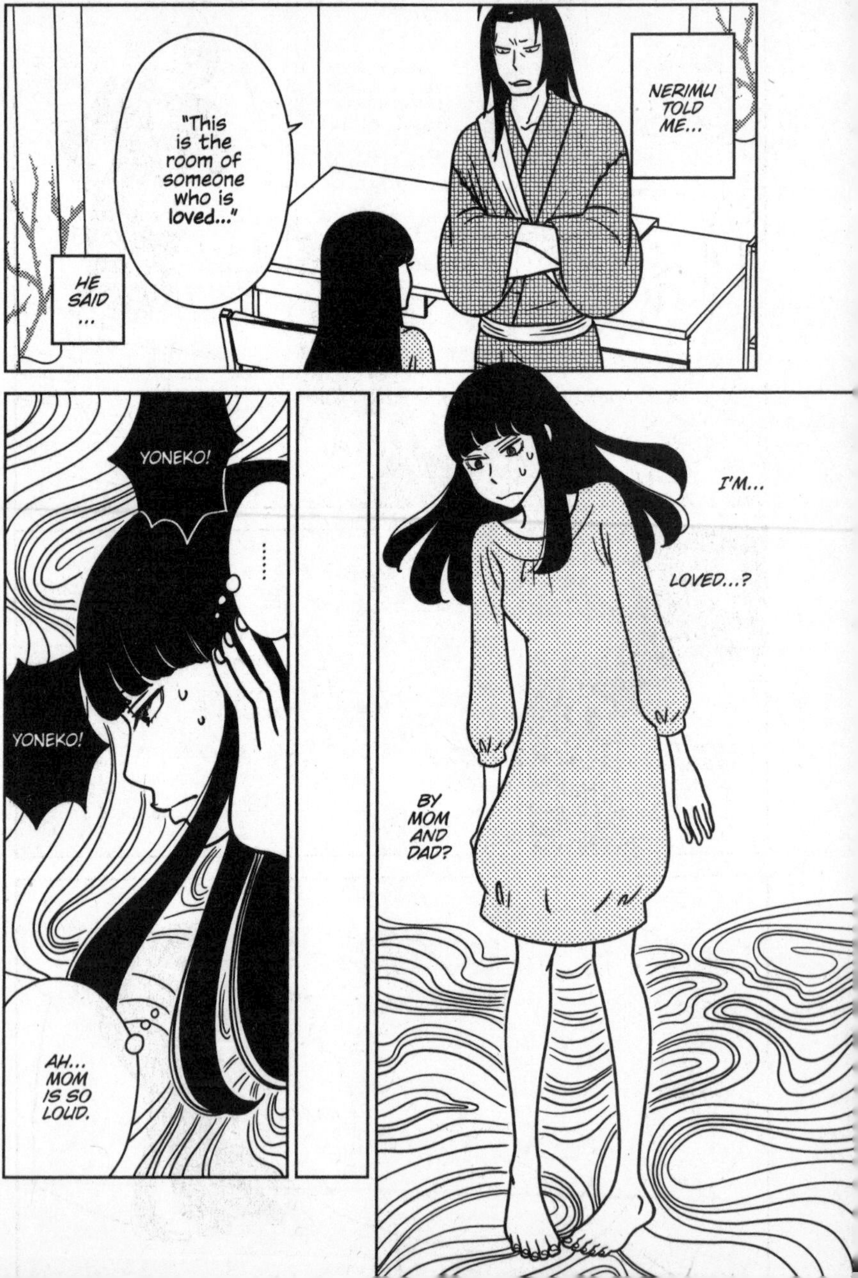

NERIMU TOLD ME...
"This is the room of someone who is loved..."
HE SAID ...
I'M...
LOVED...?
BY MOM AND DAD?
YONEKO!
......
YONEKO!
AH... MOM IS SO LOUD.

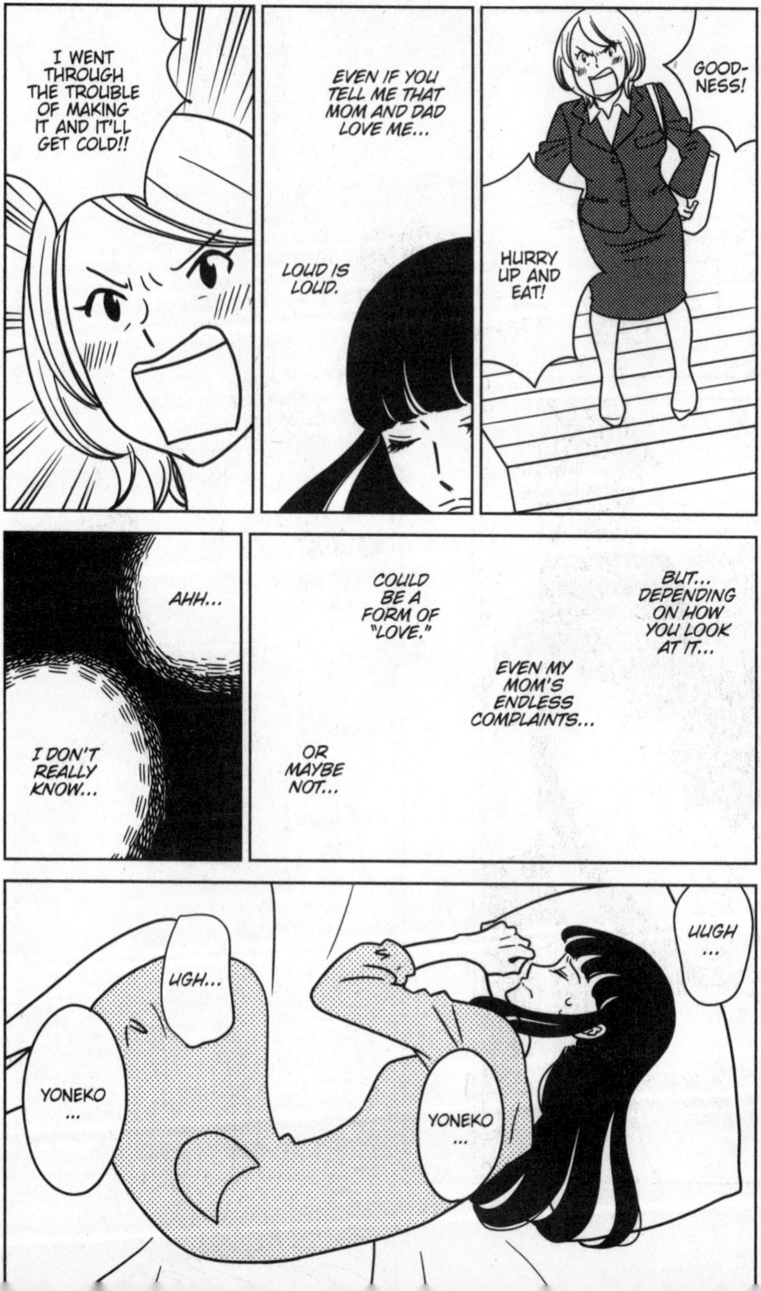
GOOD-NESS!
HURRY UP AND EAT!
EVEN IF YOU TELL ME THAT MOM AND DAD LOVE ME...
LOUD IS LOUD.
I WENT THROUGH THE TROUBLE OF MAKING IT AND IT'LL GET COLD!!
BUT... DEPENDING ON HOW YOU LOOK AT IT...
EVEN MY MOM'S ENDLESS COMPLAINTS...
COULD BE A FORM OF "LOVE."
OR MAYBE NOT...
AHH...
I DON'T REALLY KNOW...
UUGH ...
UGH...
YONEKO ...
YONEKO ...

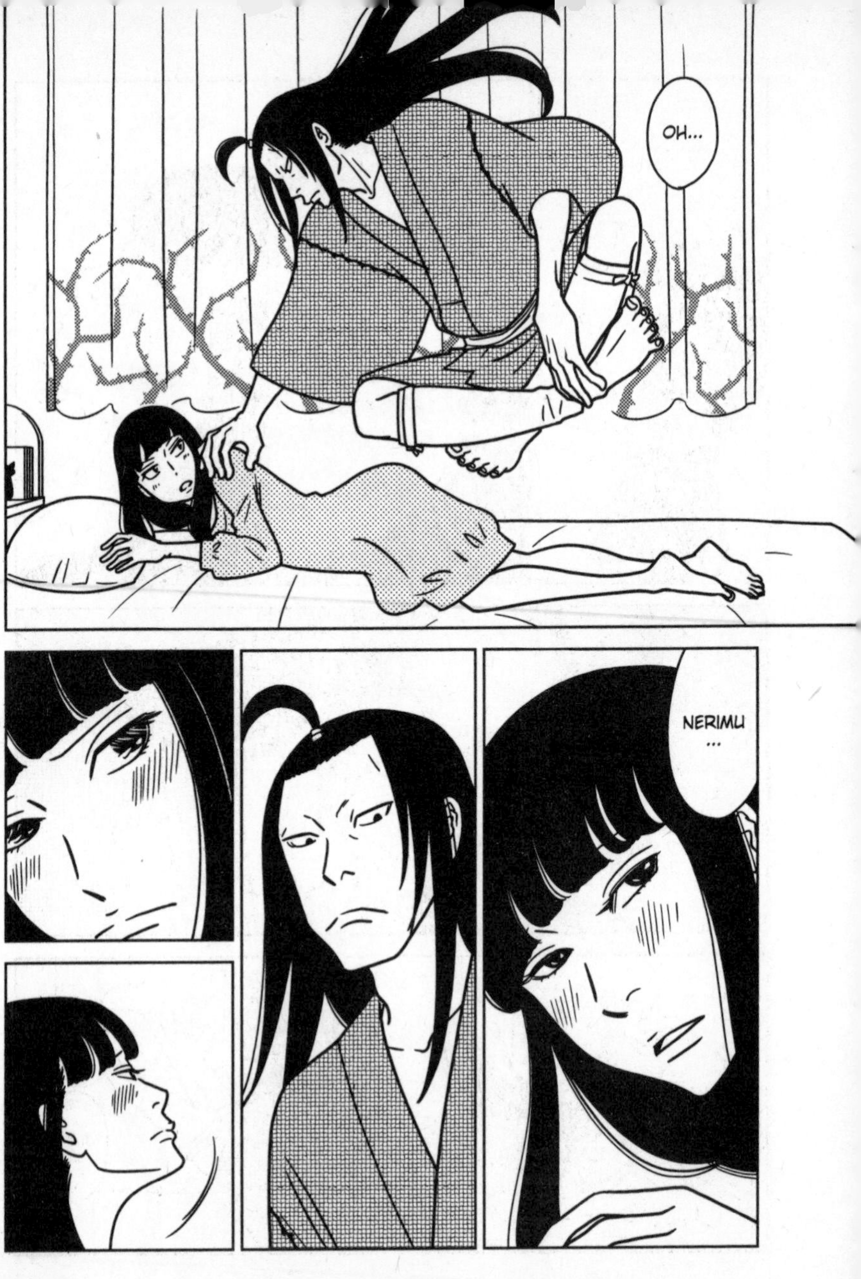
OH...
NERIMU
...

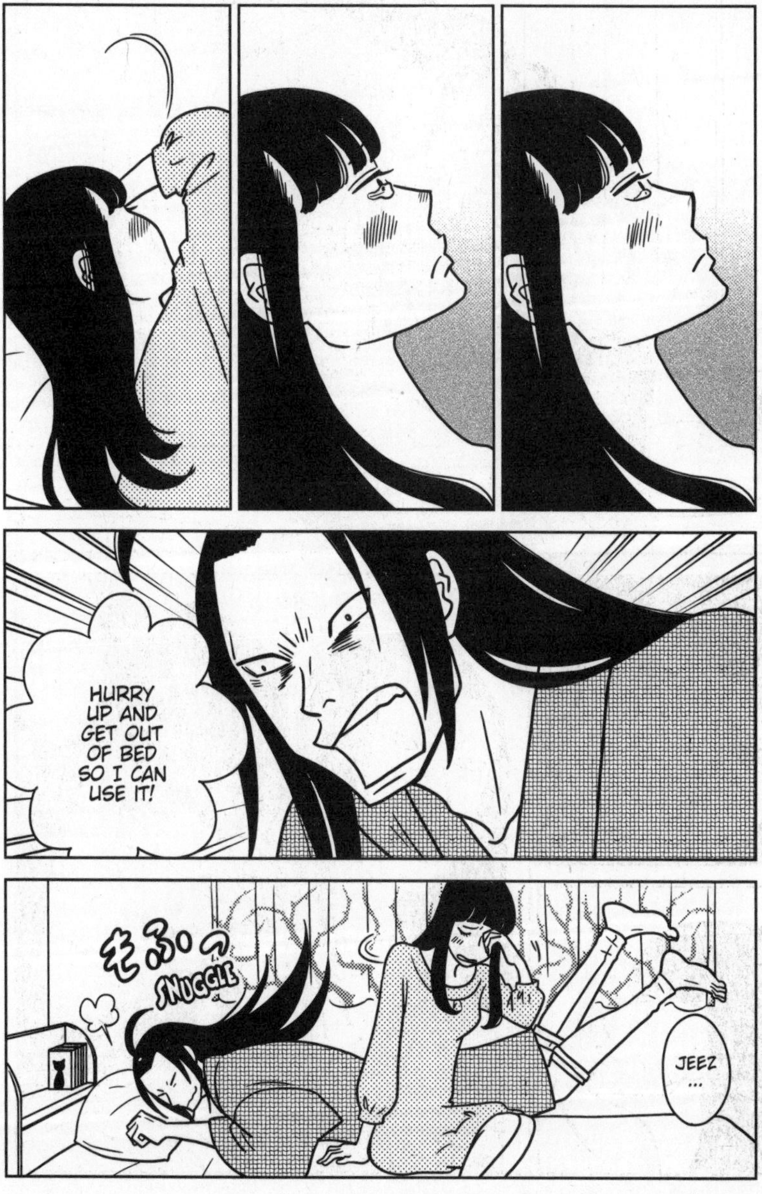
HURRY UP AND GET OUT OF BED SO I CAN USE IT!
JEEZ ...
もふっ
SNUGGLE

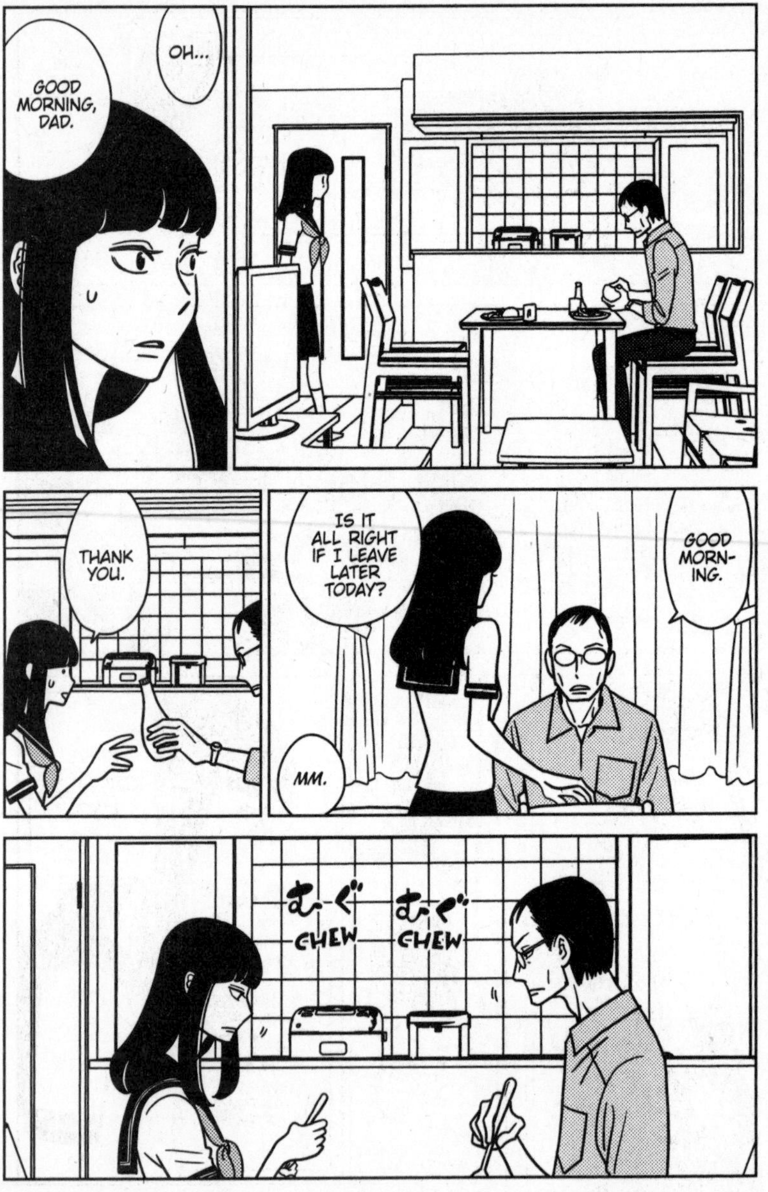
OH...
GOOD MORNING, DAD.
GOOD MORNING.
IS IT ALL RIGHT IF I LEAVE LATER TODAY?
MM.
THANK YOU.
むぐ
CHEW
むぐ
CHEW

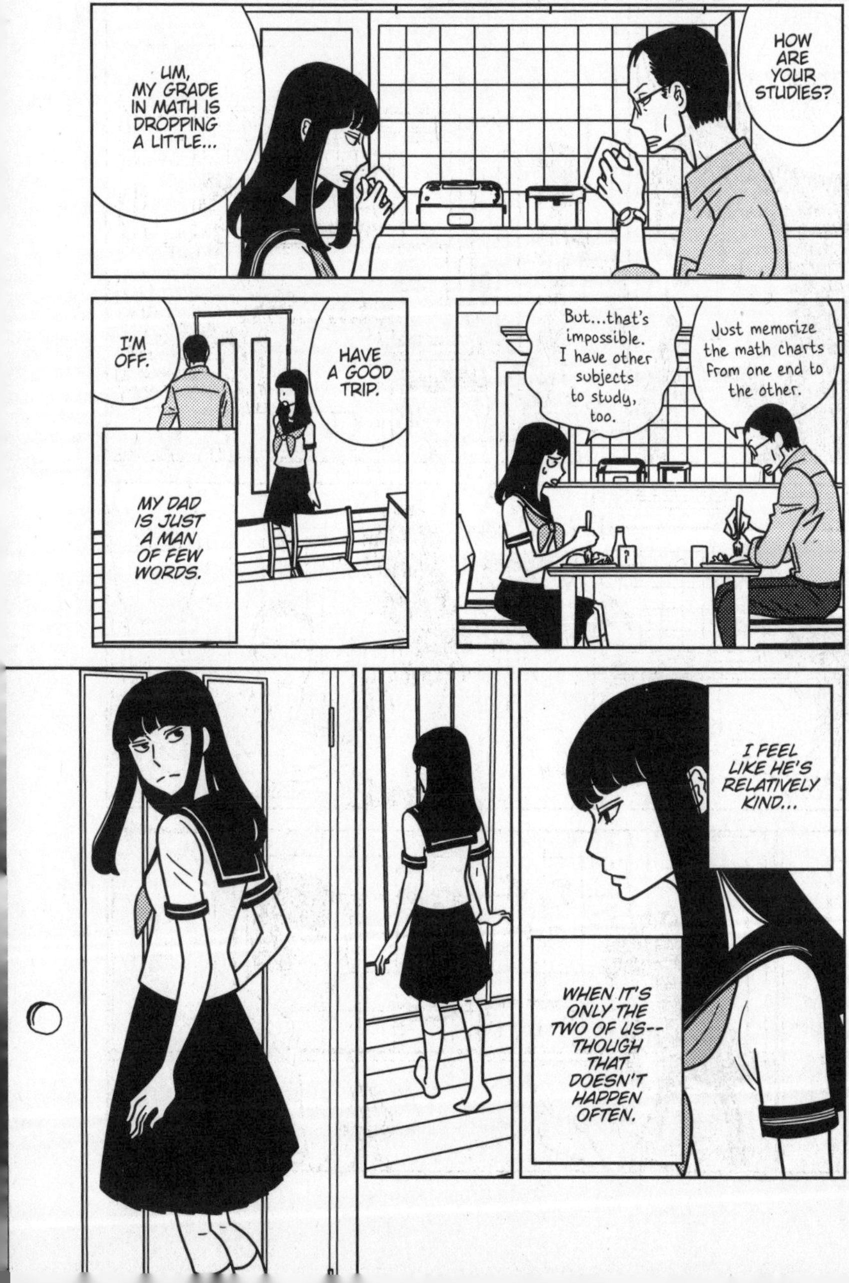
HOW ARE YOUR STUDIES?
UM, MY GRADE IN MATH IS DROPPING A LITTLE...
Just memorize the math charts from one end to the other.
But...that's impossible. I have other subjects to study, too.
HAVE A GOOD TRIP.
I'M OFF.
MY DAD IS JUST A MAN OF FEW WORDS.
I FEEL LIKE HE'S RELATIVELY KIND...
WHEN IT'S ONLY THE TWO OF US-- THOUGH THAT DOESN'T HAPPEN OFTEN.

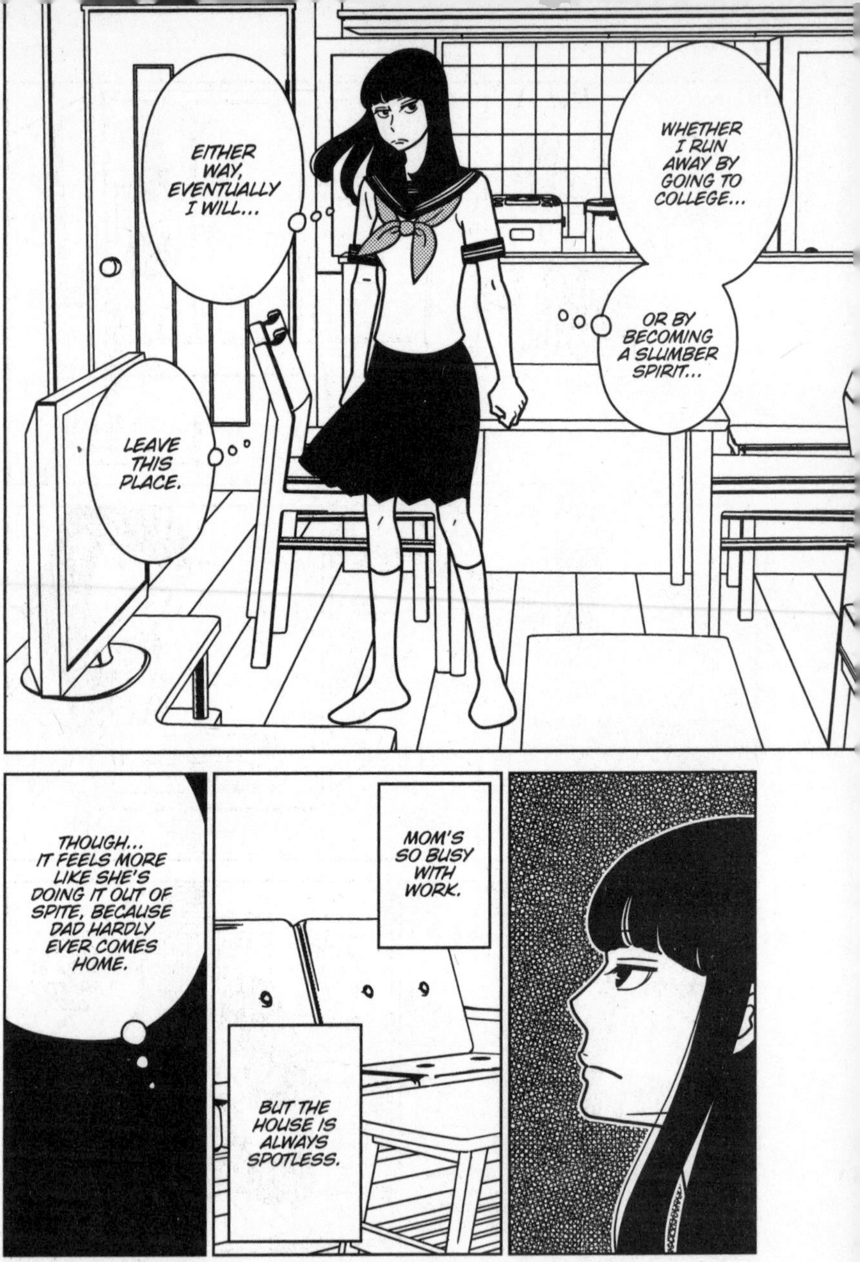
WHETHER I RUN AWAY BY GOING TO COLLEGE...
OR BY BECOMING A SLUMBER SPIRIT...
EITHER WAY, EVENTUALLY I WILL...
LEAVE THIS PLACE.
MOM'S SO BUSY WITH WORK.
BUT THE HOUSE IS ALWAYS SPOTLESS.
THOUGH... IT FEELS MORE LIKE SHE'S DOING IT OUT OF SPITE, BECAUSE DAD HARDLY EVER COMES HOME.

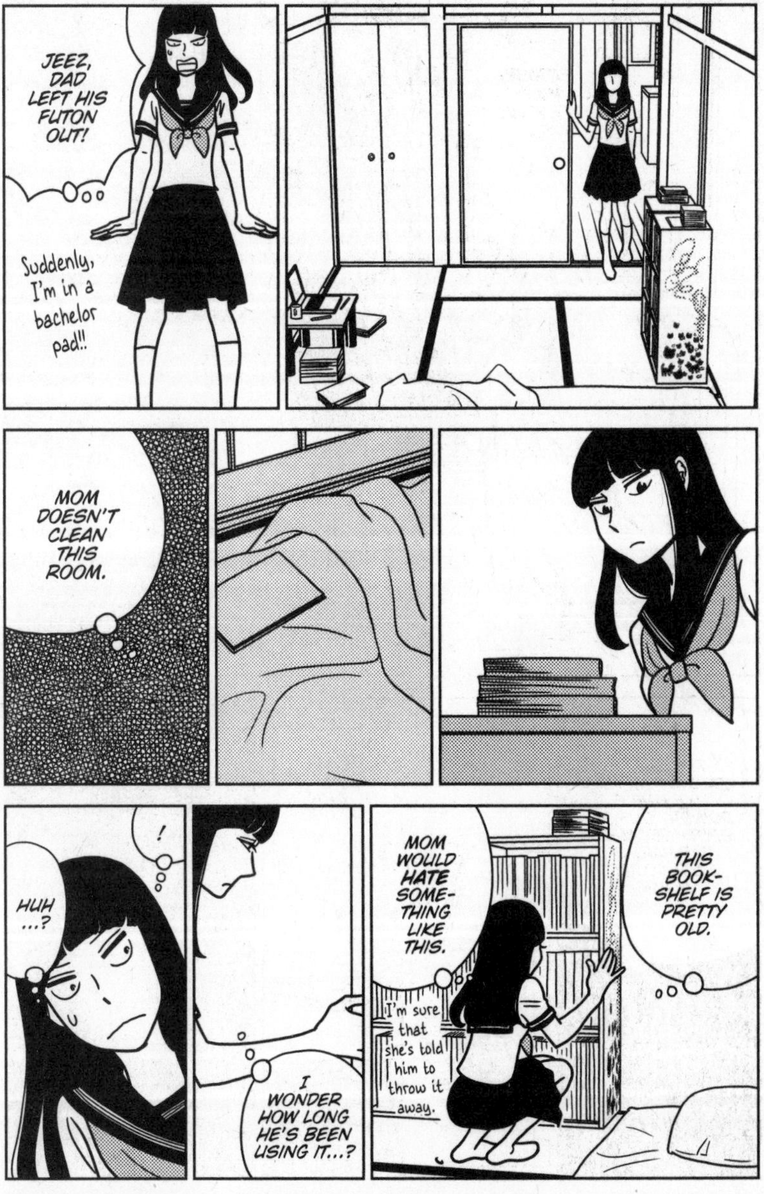
JEEZ, DAD LEFT HIS FUTON OUT!
Suddenly, I'm in a bachelor pad!!
MOM DOESN'T CLEAN THIS ROOM.
THIS BOOK-SHELF IS PRETTY OLD.
MOM WOULD HATE SOME-THING LIKE THIS.
I'm sure that she's told him to throw it away.
I WONDER HOW LONG HE'S BEEN USING IT...?
!
HUH ...?

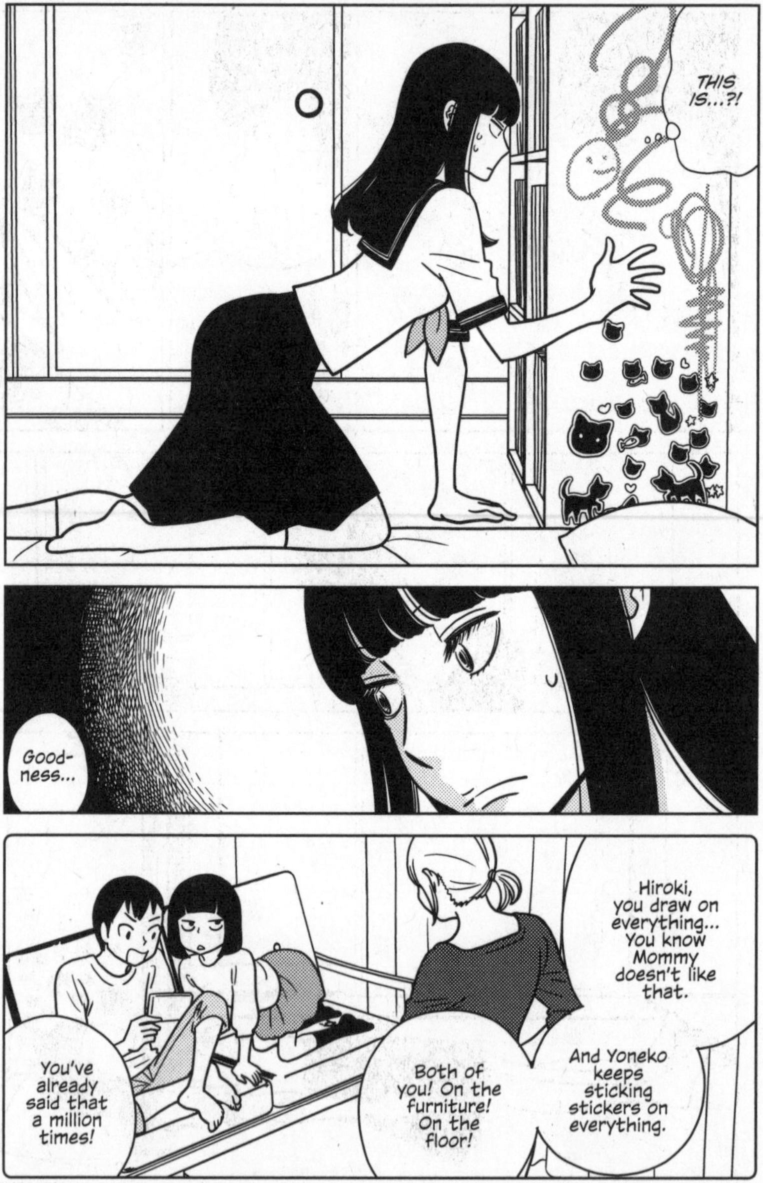
THIS IS...?!
Good-ness...
Hiroki, you draw on everything... You know Mommy doesn't like that.
And Yoneko keeps sticking stickers on everything.
Both of you! On the furniture! On the floor!
You've already said that a million times!

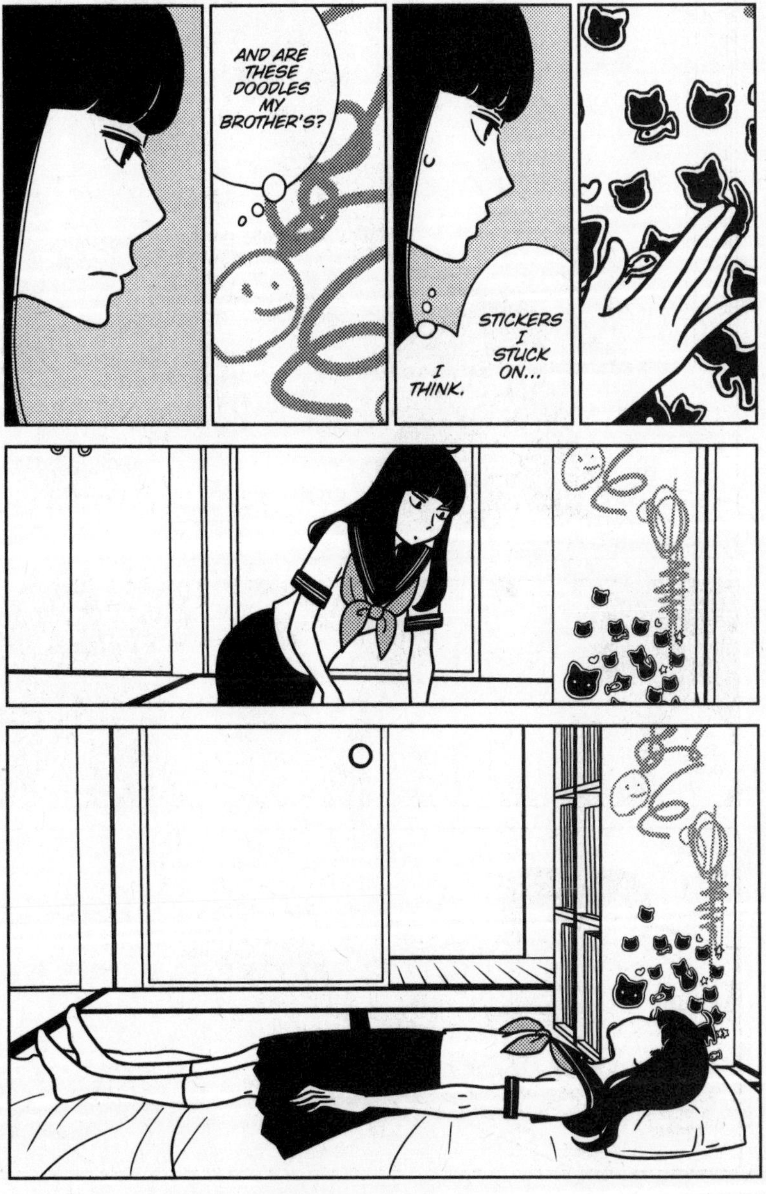
STICKERS I STUCK ON...
I THINK.
AND ARE THESE DOODLES MY BROTHER'S?

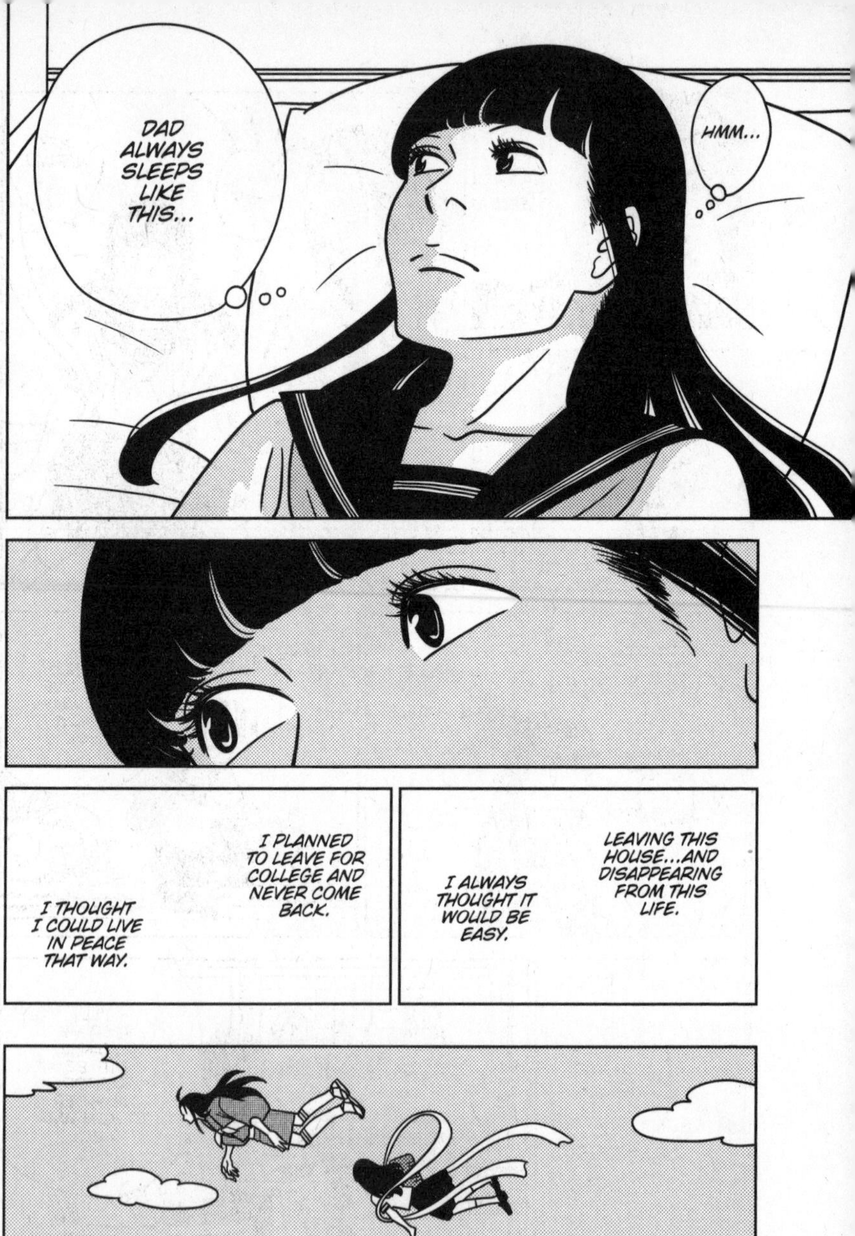
HMM...
DAD ALWAYS SLEEPS LIKE THIS...
LEAVING THIS HOUSE...AND DISAPPEARING FROM THIS LIFE.
I ALWAYS THOUGHT IT WOULD BE EASY.
I PLANNED TO LEAVE FOR COLLEGE AND NEVER COME BACK.
I THOUGHT I COULD LIVE IN PEACE THAT WAY.

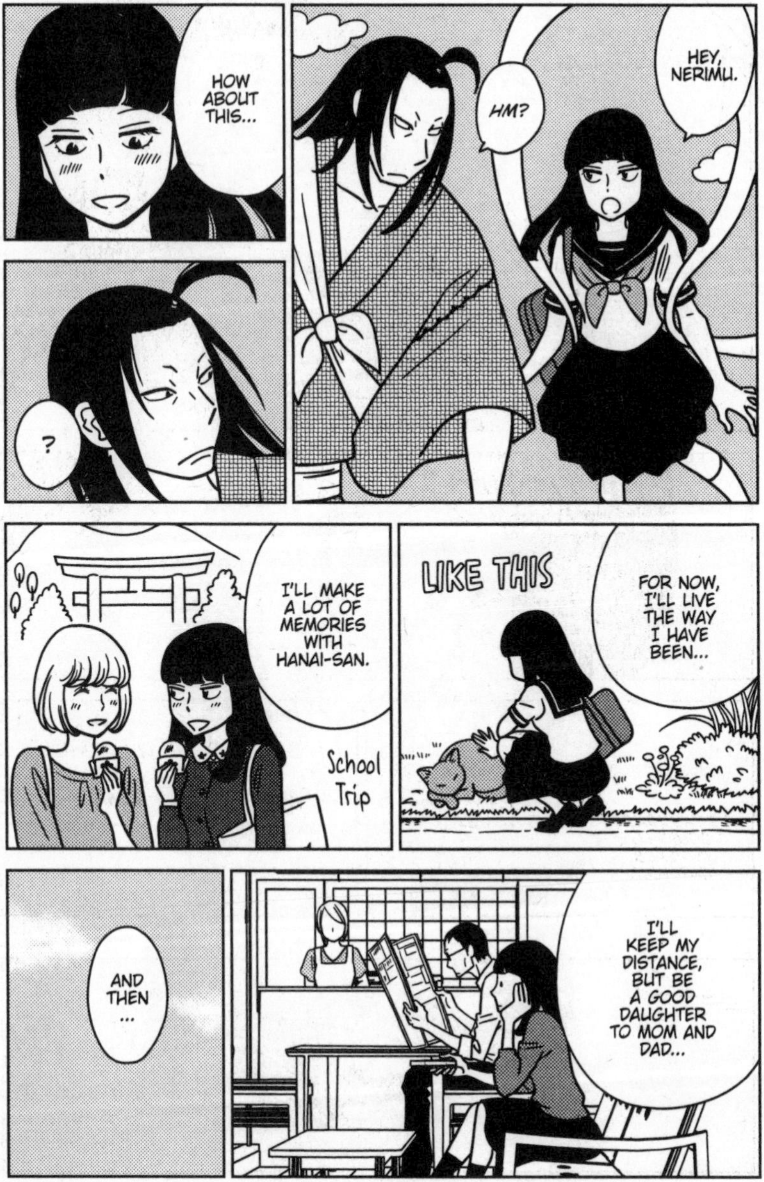
HEY, NERIMU.
HM?
HOW ABOUT THIS...
?
FOR NOW, I'LL LIVE THE WAY I HAVE BEEN...
LIKE THIS
I'LL MAKE A LOT OF MEMORIES WITH HANAI-SAN.
School Trip
I'LL KEEP MY DISTANCE, BUT BE A GOOD DAUGHTER TO MOM AND DAD...
AND THEN ...

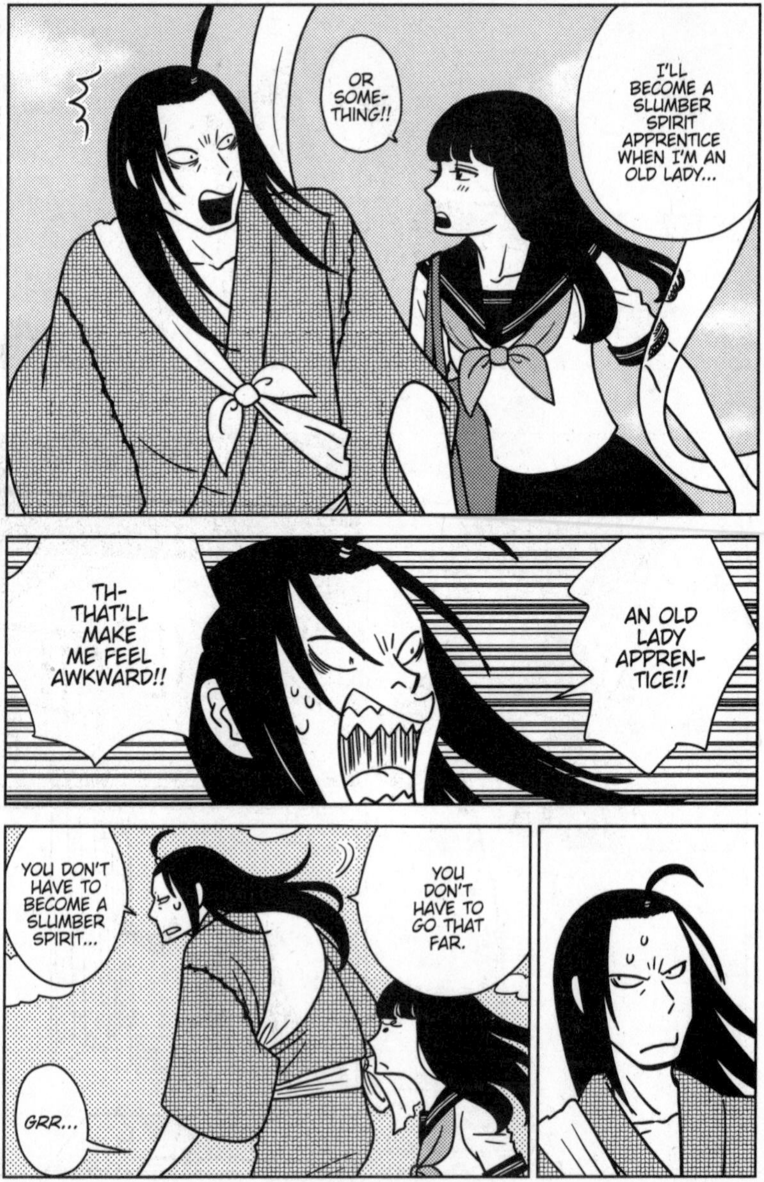
I'LL BECOME A SLUMBER SPIRIT APPRENTICE WHEN I'M AN OLD LADY...
OR SOME-THING!!
AN OLD LADY APPREN-TICE!!
TH-THAT'LL MAKE ME FEEL AWKWARD!!
YOU DON'T HAVE TO GO THAT FAR.
YOU DON'T HAVE TO BECOME A SLUMBER SPIRIT...
GRR...

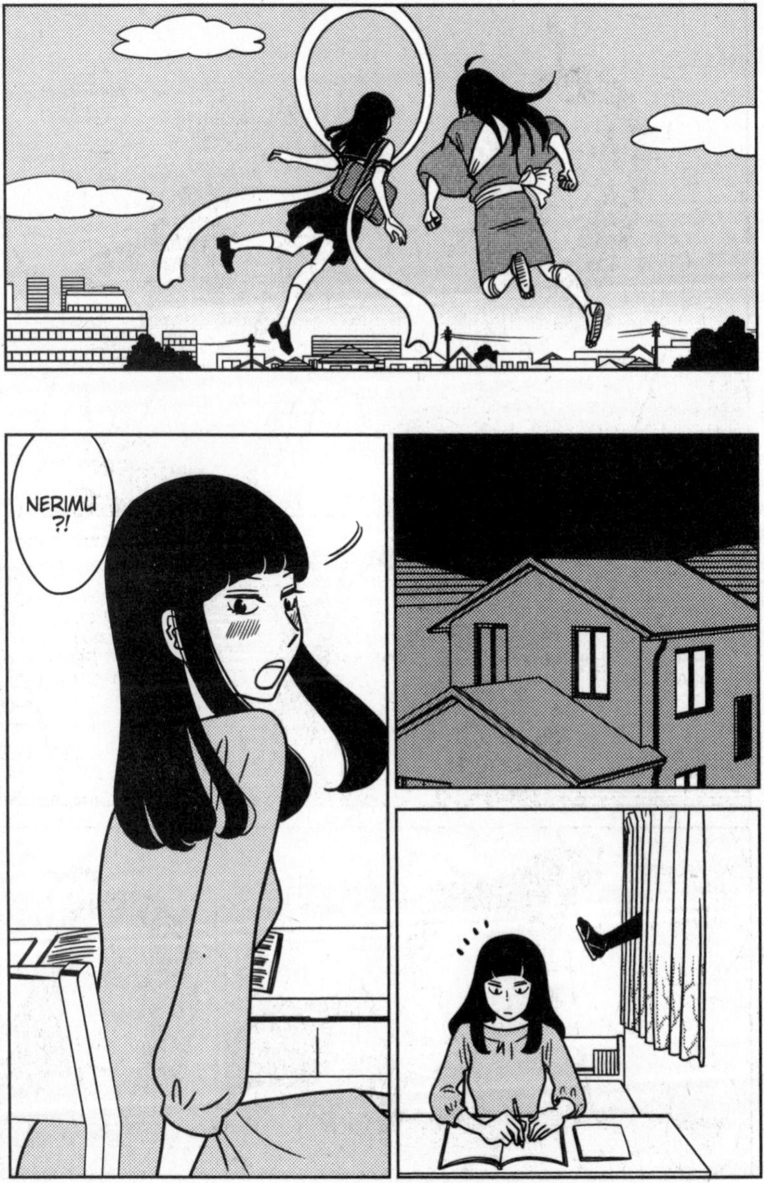
NERIMU ?!

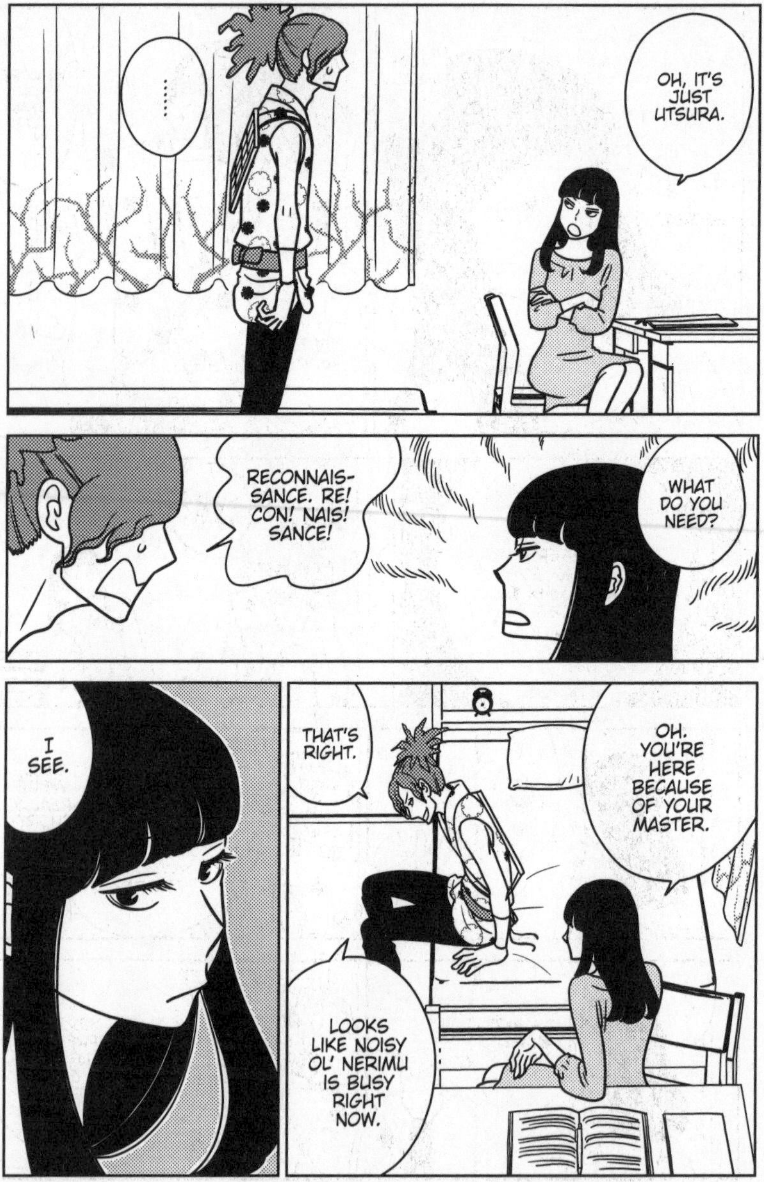
OH, IT'S JUST UTSURA.
......
WHAT DO YOU NEED?
RECONNAISSANCE. RE! CON! NAIS! SANCE!
OH. YOU'RE HERE BECAUSE OF YOUR MASTER.
THAT'S RIGHT.
LOOKS LIKE NOISY OL' NERIMU IS BUSY RIGHT NOW.
I SEE.

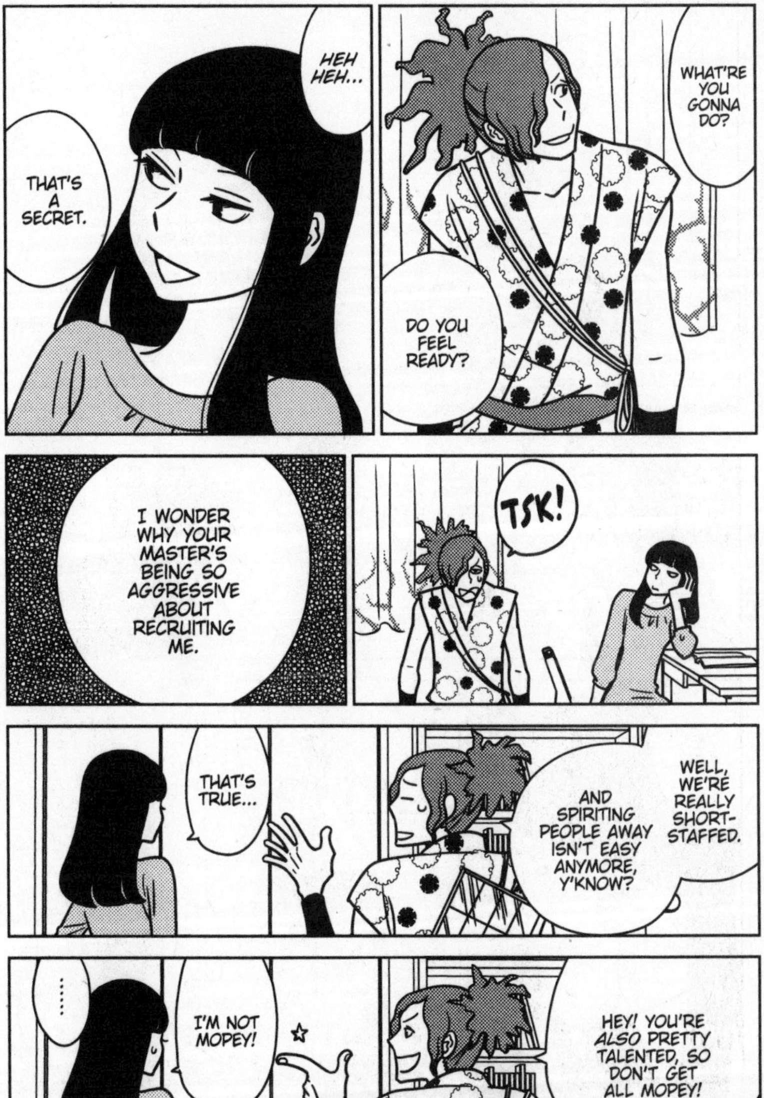

WHAT'RE YOU GONNA DO?
DO YOU FEEL READY?
HEH HEH...
THAT'S A SECRET.
TSK!
I WONDER WHY YOUR MASTER'S BEING SO AGGRESSIVE ABOUT RECRUITING ME.
WELL, WE'RE REALLY SHORT-STAFFED.
AND SPIRITING PEOPLE AWAY ISN'T EASY ANYMORE, Y'KNOW?
THAT'S TRUE...
HEY! YOU'RE *ALSO* PRETTY TALENTED, SO DON'T GET ALL MOPEY!
I'M NOT MOPEY!
......

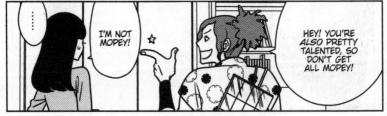

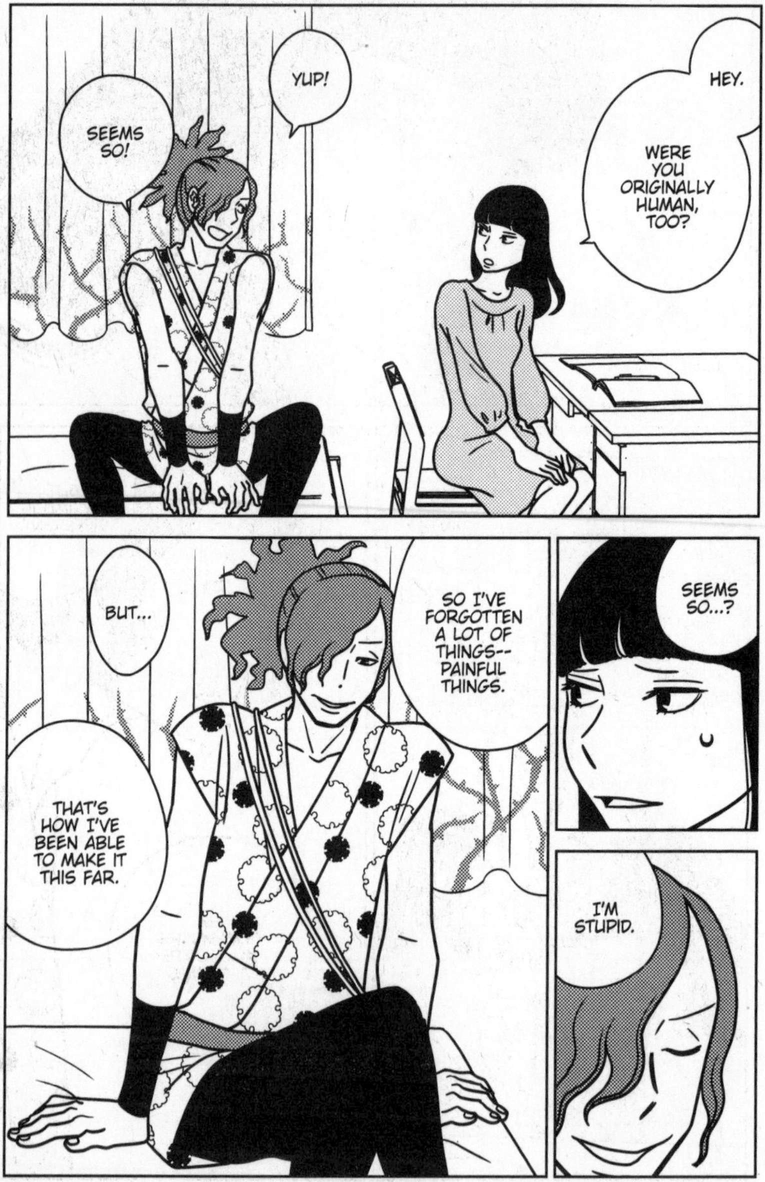
HEY.
WERE YOU ORIGINALLY HUMAN, TOO?
YUP!
SEEMS SO!
SEEMS SO...?
I'M STUPID.
SO I'VE FORGOTTEN A LOT OF THINGS--PAINFUL THINGS.
BUT...
THAT'S HOW I'VE BEEN ABLE TO MAKE IT THIS FAR.

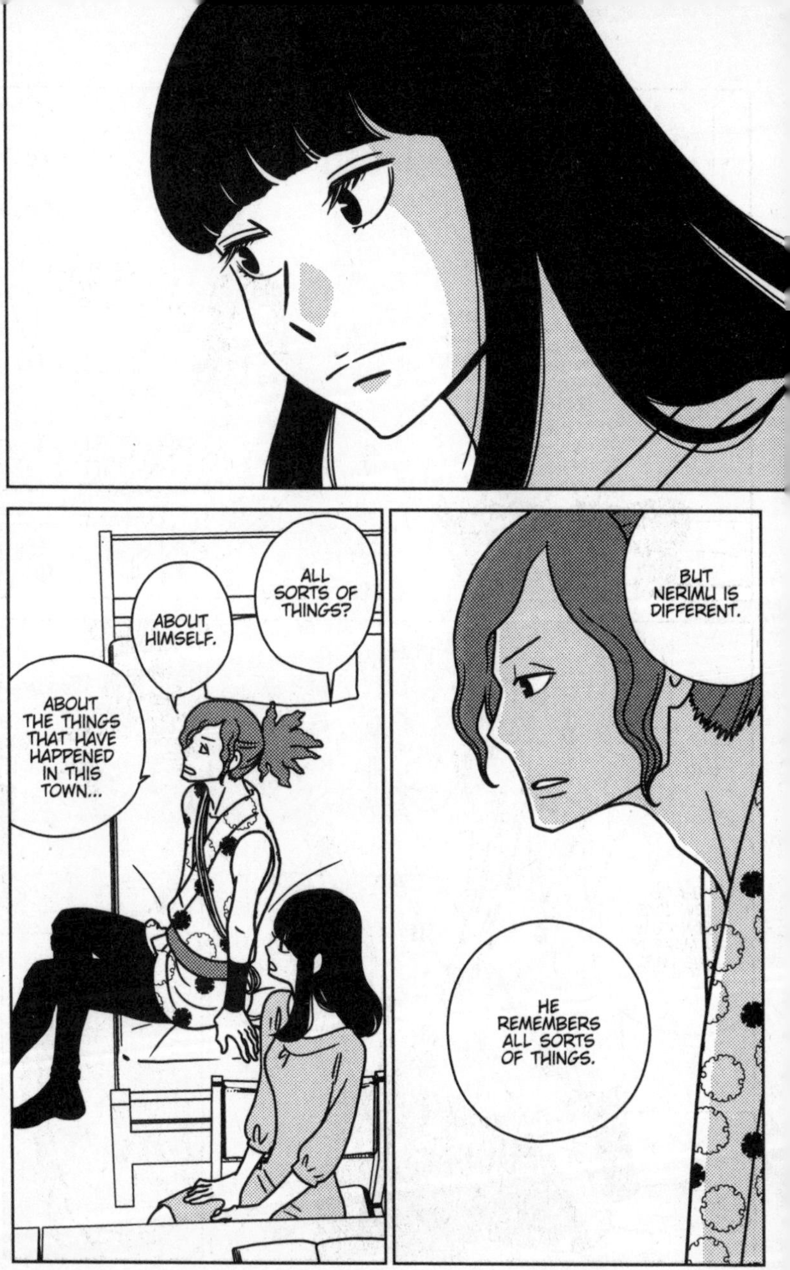
BUT NERIMU IS DIFFERENT.
HE REMEMBERS ALL SORTS OF THINGS.
ALL SORTS OF THINGS?
ABOUT HIMSELF.
ABOUT THE THINGS THAT HAVE HAPPENED IN THIS TOWN...

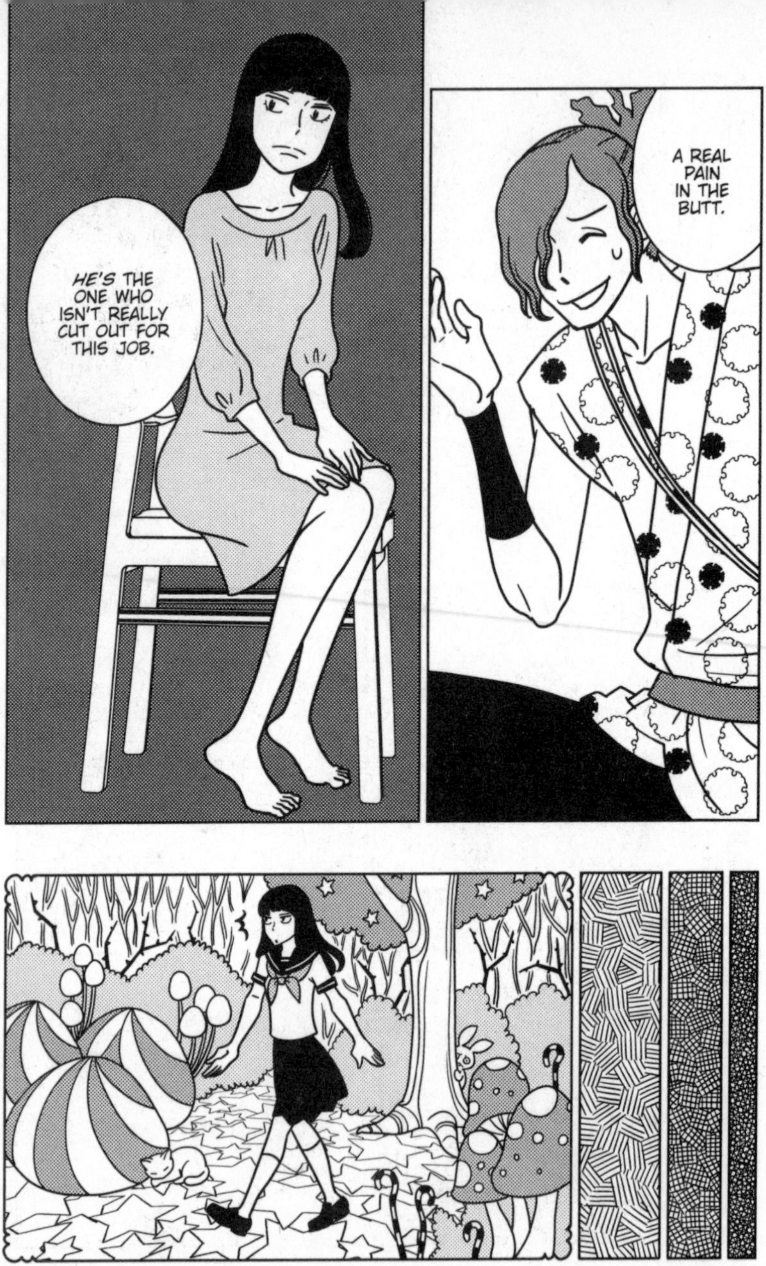
A REAL PAIN IN THE BUTT.
HE'S THE ONE WHO ISN'T REALLY CUT OUT FOR THIS JOB.

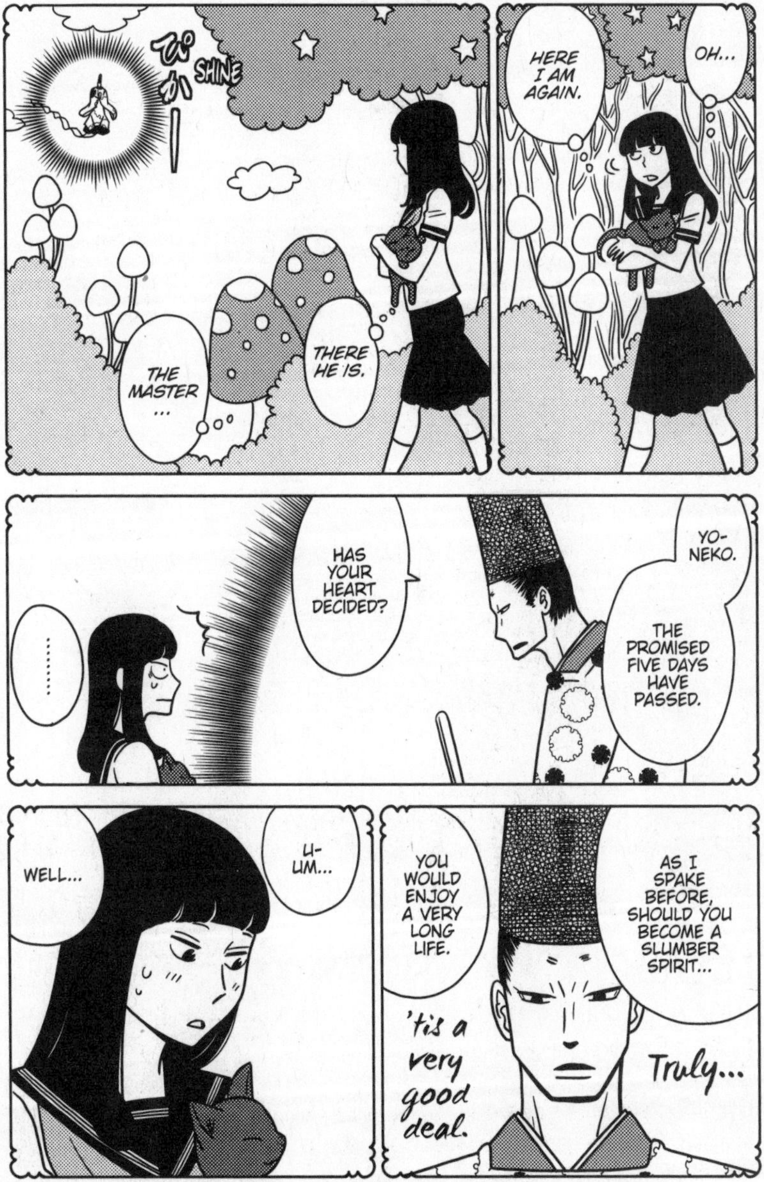
OH...
HERE I AM AGAIN.
ぴかー
SHINE
THERE HE IS.
THE MASTER ...
YO-NEKO.
THE PROMISED FIVE DAYS HAVE PASSED.
HAS YOUR HEART DECIDED?
......
AS I SPAKE BEFORE, SHOULD YOU BECOME A SLUMBER SPIRIT...
YOU WOULD ENJOY A VERY LONG LIFE.
Truly...
'tis a very good deal.
U-UM...
WELL...

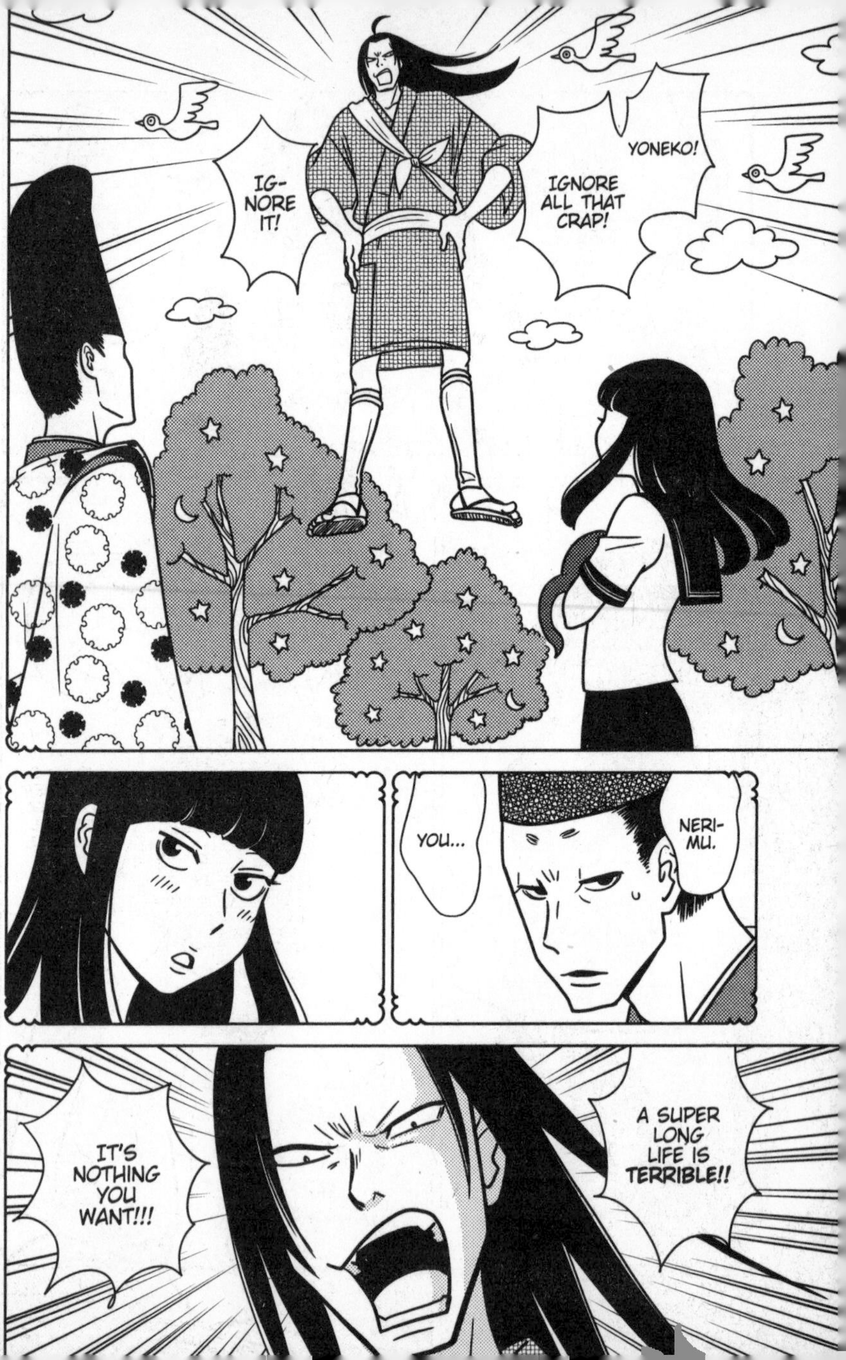
YONEKO!
IGNORE ALL THAT CRAP!
IG-NORE IT!
NERI-MU.
YOU...
A SUPER LONG LIFE IS TERRIBLE!!
IT'S NOTHING YOU WANT!!!

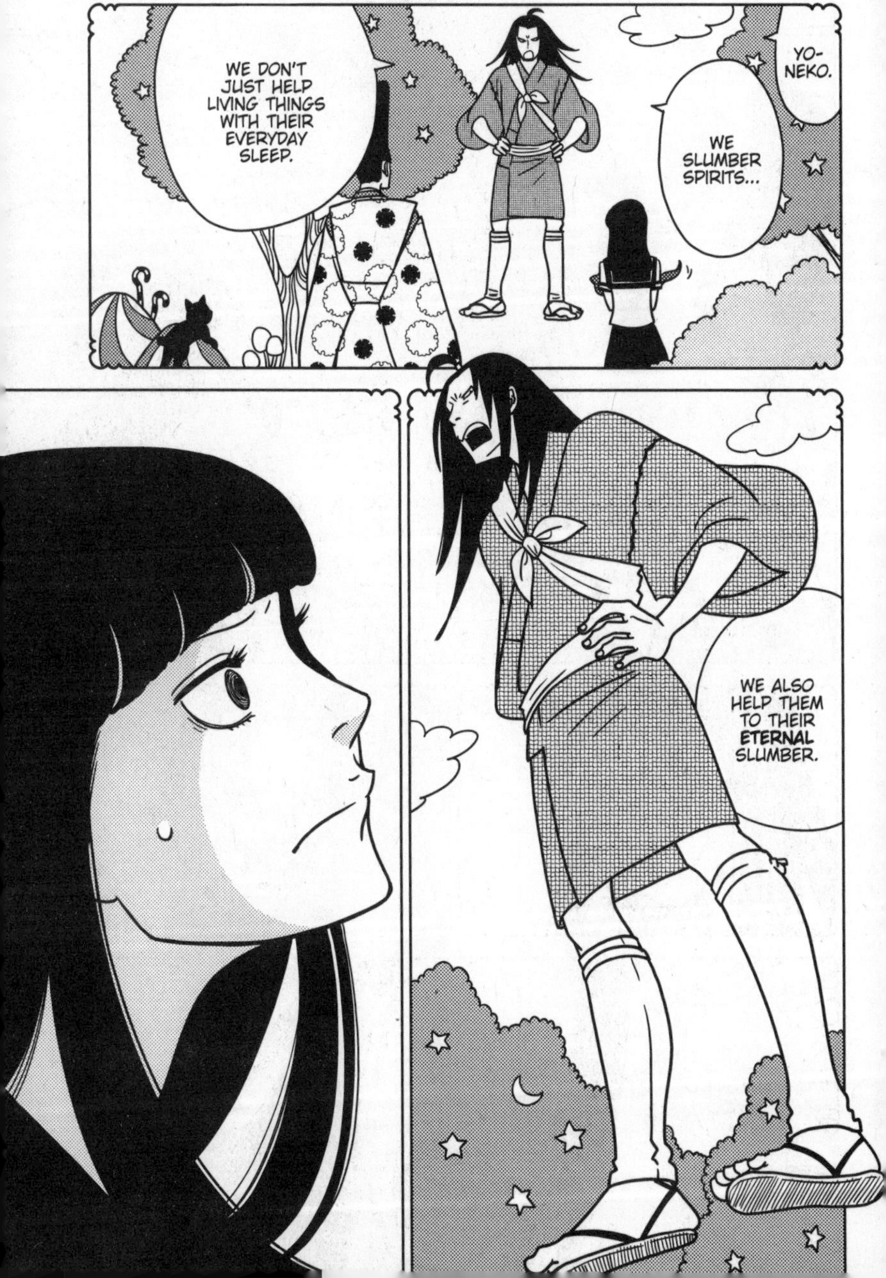
YO-NEKO.
WE SLUMBER SPIRITS...
WE DON'T JUST HELP LIVING THINGS WITH THEIR EVERYDAY SLEEP.
WE ALSO HELP THEM TO THEIR **ETERNAL** SLUMBER.

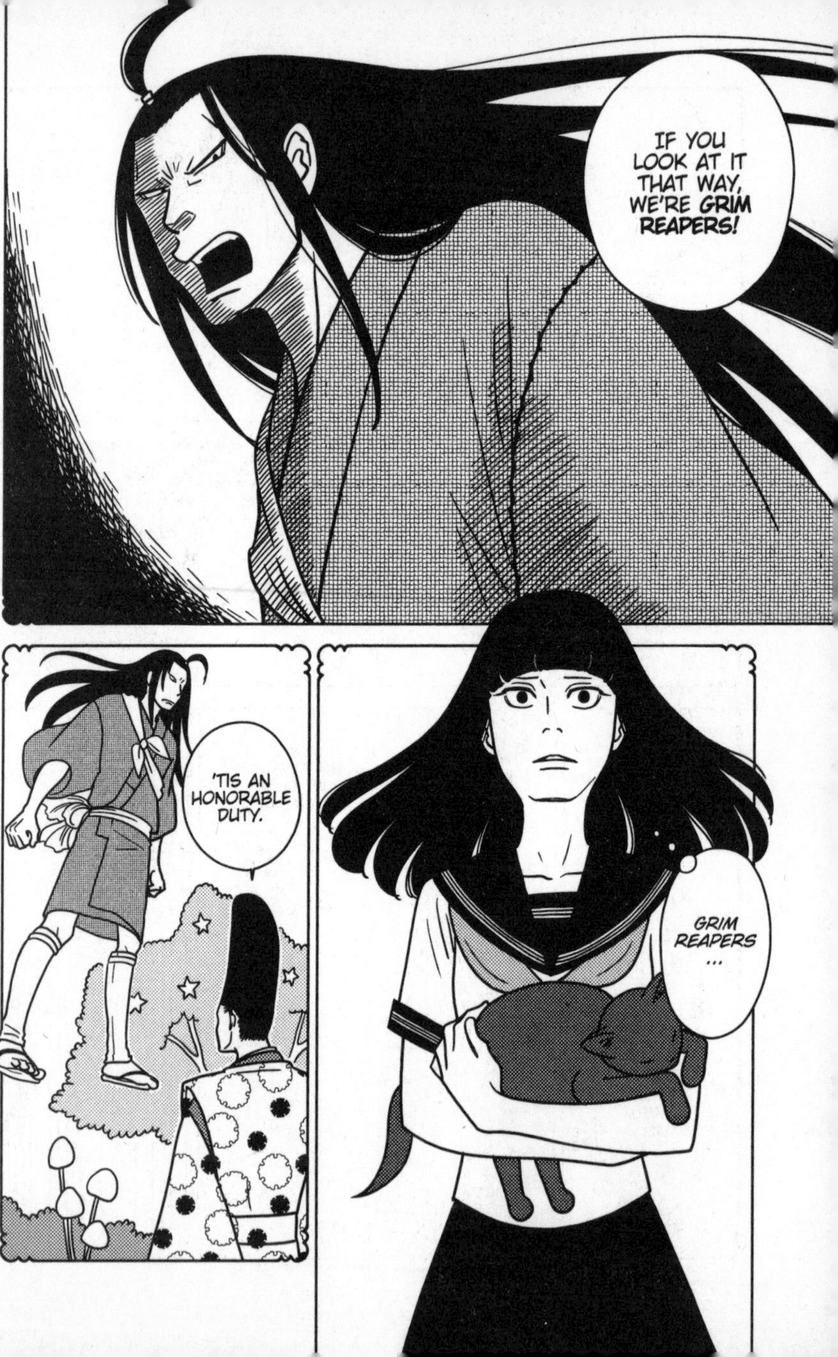
IF YOU LOOK AT IT THAT WAY, WE'RE GRIM REAPERS!
GRIM REAPERS ...
'TIS AN HONORABLE DUTY.

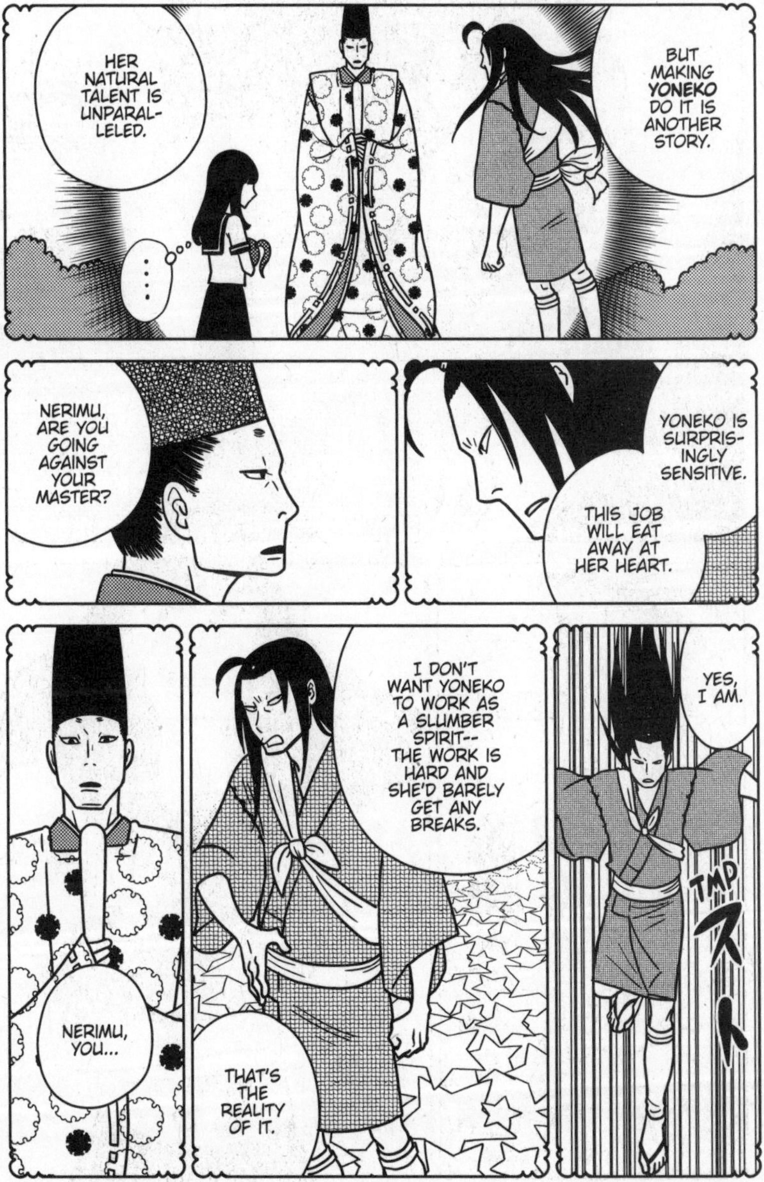
BUT MAKING YONEKO DO IT IS ANOTHER STORY.
HER NATURAL TALENT IS UNPARALLELED.
....
YONEKO IS SURPRISINGLY SENSITIVE.
THIS JOB WILL EAT AWAY AT HER HEART.
NERIMU, ARE YOU GOING AGAINST YOUR MASTER?
YES, I AM.
TMP
スト
I DON'T WANT YONEKO TO WORK AS A SLUMBER SPIRIT-- THE WORK IS HARD AND SHE'D BARELY GET ANY BREAKS.
THAT'S THE REALITY OF IT.
NERIMU, YOU...

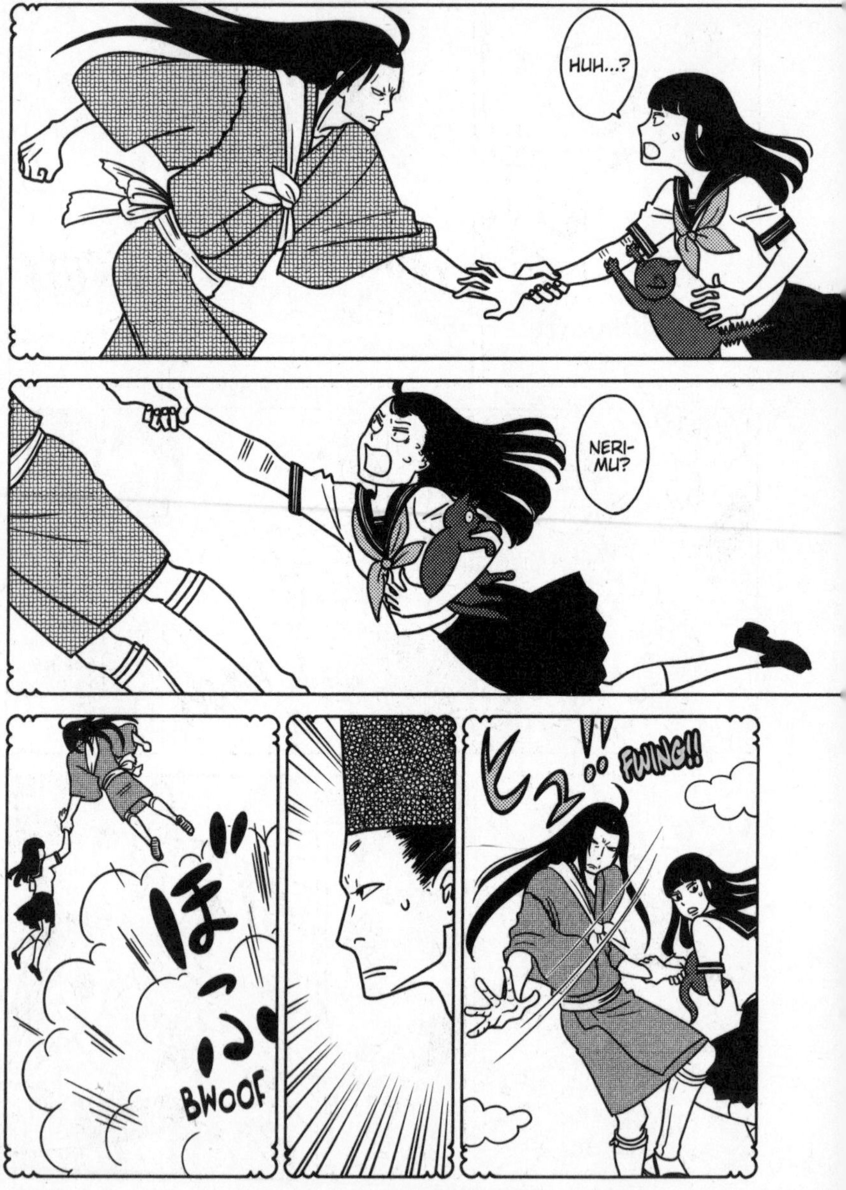
HUH...?
NERI-MU?
FWING!!
BWOOF

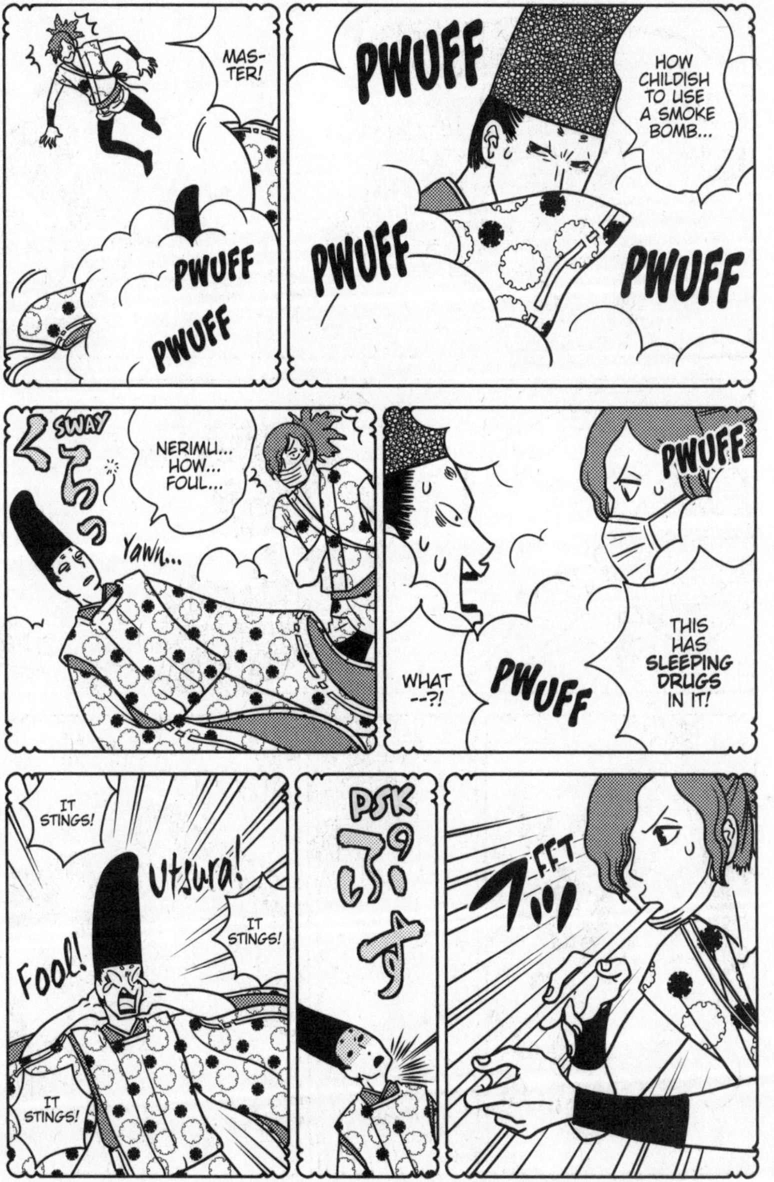

PWUFF
HOW CHILDISH TO USE A SMOKE BOMB...
PWUFF
PWUFF
MAS-TER!
PWUFF
PWUFF
PWUFF
THIS HAS SLEEPING DRUGS IN IT!
PWUFF
WHAT--?!
SWAY
くらっ
NERIMU... HOW... FOUL...
Yawn...
FFT
フッ
PSK
ぷす
IT STINGS!
Utsura!
IT STINGS!
Fool!
IT STINGS!

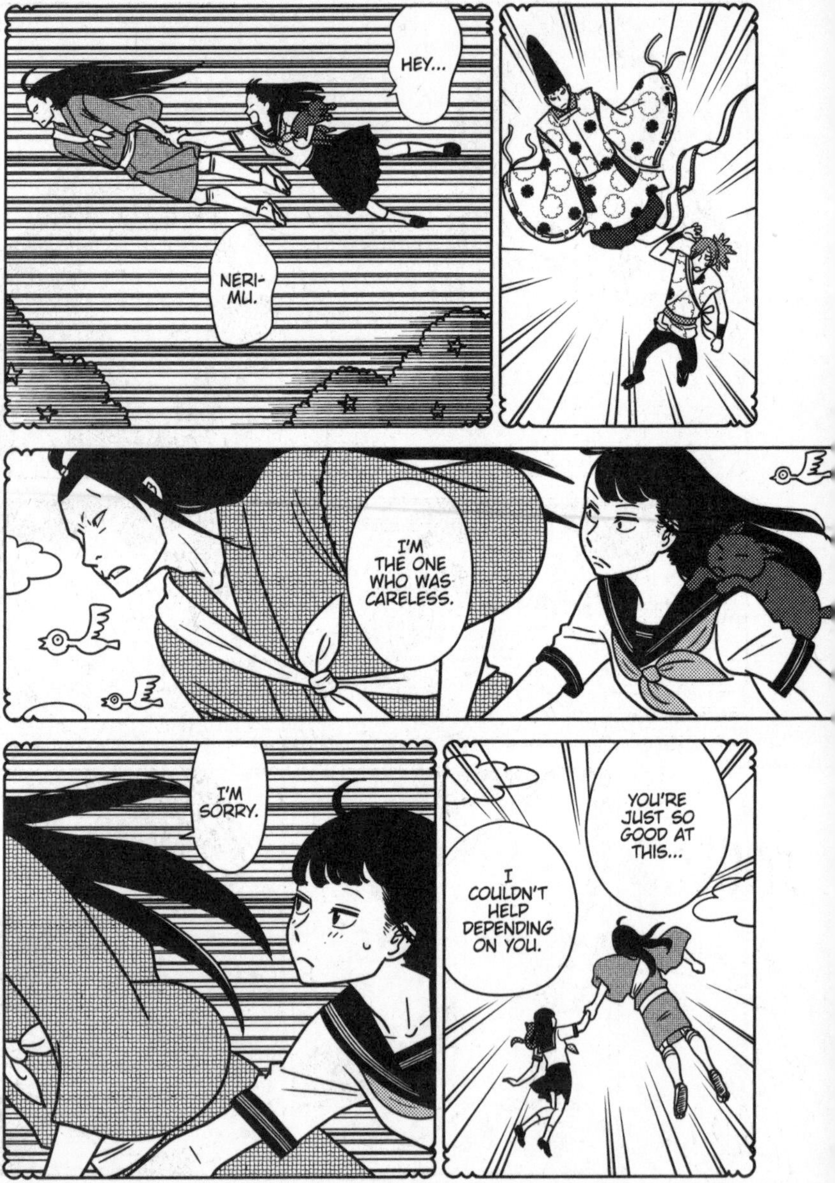
HEY...
NERI-MU.
I'M THE ONE WHO WAS CARELESS.
YOU'RE JUST SO GOOD AT THIS...
I COULDN'T HELP DEPENDING ON YOU.
I'M SORRY.

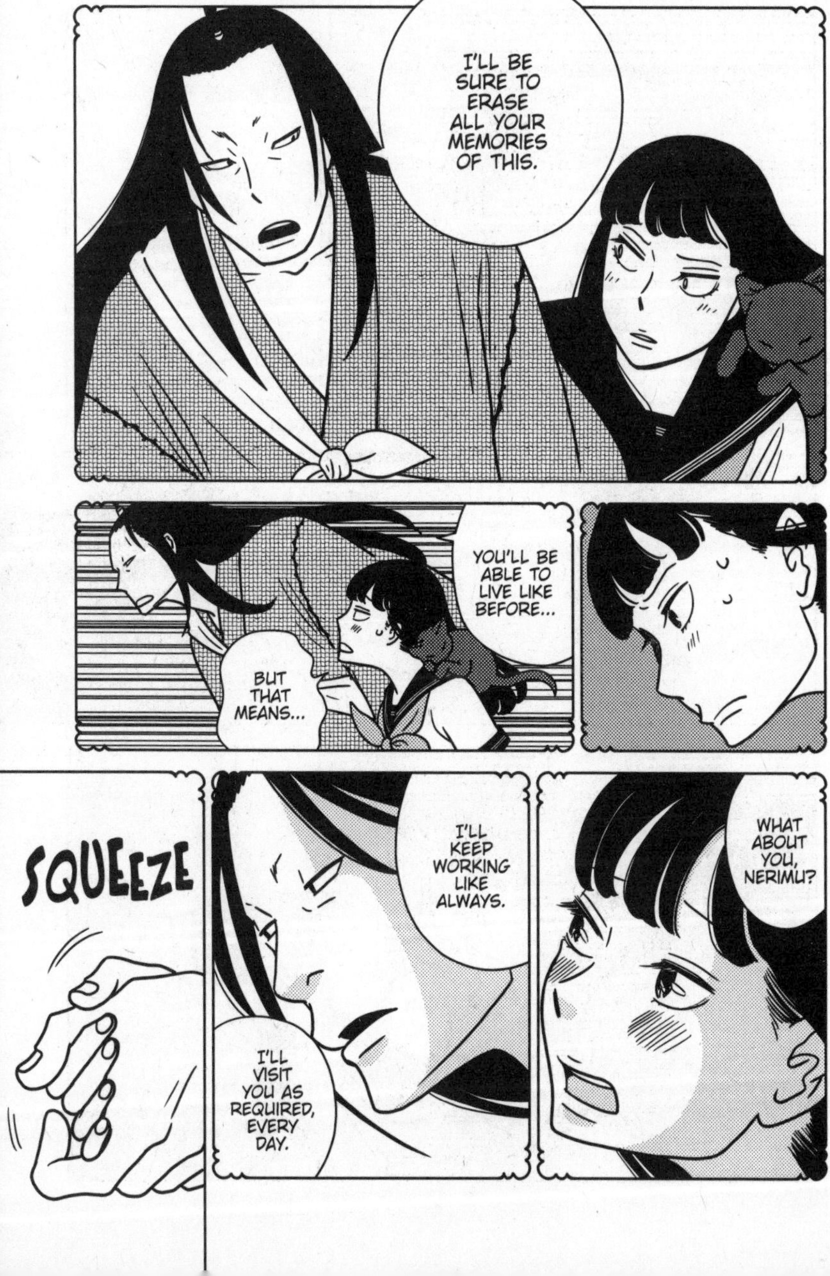
I'LL BE SURE TO ERASE ALL YOUR MEMORIES OF THIS.
YOU'LL BE ABLE TO LIVE LIKE BEFORE...
BUT THAT MEANS...
WHAT ABOUT YOU, NERIMU?
I'LL KEEP WORKING LIKE ALWAYS.
I'LL VISIT YOU AS REQUIRED, EVERY DAY.
SQUEEZE

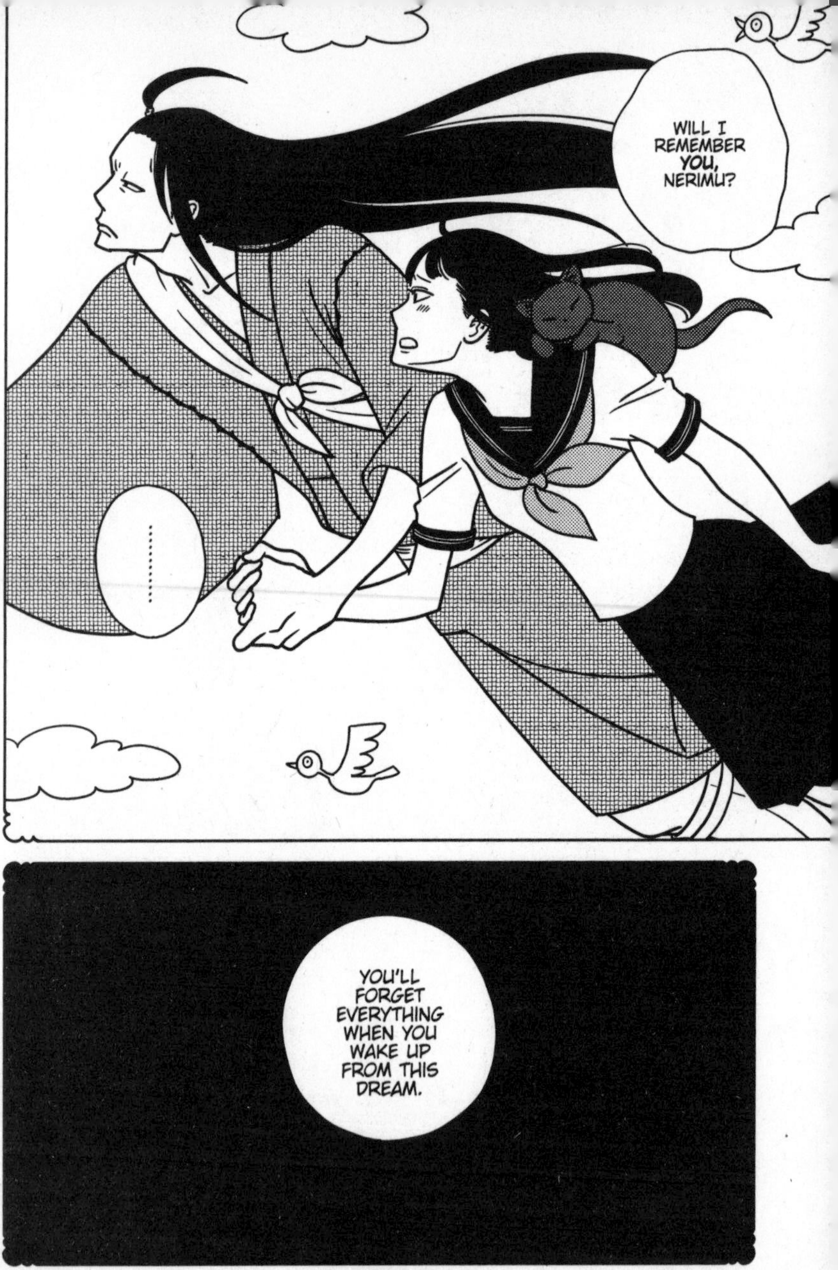
WILL I REMEMBER YOU, NERIMU?
......
YOU'LL FORGET EVERYTHING WHEN YOU WAKE UP FROM THIS DREAM.

Fin

Slumbering Beauty

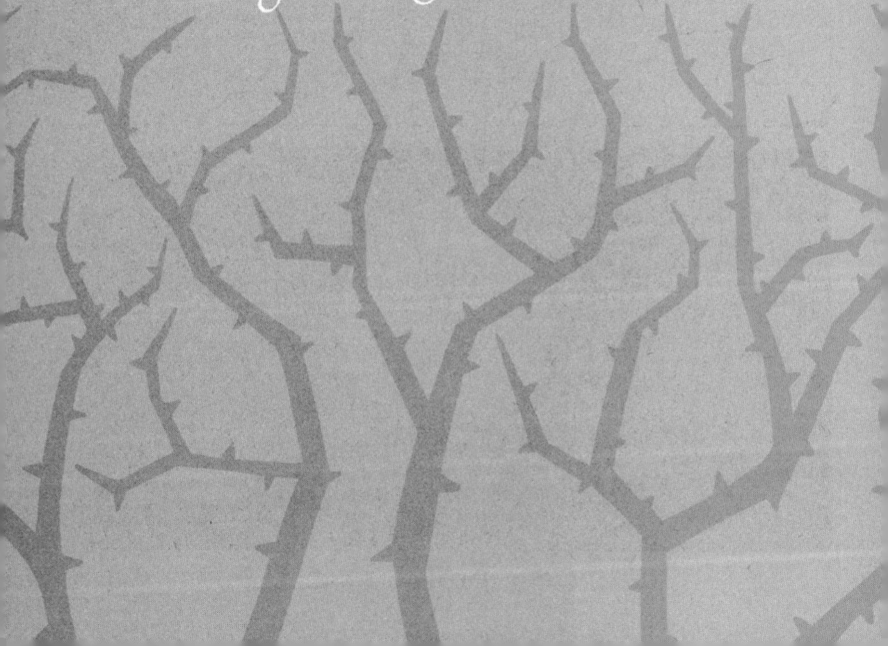

Nemurimehime by Yumi Unita

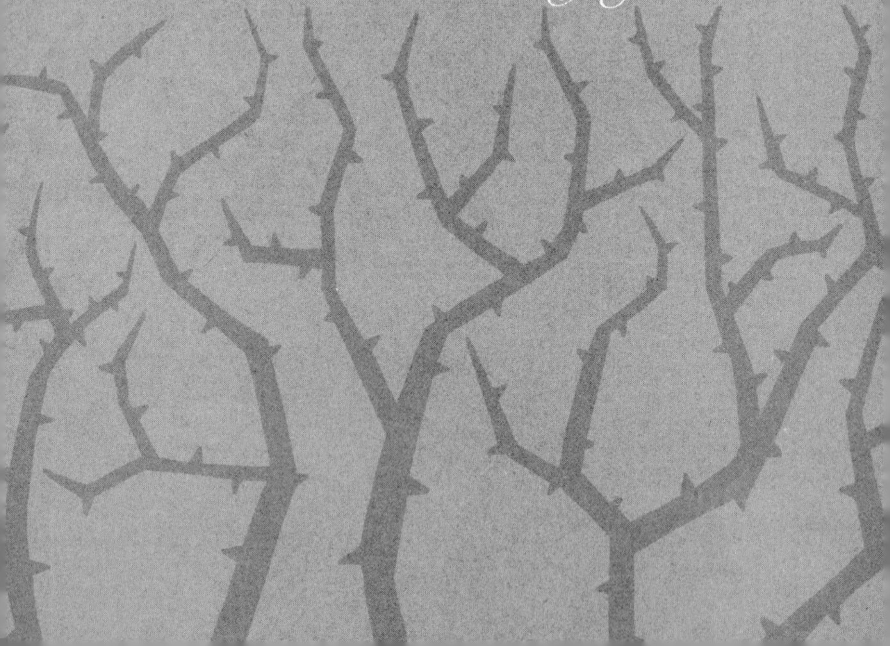

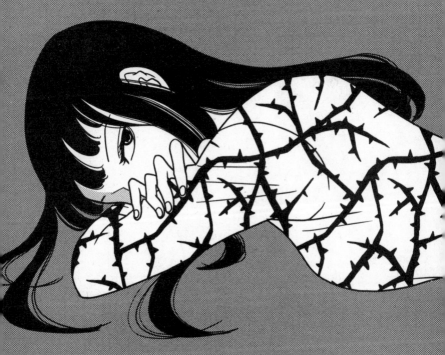

Slumbering Beauty

Last Chapter

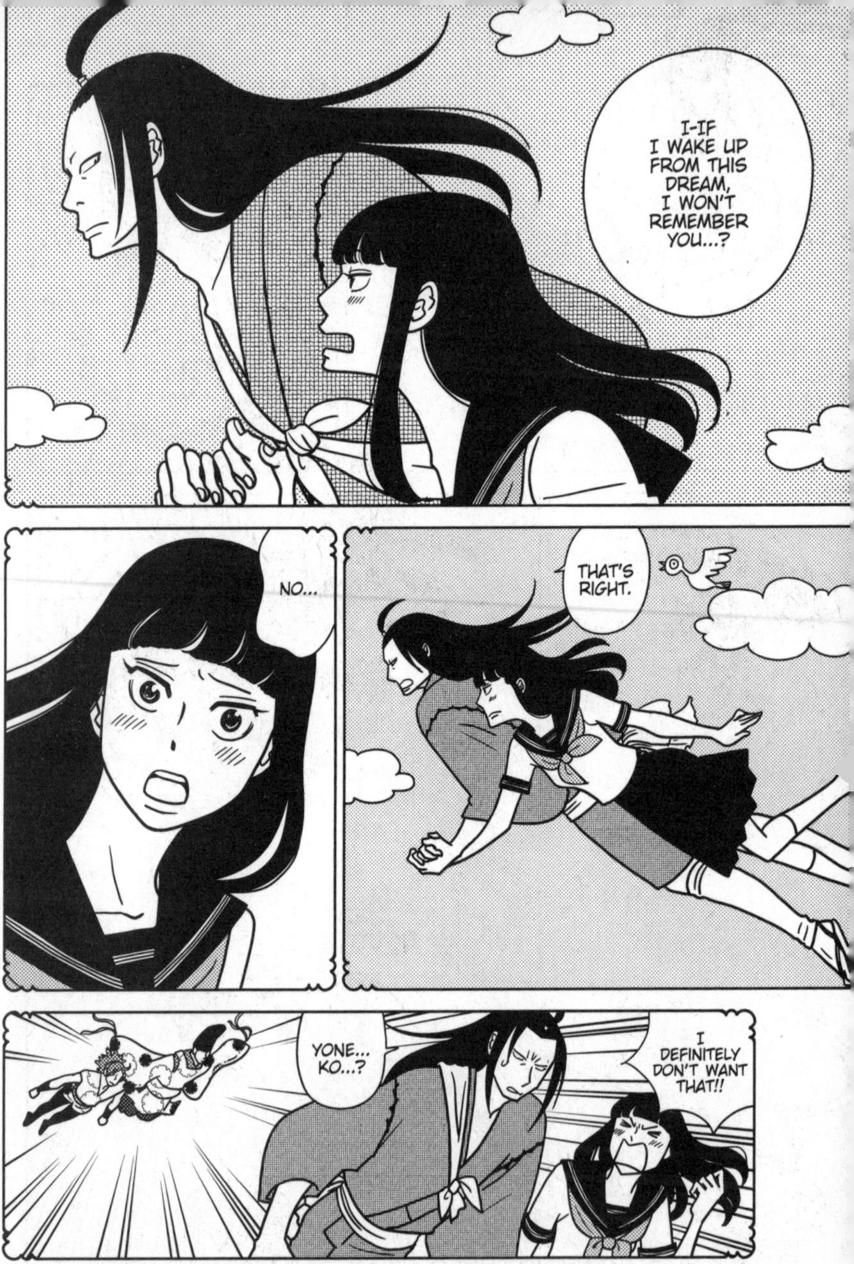
I-IF I WAKE UP FROM THIS DREAM, I WON'T REMEMBER YOU...?
THAT'S RIGHT.
NO...
I DEFINITELY DON'T WANT THAT!!
YONE... KO...?

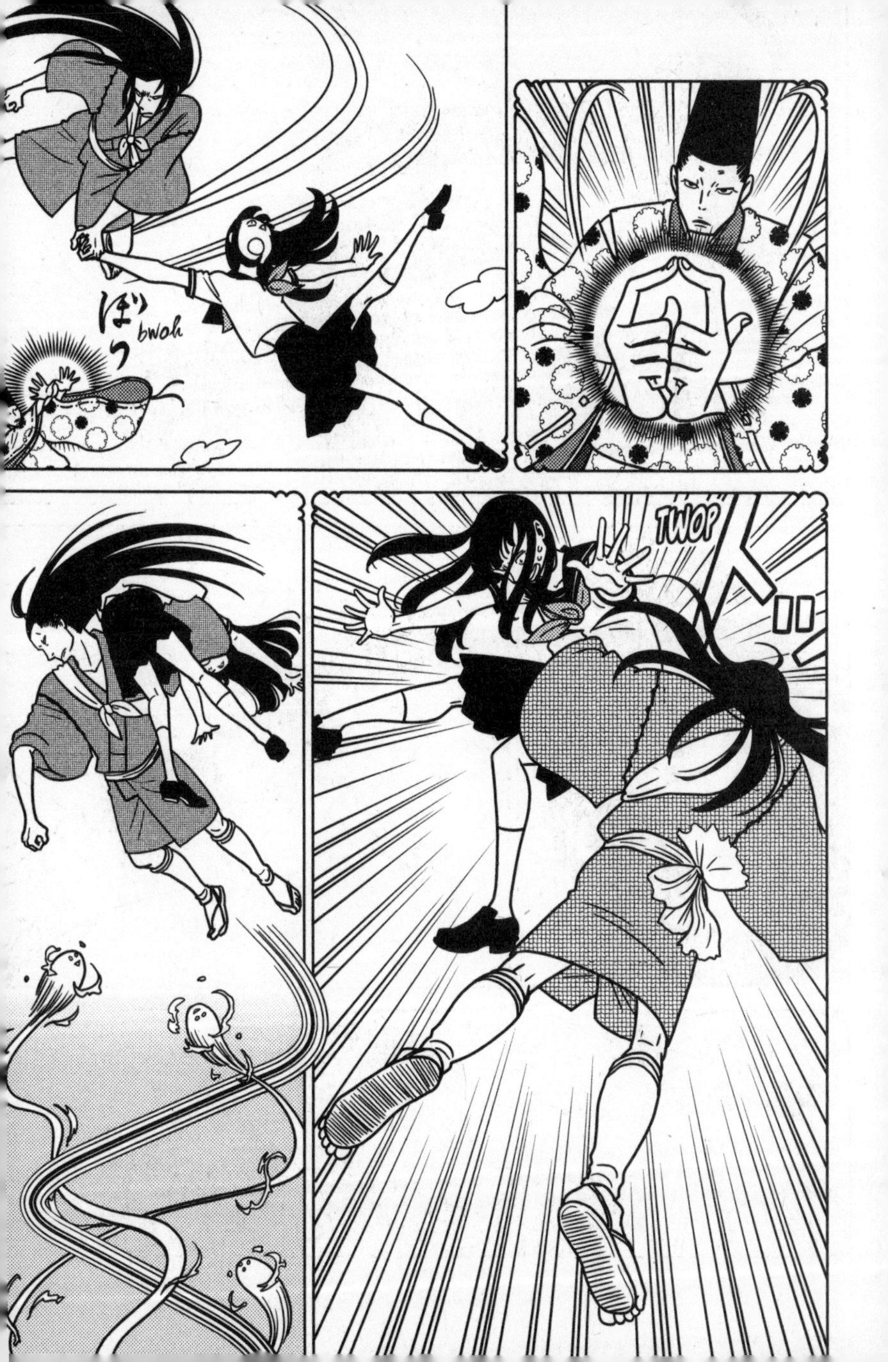
ぼう
bwoh
TWOP
ドッ

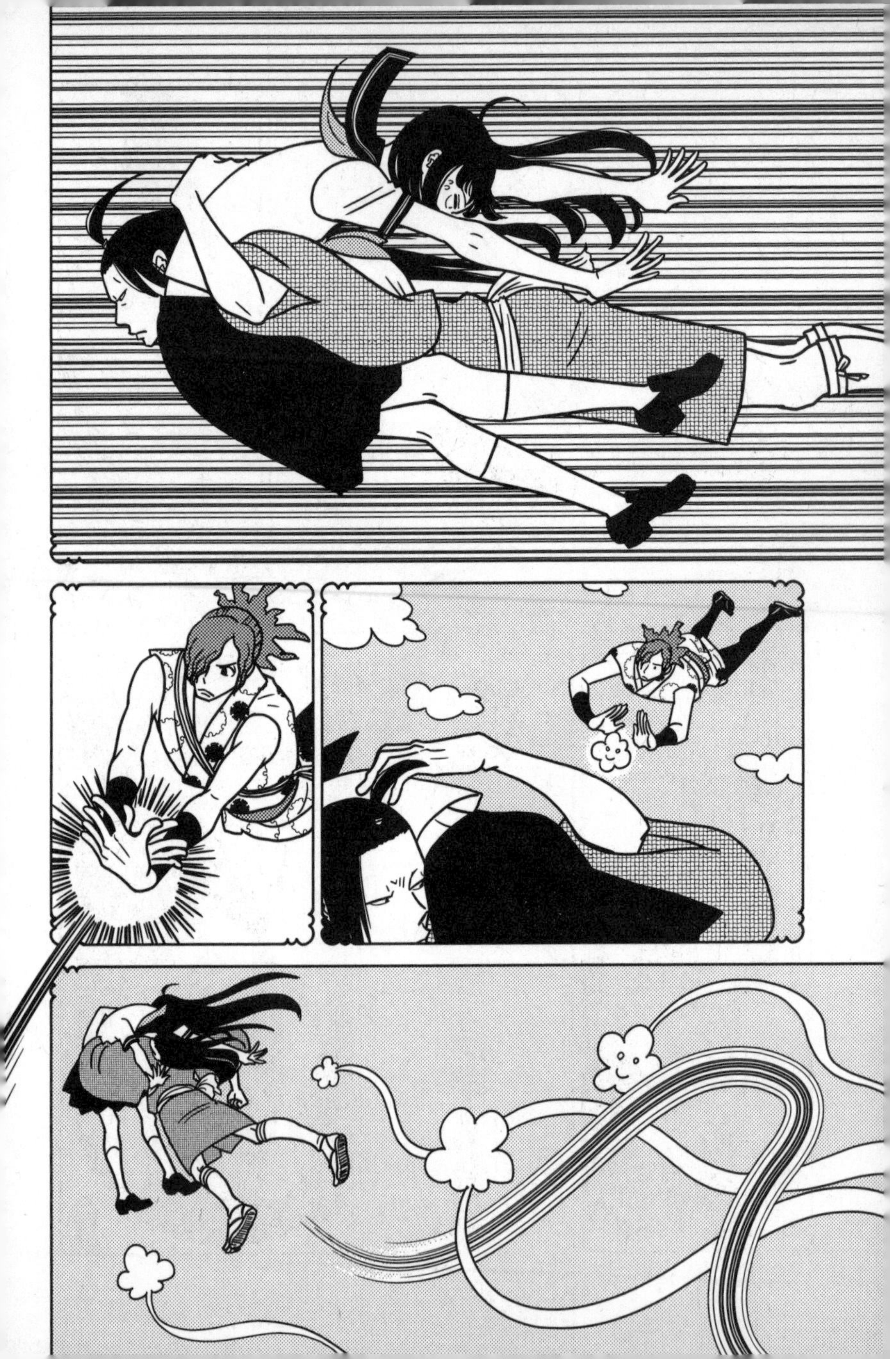

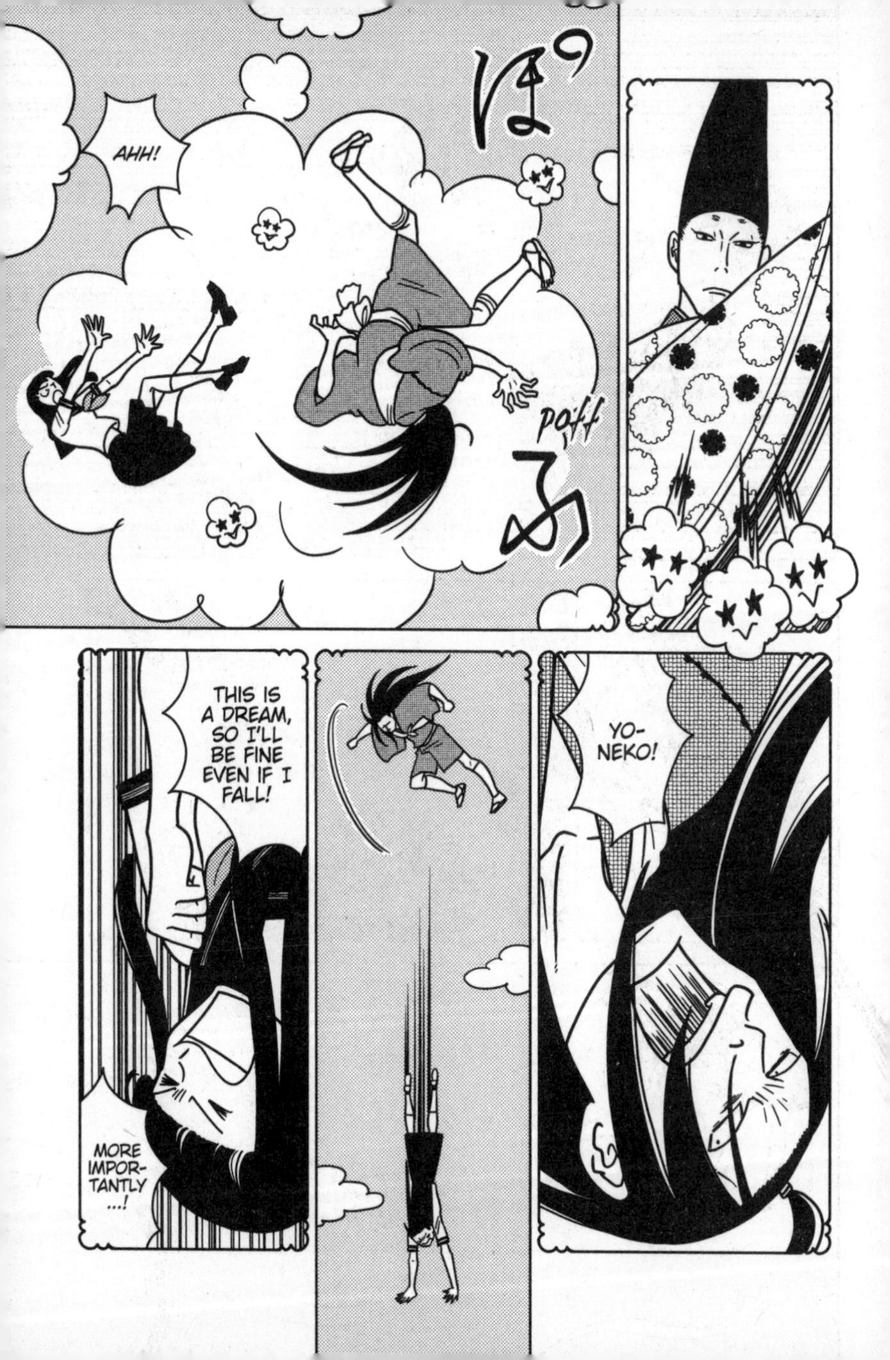
ほ
AHH!
poff
ふ
YO-NEKO!
THIS IS A DREAM, SO I'LL BE FINE EVEN IF I FALL!
MORE IMPORTANTLY ...!

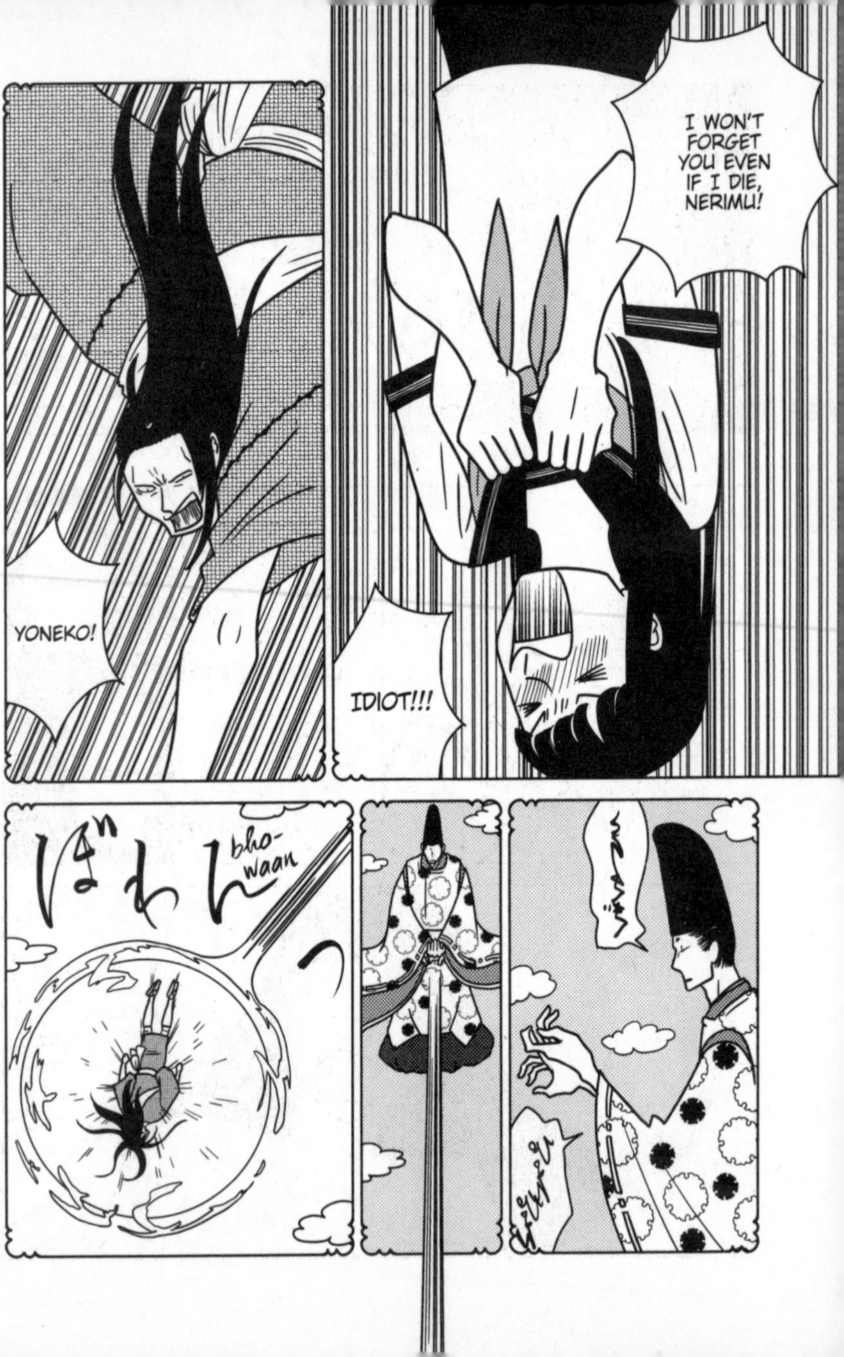
I WON'T FORGET YOU EVEN IF I DIE, NERIMU!
IDIOT!!!
YONEKO!
ぼわん
bho-waan

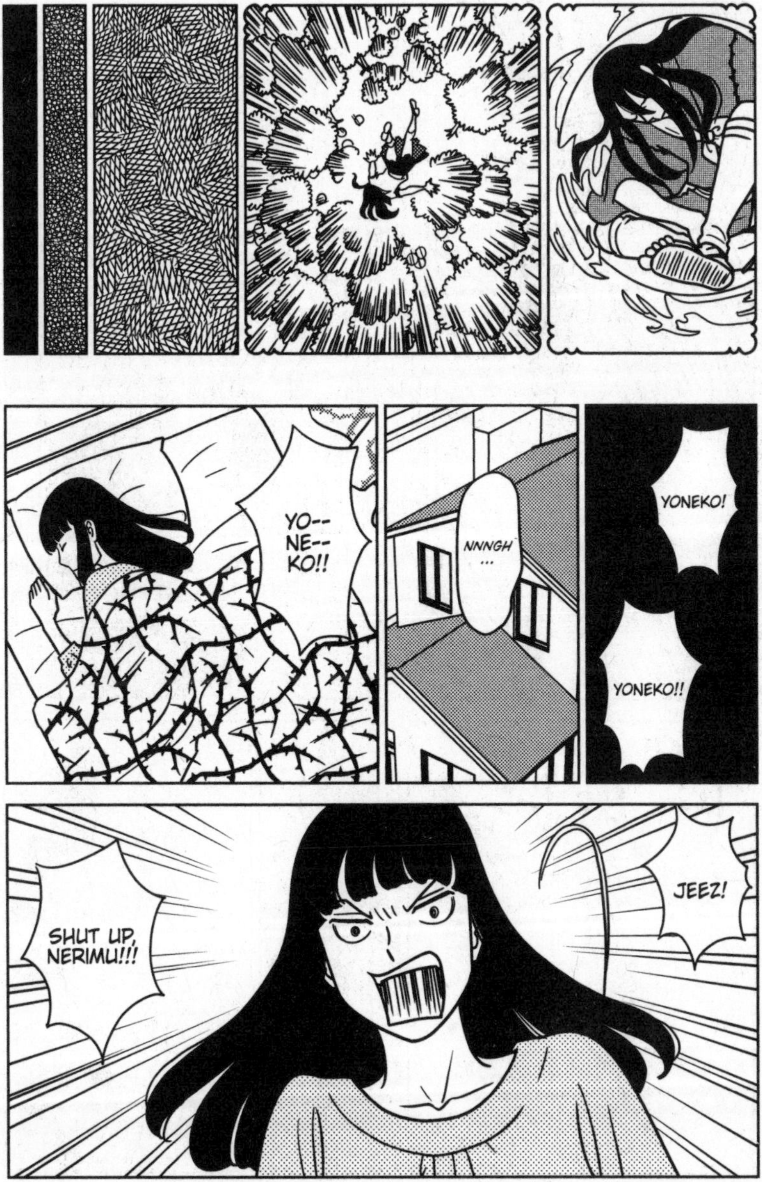
YONEKO!
YONEKO!!
NNNGH ...
YO--NE--KO!!
JEEZ!
SHUT UP, NERIMU!!!

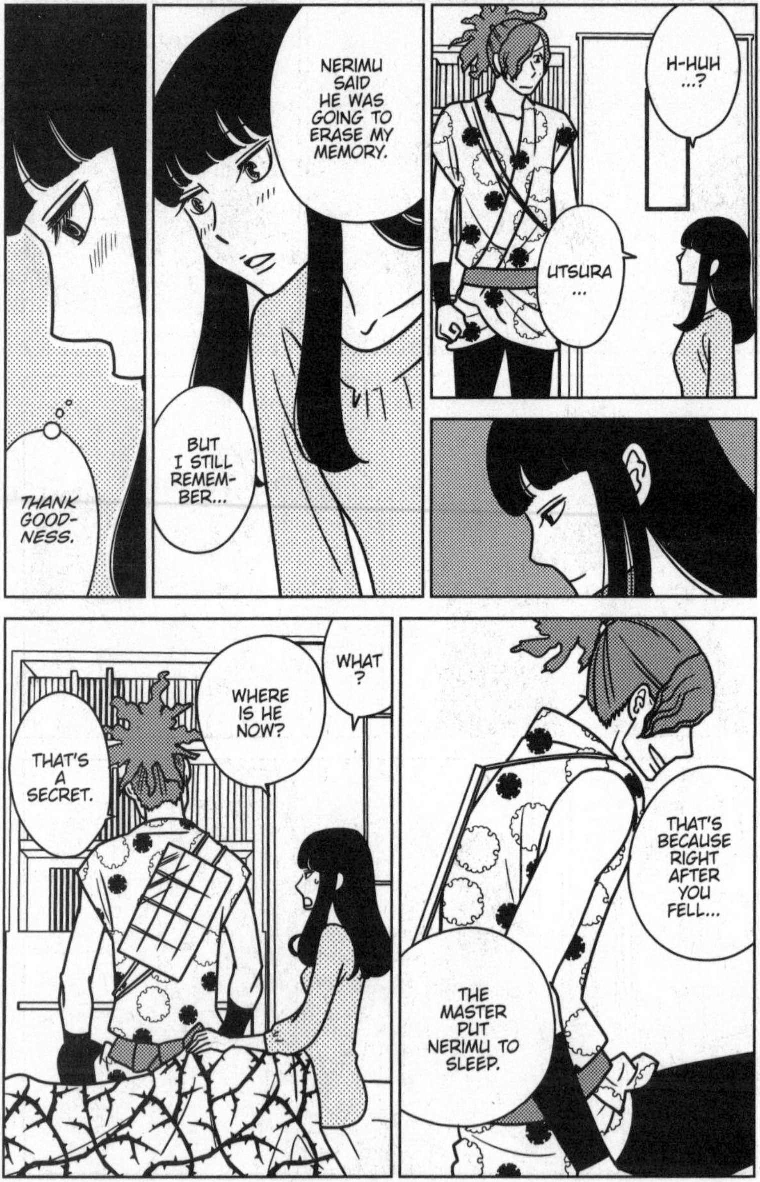
H-HUH ...?
UTSURA ...
NERIMU SAID HE WAS GOING TO ERASE MY MEMORY.
BUT I STILL REMEMBER...
THANK GOODNESS.
THAT'S BECAUSE RIGHT AFTER YOU FELL...
THE MASTER PUT NERIMU TO SLEEP.
WHAT?
WHERE IS HE NOW?
THAT'S A SECRET.

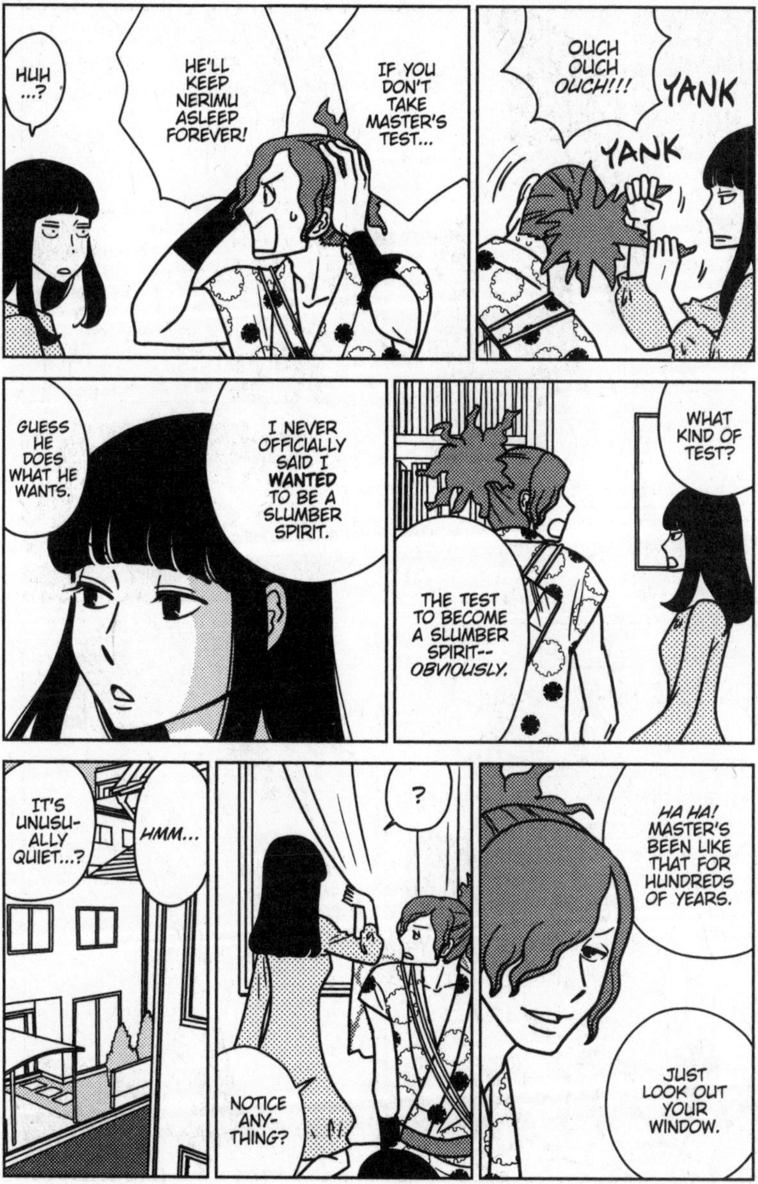
OUCH OUCH OUCH!!!
YANK
YANK
IF YOU DON'T TAKE MASTER'S TEST...
HE'LL KEEP NERIMU ASLEEP FOREVER!
HUH ...?
WHAT KIND OF TEST?
THE TEST TO BECOME A SLUMBER SPIRIT-- OBVIOUSLY.
I NEVER OFFICIALLY SAID I **WANTED** TO BE A SLUMBER SPIRIT.
GUESS HE DOES WHAT HE WANTS.
HA HA! MASTER'S BEEN LIKE THAT FOR HUNDREDS OF YEARS.
JUST LOOK OUT YOUR WINDOW.
?
NOTICE ANYTHING?
HMM...
IT'S UNUSUALLY QUIET...?

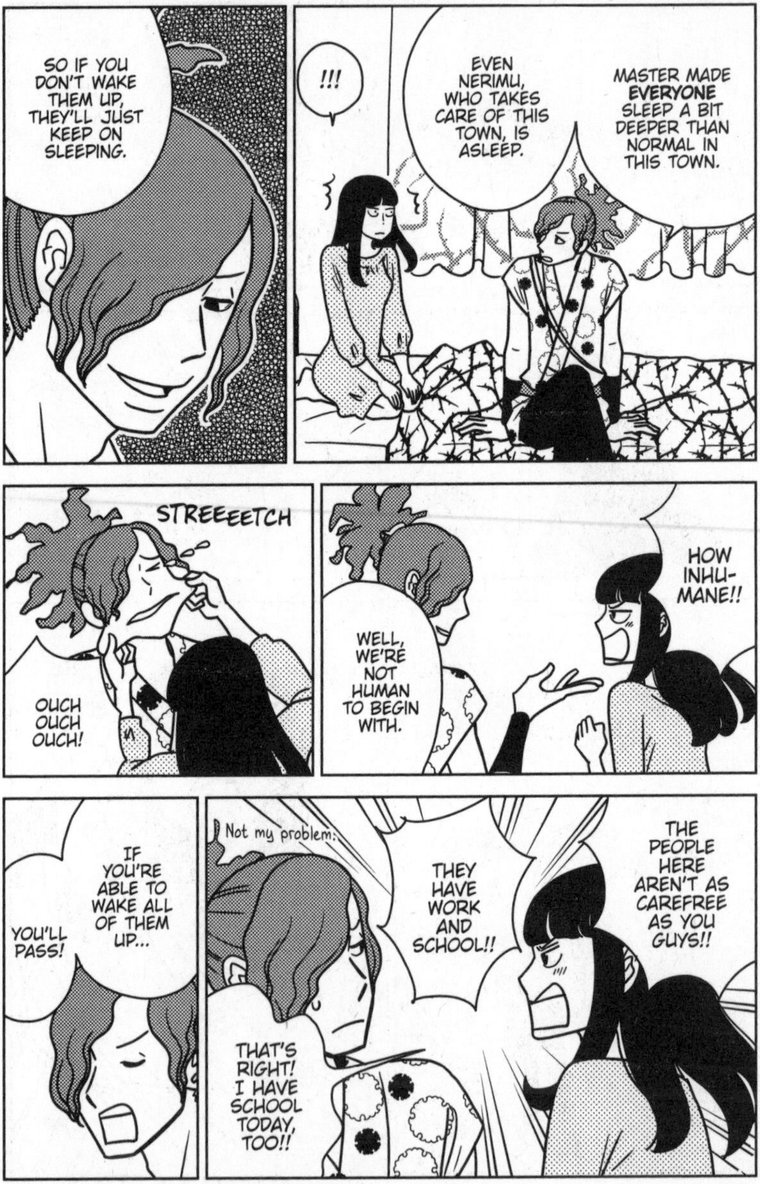
MASTER MADE **EVERYONE** SLEEP A BIT DEEPER THAN NORMAL IN THIS TOWN.
EVEN NERIMU, WHO TAKES CARE OF THIS TOWN, IS ASLEEP.
!!!
SO IF YOU DON'T WAKE THEM UP, THEY'LL JUST KEEP ON SLEEPING.
HOW INHUMANE!!
WELL, WE'RE NOT HUMAN TO BEGIN WITH.
STREEEETCH
OUCH OUCH OUCH!
THE PEOPLE HERE AREN'T AS CAREFREE AS YOU GUYS!!
THEY HAVE WORK AND SCHOOL!!
Not my problem.
THAT'S RIGHT! I HAVE SCHOOL TODAY, TOO!!
IF YOU'RE ABLE TO WAKE ALL OF THEM UP...
YOU'LL PASS!

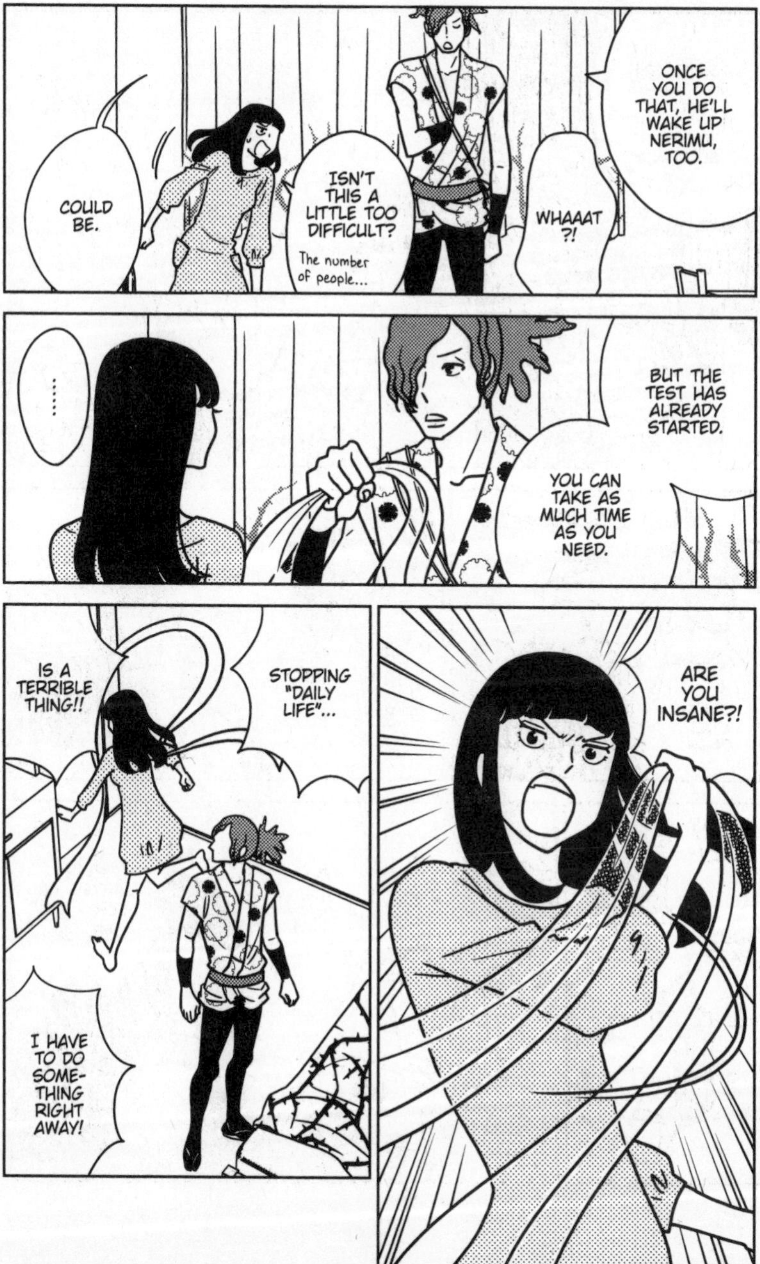
ONCE YOU DO THAT, HE'LL WAKE UP NERIMU, TOO.
WHAAAT?!
ISN'T THIS A LITTLE TOO DIFFICULT?
The number of people...
COULD BE.
BUT THE TEST HAS ALREADY STARTED.
YOU CAN TAKE AS MUCH TIME AS YOU NEED.
......
ARE YOU INSANE?!
STOPPING "DAILY LIFE"...
IS A TERRIBLE THING!!
I HAVE TO DO SOME-THING RIGHT AWAY!

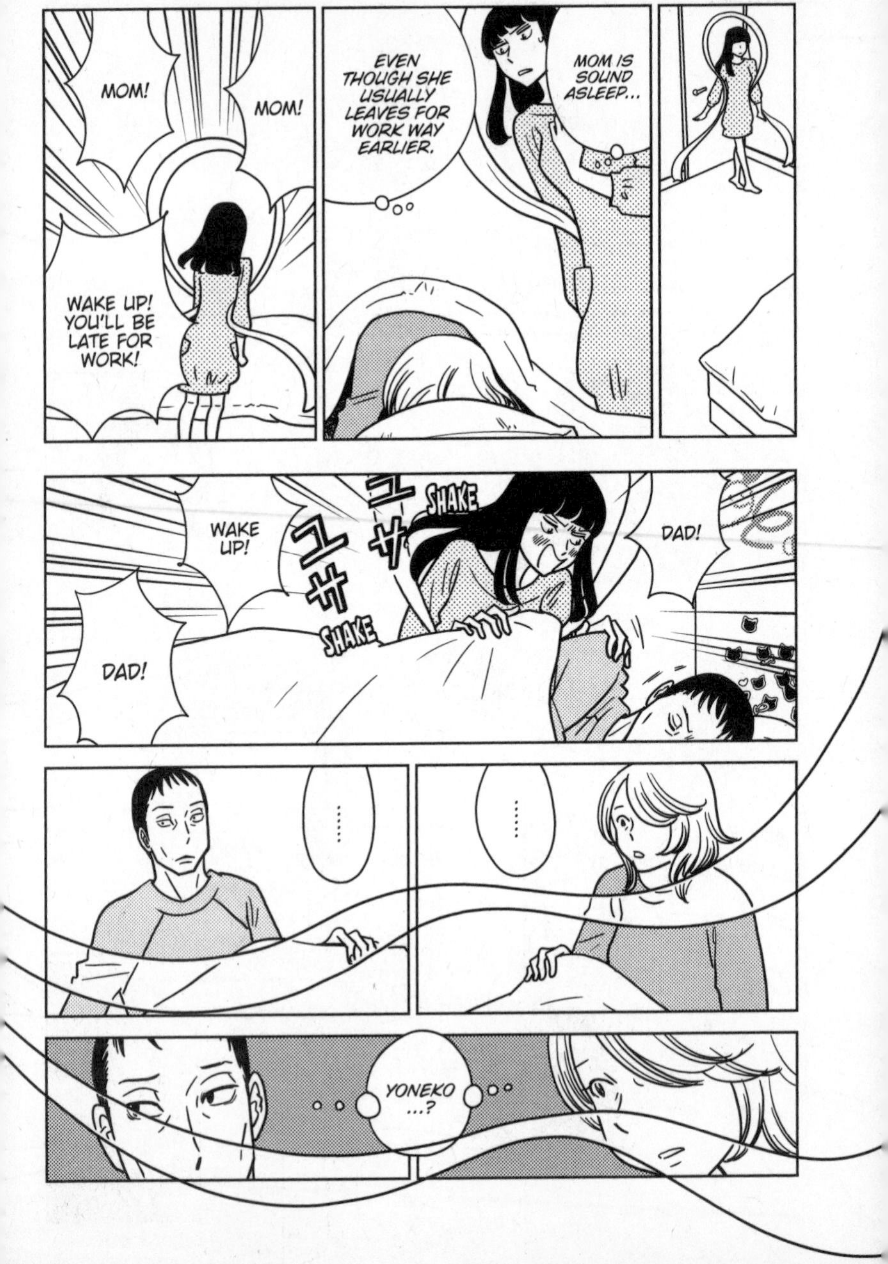
MOM IS SOUND ASLEEP...
EVEN THOUGH SHE USUALLY LEAVES FOR WORK WAY EARLIER.
MOM!
MOM!
WAKE UP! YOU'LL BE LATE FOR WORK!
DAD!
SHAKE
ユサ
ユサ
SHAKE
WAKE UP!
DAD!
......
......
YONEKO ...?

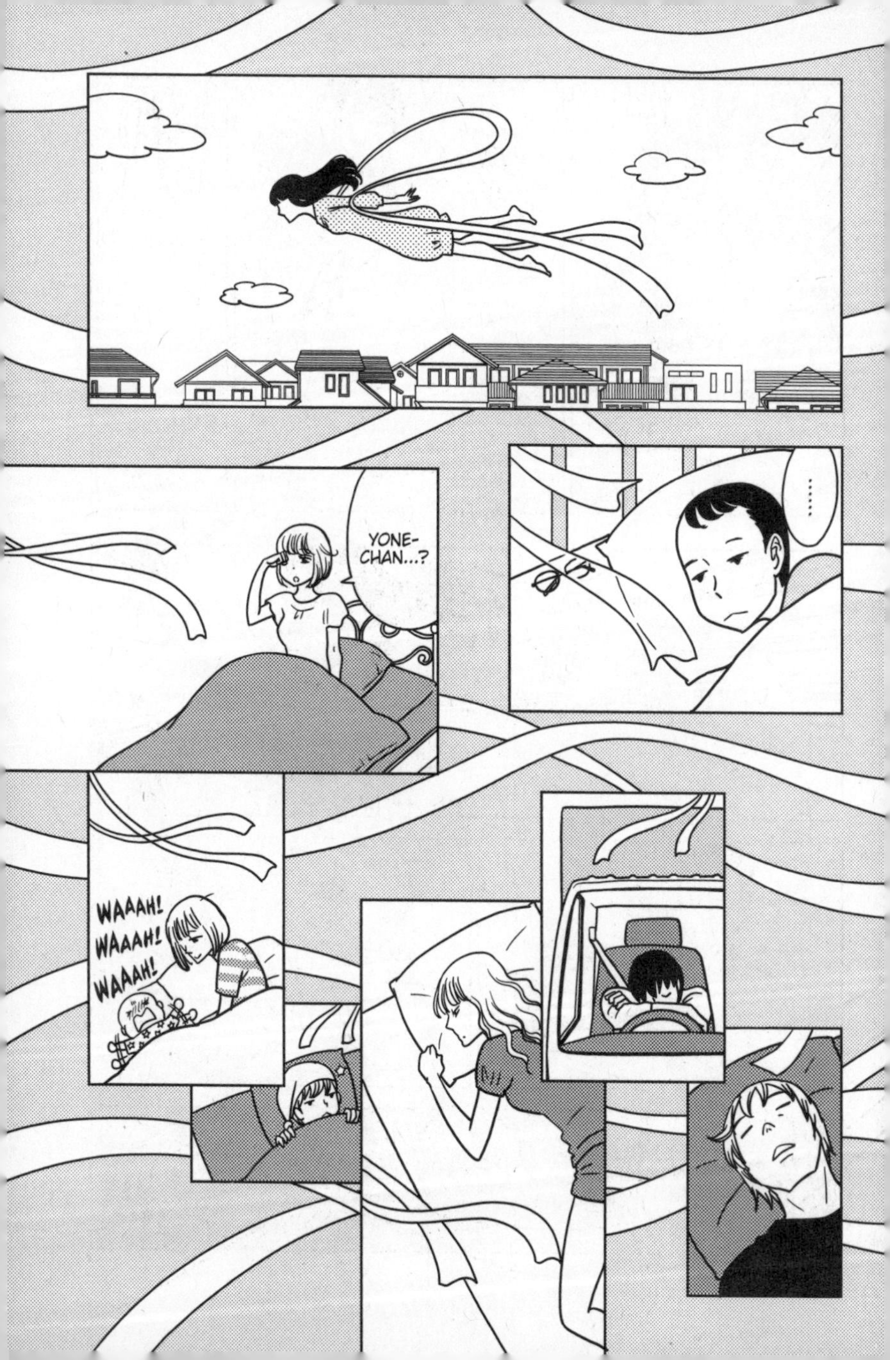
......
YONE-CHAN...?
WAAAH! WAAAH! WAAAH!

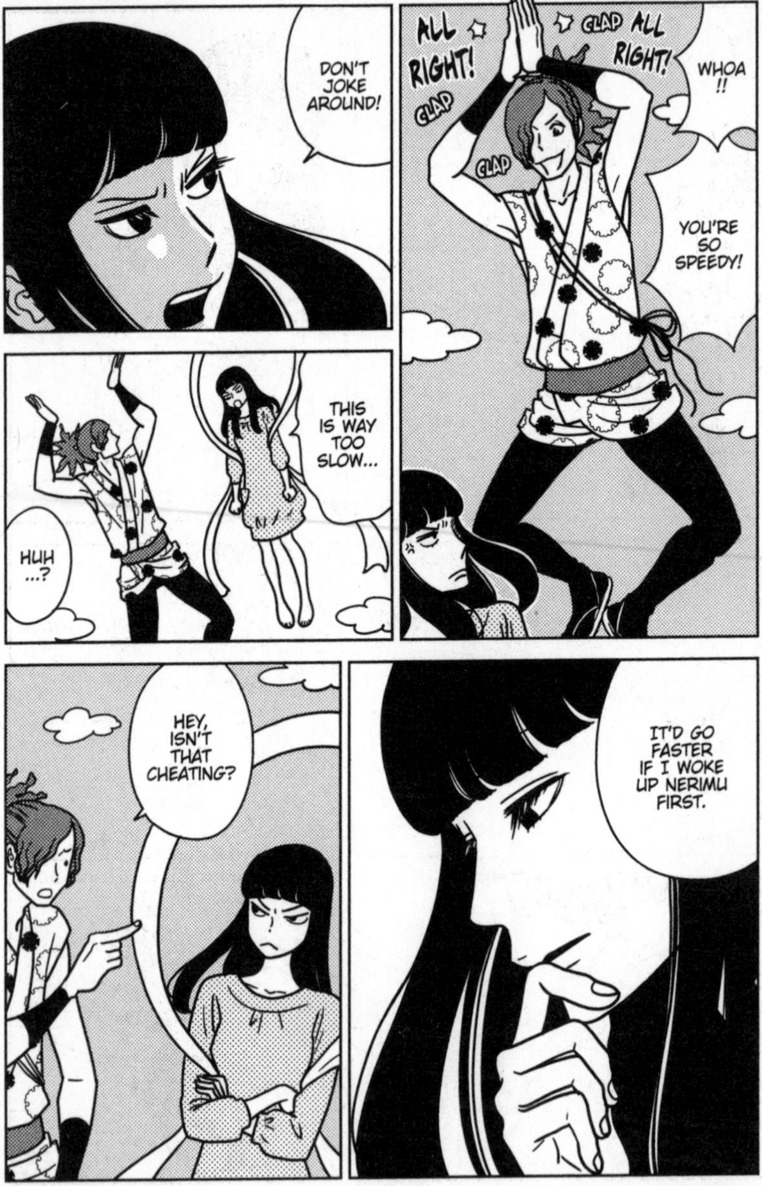
ALL RIGHT!
CLAP
ALL RIGHT!
CLAP
CLAP
WHOA !!
YOU'RE SO SPEEDY!
DON'T JOKE AROUND!
THIS IS WAY TOO SLOW...
HUH ...?
IT'D GO FASTER IF I WOKE UP NERIMU FIRST.
HEY, ISN'T THAT CHEATING?

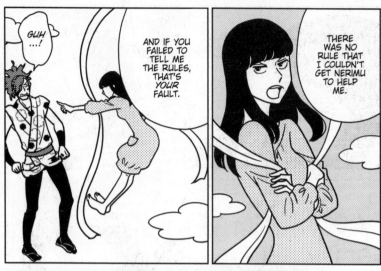

THERE WAS NO RULE THAT I COULDN'T GET NERIMU TO HELP ME.
AND IF YOU FAILED TO TELL ME THE RULES, THAT'S *YOUR* FAULT.
GUH ...!
BUT...I DON'T THINK NERIMU WILL WAKE UP.
MASTER PUT HIM TO SLEEP.
BESIDES, YOU DON'T KNOW WHERE HE IS...

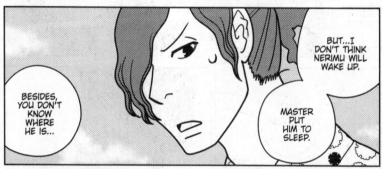

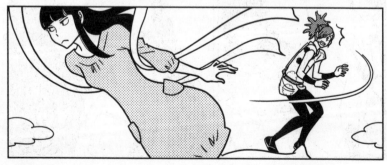

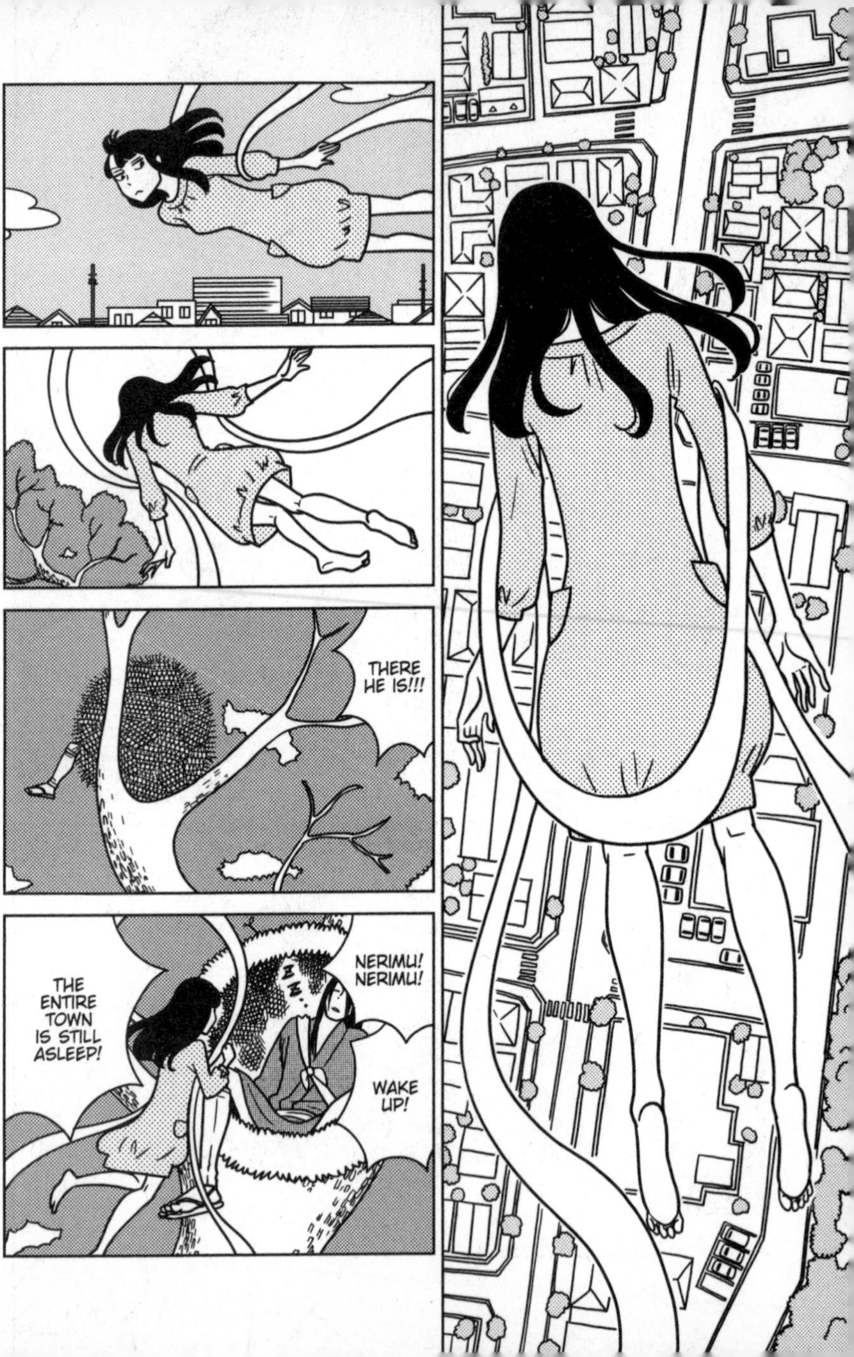
THERE HE IS!!!
NERIMU! NERIMU!
WAKE UP!
THE ENTIRE TOWN IS STILL ASLEEP!

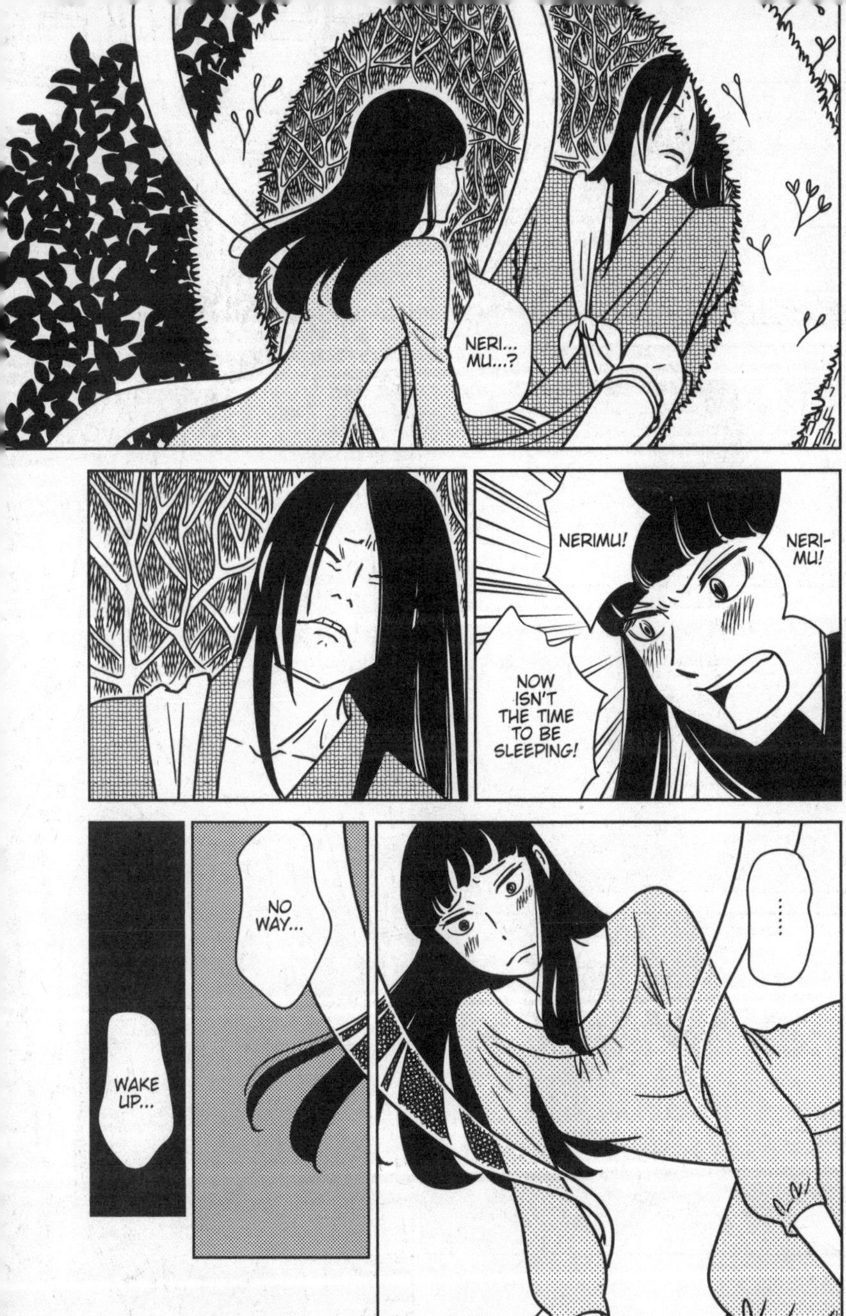
NERI... MU...?
NERI-MU!
NERIMU!
NOW ISN'T THE TIME TO BE SLEEPING!
......
NO WAY...
WAKE UP...

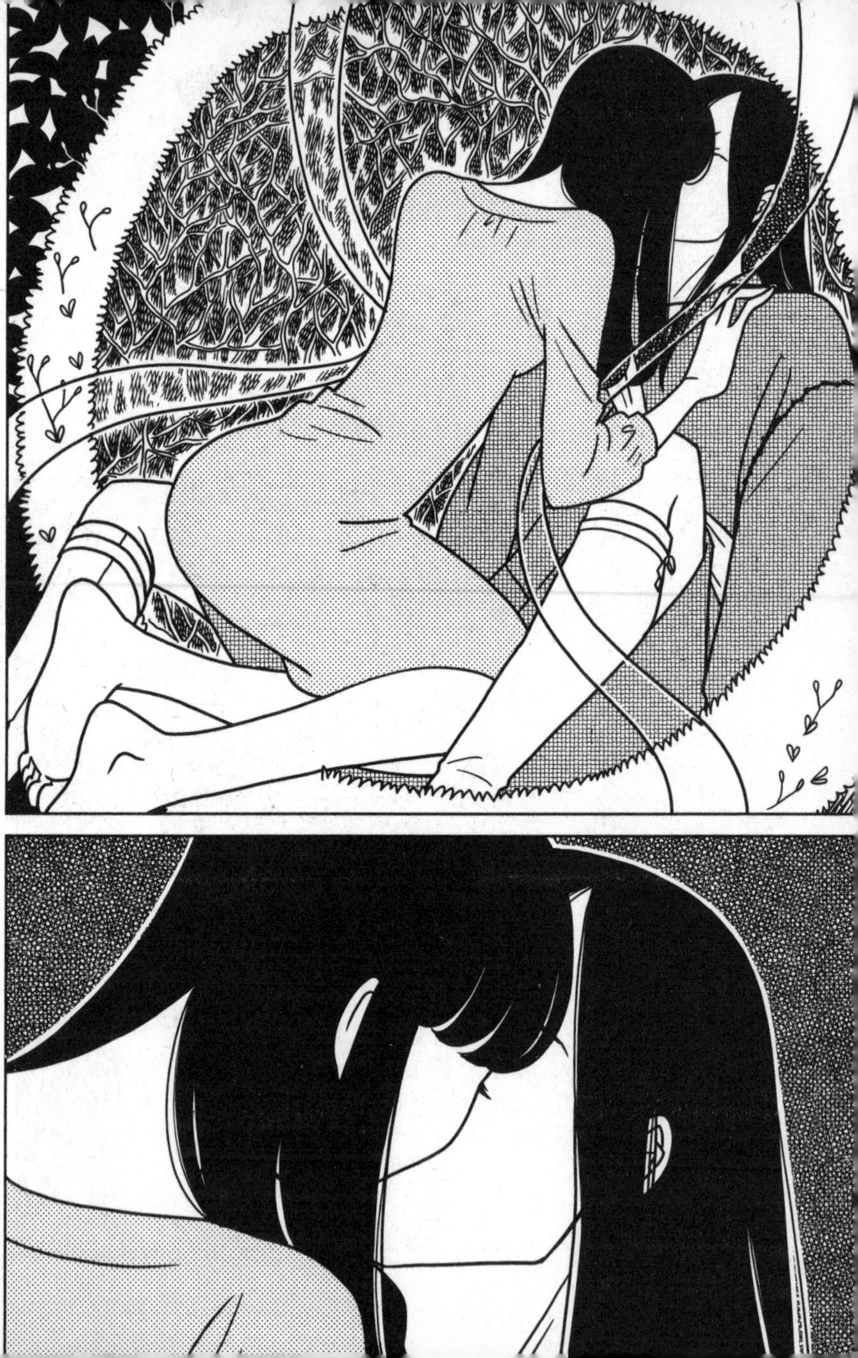

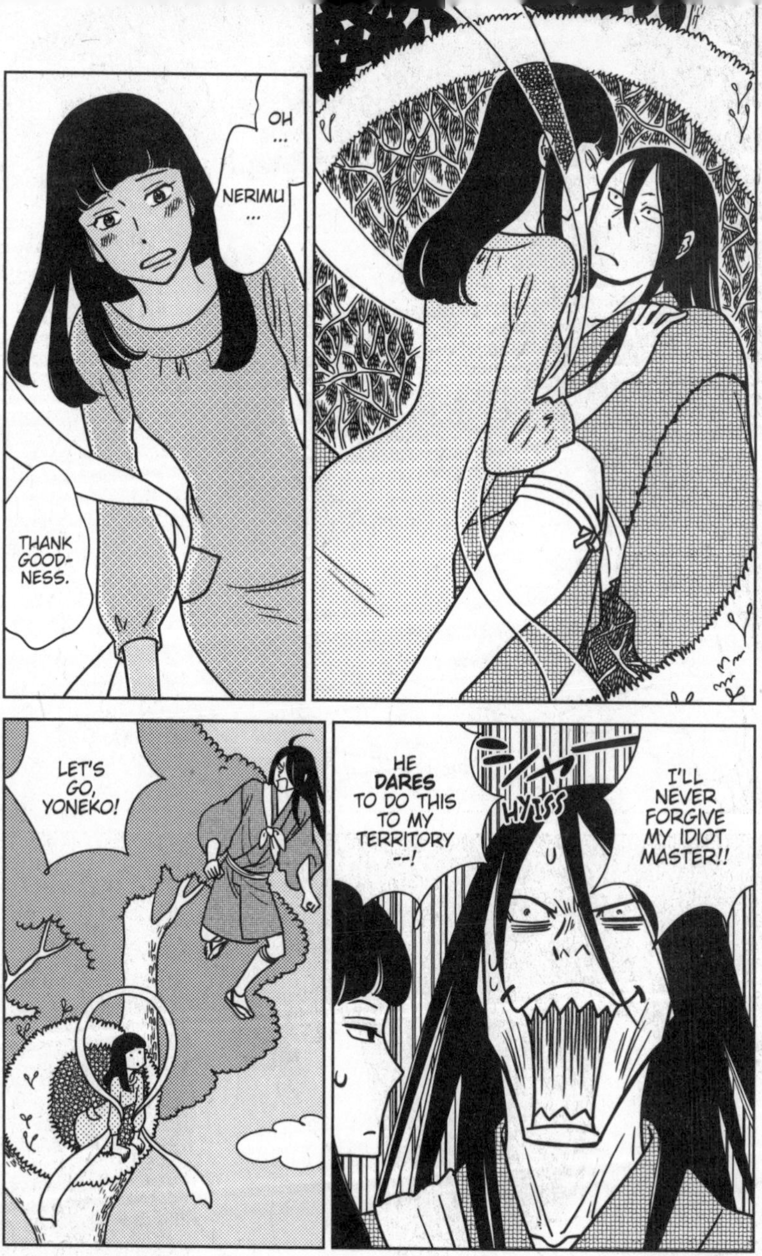
OH ... NERIMU ...
THANK GOODNESS.
I'LL NEVER FORGIVE MY IDIOT MASTER!!
HYISS
HE DARES TO DO THIS TO MY TERRITORY --!
LET'S GO, YONEKO!

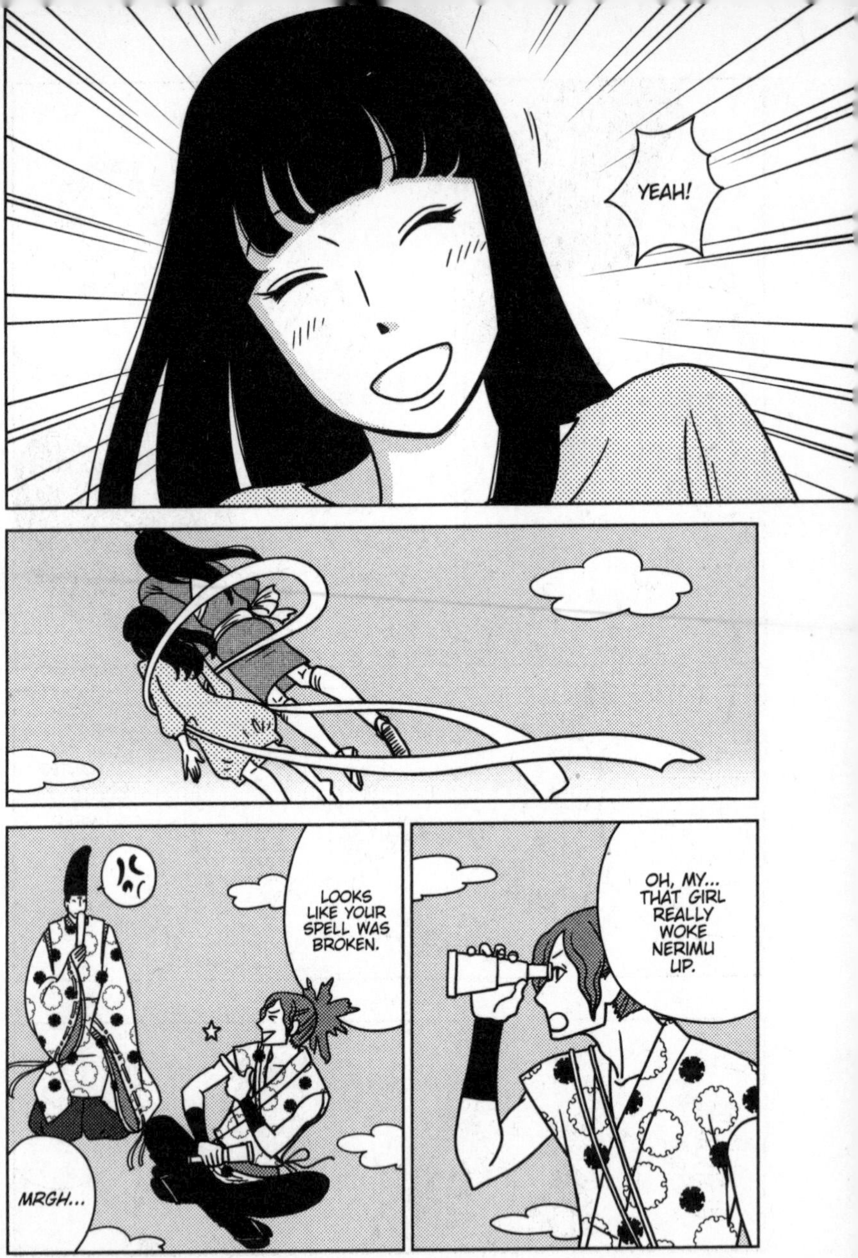
YEAH!
OH, MY... THAT GIRL REALLY WOKE NERIMU UP.
LOOKS LIKE YOUR SPELL WAS BROKEN.
MRGH...

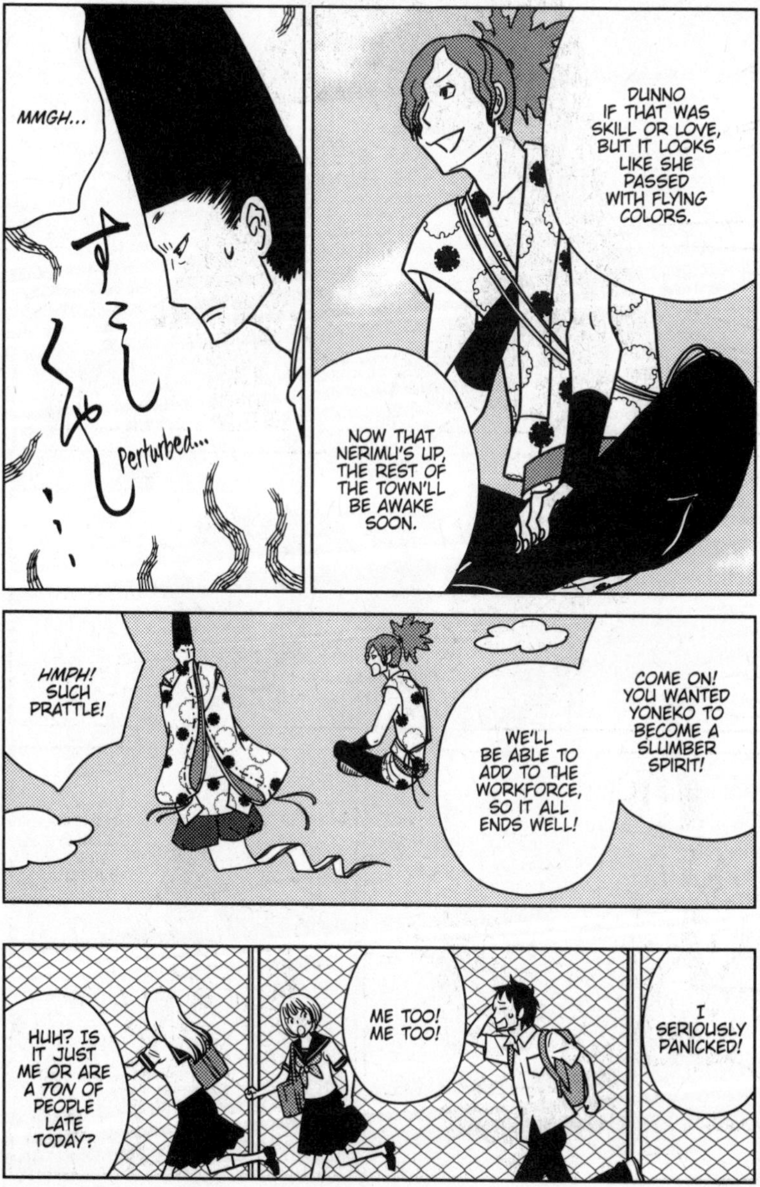
DUNNO IF THAT WAS SKILL OR LOVE, BUT IT LOOKS LIKE SHE PASSED WITH FLYING COLORS.
NOW THAT NERIMU'S UP, THE REST OF THE TOWN'LL BE AWAKE SOON.
MMGH...
Perturbed...
COME ON! YOU WANTED YONEKO TO BECOME A SLUMBER SPIRIT!
WE'LL BE ABLE TO ADD TO THE WORKFORCE, SO IT ALL ENDS WELL!
HMPH! SUCH PRATTLE!
I SERIOUSLY PANICKED!
ME TOO! ME TOO!
HUH? IS IT JUST ME OR ARE A *TON* OF PEOPLE LATE TODAY?

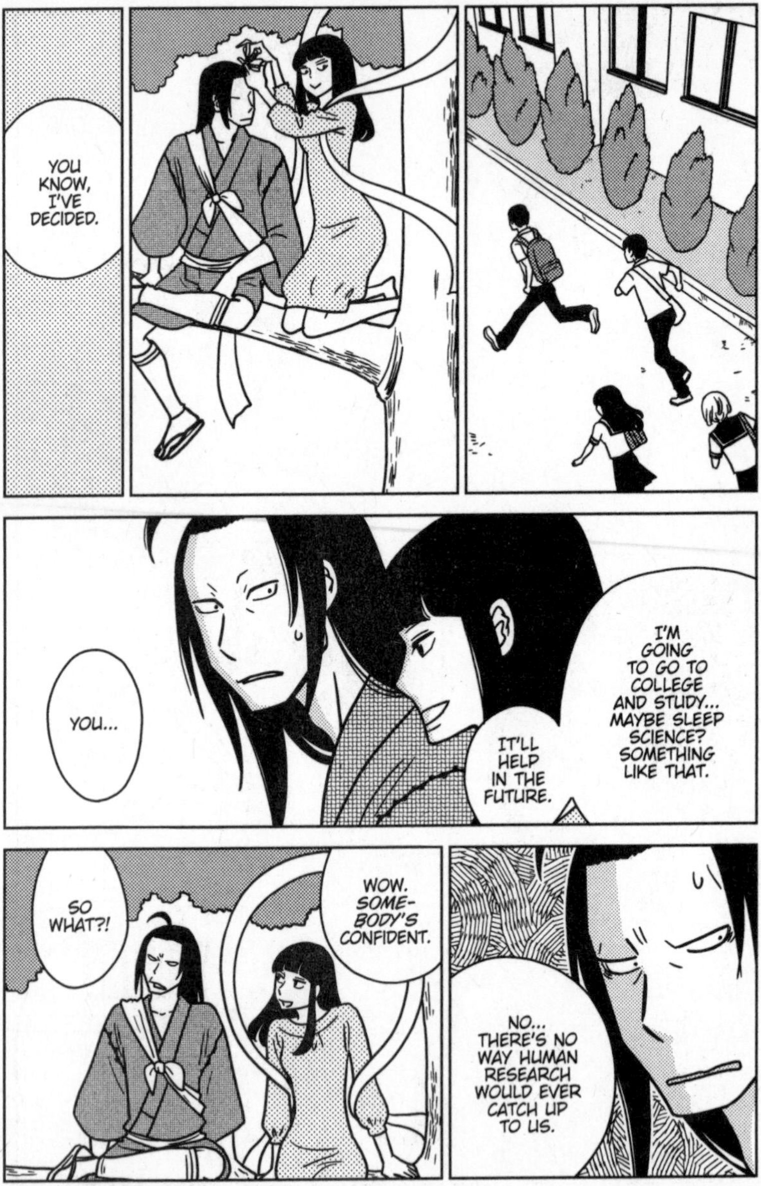
YOU KNOW, I'VE DECIDED.
I'M GOING TO GO TO COLLEGE AND STUDY... MAYBE SLEEP SCIENCE? SOMETHING LIKE THAT.
IT'LL HELP IN THE FUTURE.
YOU...
NO... THERE'S NO WAY HUMAN RESEARCH WOULD EVER CATCH UP TO US.
WOW. SOME-BODY'S CONFIDENT.
SO WHAT?!

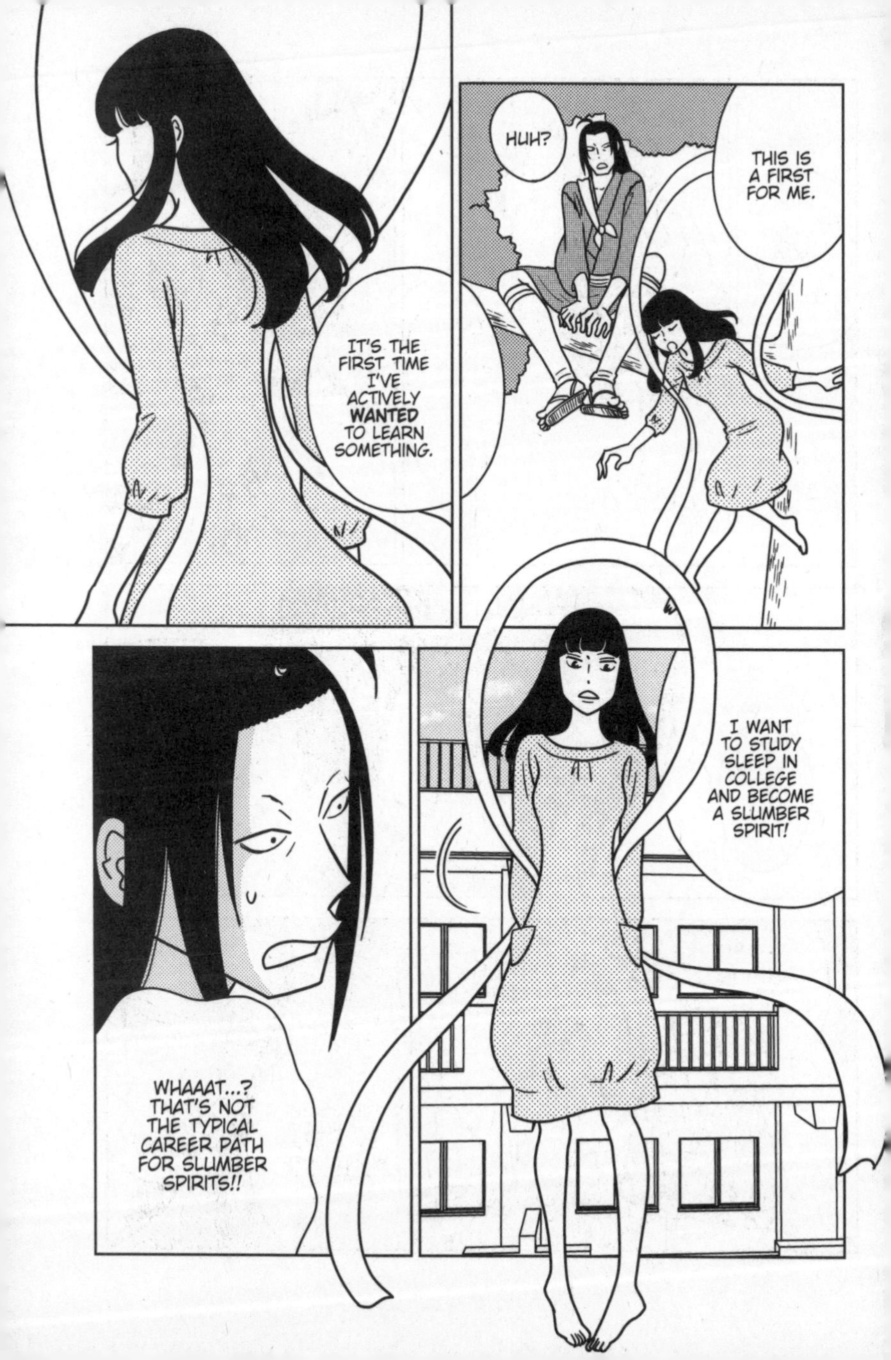
THIS IS A FIRST FOR ME.
HUH?
IT'S THE FIRST TIME I'VE ACTIVELY **WANTED** TO LEARN SOMETHING.
I WANT TO STUDY SLEEP IN COLLEGE AND BECOME A SLUMBER SPIRIT!
WHAAAT...? THAT'S NOT THE TYPICAL CAREER PATH FOR SLUMBER SPIRITS!!

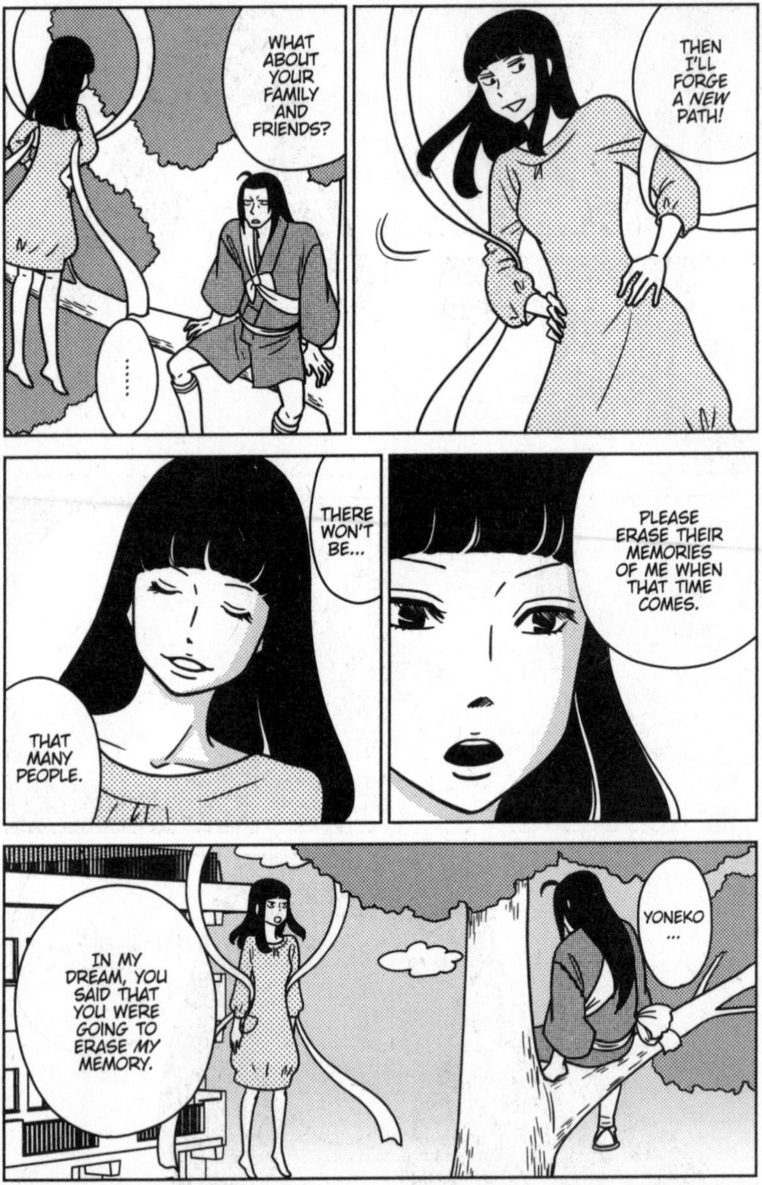
THEN I'LL FORGE A *NEW* PATH!
WHAT ABOUT YOUR FAMILY AND FRIENDS?
......
PLEASE ERASE THEIR MEMORIES OF ME WHEN THAT TIME COMES.
THERE WON'T BE...
THAT MANY PEOPLE.
YONEKO...
IN MY DREAM, YOU SAID THAT YOU WERE GOING TO ERASE *MY* MEMORY.

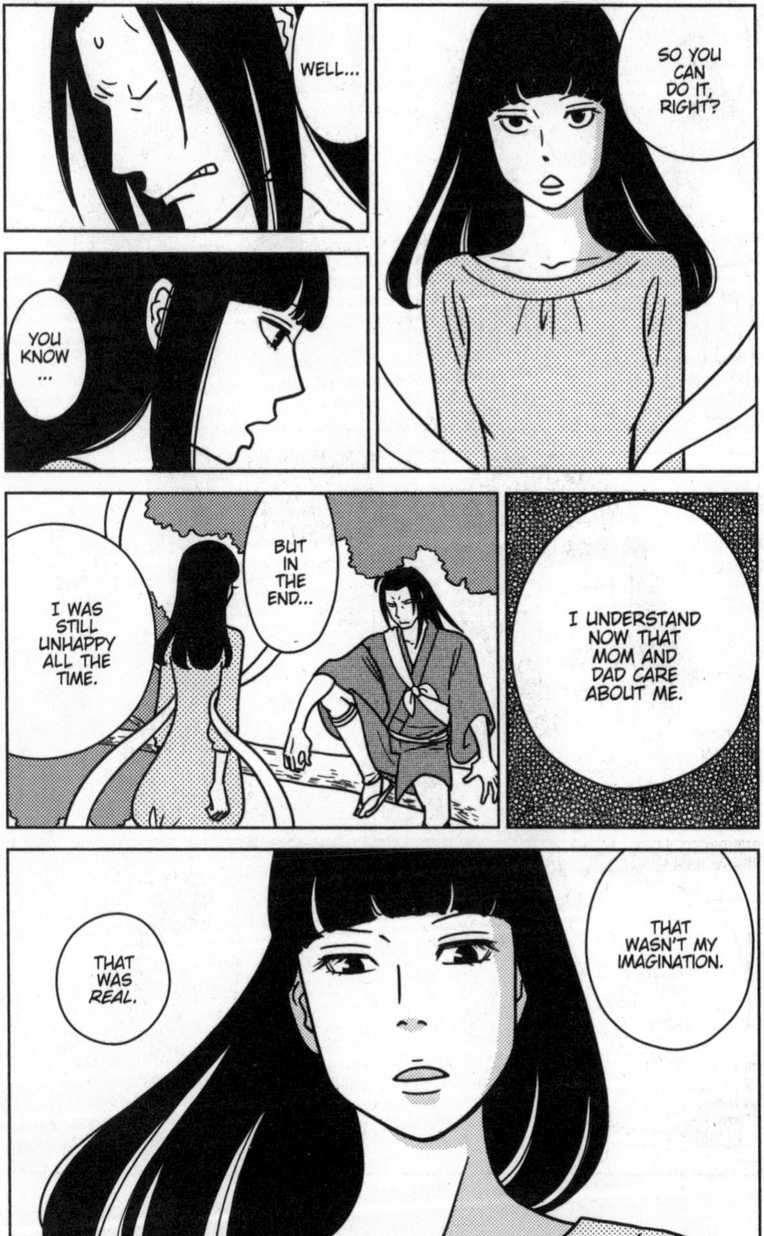
SO YOU CAN DO IT, RIGHT?
WELL...
YOU KNOW ...
I UNDERSTAND NOW THAT MOM AND DAD CARE ABOUT ME.
BUT IN THE END...
I WAS STILL UNHAPPY ALL THE TIME.
THAT WASN'T MY IMAGINATION.
THAT WAS *REAL.*

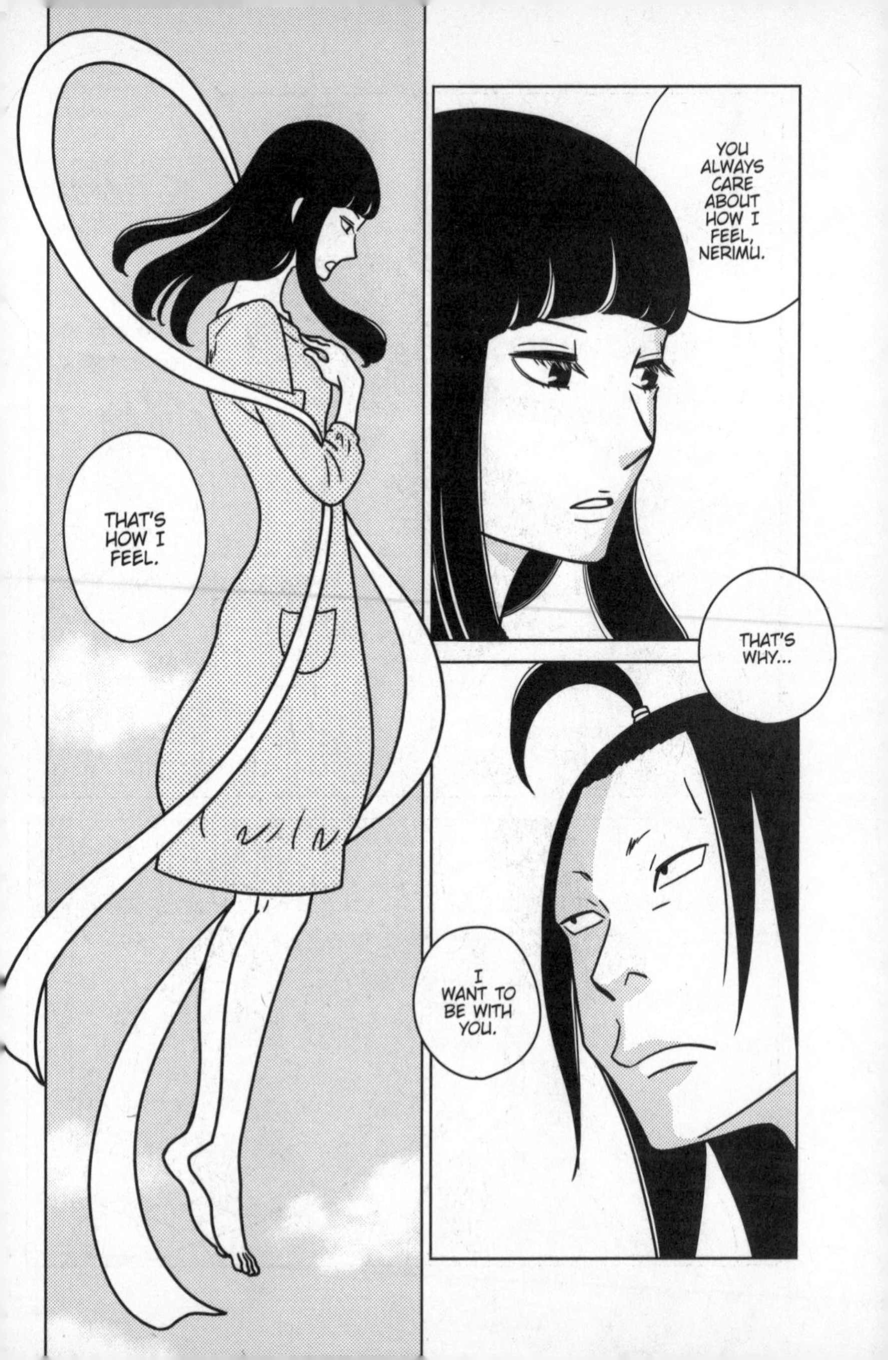
YOU ALWAYS CARE ABOUT HOW I FEEL, NERIMU.
THAT'S WHY...
I WANT TO BE WITH YOU.
THAT'S HOW I FEEL.

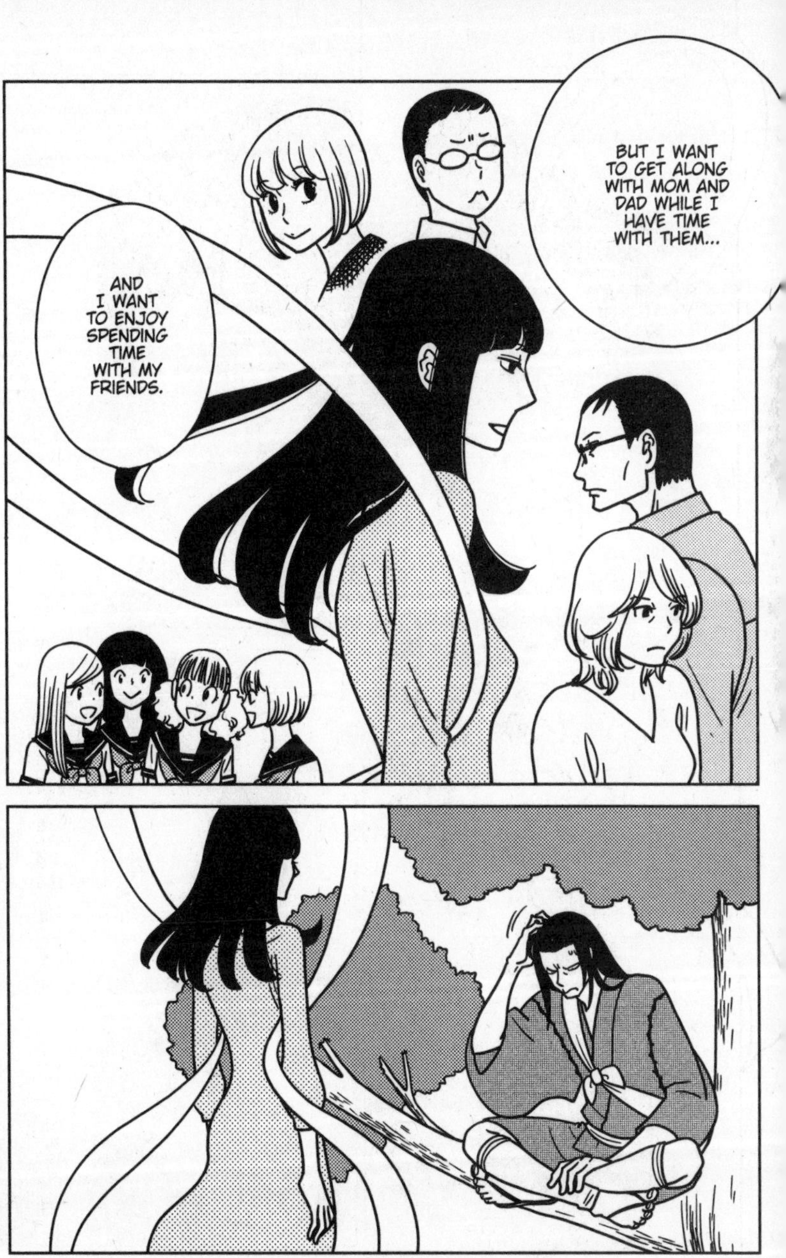
BUT I WANT TO GET ALONG WITH MOM AND DAD WHILE I HAVE TIME WITH THEM...
AND I WANT TO ENJOY SPENDING TIME WITH MY FRIENDS.

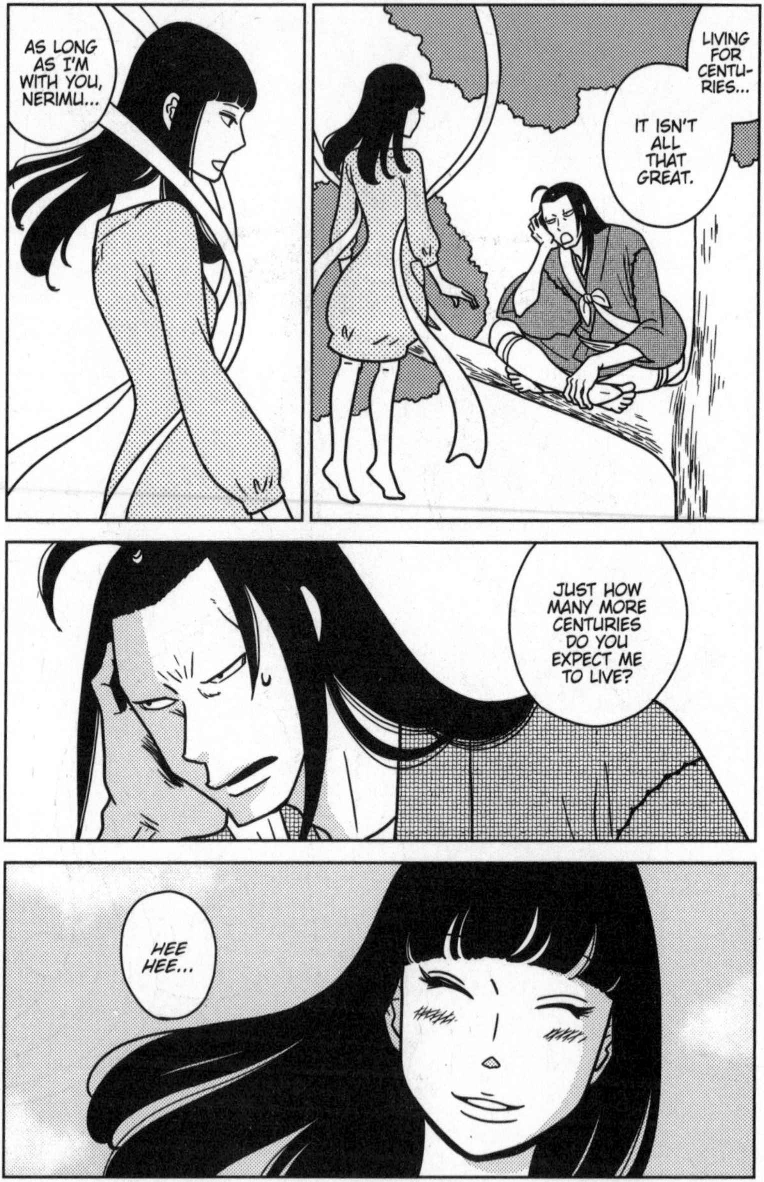
LIVING FOR CENTURIES...
IT ISN'T ALL THAT GREAT.
AS LONG AS I'M WITH YOU, NERIMU...
JUST HOW MANY MORE CENTURIES DO YOU EXPECT ME TO LIVE?
HEE HEE...

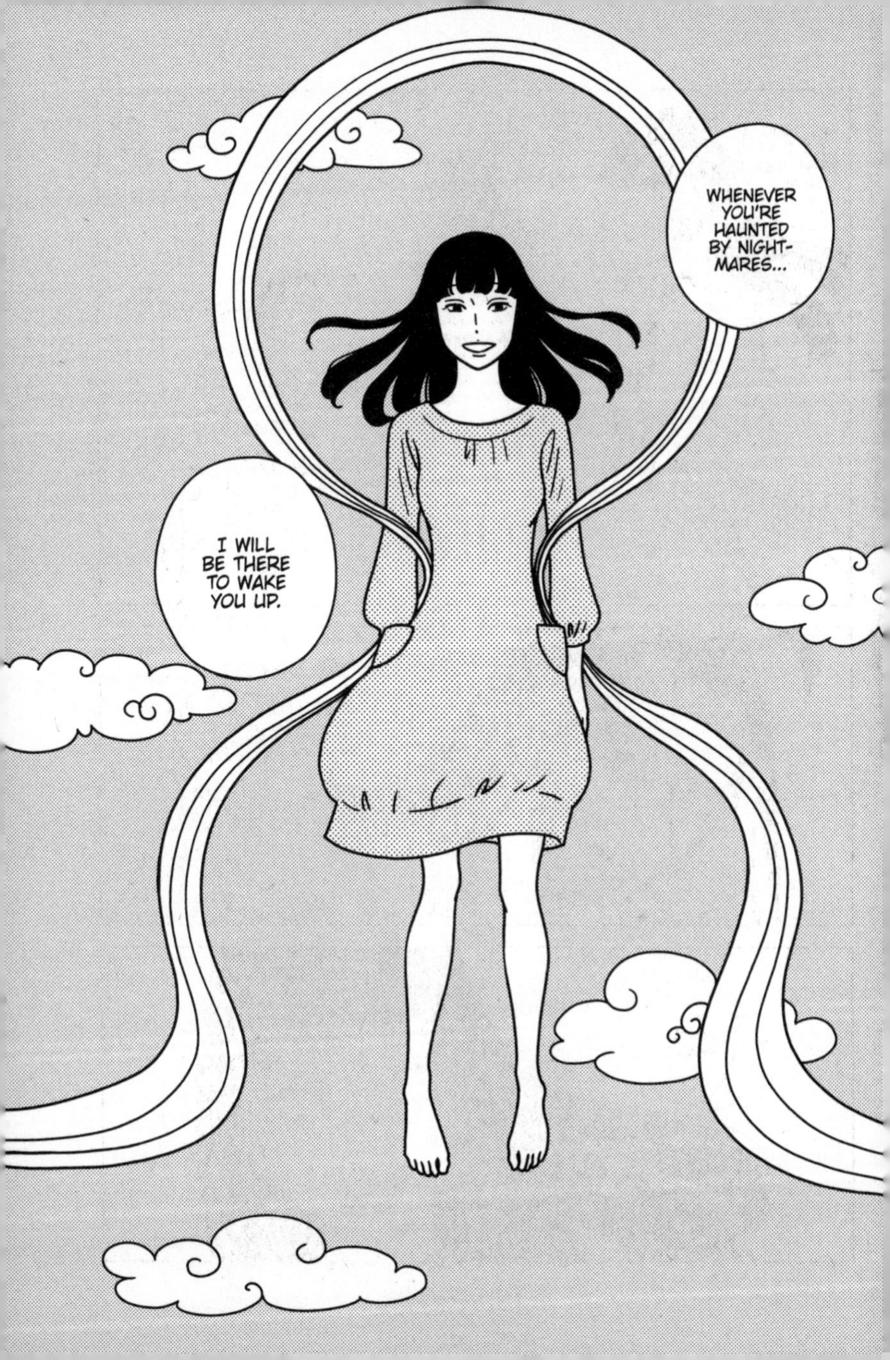
WHENEVER YOU'RE HAUNTED BY NIGHT-MARES...
I WILL BE THERE TO WAKE YOU UP.

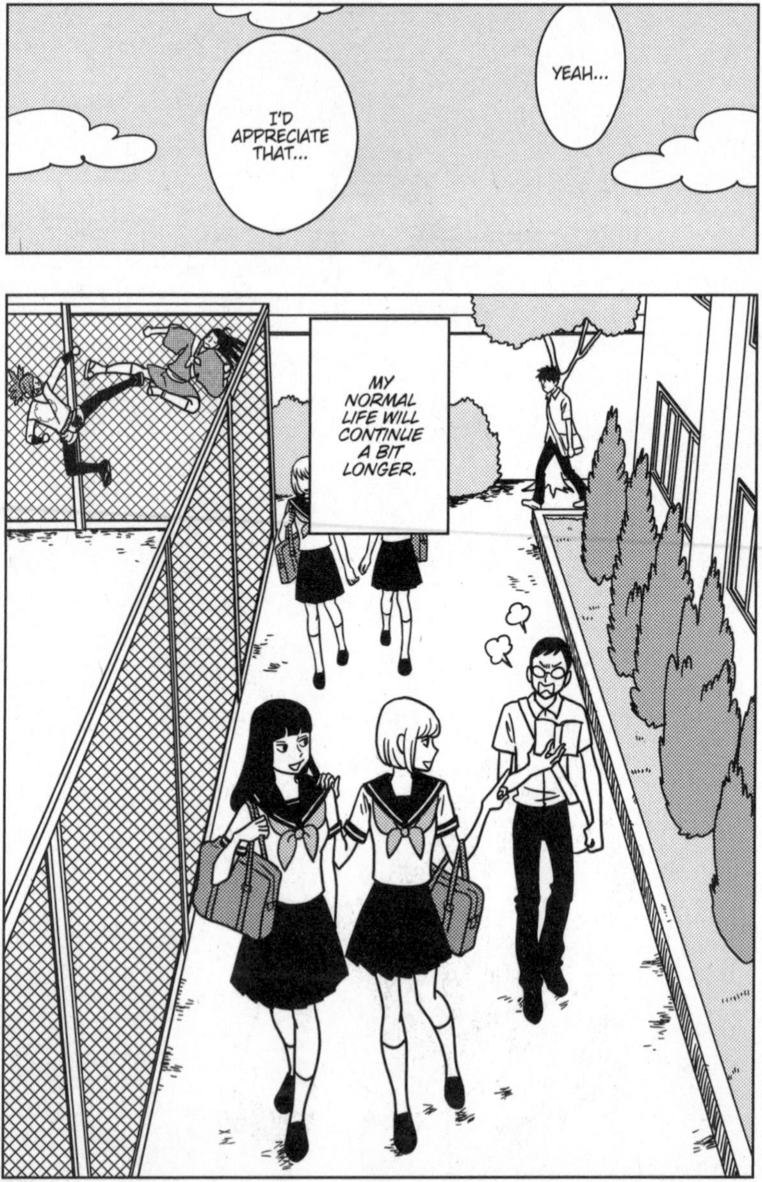
YEAH...
I'D APPRECIATE THAT...
MY NORMAL LIFE WILL CONTINUE A BIT LONGER.

Fin

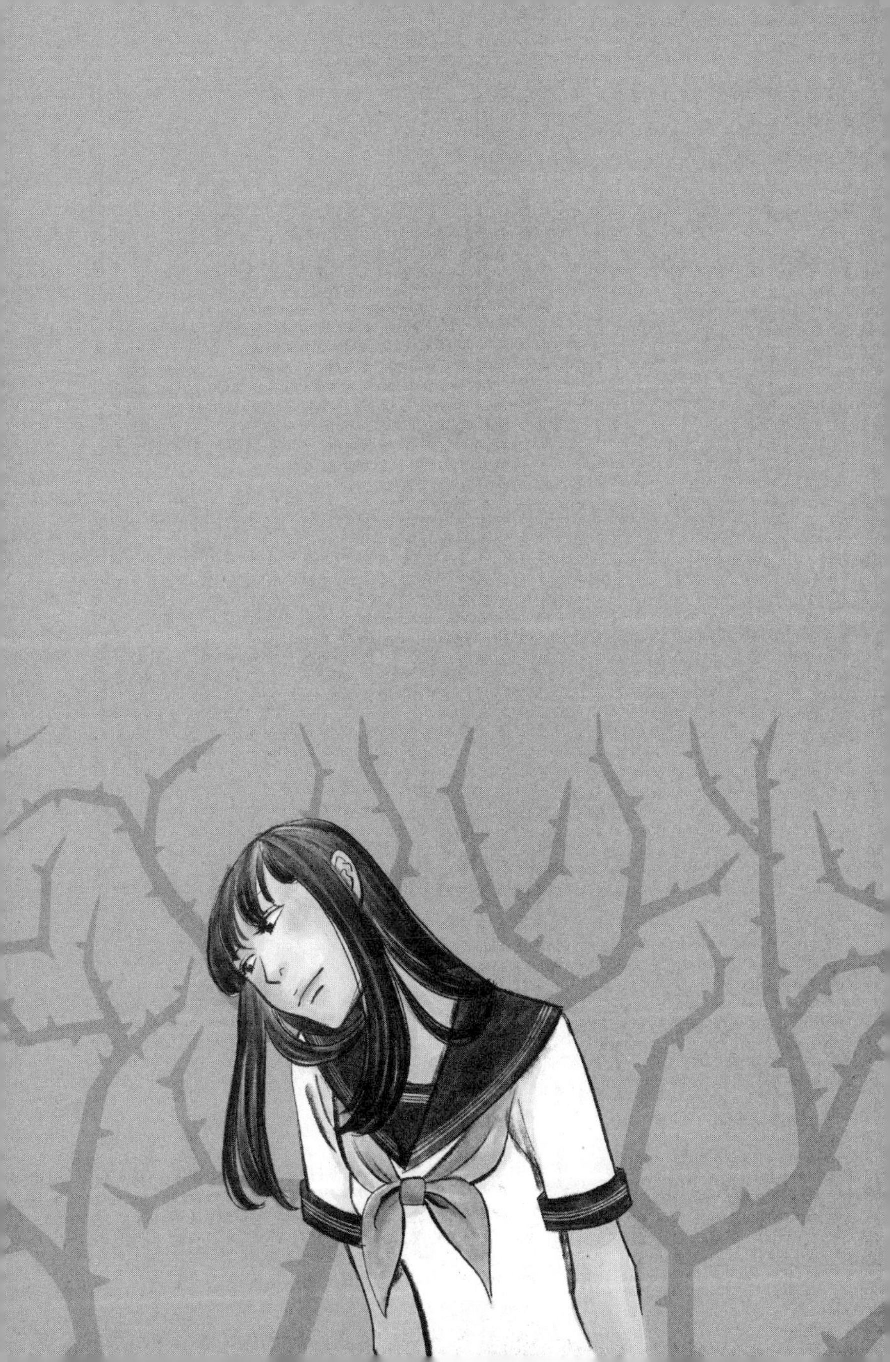

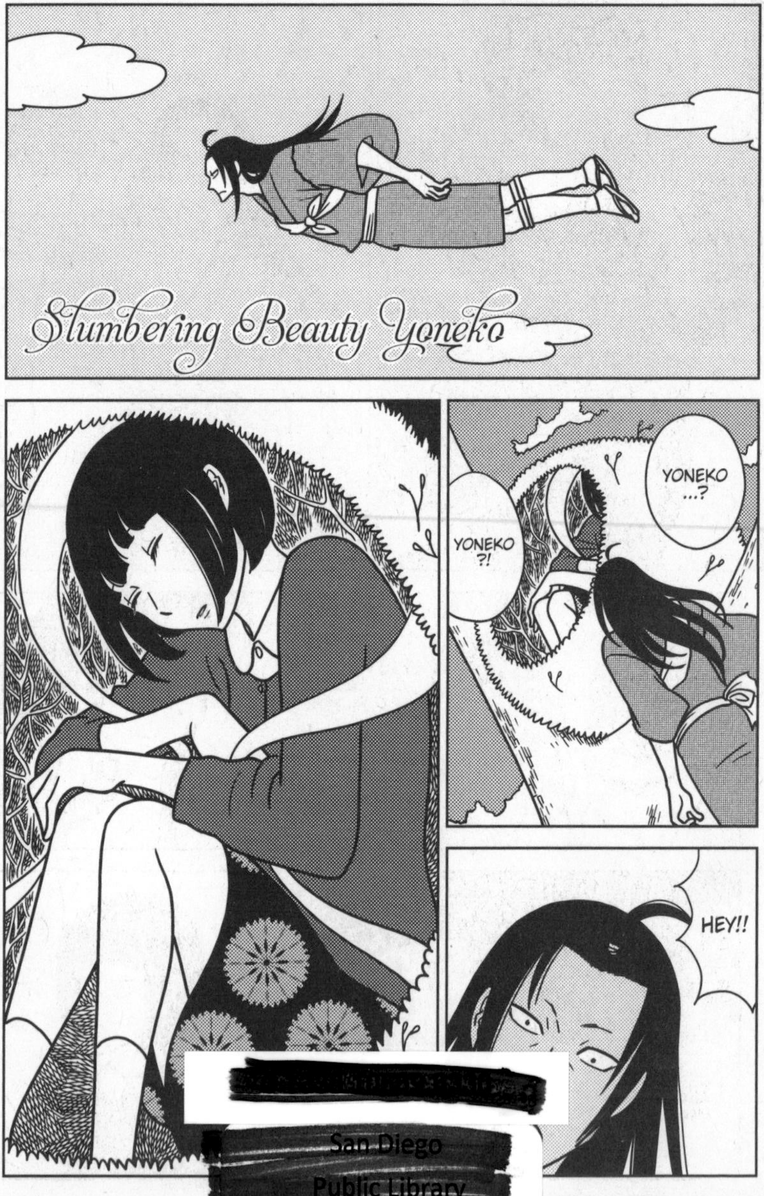
Slumbering Beauty Yoneko
YONEKO ...?
YONEKO ?!
HEY!!

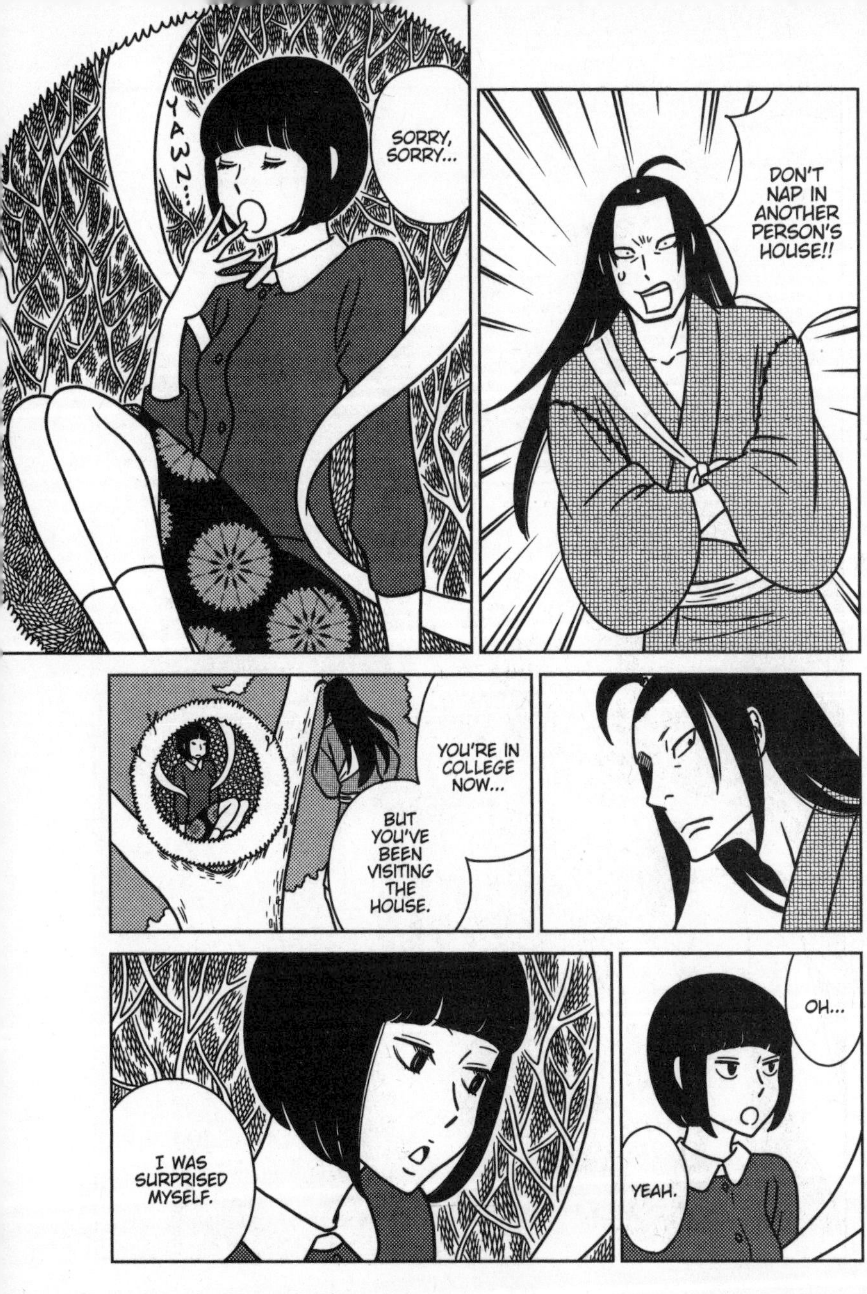
DON'T NAP IN ANOTHER PERSON'S HOUSE!!
SORRY, SORRY...
YAWN...
YOU'RE IN COLLEGE NOW...
BUT YOU'VE BEEN VISITING THE HOUSE.
OH...
YEAH.
I WAS SURPRISED MYSELF.

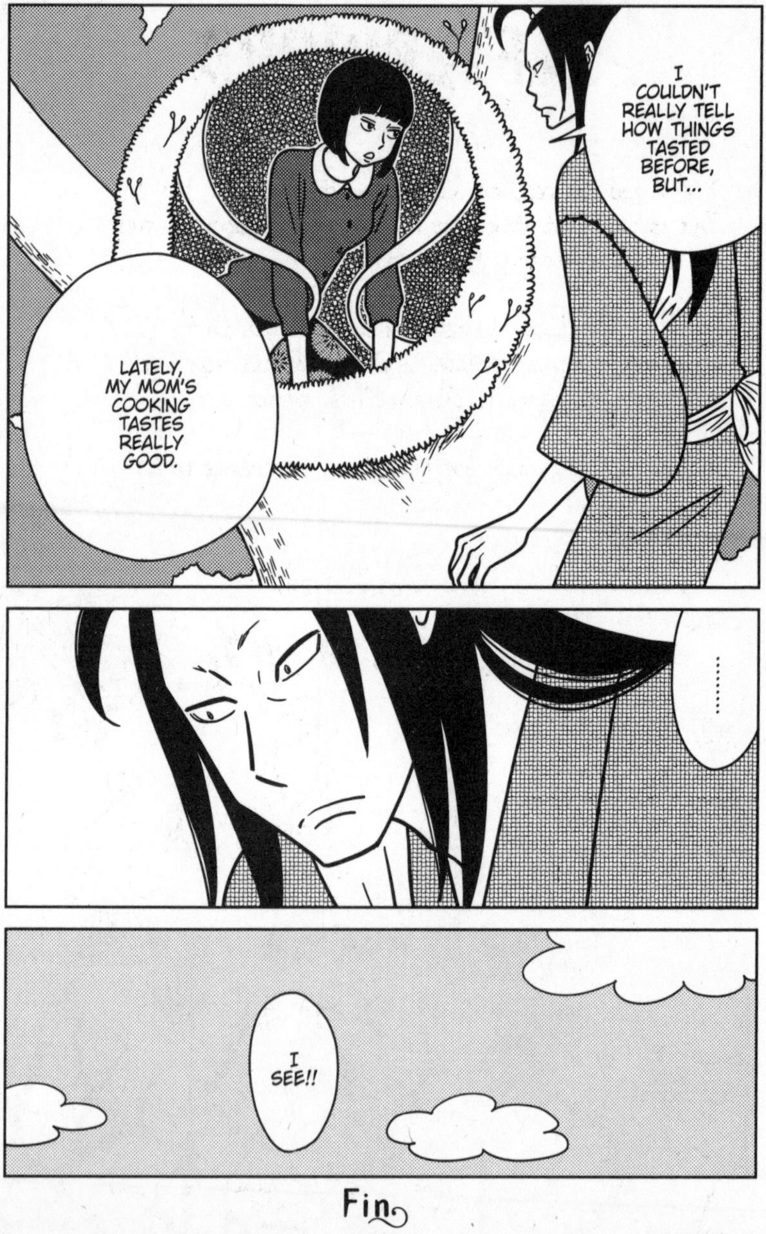
I COULDN'T REALLY TELL HOW THINGS TASTED BEFORE, BUT...
LATELY, MY MOM'S COOKING TASTES REALLY GOOD.
......
I SEE!!

Fin

AFTERWORD

Thank you for reading *Slumbering Beauty* until the end. This is the first time I've made a multi-chapter series built around strange happenings.

It made me happy, being able to draw odd things I'd never really drawn before, and strange old men I've never had a chance to draw before, either.

Thank you very much for giving me the chance to do such a thing.

March 2018

宇仁田 ゆみ
Yumi Unita

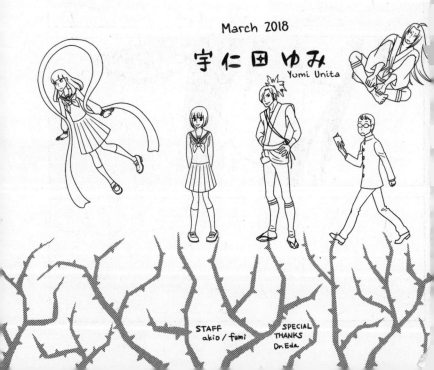

STAFF
akio / fumi

SPECIAL
THANKS
Dr. Eda

SEVEN SEAS ENTERTAINMENT PRESENTS

Slumbering Beauty VOLUME 2

story and art by YUMI UNITA

TRANSLATION
Angela Liu

ADAPTATION
Marykate Jasper

LETTERING AND RETOUCH
Lys Blakeslee

COVER DESIGN
KC Fabellon

PROOFREADER
Danielle King
Shanti Whitesides

ASSISTANT EDITOR
Jenn Grunigen

PRODUCTION ASSISTANT
CK Russell

PRODUCTION MANAGER
Lissa Pattillo

EDITOR-IN-CHIEF
Adam Arnold

PUBLISHER
Jason DeAngelis

NEMURIMEHIME by Yumi Unita
© Yumi Unita 2018
All rights reserved.
First published in Japan in 2018 by HAKUSENSHA, INC., Tokyo.
English language translation rights in U.S.A. arranged with HAKUSENSHA, INC.,
Tokyo through TOHAN CORPORATION, Tokyo.

Seven Seas books may be purchased in bulk for promotional, educational, or
business use. Please contact your local bookseller or the Macmillan Corporate
and Premium Sales Department at 1-800-221-7945, extension 5442, or by
e-mail at MacmillanSpecialMarkets@macmillan.com.

Seven Seas and the Seven Seas logo are trademarks of
Seven Seas Entertainment, LLC. All rights reserved.

ISBN: 978-1-626926-96-7

Printed in Canada

First Printing: December 2018

10 9 8 7 6 5 4 3 2 1

FOLLOW US ONLINE: *www.sevenseasentertainment.com*

READING DIRECTIONS

This book reads from **right to left**, Japanese style.
If this is your first time reading manga, you start
reading from the top right panel on each page and
take it from there. If you get lost, just follow the
numbered diagram here. It may seem backwards at
first, but you'll get the hang of it! Have fun!!

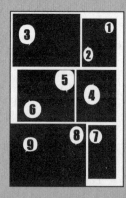